LOCAL COUNSEL

D1607999

LOCAL COUNSEL

First Women at The Citadel, and Beyond

Robert Ray Black

CAROLINA ACADEMIC PRESS

Durham, North Carolina

Library of Congress Cataloging-in-Publication Data

Black, Robert R.
Local counsel : first women at the Citadel and beyond / Robert Ray Black.
p. cm.
ISBN 978-1-61163-032-9 (alk. paper)
1. Citadel, the Military College of South Carolina--Trials, litigation, etc. 2.
Sex discrimination in higher education--Law and legislation--South Carolina-
-Charleston. 3. Black, Robert R. 4. Lawyers--South Carolina--Charleston--Bi-
ography. I. Title.

KF228.C53B53 2012
355.0071'17579--dc23

2011050119

CAROLINA ACADEMIC PRESS
700 Kent Street
Durham, North Carolina 27701
Telephone (919) 489-7486
Fax (919) 493-5668
www.cap-press.com

Printed in the United States of America

For Karen, Tonya, Pat, Liz, Angela, Shannon, Sandy, Evelyn, Ethel, Nancy, Spencer, Melinda, Mary Holland, and Blanche. And others similarly situated.

"All persons born or naturalized in the United States, and subject to the jurisdiction thereof, are citizens of the United States and of the state wherein they reside. No state shall make or enforce any law which shall abridge the privileges or immunities of citizens of the United States; nor shall any state deprive any person of life, liberty, or property, without due process of law; nor deny to any person within its jurisdiction the equal protection of the laws."

Section 1, Fourteenth Amendment to the
United States Constitution

"IT IS, THEREFORE, ORDERED, that the defendants forthwith admit Shannon Richey Faulkner to the South Carolina Corps of Cadets under such terms and conditions as this court hereinafter orders."

C. Weston Houck, United States District Judge, July 22, 1994

* * *

"As for The Citadel's status now, 'The federal courts ordered women to be admitted.' I have been observing The Citadel for over 40 years. The Citadel is in the best position it has ever been in."

The Boo, Lieutenant Colonel T. N. Courvoisie,
Charleston, South Carolina, *The Post and Courier*,
October 12, 2002

* * *

"An accurate history of this important case should be preserved for future generations.... I hope in your writing you will endeavor to paint the true picture of the scene by giving full flavor to the hatred and bigotry which was generated by so-called responsible people who did all within their power to defeat justice.... No one involved demonstrated more courage than Judge Houck and I hope he will receive the credit he deserves in your book."

Arthur G. Howe, Esq., Senior Member of the Charleston
County Bar, letter to the author, October 8, 1999

* * *

"By a faction I understand a number of citizens, whether amounting to a majority or minority of the whole, who are united and actuated by some common impulse of passion, or of interest, adverse to the rights of other citizens, or to the permanent and aggregate interests of the community."

James Madison, The Federalist No. 10

"The education and empowerment of women throughout the world cannot fail to result in a more caring, tolerant, just and peaceful life for all."

Aung San Suu Kyi,
Burmese Nobel Peace Prize laureate

"This is the only case that has bumped O. J. Simpson off the front page."

Oprah Winfrey in an interview on
September 7, 1995, with Shannon Faulkner
after she withdrew from The Citadel

"Faulkner's not the only story. You're the story too."

Nationally syndicated columnist Kathleen Parker,
telephone conversation with the author

"Que las historias fingidas tanto tienen de buenas y de deleitables cuanto se llegan a la verdad o la semejanza della, y las verdaderas, tanto son mejores cuanto son mas verdaderas."

("Fictional tales are better and more enjoyable the nearer they approach the truth or the semblance of the truth, and as for true stories, the best are those that are most true.")

Don Quixote, Chapter LXII

* * *

Contents

The Citadel Chronology of Events   xiii

VMI Chronology of Events   xix

Introduction   3

Part I

Chapter 1 • The First to Try   17
     Out of Here   17
     Tuskegee and King   21
     1989: "I Thought You Were a Black Man"   22
     1990: The Zentgraf Maneuver   29
     A Visit to The Citadel   33
     Jeanette Kellogg Wotkyns and MoFo   34
     Another Loss   36
     The Bishops' Secretary   37
     The Boo   38
     1991: The Manly Bill and Committee Hearing   39
     Tremendous Shortage   42
     Melody Lutz: Getting Serious   46

Chapter 2 • Women Veterans Pat, Liz, and Angela   49
     1992: Pat Johnson Calls an Attorney   49
     VMI: Richmond 1992   54
     God Bless the ACLU   55
     The First Shot   57
     Angela Chapman   59
     The First Hearing   61
     Call for Help   69
     Sherman Returns to Charleston   70

Vets Routed   72
Veterans Day Program? What Veterans Day Program?   78
Beaufort Bubble   80
Rodrigo Diaz   82
Public Policy   86
Antenor's Friends   87
South Carolina Commission on Women   93
Top Trainer and MacArthur Awards and NGC   94
First Defense   98
USPS   101

Part II

Chapter 3 • Dey Let De Lady In   105
1993: Si Bunting   105
Judge Johnson and Comity   108
"Unexampled Courage"   110
"Gender Was Removed with Correction Fluid": Wite-Out   113
The Strange Career of Violence   115
Concurrent Resolution   118
August 12, 1993: SRF Gets into the Day Program   121
All, All Honorable Men   123

Chapter 4 • Moses in the Neighborhood   125
1994: Moses in the Neighborhood—A Family at War   125
First Blood   133
Registration Day   134
Kick Off: January 20, 1994   141
"The Citadel Has Now Become a Household Word"   142
Von Mickel the Great   144
The Ragadier   147
"Not an Inch"   150
Show Time   151
"Surprise Attack"   152
Letters   159
Suffer Little Children   160
First Remedial Plan   162
Big Dogs' Depositions   162
Hard Hats   165
Local Counsel as Witness   166

Chapter 5 · The Trial and Right After   169
    The Trial   169
    After the Trial   177
    Faulkner I, July 22, 1994: The Big Order   180
    "Die Shannon"   183
    Bumper Stickers   185
    Hair   187
    August 1, 1994, Order   190
    The Physical Examiners   192
    August 5, 1994, Judgment and Order   194
    ROTC Options   199
    Sexual Harassment Handbook   200
    Veterans Redux: Richmond 1994   202
    SCIL Announced   206
    A Quiet Place   208
    Miss Gourdin   209

Chapter 6 · Separate and Unequal   213
    1995: "Die Nigr"   213
    Faulkner II, April 13, 1995   215
    Demand   218
    State Senator   220
    SCWLA   223
    April 7, 1995   225
    Converse Faculty   230
    "Something You Can See"   234
    NAACP and Shouting Billboard   236
    What To Do with the Girls   238
    The Court Pays a Visit   242

Chapter 7 · Honor and Good Sense   245
    The Battle of Obesity   245
    July 24, 1995, Order   253
    Death Row   255
    Band Company   257
    Security   258
    Beginning and End   262
    All Alone   263
    "Cancer to This Institution"   265
    "Honor and Good Sense"   269

Praying and Dancing   271
"Courtesy, Respect, and Dignity"   280

Chapter 8 · Mellette Steps In and Out   283
Saved by a Citadel Family   283
June 26, 1996   285
"Let Us Now Praise Famous Men"   287
DOJ Assimilation Plans   289
Messer and Mentavlos   294
"Sure I Would"   301
Loyal Sons   308
An Incomplete Conclusion   310
Payback   313

Chapter 9 · And Beyond   315

Notes   327

Index   333

The Citadel
Chronology of Events

1989

05/15/89   Robert Ray Black (RRB) calls John Banzhaf from Birmingham
05/28/89   RRB meets with a young woman and her mother in Charleston
06/26–28/89   Two young women write letters of inquiry to Department of Justice; RRB's correspondence begins with Nat Douglas at DOJ

1990

01/26/90   RRB calls Jeanette Kellogg Wotkyns, Morrison & Forrester, Washington, D.C.
02/90   RRB visits Brigadier General Meenaghan, VP, Academic Affairs, The Citadel
12/4/90   ACLU Debate on Women at the Citadel
12/11/90   Mother of Tiffany Provence calls RRB

1991

03/05/91   House committee hearings on Manly bill to admit women into the Corps of Cadets; RRB speaks in support of bill
08/21/91   Citadel admits woman ROTC student from MUSC
11/18/91   Melody Lutz and RRB visit three high school women ROTC programs

1992

01/28/92   Navy veteran Patricia Johnson calls RRB
05/05/92   Madeline Collison, Denver, agrees to serve as co-counsel
05/11/92   Isabelle Pinzler, Women's Rights Project, ACLU, agrees to serve as co-counsel
06/11/92   Women veterans Johnson, Lacey (and Chapman, 6/17/92) sue Citadel under 14th Amendment to join male veterans in Veterans Day Program
08/07/92   Women veterans' motion for preliminary injunction is denied

08/18/92	Valorie Vojdik, Henry Weisburg, Shearman & Sterling, agree to be co-counsel
09/02/92	Citadel gets rid of Veterans Day Program
09/04/92	Citadel's first motion to moot women veterans' lawsuit is denied
11/10/92	Citadel modifies its motion to moot women veterans' lawsuit
12/14/92	Two male veterans sue Citadel for closing VDP; held to be separate from women veterans' lawsuit but dismissed 01/27/93

1993

02/12/93	RRB calls Suzanne Coe on behalf of Shearman & Sterling and ACLU to represent Shannon Richey Faulkner (SRF)
03/02/93	SRF sues Citadel under 14th Amendment to join Corps of Cadets; amended 03/03/93
03/18/03	SRF lawsuit consolidated with women veterans' lawsuit for purposes of discovery
04/24/93	DOJ agrees to intervene in SRF lawsuit; permitted to intervene and names state as defendant 06/07/93
05/27/93	Concurrent Resolution adopted by General Assembly
05/28/93	SRF files motions for class action and summary judgment
08/12/93	District court grants SRF's motion for preliminary injunction to allow SRF to enter day program as civilian pending trial on the merits to enter Corps of Cadets in August, 1994.
08/16/93	Fourth Circuit stays district court Order; SRF does not enter day program. *Faulkner v. Jones*, 10 F.3d 226 (4th Cir. 1993)
09/20/93	Court grants Citadel's second motion to moot women veterans' lawsuit
09/29/93	Nine cadets move to intervene; motion denied 02/17/94
11/17/93	Fourth Circuit affirms preliminary injunction and lifts stay (J. Niemeyer, Hall; Hamilton dissenting)
12/01/93	Citadel petitions Fourth Circuit for rehearing *en banc*

1994

01/10/94	Fourth Circuit denies Citadel's petition for rehearing
01/11/94	Legislative Committee issues its report to General Assembly
01/12/94	C. J. Rehnquist grants Citadel's emergency application for stay; SRF registers as day student at Citadel
01/18/94	Supreme Court lifts C. J. Rehnquist's temporary stay
01/20/94	SRF begins biology class as day student at Citadel
03/07/94	Citadel files motion to bifurcate trial to decide justification before remedy
04/01/94	Citadel files a proposed remedial plan

05/16/94	Two-week trial begins, ends 05/27/94; closing arguments 06/16/94
06/10/94	Citadel files motion for mistrial
06/28/94	SRF files proposed remedial plan
06/30/94	Citadel files motion to reopen the record
07/22/94	*Faulkner I*: district court finds Citadel in violation of 14th Amendment and orders SRF into Corps of Cadets. *Faulkner v. Jones*, 858 F.Supp. 552 (D.S.C. 1994)
07/27/94	Citadel moves district court to stay its 07/22/94 Order
08/01/94	Hearing in district court to implement 07/22/94 Order; SRF's motions for special sexual harassment committee
08/05/94	District court orders implementation of its 07/22/94 Order; Citadel seeks stay in Fourth Circuit, pending appeal
08/09/94	U.S. marshals ordered to monitor SRF's entry into Corps of Cadets; Citadel ordered to grant marshals access to grounds and buildings, to take no action to interfere with activities of marshals, and to fully cooperate with marshals
08/11/94	Parts of transcript pertaining to SRF's medical records held under seal
08/15/94	Fourth Circuit stays district court; SRF does not enter Corps of Cadets but continues in day program
09/23/94	SRF's motions to participate in cadet extracurricular activities pending appeal to Fourth Circuit to enter Corps
09/29/94	Oral arguments on appeal in women veterans' case to Fourth Circuit
12/05/94	Fourth Circuit affirms District Court to moot women veterans' lawsuit

1995

04/13/95	*Faulkner II*: Fourth Circuit affirms *Faulkner I*, with modifications, ordering SRF to enter Corps of Cadets in August, 1995, if no adequate remedy (e.g., parallel program at Converse College) found at trial in district court. *Faulkner v. Jones*, 51 F.3d 440 (4th Cir. 1995); stay lifted
06/05/95	Citadel's motions to approve its remedial plan to put women in South Carolina Institute for Leadership, SCIL, at Converse College, to limit discovery and trial to Mary Baldwin/VMI issues already approved by Fourth Circuit, comparing Converse with Mary Baldwin; denied 06/07/95; proposed plan amended 06/12/95 and 06/16/95

06/06/95   Motions heard on SRF's medical records; under seal per 08/11/94
           and 05/22/95 Orders; and 06/14/95, 07/19/95, 07/25/95, 08/02/95,
           08/04/95
06/07/95   Citadel's request to billet SRF as cadet in Infirmary; denied
06/12/95   Hearing on SCIL
06/28/95   Court visits Virginia Women's Institute for Leadership, VWLI,
           Mary Baldwin College, Staunton, Virginia
07/03/95   Court visits SCIL, Converse College, Spartanburg, South Carolina
07/24/95   District court finds Citadel's SCIL remedial plan impossible to
           set for trial prior to beginning of classes on 08/12/95; postpones
           trial and sets new trial for 11/06/95, then 12/05/95; SRF or-
           dered into Corps of Cadets pursuant to *Faulkner I*, affirmed by
           Faulkner II
08/02/95   Citadel's motion to Fourth Circuit for stay of district court Order
           of 07/24/95
08/10/95   U.S. marshals ordered to monitor SRF's entry into Corps of
           Cadets; Citadel ordered to grant marshals access to grounds and
           buildings, to take no action to interfere with activities of mar-
           shals, and to fully cooperate with marshals
08/12/95   SRF becomes the first woman to enroll in the Corps of Cadets
08/18/95   SRF withdraws from the Corps of Cadets
08/23/95   Citadel moves to dismiss SRF's case
08/25/95   Court orders clerk to unseal record of all in-camera proceedings
08/31/95   Motion by Nancy Mellette to intervene
10/03/95   Court grants Mellette's motion to intervene and to step into
           shoes of SRF; SRF's case dismissed; Mellette denied class certi-
           fication; trial set for 11/13/95
11/30/95   Court grants Citadel's motion to stay trial pending *VMI* deci-
           sion in Supreme Court

1996
04/96   Mellette accepts place in USMAPS, prep school for West Point
06/26/96   Supreme Court rules that all-male admissions policy at VMI vi-
           olates 14th Amendment and orders women to be admitted to
           VMI. *United States v. Virginia*, 518 U.S. 515 (1996)
06/28/96   Citadel admits women; offers assimilation plan; four women
           enter in August
08/14/96   District court finds SCIL in violation 14th Amendment and or-
           ders Citadel to admit women; orders Citadel to develop assim-
           ilation plan; Citadel enjoined from continuing its all-male

admissions policy; Citadel appeals contending this order and previous others are moot

11/01/96   SRF's attorneys file petition for attorney fees; hearings 07/07–11/97

1997

01/09/07   Draft of plan to assimilate women into the Corps of Cadets

05/23/97   United States and Citadel enter Consent Decree for assimilation of women

1998

02/11/98   Fourth Circuit affirms in part and vacates in part district court Order of 08/14/96, and affirms orders of 07/22/94, 07/24/95, and 10/03/95; SCIL not inadequate because no trial of fact finding was held; Citadel not enjoined from continuing its all-male admissions policy because no evidence in record that Citadel will revert to all-male admissions policy; Mellette lacks standing because she accepted place in USMAPS. *United States v. Jones*, 136 F.3d 342 (4th Cir. 1998).

1999

03/30/99   District court orders Citadel and state to pay plaintiffs' attorney fees

2002

03/28/02   *Faulkner/Mellette* Case dismissed

2010

01/10   Veterans Day Program reopened

VMI Chronology of Events

early 1989	Letter from unnamed Virginia school girl sent to Judith Keith, CRD, DOJ
03/21/89	DOJ letter of inquiry sent to VMI; again 01/03/90
02/01/90	DOJ notifies VMI that its admissions policy is in violation of 14th Amendment and Title IV of Civil Rights Act of 1964
02/05/90	VMI Foundation and State of Virginia file declaratory action against DOJ
04/04/91	Liability trial begins in district court, Roanoke, Judge Kiser; lasts 6 days, 19 witnesses; tried under 14th Amendment and Title IV
06/14/91	J. Kiser finds all-male admissions policy at VMI constitutional. *United States v. Virginia*, 766 F.Supp. 471 (W.D. Va. 1991)
04/08/92	Arguments before Fourth Circuit Court of Appeals (J. Niemeyer, J. Ward, J. Phillips); RRB and Citadel attorney M. Dawes Cooke are present
10/05/92	*VMI I*: Fourth Circuit reverses District Court and rules that VMI is in violation of 14th Amendment; gives VMI four options. *United States v. Virginia*, 976 F.2d 890 (4th Cir. 1992)
05/24/93	Petition for writ of *certiorari* in *VMI I* denied by Supreme Court; J. Scalia comments; case goes back to J. Kiser for trial on remedy
02/09/94	Remedial trial begins in district court on Mary Baldwin College parallel program
01/26/95	*VMI II*: Fourth Circuit rules that MBC parallel program is an adequate remedy; J. Motz and J. Phillips dissent from court's denial of DOJ petition for rehearing by all members of the court. *United States v. Virginia*, 44 F.3d 1229 (4th Cir. 1995)
10/05/95	Supreme Court grants petition for writ of *certiorari* to *VMI II*
01/17/96	Oral arguments before Supreme Court
06/26/96	Supreme Court reverses *VMI II* to rule that MBC is not an adequate remedy; women ordered to be admitted to VMI, effective 1997. *United States v. Virginia* 518 U.S. 515 (1996)

LOCAL COUNSEL

Introduction

This personal account of the first women at The Citadel uses three lawsuits from the 1990s to write about the good-ole-boy way of life in South Carolina. It is as much about how the state operates as it is about the litigants and a failure of leadership at The Citadel. The lawsuits of veterans Patricia Johnson, Elizabeth Lacy, Angela Chapman, of Shannon Faulkner, and of Nancy Mellette, whose suit was folded into Faulkner's, are notable as high-profile advances in women's equal protection under the law, but they make sense only within a larger context of political, economic, and social life unique to the state. Because the issue of women at The Citadel continues for many to be as controversial today as it was between 1992 and 1996, the topic remains part of a cultural divide within South Carolina. A frank discussion of the case raises the questions: How could so many good Citadel men have behaved so badly and made so many errors of judgment? How could such a renowned place have ever brought upon itself the necessity to place United States marshals on campus to enforce the Constitution? The good-ole-boy culture anchored in The Citadel accounts for many of the ills as well as successes of the state. The Citadel in some publications is highly ranked among regional public universities, but it is also a poster boy that exemplifies James Madison's fear of state "factions" that threaten constitutional democracy.

As a primary and not a secondary source, this book contains relatively few footnotes. It is not an exhaustive legal record of something that is over and done with. The lawsuits won't go away. Animus over facts in the cases still lingers. Sides are still drawn by the general public as women continue to find their place at The Citadel. Players in the cases are remembered primarily for their role in them. As recently as spring, 2011, eighteen years after Shannon Faulkner filed her suit, the cover of *South Carolina Super Lawyers 2011*, a Thomson Reuters publication, celebrates lead defense counsel as one who "represented The Citadel in its most controversial gender discrimination case."

The stories relayed in *Local Counsel* show that the *Johnson* and *Faulkner/Mellette* cases were lawsuits that advanced the professional interests of women and therefore all South Carolinians, but the book looks at the future as well. The women's lawsuits provide a backdrop to argue that placement of non-cadets who are ordinary citizens, not just veterans, in the daytime classes will promote much-needed economic prosperity within the state and increase national security. The same kind of leadership that fought against benefits flowing to the state from the admission of women, however, resists similar benefits that will arise from the admission of ordinary citizens into daytime classes. The thrust of the book is, therefore, toward the future, not the past.

If national and international attention establishes a definition of fame, *Faulkner v. Jones* may well be one of the most famous cases ever to come out of South Carolina.[1] Second only to *Briggs v. Elliott*, precursor to *Brown v. Board of Education*, and all the cases argued by Matthew J. Perry, the *Faulkner* case is arguably the state's principal modern civil rights case.[2] It is certainly the most important gender-discrimination suit, a bookend to the racial *Briggs* and *Brown* cases and the heroic effort of 1960 Burke High School graduate Harvey Gantt to gain admission as the first black student at Clemson University. Legal aspects of the Faulkner case are discussed in law review articles by Valorie K. Vojdik, plaintiffs' lead attorney in the case and principal attorney of record. Legal issues in The Citadel case and the Virginia Military Institute (VMI) case, a companion case filed by the Department of Justice, are significantly different when seen in context of Faulkner as a named plaintiff.[3] Fundamentally, the difference is that Faulkner was a real live young woman who wanted the same benefits the young men had at The Citadel. Faulkner's case was never about single-sex education, by which The Citadel meant male-only education. It was always simply about her desire to go only to The Citadel and to wear The Citadel class ring as a graduate of the Corps of Cadets.

Shannon was 17 years old when she went to attorney Suzanne Coe in Greenville, South Carolina. She was 18 years old just days later when she met me in Charleston and talked to attorneys Isabelle Pinzler and Val Vojdik on the phone in New York on the eve of filing her complaint. I wrote *Local Counsel* to celebrate the achievements gained from a major case in the history of American civil rights in which the sole plaintiff was, legally, a child. I wrote it to give balance to The Citadel side of the case which is better known to the public. In short, the case is not about an overweight young woman who couldn't take it.

An introductory note about the bare bones of the Faulkner lawsuit is appropriate. In August 1993, Shannon Faulkner was first ordered into The Citadel day program by the district court in Charleston to sit side by side with the male cadets as a non-cadet pending trial to be admitted as a cadet,[4] but the Fourth Circuit in Richmond put a stay on that order.[5] Her admission to the Corps of Cadets was ordered in *Faulkner I* on July 22, 1994, but that order by the district court was also stayed by the Fourth Circuit on August 15, 1994. Significantly, the July 22, 1994, district court order, *Faulkner I*, required The Citadel to admit other qualified women for the 1995–1996 school year unless defendants were able to implement a plan to remedy their constitutional violation. A year later on July 24, 1995, the district court renewed its order to admit Faulkner into the Corps, pursuant to the Fourth Circuit's April 13, 1995, order in *Faulkner II* which affirmed the district court's *Faulkner I*. Pending a trial on the validity of a parallel program for women at Converse College, Shannon Richey Faulkner became the first woman to enter the South Carolina Corps of Cadets on August 12, 1995, when The Citadel failed to offer a remedy as required under *Faulkner II*. She was hazed out by August 18, 1995. Trial dates on the South Carolina Institute for Leadership, or SCIL, at Converse, initially set for November and December 1995, were continued upon The Citadel's motion pending a decision by the United States Supreme Court whether to admit women to VMI. The Supreme Court ruled against VMI and Virginia's parallel program at Mary Baldwin, the Virginia Women's Institute of Leadership, or VWIL, on June 26, 1996. Two days later, The Citadel abandoned its pursuit of the similar parallel program at Converse and began admitting the first wave of women to exploit Faulkner's success by normal admission processes rather than by admission through court order.

A bare-bones summary of the aftermath of the veteran women's law, if not the lawsuit itself, and the current status of veterans at The Citadel is also appropriate at the outset. After closing down the Veterans Day Program (VDP) in 1992 to keep women out of the Corps of Cadets, The Citadel Board of Visitors (BOV) announced fifteen years later, on April 21, 2007, its intention to reinstate a modified version of the pre-1992 VDP. According to the BOV Minutes,

> Following an in-depth discussion of the various aspects of the proposed program, the following motion was made by Colonel Dick and seconded by Colonel Love: MOTION. "That the Veterans Program be reestablished as presented by the administration." The motion carried unanimously.

What was discussed in the in-depth discussion is not reported. The Veteran Cadet Program opened in the fall of 2008.

Initially established only for veterans who were former members of the Corps of Cadets at The Citadel, pursuant to a Board of Visitors motion on June 14, 2008, the Veteran Cadet Program or Citadel Cadet Veteran Program was expanded by the spring of 2010 to include all veterans, male and female, returning from active duty. This expansion is today called The Citadel Non-Cadet Veteran Day Program. Thus, two years of litigation between 1992 and 1994 and $700,000 in litigation costs in the *Johnson* case were quietly swept under the rug.[6]

According to the Board of Visitors Minutes for June 14, 2008, Citadel veterans can get a Citadel diploma and ring, just like the ones the cadets get, if they enroll in the Veteran Cadet Program, now called The Citadel Cadet Veteran Program, following at least four semesters spent in the Corps of Cadets before they leave to go on active duty in the reserves or to join the National Guard.[7] They can return to The Citadel and get the same diploma and ring as cadets get, even though they choose to attend day classes as civilians. That is, some former Citadel veterans may finish out their Citadel education as civilians and eventually wear the same ring which the cadets wear, even though they sat in daytime classes as civilian non-cadets for up to two years or more. They may also take evening classes.

The fact that non-cadets who were formerly cadets may earn the more coveted Citadel cadet diploma and ring—an enormous economic advantage when they begin to look for jobs and seek promotions—and that other non-cadets who were not formerly cadets may not, arguably creates a violation of the equal protection clause. There is simply no rational basis for the state to confer an economic advantage to former Citadel students who are now veterans and not to veterans who have never been members of the Corps of Cadets, some of whom may or may not have also been wounded in action. Both are non-cadet civilians. It would appear, therefore, that veterans who are not formerly Citadel cadets might have a cause of action against The Citadel admission policy under the Fourteenth Amendment. Once again, all veterans are not being treated equally—not between men and women this time, but between veterans who were former cadets and veterans who were not former cadets. Some veterans are still getting the short end of The Citadel stick. Nonetheless, this book discusses only the women veterans' lawsuit and the broad educational opportunities foreclosed to hundreds of veterans, male and female, in essential core curricula when The Citadel closed the VDP for the eighteen years between 1992 and 2010.

What was the legal posture of The Citadel after the Supreme Court ruled that VMI must admit women in *United States v. Virginia*, 518 U.S. 515 (1996)? After the Supreme Court denied Faulkner's and The Citadel's writs for *certiorari*, the Supreme Court's 1996 ruling applied only to VMI. Nonetheless, both sides filed briefs in *VMI* which recognized future controlling authority of the Supreme Court's decision. VMI did not win in the Supreme Court, yet after the ruling, The Citadel appealed the critical district court orders of July 22, 1994, and July 24, 1995. Notwithstanding a passing observation by the three-judge panel in *Mentavlos v. Anderson*, 249 F.3d 301 (4th Cir. 2001), that "The Citadel was forced to abandon its male-only admissions policy and began voluntarily admitting women to its Corps of Cadets in the fall of 1996," The Citadel did not voluntarily admit women in 1996. It was forced to admit women in 1996 under the district court order of *Faulkner I*, affirmed by the Fourth Circuit in *Faulkner II*, just as it was forced to admit Faulkner alone in 1995.

Yet, in spite of its brief filed in *VMI*, if The Citadel could for fourteen years ignore *Mississippi University for Women v. Hogan*, 458 U.S. 718 (1982), the principal controlling case, it certainly was capable of continuing the fight after the *VMI* decision by ignoring *Cooper v. Aaron*, 358 U.S. 1, a 1958 case compelling state officials to integrate Arkansas public schools and thus obey federal court orders based on the Supreme Court's interpretation of the Constitution.

Yet this undeniably accurate history of the court record tracing the admission of women to the Corps of Cadets continues to be rejected by The Citadel. The Citadel claims finally to have done the right thing through a voluntary act while it continues to harbor a well-publicized lingering resentment over admitting women. Two cadets in H Company as late as November 14, 2010, while driving east on Interstate Highway 20 between Augusta and Columbia, sported a bumper sticker reading, "NO [drawing of a woman]!"[8]

For The Citadel, Faulkner does not join the long line of American civil rights leaders seeking admission to public schools. Clemson University recognizes the struggle of its first black student Harvey Gantt, but even the success of the first black cadet, Charles Foster, is given only quiet recognition at The Citadel. With regard to its admission of women, a recent history of The Citadel written by an alumnus of the Class of 1971 is typical in its rejection of Faulkner's contribution to civil rights at The Citadel: "The first women entered the Corps of Cadets in 1996."[9]

Apart from occasional references in the Board of Visitors' minutes, two small boxes of press releases and one large box of newspaper clippings marked "Coeducation," records of the *Johnson/Lacey/Chapman* women veterans' case or the *Faulkner/Mellette* case do not exist in the Department of Archives on the third floor of the Daniel Library or anywhere else at The Citadel. Sometime after the *Faulkner* case was over, Charleston professional photographer Curtis Norman, who covered the cases for *The Post and Courier*, donated his photographs to me and to The Citadel archives. On visits to the archives on July 11 and October 20, 2011, in search of photographs of the women's cases in preparation for this book, particularly those by Curtis Norman of Faulkner for which I did not have copies, I was told that no photographs from the women's lawsuits are kept in the archives. An 81-page list of categories of Citadel photographs on file contained no references to photographs of Faulkner or Mellette or of the veteran women. No written documents on Faulkner's lawsuit exist in the archives. "You don't find her name up here much," I was told. Photographs and documentation on Nancy Mace, the first woman to be graduated from the Corps of Cadets, however, are easily found.

In almost completely ignoring Faulkner, the most basic values of leadership and courage—charging the machine gun nest, being willing to make individual sacrifices, standing up for what you believe in, for what you hold to be the truth, knowing you're right before going ahead even if all others remain behind and even ridicule you—all are rejected by The Citadel which inspires a safer kind of discipline and leadership. In their place are promoted the scripted anecdotes of the daughter of a Commandant of the Corps of Cadets, a transfer student who made a safe beach landing after Faulkner had wiped out most of the initial resistance.

Local Counsel is written to reflect upon a persistent lack of leadership at The Citadel. That lack of leadership is nourished by confusion over two facts. First, The Citadel is a public university. Second, The Citadel is military only in the sense that its daytime students are cadets in a state organization. The military aspect of The Citadel exists solely to provide a liberal arts education within a military environment provided by a public state entity.

The Citadel is a college where one out of three students major in business and one out of five go into the military after graduation.

All students in the Corps of Cadets are civilians and none are military. Contrary to what The Citadel would lead the public to understand, especially in its distinction between "veteran cadets" and "veteran students," pursuant to its Cadet Veteran Program and Non-cadet Veteran Program which it announced on June 14, 2008, all cadets at The Citadel are civilians in the same sense that ordinary citizens are civilians.[10] At The Citadel, the Military College of South Carolina, a cadet is a member of the Corps of Cadets, the Palmetto Brigade, and an ROTC program in the Army, Navy/Marines, or Air Force. The composite ROTC program at The Citadel is one of the largest in the country. The status of a Citadel student as a military cadet is, therefore, merely complementary to his or her civilian status which he or she never gives up when admitted to The Citadel. Such military status is defined by his or her membership in the South Carolina Corps of Cadets, although some cadets who have signed contracts with one of the armed services are prospective members of the United States military while at The Citadel.

As few as 20% of Citadel students each year ever become truly military by serving their country when they graduate. They do so only if they are commissioned as officers in a branch of the United States Armed Forces upon their graduation from The Citadel. ROTC graduates in commencement ceremonies each year throughout America experience the same transfer to military status.

To rephrase this issue, which is a point of fundamental confusion about the military nature of The Citadel, there are two kinds of student cadets in the Palmetto Brigade: cadets who have not signed a contract with one of the branches of the U.S. military and who account for up to 80% of the Corps, and cadets who have signed a contract and/or are on a scholarship funded by one of the military branches. The latter group is compelled to take a commission upon graduation. The former may be given a commission only if they choose to seek one and are accepted by a branch of service. Commissioning usually occurs after cadets complete their undergraduate contractual obligations at graduation. Most cadets are allowed to quit The Citadel at any time without any obligation, unlike a recruit in the military. Citadel cadets with contractual obligations, however, usually cannot simply walk away from their military commitment without repaying the federal dollars spent on them so far. Both kinds of cadets take ROTC for four years. Contract and scholarship cadets are required to spend at least one summer on ROTC duties.

There are, in turn, various programs for ROTC students at The Citadel: programs for the ordinary civilian cadet, for cadets on military contracts, and for cadets holding military scholarships; the latter two groups are usually always one and the same. Those who are on scholarship or who have signed a contract are required to wear their U.S. military uniforms to ROTC class, but most cadets, because they are civilians, simply wear their Citadel cadet uniforms to ROTC. Sometimes, however, they all must wear their Army Combat Uniforms or ACUs to lab once a week. All cadets, of course, wear their Citadel Palmetto Brigade uniforms to all other classes and events.

Thus, one of the biggest mistakes one can make in understanding The Citadel is to confuse it with the military. Most observers simply allow it to pass as the private preserve of its administration and alumni. The education and training through ROTC classes for a large majority of the cadets is wasted in the sense that they do not seek a commission or do not qualify for one upon graduation. The vast majority leave to serve the private sector.

Two other kinds of students sit in class with members of the Corps of Cadets, but they are not members of the Corps. One small group includes active duty students, male and female, who have been assigned by the Pentagon to The Citadel to earn a baccalaureate degree so that they can become officers. Out of the total number of 2,089 cadets enrolled in the Corps of Cadets in the spring of 2011, including 134 women, there were five female and 63 male active duty students enrolled in MECEP, the Marine Enlisted Commissioning Education Program, and ECP, the Navy's Enlisted Commissioning Program.[11] Veterans in the Veterans Day Program make up another group. These two groups, together with ROTC staff assigned to The Citadel by the Pentagon, represent the only present and former U.S. military presence on campus. The active duty and veteran students, other than those eligible veterans who elect to return to the Corps through the Cadet Veteran Program, do not live in the barracks and are not required to participate in ROTC or Corps activities. Some members of the faculty, staff, and administration are retired U.S. military, but all are given a SCUM rank as members of the South Carolina Unorganized Militia.

Interestingly enough, the active duty Marines in class serve a very useful purpose. They unofficially help some professors keep cadets awake in class—especially the knobs, as first year students are called, who are never allowed to get enough sleep in their barracks.

The essentially non-military nature of The Citadel is, in fact, admittedly its chief characteristic. Discussing the women veterans' lawsuit filed in 1992, The Citadel's lead attorney Dawes Cooke explained, "If The Citadel's mission was to create military officers to serve in the military, that would be a valid point [to admit women into the Veterans Day Program]. It uses the military environment as its teaching method, but its goal is not to produce military officers."[12] Later, in the lawsuit brought by one of the two women cadets who were hazed out of the Corps the year after Faulkner's departure, the Fourth Circuit found that the non-military nature of The Citadel is a key point of law that not only distinguishes it from VMI, but also determines that Citadel cadets are not state actors:

> [In *United States v. Virginia*, 518 U.S. 515 (1996)], the Supreme Court described the mission of the Virginia Military Academy (VMI), a similar state military college, as "producing citizen soldiers." *Id.* at 541. As an initial premise, we note that the mission of The Citadel makes no such reference to this military-type goal; rather, the stated mission of The Citadel is to produce community leaders, not soldiers.[13]

Now, years after a woman has been admitted to the Corps of Cadets, ordinary male and female citizens who do not want membership in the Corps of Cadets seek to join the cadets in daytime classes to enjoy the same educational opportunities provided by the state. The Citadel University, for that is what The Citadel is, now fails to admit ordinary citizens who are hungry for knowledge, significantly in the sciences, math, and engineering, into its daytime classes which are reserved exclusively for the South Carolina Corps of Cadets, most of whom are not from South Carolina. The Citadel today remains largely indifferent to demands for increased educational opportunities necessitated by a global economy expressed dramatically by what can be called the Lowcountry's 2010 Boeing Effect, a blanket term for moving South Carolina into economic competition in the twenty-first century. Twenty years ago, during the women's admission cases, The Citadel suppressed women's educational opportunities. *Faulkner* dragged The Citadel into the twentieth century. Today, The Citadel continues to suppress educational opportunities for ordinary citizens. A new effort must be made to drag The Citadel into the twenty-first century.

This book is in part about Charleston—about the only city in America where a Citadel could exist—the adoration of bricks and mortar and love of an ineffable quality of life, of an old world assertion of class for anyone who claims it, of narrow fields of play and an opportunity to retire on them at birth. It is impossible to convince most white Charlestonians that states' rights include a history of oppression as well as a sense of constitutional sovereignty, that the Civil War fought 150 years ago was quite correctly for many Americans a war to end slavery. During litigation, The Citadel often described itself as the last dinosaur for its efforts to preserve an *ancien régime* in its male-only admissions policy to the Corps of Cadets. *Local Counsel* is a day-in-the-life story of a sole practitioner on a dinosaur hunt.

In the process of writing the book, I discussed peripheral facts with only a handful of people, only one of whom was a major player. One chief witness refused to discuss her experiences in the case which she described as "horrible." A research assistant who initially agreed to help prepare the text for publication withdrew after a few weeks in the spring of 2011 because she no longer felt comfortable being affiliated with research for the book. I have not discussed the book with any of the five women clients or with co-counsel. However, I did notify Patricia Johnson and Elizabeth Lacey Dawsey, two of the plaintiffs in the women veterans' case, of the reopening of the Veterans Day Program. I also discussed the current need for engineers in the Lowcountry with both of them.

Co-counsel and Shannon Faulkner were never consulted in my research and writing. Nor was Angela Chapman or Nancy Mellette. No member of my family has read the book. I mainly worked alone from personal notes and copies of court records of the veteran women's case, or simply the *Johnson* case, and the *Faulkner* case, later the *Faulkner/Mellette* case, which are kept in personal storage in Charleston. As an attorney of record, I received all copies of all court documents. I referred briefly on two occasions to the Clerk of Court's records kept in storage in Atlanta. Privileged information remains protected. As a general rule of thumb, I use only the names of major players even though many unnamed parties are also a matter of public record. An original text, more than twice the size of this one, contains most of the names of people who are mentioned here only as "a man" or "a woman." It sits in a garage full of all supporting documents for a later day and another author. A final history of the case cannot be written until Citadel records in their entirety are someday released to the public. And, certainly, until Faulkner herself tells her own story.

In discussing the history of the cases, *Local Counsel* relates many little incidental acts during the fight to win educational opportunities for the five female plaintiffs and the women who followed. I have often made reference to accounts of key incidents as they were reported in the major local newspaper, *The Post and Courier*. Anyone who reads only the local newspaper, however, might have scant knowledge of what really happened in the women veterans' and the *Faulkner/Mellette* suits. This book brings to light facts not previously published. It talks about some of the little things that are most telling about a lawsuit.

Everything in the book is accurately related to the best of my ability. It is partly anecdotal. It skims over many events and tries to sail through the Scylla and Charybdis of being whiney or too critical. Conversations set in quotation marks are my recollection of those conversations to the best of my ability. It is possible that others could have differing recollection of the same conversations.

Local Counsel is written as a primary source, yet the marriage of memory and history, as Yale Professor David Blight might say, is here conspicuously one of conflicted companions.[14] Court documents and written correspondence are quoted verbatim, with a few minor exceptions. Not all important legal events are recognized. Anyone can tell that I have not used the federal courts' docket sheets as an outline.

Within a range of legal issues and strategies, the book raises the kind of questions that lawyers and law school students deal with every day: What are the ethical bounds of professional responsibility that mark the extent to which an attorney may zealously go to represent a client who brings a suit against a powerful and obdurate defendant? When, if ever, does a civil rights case become no longer just the client's, but the lawyer's as well? To what extent is a civil rights lawyer a "social engineer"? And, from the defense side, the same collision of passions: What can be done short of court-ordered sanctions to enforce court orders and the rules of discovery under the Federal Rules of Civil Procedure? What are the bounds of civility toward a plaintiff in a fiercely protected cause?

This book is also an account of personal reasons or motives for entering a protracted civil rights litigation and the price paid for zealous representation. I wrote the book to serve as a historical record from the unique point of view of a participant who had a better perspective of the case, albeit necessarily limited, than most. Serving as local counsel in efforts to get women in The Citadel— or as a reviewer for the University of South Carolina Press put it, my "attitude"—effectively put an end to my law practice.

The numerous short subsections used in drafting the text over a period of ten years have been retained somewhat in the manner of the 65 short chapter headings in *Eyrbyggja Saga*. That story is about a Norwegian during the arrival of Christianity in Iceland. The thirteenth-century author resorts to brief interrelated accounts to report the complex social and political reactions to a new idea among people living in small communities bound by duty, honor, and tradition.

The book, *Local Counsel,* was already at press in the fall of 2011 when failures by college officials to report alleged incidents of sexual abuse at Penn State and The Citadel appeared in the national news media. The cover-up at Penn State arose in violation of state law requiring that such allegations be directly reported to the police. The cover-up at The Citadel broke no state law since, The Citadel argued, no law at the time expressly required that such a report be made by a university to the police, but the cover-up did throw more light on the meaning of honor at The Citadel. From reports in *The Post and Courier*, which broke the story after strong resistance by The Citadel, general counsel at The Citadel was charged by the Board of Visitors in 2007 mainly with the responsibility of protecting The Citadel from any potential lawsuits if and when any alleged incidents of sexual misconduct by Louis "Skip" ReVille as early as 2002 ever came to light, as indeed they did in 2011. ReVille, 2002 Chairman of The Citadel Honor Committee while a cadet, had been hired by The Citadel as a camp counselor in its summer program for young boys. By early 2012, several victims filed lawsuits against ReVille as perpetrator and The Citadel as enabler of sexual abuse. Plaintiffs included victims in schools and youth programs where ReVille worked after he left The Citadel without disclosure made by The Citadel of the allegations made during or shortly after his employment at The Citadel. Some plaintiffs alleged that when the president and The Citadel police, a law enforcement agency of the State, failed to report the allegations either to the City of Charleston police or to SLED (South Carolina Law Enforcement Division), The Citadel violated, in both spirit and letter, South Carolina Code of Laws, as amended, Sections 63-7-10(A), 63-7-20, and 16-15-365. By failing to report, The Citadel hoped to protect its honor if not young boys—ironically, even when the reporting party could choose to remain anonymous. In a letter to the editor of *The Post and Courier*, which I drafted on November 24, 2011, but never mailed, I said that two things would happen as a result of the cover-up: no one at The Citadel will be fired, and complete disclosure by The Citadel will never be made.

Finally, this book is not written simply to praise Faulkner, Mellette, Johnson, Lacey, and Chapman. Nor is it written to bash The Citadel. The chairman of The Citadel Board of Visitors correctly characterized litigation in the women's cases as one over which reasonable men may differ. If not clear on every page, this book recognizes that fact. It is written, however, to record the manner in which The Citadel defended. The Citadel lacked leaders in the 1990s, a problem that continues today. In the early 1960s, as colleges and universities all over the South began to admit African Americans, South Carolina's response was largely different from that of most states, notwithstanding the Orangeburg Massacre. Clemson, the University of South Carolina, and The Citadel were racially integrated without serious incidents of violence. The likes of George Wallace in Alabama, Ross Barnett in Mississippi, Orval Faubus in Arkansas, and Lester Maddox in Georgia were not in major leadership positions in South Carolina. Instead, the governor of South Carolina from 1959 to 1963 declared that South Carolina had "run out of courts" to continue to resist compliance with the law and sought wisely to begin the decade with order and civility. He was a Citadel man, Fritz Hollings, Class of 1942.

I am grateful to Professor Jay Bender, University of South Carolina School of Law, and Professor Nathan Crystal, Charleston School of Law, who kindly reviewed portions of the manuscript and offered comments, but I alone bear complete responsibility for its contents.

I also wish to thank Ms. Wendy Hustwit, copyeditor; Ms. Laura Dewey, who compiled the index; and Ms. Darla Walls for help with gathering photographs by Wade Spees, Curtis Norman, Brad Nettles, Gabriel Tait, and Roger Cureton, most of which are on file at *The Post and Courier*. Regrettably, many other newsprint photographs taken during the cases were not able to be reprinted from the newspapers in which they first appeared.

My appreciation also goes to Zoë Oakes, Suzanne Morgen, Tim Colton, Karen Clayton, and Rachel Smithson at Carolina Academic Press for their work on this project.

PART I

Chapter 1

The First to Try

Out of Here

Montana does not have the 54 fourteeners that Colorado has, but from the top of ski lifts 12,000 feet up at Big Sky Resort you can see enough of the Gallatin Valley to get some perspective on things. The river that runs through it is just to the east. It was January 2006. The rich were bundled in their gear and the richer were hiding somewhere within the Yellowstone Club just west of the black diamond ski runs. I had been lifted high enough on one of the ski lifts to look down and see the tiny images of people below and stood bemused at us all. It was exhilarating. Grizzlies, wolves, bison, mountain goats, and elks were in the neighborhood. By leaving Charleston for four months I was getting a different point of view. I wasn't practicing law. I was trying to get over being sued by The Citadel for a suit I filed on behalf of a cadet after Faulkner's case ended.

"I got to get out of here," I told Melinda a few months earlier. "They sued me for suing them and I barely got away. Now I've got to get out of here."

"Go where?"

"Bozeman. Montana State will let me teach for the spring semester. I'll look for land. If you wouldn't move to Colorado after the case in '96, maybe you can see now that I'm really done for here. I really can't practice law in Charleston anymore."

"That cadet case was just bad luck on your part. You did everything you could," she said.

"You know I lost on summary judgment, on two state statutes that clearly say he did not haze those girls. The South Carolina law says you've got to have intent to injure or punish for it to be hazing, and even The Citadel admitted there wasn't any intent on the part of my client. But now they can interpret hazing as it's defined by The Citadel, straight out of their own regulations that don't require intent for it to be hazing. So I'm thrown out of court, and they immediately turn around and sue me for filing a frivolous lawsuit."

"You won against the frivolous lawsuit," she said. "The judge threw it out. There should be something in the rules that would have allowed you to sue

17

them right back for filing a 'bogus' lawsuit against what they called your client's 'frivolous' one. Anyway, under state law every cadet could always argue that he didn't really intend to do any harm—and get off scot free."

"The Fourth Circuit affirmed," I went on, "and I had to pay $136 in costs. The law's what counts. The district court wrote a good opinion. I have no gripe with that, just with the suit filed after I lost. They need to change the statutes. As it stands now, the Citadel regulations are the law. I can't just sit around and whine. I need a break. I can't hang up my own shingle. 'How's he going to draw a jury?' That's what the judge asked about me during the attorney fee fight after the *Faulkner* case. At any rate, I need a break from the Holy City."

That was one of the last times my wife and I talked at any length about the case. Not only on the town but also at home the case took its toll. I had heard that really famous lawsuits include desperate acts, a bunch of divorces among the lawyers, and even a suicide or two. All in all this was not one of them. And it never got anywhere near the violence of the racial discrimination cases a generation or two earlier, notwithstanding Shannon Faulkner's own account of a death threat against her parents as the reason for her dropping out.[1] By 2008 I had even heard from friends on The Citadel faculty that the women admitted into the Corps of Cadets since Shannon Faulkner were gradually thriving under a new administration. I didn't believe it, but that's what I heard.

First, how is The Citadel doing after getting rid of the Veterans Day Program in 1992? Admittedly, eighteen years later, The Citadel is now trying to make amends with veterans and society at large by reopening the VDP. Nonetheless, The Citadel's decision in 1992 to close the VDP to keep women out of the Corps, for some, still represents a force greater than its sense of patriotism and national defense. Columbia University, the home of Rudy the Red and site of violent demonstrations during the Vietnam War, never shut down its undergraduate School of General Studies to keep out veterans as The Citadel did its Veterans Day Program. Both the VDP at The Citadel and the School of General Studies at Columbia University were created after World War II to educate veterans on the G.I. Bill. In the fall of 2009, Columbia University was educating 210 veterans, 88 of whom were on the G.I. Bill. They had access to all courses taught at any time.[2] In the spring of 2011, The Citadel was educating 28 veterans, eight "veteran cadets," presumably former members of the Corps of Cadets admitted pursuant to the Board of Visitors' decision on June 14, 2008, and 20 "veteran students" admitted pursuant to a Citadel news release to the public on November 16, 2009. No women were among the 28 veterans, but women would have been admitted after 2010 if they had met the same admission qualifications the males had to meet.[3]

In further contrast, veterans in the Lowcountry have always been welcomed at Trident Technical College, a two-year community college in North Charleston that tries to satisfy veterans' basic academic requirements for the first two initial years toward a four-year baccalaureate degree.[4]

Secondly, how is The Citadel doing after Faulkner was admitted in 1995? How is it doing since the district court ended the case in 2002 and no longer ordered The Citadel to file remedial quarterly reports with the court?

In 1999 when the first woman was graduated among some 2000 total cadets in the Corps of Cadets, there were more than 40 women enrolled, 27 rising sophomores, 12 rising juniors, with one woman entering her senior year. Thirty years after the federal military academies admitted women, 14%–16% of the cadets at the academies are women. Fifteen years after Faulkner's departure, the percentage of women, around 6%–8%, remains low at The Citadel but matches the percentage of African Americans. It is about one-third the percentage needed to establish a critical mass of 20% for successful integration and assimilation.[5]

What subjects are mainly being taught at The Citadel, a liberal arts college in a military environment? In a recent year, 2008–2009, for example, the Office of Institutional Research at The Citadel reported that Business/Marketing was again the most popular major by far. But in most universities, business administration majors make up only about one-fifth of the total number of graduating seniors.[6] Out of the 2098 cadets in the Corps of Cadets, nearly one-third chose Business/Marketing, down somewhat from the usually high percentage of 35%–40% in previous years. Criminal justice came in second with 14%, for a staggering combined percentage of 43% of the cadets majoring in either business administration or criminal justice at The Citadel in 2009. More than 150 cadets majored in Health, Exercise, and Sport Science. Engineering and the sciences hardly registered. Although actual numbers taken from commencement programs vary by one or two percentage points, according to the website, 10% of the cadets majored in civil engineering and 6% in electrical engineering. Five percent majored in biology. Thus, the 7% who majored in Health, Exercise, and Sport Science were about as many as those who majored in biology and electrical engineering. Chemistry and physics majors were 1% of the Corps, but math did not even register a full percentage point. Three-tenths of 1% of the cadets at The Citadel majored in math in the fall of 2008.[7]

According to a survey conducted by Clemson in 2010, there are approximately 8000 "home bound" engineers who would like to continue their studies in engineering beyond a baccalaureate level in the Lowcountry.[8] A home-bound student is one who, for reasons typically related to family commitments, cannot leave his home town to study elsewhere. There is arguably at least that number of prospective home-bound non-cadets who would welcome a chance to take undergraduate engineering courses at The Citadel in classes taught between 8:00–5:00, if offered.

At the United States Military Academy (USMA) at West Point, engineering and engineering technologies are the major subjects for 27% of the cadets; only 9% are business/marketing majors.[9] Two USMA women won Rhodes scholarships in 2009. The Citadel has never had a Rhodes Scholar. At the Naval Academy, 27% of the students majored in engineering in 2007 and 18% majored in science, computer science and engineering, and math. The same strong emphasis is given to the basic sciences and engineering at the Air Force Academy. The Naval and Air Force academies both have about 20% women, and West Point has 14%, still more than twice the percentage of women at The Citadel.[10]

Nor is The Citadel's minimal contribution to national defense through the study of engineering, math, and the sciences tempered by instruction in foreign languages other than French, Spanish, and German. Mandarin and Arabic, for example, are not taught as they are at West Point.

Numbers available on The Citadel cadets are set in relief by numbers available on the Active Duty Students, those students sent to The Citadel on orders from the U.S. military. Each service branch approves the subjects they major in. Out of the 32 Active Duty Students at The Citadel in the fall of 2008, one was a woman.[11] Nineteen percent majored in Business Administration and 6% in Health and Wellness, but 27% majored in engineering and 42% majored in engineering, math, or physics. That's roughly the same percentage of cadets in the Corps who majored in business/marketing and criminal justice.

In 2008–2009 South Carolina tax payers helped educate more Citadel cadets from out-of-state (55.3%) than from in-state (44.7%).

In the last five years, there has been a 5.8% decline in enrollment of women cadets in the Corps.

The Office of Institutional Research at The Citadel keeps no records prior to 1998. The South Carolina Commission on Higher Education is not charged with the responsibility to maintain data marking the progress of women at The Citadel. The early progress of women is marked in the reports in the *Faulkner/Mellette* case which were filed by The Citadel under court order between 1995 until the case was closed in March, 2002, but the reports are available only from federal court archives in Atlanta. Presumably, what is not documented by the Office of Institutional Research and available to the public on The Citadel website has not been documented at all or is simply made available only to the administration and the Board of Visitors.

In September 2009, The Citadel responded to a Freedom of Information Act request with the reply that documentation according to gender (e.g., average SAT score and GPA of female/male cadets, average female/male graduation rates, average female/male drop-out rates, average female/male business majors, engineering majors, etc.) is not readily available and that preparing such essential information would require several days of programming time, a cost-prohibitive procedure billable to the inquirer.

Tuskegee and King

Experiences that led me to the *Faulkner* case and my role as a civil rights lawyer started in 1958 when, as a high school student, I asked my mother for permission to go to Tuskegee to help integrate the Episcopal Young Churchmen. "Go ask your father," she said.

Professor Ray Black of Birmingham-Southern College, a couple of years earlier, had gone over to get the family car that my sister somehow managed to get stuck in a ditch in front of Arthur Shores's house in College Hills, not too far from Condoleezza Rice's and Alma Powell's old neighborhood. Ty Cobb's too. Arthur Shores was co-counsel with Thurgood Marshall and Constance Baker Motley when they represented Autherine Lucy in her effort to become the first black undergraduate at the University of Alabama. Professor Black's teenage daughter, Mary Holland, had been rubbernecking around a large crater in the yard left by a bomb planted by the Ku Klux Klan the night before. They were bombing his house long before the 1963 bombing of the Sixteenth Avenue Baptist Church. She left our 1955 Chevrolet in the ditch and walked the few blocks back home.

"Bob," my father said, "these are not easy times for you children to be out there the way you are."

The professor drew out his Sir Walter Raleigh tobacco and packed his pipe in the kind of way that always kept it lit. "But I'll let you do this because you want to and it's right."

And then he paused and said something unforgettable. "I'd go too, but I can't. I've got a job and family to think about." Those sentiments rang throughout the *Faulkner* litigation with men and women of good will.

A handful of Episcopal Young Churchmen of the Diocese of Alabama in the spring of 1958, with Youth Director Peggy Horn leading the charge, drove to Tuskegee, convinced that any racial problem could be solved with a little light on the subject, a little mutual understanding. During our meetings with black members in the church, I and others, black and white, even took umbrage at the idea that an outside agitator might come over to Alabama to help.

"We can solve our own problems here in Alabama," we said, "and we don't need any help from folks in Atlanta." We had never heard of Martin Luther King until then.

At about the same time in 1958, Bud Watts, Lewis Spearman, and Jimmy Jones, future leaders in the fierce defense against the admission of women into the Corps of Cadets, were being graduated from The Citadel.

1989: "I Thought You Were a Black Man"

Melinda was to become the better lawyer. She was smart and had a gift for negotiation and getting along with everybody. After we got married at St. Michael's Church, I put aside my new Charleston practice on Broad Street for a couple of years to accompany her to Birmingham while she went to Cumberland Law School. I was back in my home town.

"Honey, look at this," Melinda said, handing me *The Birmingham News* with her finger pressed on a small column of print. "The Justice Department is suing VMI to let in women. There's even some talk about a future lawsuit against The Citadel as well." She paused while I read. "It's about time," she added.

She was excited and at the same time surprised.

I took a hard look at the paper and realized that this was not simply a matter of the State of Virginia dealing with its own problems with women in higher education.

"So?" she asked. "Why don't you call him, the guy in the paper?"

"Why?" I asked.

"Why? You know why. The Citadel."

I reread the short article. A lawyer in Washington, D.C., John Banzhaf, was quoted in his discussion about a Virginia school girl who complained about not being able to go to VMI.

"Now that's a brave girl," Melinda said. "Think of all the attention on her now."

After Melinda left for class at Cumberland Law School and Spencer was off to kindergarten, I wrote Banzhaf on May 15, 1989, from Johnson & Cory, the law firm where I was working in Birmingham.

"This is a follow-up letter after calling your secretary this morning to leave my name and address as one willing to help you in your suit under the Civil Rights Act of 1964 against The Citadel," I wrote.

> Furthermore, I think The Citadel has been preparing for your lawsuit since the early 80s when rumor had it that it received a large benefaction from someone in Atlanta who had been to The Citadel for only a year back in the 1930s. That amount was never made public and I suspect that there are other hidden gifts that could be discovered.... Now that General Mark Clark is dead the time has come for your law-

suit. Perhaps you are already in touch with attorneys such as Armand Derfner and Ray McClain in Charleston. At any rate, please let me know if I can be of any help.

Banzhaf returned my call, but I did most of the talking.

"The reason I called, Mr. Banzhaf, is that I want to offer my services if you ever need help on your companion case to get women in The Citadel. The paper said you wrote a letter of complaint to the Justice Department about the all-male admissions policy at The Citadel as well. I'll help you with the facts if I can."

I thought that bold offer would put me on record as being there when it counted. I would play a minor cameo role.

"What do you need me to do on your case against The Citadel?" I added.

"Well, do you know of any young woman who wants to go to The Citadel?" Banzhaf asked. "The article you read must not have made it clear that I'm really not suing The Citadel at all. In fact, I personally am not even suing VMI," Banzhaf said.

"How's that?" I asked.

"The United States—the federal government, the Department of Justice—is suing VMI, not me. The high school senior who wrote DOJ about The Citadel is my niece. I wrote the letter and she signed it." Banzhaf said. "So DOJ is not suing The Citadel. It's just suing VMI."

"I thought you were the plaintiffs' lawyer in cases against both VMI and The Citadel, or at least with a case already going against VMI and one about to be filed against The Citadel," I said.

"You know," Banzhaf said, "DOJ doesn't do everything on its own. In some cases, they don't act upon a complaint of a Fourteenth Amendment violation unless it's made from a private citizen, unless the private citizen raises it first in his or her own letter of complaint. That's possibly what another school girl in Virginia eventually did. Somebody I don't know may have eventually written her own letter of complaint. Either that or DOJ chose to act on my niece's letter about VMI and not on the one I wrote about The Citadel. I don't know. All I know is that DOJ is suing VMI but not The Citadel. At any rate, the legal issue is one of standing. Whoever gets DOJ to write The Citadel a Letter of Inquiry has got to have standing, and only a girl who writes a letter for herself will have it."

Banzhaf added a bit more. "The girl who wrote the DOJ from Virginia gets to remain anonymous since the plaintiff is the federal government if a lawsuit if filed. The statute under which the government brings these kinds of cases is set up that way to encourage the little guy—or girl—to speak up without fear of reprisal if she feels she has been deprived of her equal rights. Fear of reprisal is the beginning and the end of these civil rights cases. VMI will never know her name unless she tells them some day. The DOJ will keep it a secret. Even if DOJ wins and she gets to enroll in VMI, the people there won't know that it was she who got it all started in Virginia."

After Banzhaf rang off, I called two women in Charleston who I thought might know of young women interested in going to The Citadel. They scarcely comprehended the question. I then called Edmund Robinson, ACLU president in Charleston. Although I did not know about it at the time, in a four-page memorandum dated two years previously, on September 20, 1987, Armand Derfner, a well-known civil rights attorney in Charleston, had outlined for Robinson the arguments that could be made in a suit to admit women to The Citadel. The memo briefly discussed *Williams v. McNair*, 316 F. Supp. 134 (D.S.C. 1970), *aff'd*, 401 U.S. 951 (1971), a case in which Judge Donald Russell upheld under a rational basis analysis the all-female admissions policy at Winthrop, a case which The Citadel would fondly cite in the *Faulkner* litigation.

"Edmund, I need your contacts in the Holy City. I need the names of young women who might want to go to The Citadel now that VMI is being sued. What's the word on that?"

Robinson was slightly taken back. "Nothing. Nothing's going on. Nobody has taken much notice of the *VMI* case, I guess. I'm not even sure if I know a lot about it. Not much in the paper here about it. Of course, they wouldn't want to publicize such radical mischief anyway," he laughed. "I don't know of any woman trying to get in The Citadel. This is Charleston, you know."

But he offered to look around among the black community for a prospect. It would be from that community, I thought, that the best candidates would be found. The Citadel would have to fight blacks as well as women.

"Edmund, do you think you could represent her if you find her?" I asked.

"Bob," Robinson said without a pause, "you know I can't do that. Bill Ackerman in my firm could not be a bigger supporter of The Citadel. He's 'Mr. Citadel.' Word about Bill is that he never met a person he didn't like. But I can tell you that if I represented a woman to get in The Citadel, I would be the first exception. And I would be a dead man professionally—and socially, as any lawyer would be."

A few days later Robinson called back and gave me the names of David J. Mack, Jr., Joseph G. Thompson, and William Glover, major players in the black community in Charleston. Taking a line from Freud on the unconscious, I wrote Mr. Mack on May 17, 1989, "As I mentioned on the phone, I am not trying to 'invent' a plaintiff but rather hope to 'discover' a young girl who wishes that her state's tax dollars could be used on her at The Citadel. I welcome any information from you or your high school guidance staff about such a person."

I went on to say that I would be at Kiawah over Memorial Day for an annual reunion at the beach with two of my old Army buddies.

Mr. Mack organized the meeting but dropped out of all future inquiries. Mack was area supervisor of District 20, the school district of the peninsular city. District 20 was made up of many black students and had been in the middle of a federal lawsuit forcing Charleston schools to integrate.

Thompson was one of the first black students to integrate North Carolina State University. Glover was the NAACP president. Both Thompson and Glover were NAACP educational coordinators for South Carolina and Charleston.

I met with them on Memorial Day 1989, at the Old Citadel on Marion Square in downtown Charleston. The men were waiting in a room on the top floor of the Old Citadel when I arrived. How fitting, I thought, as I climbed the stairwell. Thousands of Citadel cadets ran up these steps from 1842 till 1922 before the new buildings were constructed on the Ashley River.

They were understandably wary of me at first. Neither really trusted a white guy who wanted to use a young black woman to be the "First Woman in The Citadel." Mr. Glover especially was mindful of the tuition costs to go to any college, and both knew of the emotional costs to be paid by such a woman.

"We can talk to a couple of parents we know. We think their girls might be interested," Mack confided after we talked for a while. "They both seem to be good students, and are both interested in the military."

"They have to be first rate," I said, knowing full well that any woman of just average abilities would do well enough.

"Someone ready to go next August 1990, is whom we're looking for," I added.

"Well, where can they meet with you?" Glover asked. "They'll be there with their mothers."

"I can't taint any lawyer friends here, and I don't have a Charleston office anymore, so what about the public library on King Street?" I asked.

After I returned to Birmingham, I dictated a letter dated May 31, 1989, to Banzhaf to report on my meeting with representatives of the NAACP.

On May 23, again copying Banzhaf, I wrote a woman interested in the Veterans Day Program at The Citadel, a 41-year-old reservist with eight years active duty in the Navy and a 16-year-old son. After completing a two-year program at the City College of Chicago extension center in North Charleston, she would soon have to transfer to a four-year college. Her interest faded, however, after she moved out of town.

When I met the first young woman, Karen, and her mother at the King Street Library on a return visit to Charleston, I saw an attractive young woman still in her sophomore year at Burke High School, not at all ready to make application to The Citadel.

"Mr. Thompson and Mr. Glover tell me you want to go to The Citadel," I said. "Why is that?"

"I'm in Junior ROTC. I just want to go," she answered. "Really, I want to go because I was a cadet there already. They let us stay overnight one time when I was in Junior ROTC, and ever since, I've wanted to go. But they didn't let us girls wear our uniforms there. Only the boys got to wear their JROTC uniforms while in the barracks."

She was ready, willing, and able, for a time, to give all she had to go to The Citadel. Her mother realized the importance of her daughter's aspirations and was fully in support, but she did not force her. I would eventually pick her up at her mother's apartment at 119 Coming Street and drive her to The Little Professor west of the Ashley River in South Windemere Plaza for tutoring lessons. Her grandmother paid for the lessons.

Tonya, the second young high school girl recommended by Mack and Glover was one I knew less well. She and her mother didn't make it to the meeting at the King Street Main Library the day after Memorial Day 1989. Instead, I was told to call on her before I returned to Birmingham.

When I arrived at their house, I knocked for a good five minutes on the front door before yelling up to an open window. I felt like Walter de la Mare's traveler. "Hello, I just talked to you on the phone a minute ago. Is anyone home?"

Finally, a head stuck out of the window of the two story house and yelled back, "I'm up here, Mr. Black. We'll be down in a minute."

I chatted with the young woman and her mother for about 30 minutes. She was a striking, tall, young woman who also would have made a good cadet. Her grades at Stall High School were good enough for The Citadel. Just one slight problem. The gold ring through her nose would probably have to go. But a major problem was that she probably didn't want to go.

Before I left, I turned to her mother. "Just wondering, but why did you make me wait so long before coming to the door?"

"The way you talked on the phone," she replied, "I thought you were a black man."

In a letter dated July 5, 1989, I reminded both young women that their names would be kept confidential when they wrote letters of complaint to DOJ, unless either of them personally identified themselves. Later during discovery and trial in the veteran women's case, their identities would become a part of the public record.

A week later, on July 12, 1989, I responded to a call by Nat Douglas, Civil Rights Division, Department of Justice, Washington, D.C., and immediately sent out a letter to DOJ explaining that I was definitely not the girls' attorney since it meant that DOJ could not pursue an investigation of The Citadel's all-male admission policy if I were their attorney. I simply had not understood that my effort to get DOJ to represent Karen and Tonya meant that I could not also represent them. So I quickly backpedaled to get out of any potential lawsuit.

Douglas also gave me the name of an associate who would become the principal attorney from DOJ, Sandy Beber, chief litigator in the educational section of civil rights in Washington.

On July 14, I sent Beber information on the young woman. "But I'm out of it," I said.

News of the girls' letters being received in Washington and the DOJ's response by way of a Letter of Inquiry to The Citadel quickly made the Charleston *News and Courier* and *The Evening Post*, the two family-owned dailies which merged in 1991 into *The Post and Courier*. By July 10, 1989, a cartoon by a member of the Class of 1966 was submitted as a letter to the editor. It showed two male cadets hovering over a chesty female cadet thinking, "Why can't they just love me for my mind?"

Nearly a year went by. The March 1, 1990, Letter of Inquiry sent from Justice to The Citadel announced to The Citadel that a formal complaint had been received, alleging a violation of the 1964 Civil Rights Act, and that The Citadel by law was required now to explain its all-male admissions policy.

The Citadel responded to Justice without divulging the particular contents of their letter to the press. Their all-male admission policy, they no doubt replied, was clearly supported by existing law. The Charleston papers carried little information about it, but the men in Bond Hall, the administrative bunker at The Citadel, knew the ball had started to roll. *The New York Times* as early as August 2, 1989, had captioned a lengthy article, "Citadel's Lonely Battle to Keep Women Out."

I called Armand Derfner to talk about strategy. Armand had successfully litigated civil rights cases throughout the South and in Washington, D.C., before coming to Charleston. I thought that the case to get women in The Citadel would go best if Armand, instead of out-of-state lawyers, had the unlimited resources and inclination to represent women seeking admission. No charges of cultural intrusion, outside agitation, and so forth could be made by The Citadel against one of Charleston's own.

But Armand would not touch the case as an attorney of record. Instead, always in the background, he would remain throughout the case a principal source of law and moral support. The platoons of attorneys who would eventually join the case against The Citadel would bring to the game the very best minds and talent in New York and Washington. Locally, I would have one person, even better, a phone call away.

I then made fruitless calls to other civil rights lawyers, Jim Blacksheer and Ed King in Birmingham, for names of lawyers to represent the two young black women in Charleston. While in David Cromwell Johnson's law office, I had defended against clients of Blacksheer and King in my representation of the Shelby County Republican Party in a voting rights case filed by the Democratic Party in the Eleventh Circuit.

Banzhaf caught up with me in Birmingham shortly after that. "Bob, the press wants to know if I am the one behind the two letters from South Carolina school girls wanting in The Citadel. I'm going to tell them it's you, not me."

I panicked. For the first time, the weight of the case began to settle in. I knew people at The Citadel and in Charleston and throughout South Carolina. Like my father 30 years previously, I was afraid.

"No, wait a minute. Don't tell them my name, don't tell the press that I'm behind all this. I don't want my name in the papers," I said. "I think I can be of more use behind the scenes with this thing. Anyway, Justice will soon take it over and run with it any day now. I just need quietly to be in this a little longer to set it up. Then I'm out." Following Robinson's and Armand's lead, I added, "I've got to go back to Charleston when Melinda finishes law school."

After ringing off with Banzhaf, I conveyed my fears to Armand—just in time. The press called Armand looking for the rat and asked him if he knew who was representing these anonymous women who wrote letters against The Citadel, if the women were represented by, as the reporter asked the question, "a lawyer in South Carolina."

"No," Armand answered as if on cross examination, knowing that I was a South Carolina lawyer but residing in Alabama at the time.

True, there had been a few other women in the past to make a stab at being admitted to the Corps, but their efforts fizzled out. Charleston attorney Gerald Kaynard knew of some early efforts by young women, and perhaps Bill Ackerman's daughter Connie knew women who were ahead of their time when they too tried to get in during the 1960s and 1970s. Also, one of Armand Derfner's secretaries told me that her sister had applied and been erroneously admitted. The actual names of women applicants prior to 1993 would not be known until later through discovery under the Federal Rules of Civil Procedure, and the names of others would never be known at all.

The real aspirations of the first women to make a try at integrating the Corps of Cadets with women—to go far enough to put themselves in a position that might have led to admission—were to be put into perspective by the guidance counselor at Burke High School. Throughout the fall of 1989, while still in Birmingham, I occasionally called her to ask how one of the women was doing and to express my concerns about the number of hours and kinds of courses she was taking. Maybe too many and too hard, I thought.

"Mr. Black," the guidance counselor said, "don't you think that it's you, not she herself, who really wants her to go to The Citadel?"

I was genuinely shocked. I had not thought of it that way at all. I thought that what I was doing was making it possible for her to fulfill a dream, to do what she wants to do.

"You need to back off for a while. You need to let her alone," she said.

Ultimately, she could have been right. But I also knew that there was something about this whole thing that brought out the most timid in everybody, including myself. Throughout the case I kept in mind my father's remarks about my trip to Tuskegee. When I saw the close ties between the Burke administration and The Citadel, the special tutorial programs run at Burke by the Education Department at The Citadel, the Adopt-a-Buddy program run by The Citadel in which a cadet took a Burke student to tutor, the fact that the high school was right across the street from The Citadel. It all added up. The Citadel was an awesome place that imposed a master-servant relation on everybody, like falling in love with your jailor. Intimate and close to the heart of the city and state, and even the nation. On the day they graduate, Citadel cadets say the best thing about The Citadel is looking at Lesesne Gate, the main access to the campus, in the rear-view mirror. Love at last sight. Loved and feared and the heart of the good-ole-boy culture.

1990: The Zentgraf Maneuver

I wrote one of the young women and her mother on August 10, 1989, to mention that following our meeting, I had spoken to the King Street librarian, Catherine Boykin, an Alabama native who was my oldest acquaintance in Charleston. Catherine gave me the names of two women who she thought might be of help to the Burke and Stall high school women in an effort to go to The Citadel. They were Barbara Ferer, President of the South Carolina Commission on Women and the Lowcountry Coalition of Women, and Millicent E. Brown, the well-known civil rights professor who was then at the Avery Research Center for African American History and Culture at the College of Charleston. Brown, later at Chaflin University, had been the first African American to integrate the Charleston public schools in downtown District 20 in 1963.

In my letter to Professor Brown on August 11, 1989, I asked her to help one of the young high school women to fill out The Citadel application for admission. I drew attention to the news that Colin Powell had just been named the first African-American Chairman of the Joint Chiefs and that Kristin Baker had become the first female First Captain in the Corps of Cadets at West Point. Kristen Culler would become first female Brigade Commander at the Naval Academy in 1992.

A former Roman Catholic nun, Ferer owned or managed Insty-Prints, a printing business on the Savannah Highway in West Ashley, so the financial costs of my "position papers" to Marilyn Henderson at the League of Women Voters and to the Lowcountry Coalition of Women on November 1, 1989, and on January 20, 1990, were borne by Ferer. Her contacts with other women, notably with Susan Davis, then director of South Carolina Commission on Women, were equally invaluable in the early efforts to identify women of South Carolina who would actively take roles to get women in The Citadel.

I sent Ferer a single-spaced, three-page memorandum on The Citadel on August 25, 1989, in which I tried to set out the basic legal issues in which a case could be brought under 42 U.S.C. Section 1983 for violation of the equal protection clause of the Fourteenth Amendment, Title IV of the Civil Rights Act of 1964, which was available to DOJ in its suit against VMI, Title IX of the Education Amendments of 1972, and *Mississippi University for Women v. Hogan*, a controlling case decided in 1982. The Justice Department had used Title IV and the equal protection clause successfully in its 1985 suit against Massachusetts Maritime Academy to force it to admit women. Only The Citadel and VMI among state military colleges were holdouts. All federal military academies had been admitting women for the last 20 years—West Point, Annapolis, the Air Force Academy, Coast Guard Academy, and the Merchant Marine Academy.

In *Hogan*, Justice Sandra Day O'Connor elaborated on the intermediate scrutiny test recognized in *Craig v. Boren*, 429 U.S. 190 (1976). The court used the test to establish whether a gender classification by a state is substantially related to an important state purpose within the meaning of the equal protection clause. This would be the test used in *Faulkner* and *VMI*:

> Our decisions also establish that the party seeking to uphold the statute that classifies individuals on the basis of their gender must carry the burden of showing an exceedingly persuasive justification for the classification. The burden is met only by showing at least that the classification serves important governmental objectives and that the discriminatory means employed are substantially related to the achievement of those objectives.

The critical language in *Hogan*, I said in the memo to Ferer, language that each side would try to construe to its favor, was from the famous footnote 17:

Since any gender-based classification provides one class a benefit or choice not available to the other class, however, that argument begs the question. The issue is not whether the benefitted class profits from the classification, but whether the State's decision to confer a benefit only upon one class by means of a discriminatory classification is substantially related to achieving a legitimate and substantial goal.

In other words, not what benefits just one sex or another, but what benefits the state — both sexes — is the constitutional issue.

"In short, in South Carolina there are few greater steps to be taken to put women in the business community than to put women in The Citadel," I wrote to Ferer.

Melinda, my step-daughter Spencer, and I had Christmas dinner in 1989 from a vending machine at an Exxon service station in Mountain Brook, a Birmingham suburb, while en route back to Charleston. Melinda was leaving Cumberland Law School to transfer to the best law school in South Carolina and Spenceroo was headed to the second grade at Mason Prep and, later, to Porter-Gaud School.

By the following month, it was becoming clear that DOJ had no real interest in the two young women I identified in Charleston. A new strategy had to be devised. I still felt that I could not sue The Citadel because I did not have the expertise and an enormous law firm at my disposal necessary to run such a case and, more to the point, I did not want to be alone in a monumental fight.

So I continued to nag Nat Douglas. "Nat, I do not understand why you guys care only about VMI in Virginia and not about The Citadel in South Carolina," I told him in a call in March 1990.

"Well, you can always do this," Douglas said. "You can always sue The Citadel yourself. By that I mean that you can bring an action on behalf of a plaintiff who you know wants to go there and can get in."

"Nat, I've always told you I don't have the resources to do that, and I never wanted to be anything other than be the government's little helper," I replied.

"No," Douglas went on, "I mean that if and when you file a suit against The Citadel, you would presumably name the active-duty colonel in the ROTC program there. That's the same as naming us, the USA. So this department, the Department of Justice, would either have to defend the colonel as an agent of the federal government supporting The Citadel's all-male admission policy or move to realign and become co-plaintiff with your plaintiff."

All of this sounded like high-stakes gambling. I saw right away that it was risky business, a notion Douglas quickly supported when he confided, "But don't count on us to realign. We could leave you hanging."

When has one ever heard a more political statement than that? DOJ could end up on opposite sides of the all-male admissions policies at VMI and The Citadel if it chose not to realign. Furthermore, the realities of the influence of "ole Strom," as Senator Thurmond was affectionately called, whose own sons may have already made their unofficial applications to The Citadel as infants, presented a bigger picture than one made under a procedure of intervention in the Federal Rules of Civil Procedure.

"Talk to Gregg Meyers," Douglas finally said. "You probably already know him. But you may not know that he worked for the Justice Department when we sued Texas A & M University (TAMU) to get women in there in 1978. We used the same procedure and realigned after attorney Carol Nelkin sued on behalf of her client Melanie Zentgraf."

I knew Gregg as an attorney who was highly regarded among the Charleston bar. He had real life experiences north of Beaufain Street.

Myers told me an anecdote that helped me understand what I may be getting into. A while after he was with the Justice Department in Texas and after DOJ put women in A & M, an Aggie came up to him at a party and took a swing at him. The guy was still mad long after the case was over.

I first got in touch with Nelkin in Houston on January 29, 1990. I asked for the pleadings in the Texas A & M case on three occasions but never got them. I did, however, get a copy of the 12-page docket from her and enough documentation from Nat Douglas to know to name the Air Force colonel at The Citadel as a defendant in a complaint.

Melanie ZENTGRAF, Individually, and On Behalf of All Others Similarly Situated, and the United States of America, Case No. H-79-943, was filed in the U.S. District Court on May 11, 1979. Judge Ross N. Sterling presided. Under the same cause of action used in The Citadel case, 42 U.S.C. Section 1983, Nelkin named Army Colonel Robert J. Kamensy, Cadet Colonel of the Corps of TAMU, as one of the defendants, along with the university, its president and vice-president. The USA moved to realign as plaintiff-intervenor six months later. Six years of litigation led to a five-day trial in March 1985. The plaintiff won. Women were admitted to the TAMU Corps of Cadets, and the case was dismissed on January 19, 1989. The effort to get women in the Corps of Cadets at Texas A & M took ten years.

The Citadel was probably well aware of the *Zentgraf* case, the time and expense it took, and its ultimate resolution in favor of women cadets. However, at no time in The Citadel case—other than Nat Douglas's comments to me in 1989 or 1990—did anyone mention the *Zentgraf* case.

In the early days I thought that the best strategy would be to forget the two young Charleston women, find another plaintiff, and sue using the *Zentgraf* maneuver. On February 11, 1990, I began to cast a wide net outside the South and wrote a former colleague at the University of Denver who had become a Colorado State senator. If anyone knew of women who did not get into the Air Force Academy and might want to come to The Citadel, Pat Pascoe probably would. She was a friend of U.S. Representative Patricia Schroeder and Gail Schoettler, Lieutenant Governor of Colorado, twin sister of a close friend of mine and valuable public servant who eight years later barely lost the governor's race to Bill Owens. I wrote to Schroeder and Schoettler without success. By February 25, Pascoe also wrote back that she too knew of no one. I would have to cultivate my own back yard.

A Visit to The Citadel

By January 4, 1990, Captain Linda L. Bray in Panama had become the first woman to command American soldiers in combat. What was omitted in the Charleston *News and Courier* front page article but carried in *The New York Times* was a remark by the Pentagon: "What has been demonstrated is the ability of women to lead, for men and women to work together as a team without distractions and for women to react in an aggressive manner."

In the 1970s The Citadel proudly described itself as what it truly is, a "liberal arts college in a military environment." Whether the liberal arts could be taught in a military environment was not a topic for debate. Courses were assigned to the faculty according to a professor's military college rank, not according to his academic degree. Many of the upper-level courses were taught by colonels with seniority and an M.A. degree, not younger captains with a Ph.D.

Ironically, I had been asked by the acting president, Wallace Anderson, in the fall of 1981 to write a new history of The Citadel. I declined. The president of The Citadel had sent out an inquiry to Princeton Professor Willard Thorp who knew I was teaching at The Citadel and knew that I had been a first lieutenant in the Infantry and Military Intelligence in Korea and Germany. I had rented a room from Professor Thorp in Aaron Burr's father's house on Nassau Street. For my history of serving on the faculty and later fighting to admit women, some would later call me a traitor.

The faculty was known as the South Carolina Unorganized Militia or SCUM. The only visible difference in the real thing and the fake was that U.S. military officers wore the insignia "U.S." on their lapels and SCUM wore "S.C." The real difference, however, was one between lightning and the lightning bug, although the rationale for wearing U.S. military uniforms on The Citadel campus was simple. The Pentagon had no objection with members of SCUM walking around in Army or Navy uniforms any more than it had with actors in a stage production of, for example, "Mr. Roberts."

In February 1990, I paid a visit to Citadel Brigadier General George Meenaghan, Vice President of Academic Affairs and Dean of Academic Affairs, the number two man at The Citadel, and someone I admired.

"General Meenaghan, I want to keep this visit confidential if I may. But you should know that I am in touch with two young high school women, both black, who want to be admitted into the Corps of Cadets next fall 1990."

I did not let on that the young women were probably already non-starters. "They are the ones who wrote the letters of complaint to the Justice Department last June 1989."

Meenaghan said nothing.

"They are both good students," I went on. "Do you think you can relay their personal individual stories to the Board of Visitors so that we can avoid a lawsuit?"

Meenaghan looked at me like a calf at a new gate. Calves don't go through new gates, a rancher from Big Timber, Montana, later told me.

"There's no chance whatsoever and you know it," he replied. "If I know this place, the Board will never admit a woman into the Corps. That's what The Citadel is, an all-male Citadel. I could go on and on. Everything would be lost if we let a woman in, the egalitarian environment, the high military standards, the bonding, everything. All our distinct values. The networking afterwards."

To make it a touch more specific, the general reflected on his own experience with an anecdote he would later give in his deposition.

"I've seen what can happen to an all-male school when it admits women," he said. "The first time I personally was in a classroom with women, in chemistry at VPI—Virginia Tech—all the boys in the lab exercises tried to help this one particularly pretty young girl so badly that we were falling all over ourselves. Nobody, including that poor little girl, got anything done. Nobody learned a lick. It just won't work in some colleges—at Princeton and Yale, yes, but we don't have the same mission as a those places. I think we are comparable in most respects to those places, but we just don't have the same mission."

Jeanette Kellogg Wotkyns and MoFo

After a slow start in finding a *Zentgraf* plaintiff through Colorado contacts close to the Air Force Academy, I began to doubt if I could even get a case up to speed with the hope that Justice would intervene and take it over. If they did not, I alone would be unable to go forward. Yet what big firm would initially handle the case only to yield to DOJ if a young woman were ever found for a *Zentgraf* maneuver? Would a big firm want to hang on as co-plaintiff after DOJ intervened? And at the same time it occurred to me that maybe with a heavy-weight law firm to represent a young woman, DOJ intervention would not even be necessary. The *Zentgraf* strategy was beginning to take a back seat to a new interest in finding counsel. On January 26, 1990, I called a buddy from my Princeton days.

Jeanette Kellogg Wotkyns was clerking for Judge Ken Starr at the time, but she still had connections at the offices of the big firm of Morrison & Forrester—MoFo for short—where she had earlier worked. Jeanette was in the first class of women at Princeton in 1969.

Conversations with two female attorneys at MoFo were less than satisfactory, however. They were interested, but I thought it would not be easy for me to stay in the case and work with them if MoFo decided to take the case.

Shortly after DOJ sued VMI a few weeks later, in March 1990, the MoFo lawyers called back on a conference call in my Broad Street office. They never had been so lively in their conversation.

The two MoFo lawyers knew what the Burke High School young woman and I also knew, namely, that The Citadel had just rejected the application of an anonymous high school girl in Charleston three days after DOJ sued VMI. Her identity would remain unknown to the public until it was later disclosed through the process of discovery to be Tiffany Provence from nearby Dorchester County.

In a November 15, 1990, letter addressed to John Dunne in the Civil Rights Division of DOJ, I again expressed frustration at the government's lack of response to the letters written 16 months previously by the two young Charleston women. I offered an excuse for there not being much evidence of strong support from Charlestonians either. "The problem," I wrote, "is that the people of Charleston are not very courageous when it comes to protecting the civil rights of high school girls who want a 'liberal arts education in a military environment.'"

By November 28, 1990, I had received all relevant *VMI* documents from the Clerk of Court of the Fourth Circuit. I had also gotten strategy tips and key facts on the *VMI* litigation team from Sylvia Clute, a Richmond attorney, by December 6, 1990. Harriet McBryde Johnson in Charleston, a law school classmate, had earlier, on March 6, 1990, researched relevant case law, without charge, a nice break from the rising costs of pretrial discovery that would eventually be astronomical and the solitary burden for Shearman & Sterling to bear.

Another Loss

"Is this the man who helped the young women write the Justice Department to get in The Citadel?" a very pleasant voice asked on December 11, 1990. I knew that I had been talking too much. My identity was out.

"I got your name from the League of Women Voters. I just wanted you to know that it was our daughter who applied to The Citadel last February 5 and was rejected." I later would learn that I was on the phone with Tiffany Provence's mother.

"That was just a few days after we heard about those two other girls who had written letters to the Department of Justice. I think my daughter was the first female applicant to The Citadel. I wanted to tell you why she withdrew her application and decided not to sue the college.

"It got so bad, Mr. Black, that our daughter withdrew her application. Being the target of ridicule on the radio, having even our neighbors—they didn't know it was our daughter who applied—speak so ugly about our daughter got too scary. We were just afraid. And my husband's a Citadel alumnus, too."

Great! I thought. This kind of fact was exactly what I needed to bring DOJ back to the table and get them to sue The Citadel on their own. They would act upon evidence of this kind of intimidation.

"If you don't mind, ma'am," I said, "would you please write to Mr. Dunne at the Department of Justice and tell him your story? Will you tell him what you're telling me, that your daughter withdrew her application because she was afraid of The Citadel and the people of Charleston?" I asked.

After I gave her the address and hung up, I wrote Dunne at DOJ and put everything down secondhand:

> It turns out that the family was genuinely fearful of its reputation and well-being after word got out last March 1990, that a female had applied to The Citadel. The news media, friends, and strangers alike were calling various Charleston high school counselors to find out who she was. Disc jockeys were making vulgar remarks over the radio about what kind of girl would actually want to go to The Citadel and for what reason. Without knowing the daughter's identity, friends made unkind and absurd observations.... This is an issue which requires federal prosecution as soon as possible. This is not a violation of civil rights which can be met by local confrontation and litigation. The Citadel is like Central High School in Little Rock—indeed, separate but equal is apparently its main defense. The Citadel alumni and Board of Visitors have too great of an emotional control over parts of South Carolina that do not represent its better parts, and we need your help.

Tiffany Provence's record as a high school student demonstrated what kind of exceptional young women The Citadel was rejecting: Beta Club at Summerville High School, National Honor Society, captain of the tennis team, SAT Scholar Award, and so on. A Barbizon model as well. Through occasional telephone calls and a letter from her mother, I continued to hear about the young woman during her college career. She was on the Dean's List and the varsity tennis team at the University of Florida. During the summer of 1992, she worked as an intern in Senator Hollings' office in Washington, D.C. In June 1998, she became a probate judge in a neighboring county. I never met her but was invited to attend her wedding in The Citadel chapel. It was clear that The Citadel lost a great student three years before Shannon Faulkner arrived on the scene. But she did not want to fight to get in.

The Bishops' Secretary

With MoFo gone and no real chance at the time for DOJ to move forward on its own with the three high school students identified so far, I was stuck again in a fantasy of finding a *Zentgraf*-type plaintiff to file a case against The Citadel. I wrote Nat Douglas on September 7, 1990, complaining that the lack of response by DOJ "reminds us all of Martin Luther King's classic letter from the Birmingham jail."

The analogy was a good one. Thirty years previously, several well-respected religious leaders had worked hard to hammer out a gradual but steady plan to integrate key facilities in Birmingham, and they were concerned that King might upset their progress with his call for immediate reforms. Several years before the 1964 Civil Rights Act became law, they hoped for the city, over time, to integrate voluntarily. A young woman named Catherine George dutifully typed out the bishops' and rabbis' letter to be sent to King in jail. She worked for Bishop C. C. J. Carpenter and Bishop George Mosley Murray in the office of the Episcopal Diocese of Alabama on Twentieth Street in Birmingham, adjacent to the Church of the Advent. As a secretary, she had the job to get the letter ready for the signatures of the religious leaders before sending it on April 13, 1963, to *The Birmingham News* and to King.

When she finished and handed the letter to Bishop Murray, young Catherine had no idea that the letter would provoke one of the most famous responses in the history of American civil rights. The civil rights battle cry that "a right delayed is a right denied" would later emerge full blown from King's letter to be used in future civil rights rulings, including Shannon Faulkner's.

"Bishop, here's your letter," she said politely. "But if you don't mind my saying so, I think we will all someday be grateful to Dr. King," an understanding the bishop fully shared. He, too, would soon have a cross burned in his yard.

Later, but still years before she married a Citadel political science professor and became the King Street librarian who gave me the names of Millicent Brown and Barbara Ferer, Catherine George Boykin, granddaughter of a Confederate officer, was, while still employed by the bishop, one of the very few white people at the funeral of the four little girls who died from the September 1963, bombing of the Sixteenth Avenue Baptist Church in Birmingham. The other white women who joined Catherine at the funeral, Peggy Horn and Estelle Warren, were the same women who sent me to Tuskegee in 1958. Women, both white and black—like Daisy Bates who guided the Little Rock Nine—were always on the front lines of the battle for civil rights in the South.

The Boo

> "Why does the lamb love Mary so?
> The eager children cry.
> Why, Mary loves the lamb, you know,
> The teacher did reply."

Knobs, freshmen at The Citadel, are taught that the most dangerous place at a military installation is the arsenal where rifles and ammo are locked up. It was the arsenal at Fort Sumter, they are told, that exploded when a Confederate fireball hit it, forcing Major Anderson's retreat. But it is the Daniel Library at The Citadel that is the most dangerous place, even if most of the books there are used only to get a cadet up to a 2.0 GPA and no further: "2.0 and go."

When I arrived at The Citadel to begin my first year of teaching there, I called The Boo, Lieutenant Colonel T. N. Courvoisie, to ask for more bookshelves in my office. What I had were real pretty shelves for just a few books, like what one would see in the lounge of a Hampton Inn or the lobby of a lawyer's office. The Boo was a much beloved figure at The Citadel, at least to cadets, whom he called his lambs. By August 1968, he had provoked enough jealousy within the administration, as the cadets saw it, to cause him to be moved from Assistant Commandant of Cadets for Discipline to Provost Marshal to Supply and Property Officer. There he would live out his career at The Citadel. Yet nobody was more popular with the cadets than Lieutenant Colonel Courvoisie. Nobody was more identified with the best it offered.

The Boo patiently listened to my problem and told me to keep my books boxed up. He told me not even to take them out of their boxes. He told me that I was at The Citadel now. Told me I didn't have any more use for them.

I guessed at the time that he was joking and that he would get back in touch at some point with a solution. I didn't fully get the humor until months later, after I never heard from him. That's when I got what he may have meant. It wasn't just a college. It was a network.

1991: The Manly Bill and Committee Hearing

"Now, let me mention one other view that I hear. 'Wait and let the courts decide in Virginia.' Dear friends, must we always have to be forced to do what we know we must?"

Representative Sarah G. Manly,
Journal of the House of Representatives,
109th General Assembly of the State of South Carolina,
Vol. II, March 14, 1991

By January 1990, Virginia Senator Emilie F. Miller's bill to put women in VMI had already been voted down when Representative Sarah G. Manly proposed a similar bill in the South Carolina House of Representatives to admit women in The Citadel. Senator Miller had done enough to stir up the VMI alumni forces to get her voted out of office in Virginia. The same would happen to Representative Manly, District 25, Greenville, South Carolina.

Miller and Manly proposed timely legislation, however. Twenty-three thousand women had made applications to go to the federal service academies in the preceding five years, and over 8,000 women were enrolled in ROTC programs during the 1992–93 school year.

In 1984, South Carolina Representative Virginia Crocker introduced a similar bill that was intended to add an affirmative action statement to higher education, but The Citadel handily defeated it in the education subcommittee. Manly's bill six years later was to allow all of the state's few resources to be used to educate the citizens of South Carolina without regard to race, color, religion, national origin, or sex. It did not mention The Citadel by name, but it had the obvious effect of admitting—and was drafted to admit—women in The Citadel.

Manly's bill was drafted in part by two other women in the House of Representatives, Representative Harriet Keyserling, and Representative Lucille Whipper. Manly, a doctor's wife, was graduated cum laude from Furman, took an M.Ed. at Clemson, and studied at MIT and Cambridge University. She taught physics for nearly ten years in the Greenville school district and later taught at MIT and was affiliated with NASA. Representative Whipper, who had an M.A. degree from the University of Chicago, was a highly respected black legislator who had a long history of active support of racial issues in Charleston. She understood the effort to get women in The Citadel. She understood as well as anyone what it would mean to the social fabric of Charleston and the state if women were allowed to join the Corps of Cadets.

Representative Keyserling from Beaufort was a Barnard College graduate in economics and the kind of woman who, like Whipper and Manly, if she had been living at the time of the suffragettes, would have fought toe to toe against the good ole boys on voting rights. But at the time the Manly bill was presented at committee there were only a handful of women in the General Assembly and some of them were definitely determined to keep women out of The Citadel. In the history of South Carolina there had been only a few powerful women in the General Assembly—like Mrs. Caroline Frederick in Greenville who with Mrs. Virginia Gourdin from Charleston forced the ratification of the Nineteenth Amendment in the South Carolina General Assembly in 1968. South Carolina elected its first woman governor in 2010, but in 2011 there are no women in the state senate.

The Manly bill sought to educate women, black and white. At the time of her bill, over 60% of black children living in families with women as head of the family lived in poverty in South Carolina. Over 13% of all South Carolina families lived in poverty. More women in South Carolina with children at the critical ages under six worked outside the home than in any other state: nearly 60%. And 70% with children age 6–7 worked outside the home too. A woman working in the Palmetto State made 60 cents to the dollar that a man made. Women had nowhere to go but up. At the time it was also not illegal for a man to rape his wife in South Carolina.

In the Palmetto State at the time of the Manly bill, education was not important enough to have its own standing committee in the House of Representatives. Any bill having to do with education was pitched in with other bills on Highways, State House and Grounds, Railroads, and Aviation and sent to the Standing Committee on Education and Public Works. Its chairman was Olin R. Phillips, a high school graduate from Gaffney who had spent an additional two years at Cecil's Business College. The same set-up remains unchanged today.

The public hearing on House Bill 3150 sponsored by Representatives Manly, Whipper, and Keyserling was held before the committee on March 5, 1991. The proposed bill was loaded with sex. Manly had simply added the word "sex" into an existing state statute, South Carolina Code of Laws, 59-107-10, to amend it with generic equal rights language: "A BILL TO REQUIRE THE STATE-SUPPORTED

INSTITUTIONS OF HIGHER LEARNING ... TO ACCEPT APPLICANTS RE-
GARDLESS OF RACE, COLOR, RELIGION, SEX, OR NATIONAL ORIGIN...."

The VMI trial was scheduled to begin the following month in Richmond.
There was a sense of urgency on both sides. Those speaking at committee in
support of the bill included Steve Bates, state director of the ACLU, Candy
Kern, President of the National Organization for Women (NOW), and representatives from the South Carolina Commission on Women, Winthrop College,
South Carolina American Association of University Women, the South Carolina American Association of University Professors, the South Carolina League
of Women Voters, two women graduates of West Point, and me. A female retired Naval officer also was invited by Manly to speak. Representative Whipper, and Representative Terry Haskins from Greenville were scheduled to speak
as members of the House.

The Citadel sent only two speakers, the chairman of the Board of Visitors,
and the president of the Association of Citadel Men. A member of the House,
a Cheraw High School graduate on The Citadel side, failed to show up.

The Citadel was not outgunned, however. They could have had no speakers at all and still have won the day. The hearing was, for The Citadel, a non-
event, all work having been done behind doors and in heaven prior to the
event, even though there were only eight Citadel graduates in the House and
one in the Senate in the entire 170-member legislature.

Citadel opposition to the bill was partly orchestrated by Representative Ron
Fulmer, a devoted and well-placed alumnus, Class of 1967, whose very presence in the House made sure that no bill supporting the admission of women
in The Citadel got passed. Fulmer served in the House to help Citadel lobbyists. The Citadel got ready to defend not long after VMI was sued in 1988. In
1992 Ben Legare left the office of public relations at The Citadel and moved to
Columbia to act as a lobbyist for the cause. Perhaps as early as 1989, seven
years after the *Hogan* decision, The Citadel went in just the opposite way and
got ready to defend against the admission of women rather than to get ready
to admit them. At the committee hearing itself, Citadel supporters spoke forcefully of their love of The Citadel just the way it was. With no tear out of place,
one apologized for his emotional speech.

"You don't know how many great things go on at The Citadel and they all
would be lost if women were admitted to the Corps," he said. "You know, I get
very passionate when I talk about The Citadel being all male."

Manly, who was sitting next to me, turned and quietly whispered, "What
if I said something like that? Wouldn't it be just another woman crying?" With
that simple observation, like a mother about a child, Manly got the essence
of the entire case: a lack of maturity among men in the state and at The Citadel

specifically. Manly later died while on a trip to India, her daughter told me, while trying to help women improve their lives and raise their standard of living.

When the bill did ultimately get to the House of Representatives on March 14, 1991, it failed to pass by a vote of 68–29. Voting against the bill were all five Charleston Republicans in the House, Ron Fulmer, Roger Young, later a state Circuit Court judge, Harry Hallman, later the Mayor of Mount Pleasant, Stephen Gonzales, and John Rama. They were joined by other Lowcountry members, George Bailey, Don Holt, Sandra Wofford, Annette Young, and Henry Brown, later a member of the U.S. House of Representatives. Voting in favor of the bill were Lucille Whipper, Daniel Martin, Sr., Jimmy Bailey, and Robert Barber from Charleston, and John Williams from Moncks Corner.

In the spirit of good manly fun, the five Charleston Republicans gave their defeated colleague in the House, Lucille Whipper, a certificate signed by House Speaker Bob Sheheen that made her an honorary cadet. This was about the time a flyer was distributed by some members of the House suggesting that certain meetings be held at Hooters.

A few days later, I send a copy of the bill to U.S. Representative Emily Van Tassel, Committee on the Judiciary in Washington, D.C., urging her to make more explicit the rights of women in education as well as employment as her sub-committee worked on proposed amendments to the Civil Rights Act of 1964.

Tremendous Shortage

On August 12, 1991, Brigadier General Julius F. Johnson, U.S. Army ROTC Cadet Command, Fort Bragg, North Carolina, wrote to Lieutenant General Watts, President of The Citadel:

> The United States Army is experiencing a tremendous shortage of nurses.... I request that you allow the use of The Citadel facilities and ROTC detachment to train Army ROTC nurse cadets enrolled at the Medical University of South Carolina. The nurse cadets will not be required to enroll at The Citadel or take classes with The Citadel cadets. My staff has discussed this arrangement with Colonel Zinzer and he feels it is achievable pending your concurrence.

The Army was calling upon The Citadel to help fight the Gulf War. I and the rest of Faulkner's lawyers would not learn exactly how The Citadel responded until the deposition of Zinzer, Professor of Military Science and Commandant at The Citadel, two years later.

On August 19, 1991, Watts sent out a memo in which he said, "I need to understand our arrangement and commitments," and again on the 22 he expressed concern to Zinzer about a woman in "ROTC cross registration."

On August 28, 1991, Colonel Roy R. "Rick" Zinzer recommended that Watts support Johnson's request. In his memo Zinzer reiterated Johnson's critical shortage of nurses. "The Cadet Command DA mission for School Year 1990–91 was set at 310 nurses and only 125 nurses were commissioned," Zinzer wrote. He added:

> MUSC [Medical University of South Carolina] provides an unexploited source of nurses to decrease the shortfall.... To initiate this program an informal enrollment agreement between The Citadel and MUSC will need to be established. The administration organization will require The Citadel to be identified as the "Host Institution" and MUSC as the "cross enrolled" school.

To hide the presence of women on campus at The Citadel, "The MUSC nursing students will be carried on the Cadet Command computers as MUSC students, not Citadel students/cadets."

An Agreement among The Citadel, Medical University of South Carolina, The Army ROTC Instructor Group, and First ROTC Region was drafted on Veterans Day, November 11, 1991. The agreement stated,

> The Citadel Army ROTC Detachment is offering the required 2 years of Military Science to nursing students enrolled at The Medical University of South Carolina. The 2-year program will require the student to attend classes one night a week, major field training exercises, as well as a 6-week summer training program between their junior and senior years. Upon completion of both graduation and ROTC requirements, the nurses will be commissioned a 2LT in the United States Army.

The ROTC nurse cadets at The Citadel would attend courses from 1700–1900 hours once a week in Jenkins Hall, while The Citadel would "process students on the cross-registration form as full-time transfer students, charging no tuition or fees" and, further, "upon satisfactory completion of courses, award appropriate college credit, and maintain ROTC grades on Citadel transcripts only."

The gun was loaded. As Major Paul Kotakis, spokesman for the Army ROTC at Fort Monroe, Virginia, explained to me on November 17, 1992, ROTC regulations exempt The Citadel and VMI from requirements of admission. But the problem was not so much with the Army's AR 145-1 UPDATE paragraph 2-1

(Cross Enrollment) which allowed enrollment of a student who does not have to meet The Citadel's admission requirements, but rather with The Citadel's own admissions policy in its Catalogue, p. 27, which required all non-cadets taking ROTC to be "accepted as a degree seeking student in the day program at The Citadel." Thus, The Citadel was in violation of its own admissions policy by allowing women nurses to attend ROTC classes one night a week. As Citadel witnesses Professor Patricia Ezell testified in her deposition and Colonel James Woods wrote in a letter of July 13, 1978, there was no ROTC program in the Evening College.

One of the reasons the Supreme Court in *Mississippi University for Women v. Hogan* ruled that Joe Hogan should be admitted to the all-women's nursing school at MUW was that Hogan had already been auditing nursing courses there. A precedent for women to be admitted to The Citadel Corps of Cadets was exactly on point. After some deliberation, The Citadel realized it could not completely refuse to admit nurses to audit ROTC on campus.

Therefore, to keep the numbers down as much as possible and hope not to be discovered at all, The Citadel would allow under great secrecy only one woman to participate in ROTC. But a deep-throat call to me blew her cover.

One of the issues in the *Johnson* and *Faulkner* cases was whether The Citadel was truly "military," or to what extent it was military. The most conspicuous examples of The Citadel not being truly military were the expulsion of veterans from the daytime classes in 1992 and, later, the refusal of the administration to follow the spirit of judicial orders to admit women after Faulkner's admission was effectively sustained by the Supreme Court's *VMI* decision in 1996. More immediately, the ratio of graduating commissioned officers to the total number of graduates each spring defines The Citadel simply as another university with ROTC programs.

The exact commission rate at The Citadel is confidential, presumably because it is so low. In the spring of 2011, an Army ROTC office refused to release the number and referred all inquiries to the Public Affairs Office. I found out later, however, that among the 483 cadets in the Class of 2011, 64 men and 3 women, a total of 67 or approximately 14% of the Class of 2011, were given commissions as Second Lieutenants in the United States Army at The Citadel graduation on May 7, 2011. Commissions by the Air Force and Navy/Marines would have added to that figure.

The current Citadel website claims, "About a third of the graduating classes accept military commissions."[12] This rate may reflect a range of 20%–40%. During litigation of *Johnson* and *Faulkner*, 20% was the accepted rate. While all cadets go through ROTC training at The Citadel, many in a casual fashion, not all are eligible for a commission after they graduate. A majority of Citadel alumni thus never end up serving their country in the United States armed forces. They are like alumni of every other university, except they all go through ROTC even if they do not take a commission after graduation or are not offered one.

"You would be very wrong to think that The Citadel is 'military' in the same way the real military is," the voice at the other end of the line said. It was the first of several deep-throat calls that I would receive during the *Johnson* and *Faulkner* cases. "I know. I'm teaching here in the ROTC program at The Citadel, and it ain't anything like the military."

The deep-throat went on to make a startling announcement. His call and letter in 1992 would initiate the unraveling of The Citadel's deception to hide a female nursing student in ROTC after Brigadier General Julius F. Johnson made his call to The Citadel for help in putting nurses in ROTC classes on August 12, 1991.

"Let me tell you this, there's a woman taking ROTC right now at The Citadel, and nobody knows it because they don't want it to be known," he said. "She's a secret. She's also military, the real thing."

"What do you mean?" I asked.

"A nurse from MUSC. She's set to get her commission at The Citadel in December 1992. She's here because Fort Bragg told The Citadel that they had better take her. They make her slink in after 5:00 p.m. and don't let her train with the all-male Corps."

"The night school doesn't offer ROTC," I told him.

"Right," the caller said. "They're breaking the rules."

"Well, tell me your name," I said. "We could use you as a witness."

"Not on your life. I'll send you the name of the woman in ROTC now but I have to ask you not to let anybody see the documents I send you. People here would know right away who sent them to you."

"I can appreciate that," I told him. "I got a call last month from a woman who told me that she was also being given separate individual instruction in AFROTC at The Citadel, so evidently at least the Air Force and Army are running ROTC programs for some women on the sly."

When I called the nurse, she was anything but helpful. She was completely unwilling to get involved as a witness. The plaintiff's pleadings later used the fact that a woman was taking ROTC at The Citadel, but The Citadel skillfully suppressed the significance that should have attended the fact and made it into an irrelevant footnote. The Citadel was able even to divert attention away from the presence of another woman in AFROTC.

Was the value of having no women in the South Carolina Corps of Cadets, one had to ask, greater than training women nurses for the Gulf War? The Citadel's clandestine and limited response to the "tremendous shortage" of trained ROTC nurses from MUSC would come to mark a questionable point about the mission of The Citadel, one as troublesome as The Citadel's termination of the Veterans Day Program a year later.

Melody Lutz: Getting Serious

I met Melody Lutz, a retired Army captain, when we both spoke in support of Sarah Manly's bill in March 1991. Lutz was the first woman from South Carolina to be graduated from West Point. She would gladly have attended The Citadel if women had been admitted in her day. If there seemed to be something contradictory about a woman soldier, Lutz put that thought to rest. Women were in the Gulf War but not in The Citadel at this time, a fact that Sarah Manly exploited when she passed out blue and white buttons that read, "Women are in the War. Why Not The Citadel?" Charlestonians had also read the previous March 29, 1990, such Associated Press releases that began, "Women guerrillas of the Tamil Tigers, cyanide capsule around their necks and assault rifles ready, have moved out of the jungles and into the towns since Indian peacekeeping troops went home," just as they would read "Female Troops Form a Bond With Afghans," ten years later, May 30, 2010, in *The New York Times*.

Women have been fighting alongside men in America since the Revolutionary War. My ancestor from the Piedmont in South Carolina, Fanny Bealle, daughter of Captain William Bealle, may have been among the few women known by name to have actually fought with weapons during the Revolutionary War. Others are Nancy Ann Hart, Mary Bobo Musgrove, and Mary Rammage Dillard. Hart was so cross-eyed that the British complained that they did not know at whom she was shooting.[13]

I called retired Captain Lutz on the phone. "Melody, can you come to Charleston just to wave the flag and let these high school Junior ROTC girls down here know that it's OK to want to go to The Citadel? That it's OK to try to get in? You were a pioneer in your own right. Girls here would listen to you. They would take courage to hear you talk about going to a military academy. We need a plaintiff, and you could drum one up for us.

"Armed Forces Day this fall is the perfect time to visit women ROTC classes in some of the high schools in Charleston," I went on. "You can make a speech to the ROTC classes, both men and women, about the new emerging role of women in the military. I'll sit in the back of the class and never say a word."

The plan seemed innocuous enough: just mix women's JROTC with the *Zentgraf* maneuver. I began to call the various high schools around town to ask if Lutz could speak about her experiences at West Point and her tour of duty that followed. I knew that Lutz would impress the students simply by virtue of being someone who made it through West Point. I also knew that in spite of The Citadel's ridiculous claims of superiority over West Point, The Citadel said that 18 to 24 percent of each class at The Citadel dropped out before graduation. The Class of 1970 claimed that 47% left. West Point lost about 25 percent.

I lined up three high schools to visit during the Friday that Lutz would be in Charleston. Others were reluctant to get involved. On the November Friday morning nearest to Armed Forces Day 1991, Lutz and I set out for Wando, John's Island, and Burke high schools. I picked those as the most appropriate based on the fifteen or so high school ROTC instructors and guidance counselors I had earlier called on the phone.

The all-white students at Wando High School scarcely paid attention. But like Johns Island High School, Burke High School was nearly all-black, and some of the students there had real aspirations to make the military a career after college. They also needed the scholarship money that might come with enrollment in ROTC.

The issue as always was to see if there was enough of an initial demand among high school females for JROTC, enough to argue that they would indeed pursue ROTC in a military college curriculum if afforded the chance. I found out that there were plenty of high school females taking JROTC. Interest in The Citadel was another matter.

Yet behind the frustration in proving that some young women were interested in a military college lay an irony created by The Citadel itself. Through intimidation created by neglect and indifference toward young women high school students, even those in JROTC, The Citadel was always able to say that there were never many women who were interested in going to The Citadel because none had ever applied. This was the issue of "demand" which was to grow into the keystone argument to The Citadel's defense to keep women out.

Chapter 2

Women Veterans
Pat, Liz, and Angela

1992: Pat Johnson Calls an Attorney

On June 14, 1991, in the trial on the merits in *United States v. Virginia*, 766 F.Supp. 1407 (E.D.Va. 1991), United States District Court Judge Jackson Kiser, who was appointed to the Western District of Virginia by Ronald Reagan, ruled that VMI was not in violation of the equal protection clause of the Fourteenth Amendment. Paul Davis, a witness for VMI, testified at the trial that began the previous April that men were better, more or less, than women in every way except in "having babies and giving milk." I gave an early release of Judge Kiser's order to the nationally syndicated columnist James J. Kilpatrick as we checked our mail at the post office located at the Four Corners of Law at Broad and Meeting Streets in Charleston. We sometimes exchanged brief comments about The Citadel case. He reluctantly concluded in his column that women would eventually be admitted to the Corps of Cadets at both state colleges.

On January 24, 1992, events leading to litigation began against The Citadel. They came not from high school girls but from an adult Navy veteran. Patricia Marlene Johnson called attorney Terry Rickson, vice-president of the Charleston branch of the ACLU, to ask for help to get in the Veterans Day Program (VDP). Before her call to Rickson, Johnson purposefully had called attorneys only in Columbia. She didn't think that anybody in Charleston would touch the case. But even in-state lawyers 100 miles away wouldn't help. One of them in Columbia simply laughed.

Rickson told Johnson that I might be interested in it. I found a message in my office at 23 Broad Street: "1/24/92. 4:17 p.m. Pat Johnson. A female plaintiff who is interested in going to The Citadel." I carried it around in my billfold for of the duration of her case.

Patricia Johnson and Liz Lacey filed their women veterans' case on June 11, 1992. The complaint was signed by Izabelle Pinzler, associated attorneys in

49

Denver, and me. After Angela Chapman joined Pat and Liz six days later, the case was consolidated the following year on March 18, 1993, with Shannon Faulkner's case for purposes of discovery. The women veterans' case would last for fifteen months, until September 20, 1993, and would remain on appeal for an additional fifteen months, until December 5, 1994, when the Fourth Circuit affirmed the lower court ruling to dismiss the case for mootness.

Pat Johnson was a retired Navy veteran with over nine years of active duty and two years in the Reserves, an E-6 Petty Officer, First Class, with the most sea-time, seven and a half years, of any woman in her instrumental rating, "IM-1." Johnson was scheduled to go before the Selection Board for the rank of E-7 in August, 1992. She had been awarded two Good Conduct and Battle Efficiency medals, three Meritorious Unit Commendations, and on November 6, 1991, the National Defense medal, although she had been a reservist and not activated during the Gulf War.

Unlike the first young black women and Tiffany Provence, Pat Johnson— also called Trish—was an adult in her 30s. And unlike the others, Johnson wanted to get into the Veterans Day Program, not the Corps of Cadets. The Veterans Day Program was a misnomer. It was actually the Male Veterans Day Program which was started after World War II to allow male cadets whose education was interrupted by the war to return to The Citadel as day students under the G.I. Bill.

Classes for the VDP were the same as those for the Corps. The male veterans sat in classes side by side with the cadets from 8:00 a.m. until 5:00 p.m., but the veterans were not members of the Corps and did not live in the barracks, wear uniforms, or participate in cadet life. Women veterans, on the other hand, had to go to class in the Evening College (EC) with all the other women. There were some male veterans as well as other males in the Evening College. The Citadel Evening College offered only four majors, education, history, business, and engineering, as opposed to the daytime classes which offered a whopping 17 majors. Classes began in the EC at 5:00 p.m. Cadets, of course, could not attend the EC and mix with women and males who were not veterans.

On August 4, 1992, the Commission on Higher Education faxed me a printout of the total number of men and women at The Citadel, including both the Corps and Evening College enrollments, as reported by The Citadel. Full-time men accounted for 1857 students and full-time women for 58; part-time men for 425 and part-time women for 1115. The number of women in the EC allowed The Citadel to claim that it taught both men and women, notwithstanding the fact that the Corps itself was for men only. Then, as now, the EC offered a master's degree in education. Yet, there has never been any doubt that the centerpiece of The Citadel is the Corps, and for that reason The Citadel has always rejected formal efforts to be called a university, an educational institution that offers a graduate degree as opposed to a college which does not.

The trick at The Citadel in 1992 was to hide the real facts, or at least make it difficult to figure out where the women were buried among the composite numbers of both sexes attending classes. All part-time men and all women were in the Evening College, a total of nearly 1600 students. The only full-time men were the 1857 cadets in the Corps. Nearly 75% of the students who attended night school were women, and they were getting education degrees to become teachers. The Citadel was proud of the fact that so many women attended The Citadel after dark and were severely limited to courses in the stereotypical mold of a teaching career. Figures posted even today may mask a distinction between the 2000 students in the Corps and the 1000 in the Evening College or The Citadel Graduate College (CGC), as it is now called. The CGC offers three baccalaureate undergraduate programs.

Pat Johnson told me at first that she wanted to be an engineer. She was incensed about the fact that some of her male veteran friends in Naval Reserves could attend day classes in engineering and she could not.

"And did you know that the Evening College is not even accredited in engineering?" I asked. "The first ever to be graduated in Civil Engineering from the Evening College are supposed to be graduated this May 1992. And there have never been any graduates in Electrical Engineering from the EC, so that program is still unaccredited. You know that ABET, the Accreditation Board for Engineering and Technology, treats the two programs—the engineering program for the Corps of Cadets and the miniature version set up for the Evening College—as two separate programs at The Citadel."

It took women in the Evening College about eight years to get an engineering degree instead of four or five years for the cadets and male veterans. The number of engineering courses offered in the EC was fewer than half of the courses offered in the day program.

"So, understandably," I added, "not many women or even male veterans get through the engineering program offered at night. And, of course, there's the irony that not enough of the cadets themselves major in engineering.

"Both disciplines in the department—the civil and electrical sides—include a disproportionate number of veterans. And about half, approximately 15, of the Electrical Engineering and Civil Engineering majors are veterans, and they are some of the best students in the department. Faculty members will tell you that.

"At any rate," I said, "I got a call from someone who wanted to tip me off about what really is being hidden over there. Someone from Baltimore called me not long ago to tell me to ask for the ABET report that is supposed to be filed in July 1994. The engineering program at The Citadel is slated to be accredited around the end of the year in 1995. But The Citadel has never made it clearly known that its engineering courses offered in the Evening College for non-cadets are unaccredited. They keep that crucial ABET evaluation a fuzzy issue.

"Ironically," I said, "when we need engineers more than ever, there was even some talk of terminating the Evening College engineering classes. The Commission on Higher Education was thinking of recommending that engineering be taught only at Clemson and USC where people had freer access to public education. Either that or have courses piped in at Trident Tech in North Charleston."

After a few more dire forecasts which only increased her indignation at being shut out at The Citadel, I surmised that Johnson was a woman with heart and courage enough for the job. She was tough. She had worked on the same jobs as men in the Navy, even cleaned latrines side by side with men. I got her to write Nat Douglas to ask if DOJ would represent her.

Johnson left my office and called back a few days later. "I have a friend who wants to go to The Citadel too. Can you call Liz Lacey and tell her what she needs to do?"

Navy veterans Patricia Johnson and Elizabeth Lacey, center, front row, among Navy personnel on the day of their reenlistment on the USS Frank Cable in 1985. Used with permission, Patricia M. Johnson.

Elizabeth Anne Lacey, a fellow reservist with Johnson, was even a better plaintiff on paper than Pat was. She had made an inquiry about going to The Citadel in 1989 but was told that it was for men only. She couldn't believe the culture of Charleston and South Carolina to have such a preserve in which important training was off-limits to women. Completely dissuaded, she didn't even bother to make application. Three years later, she was ready to fight.

Lacey was a Navy veteran with about eight years service, also a decorated veteran of the Gulf War era, but unlike Johnson, she had already done some work at Trident Tech and simply wanted to take advantage of the Veterans Day Program in order to take Physics II which she needed for an engineering major. She was further along than Johnson, and the crunch of getting the courses needed for an engineering degree was getting to be more critical.

Johnson and Lacey needed the very courses that were not taught anywhere else in Charleston, engineering courses that would have required them to move to Columbia to take classes at the University of South Carolina. I knew that that was a big issue for the Supreme Court when it ruled that plaintiff Joe Hogan did not have to travel to Jackson to take the nursing courses he needed if he could get them at Mississippi University for Women, the "W," as it was called. Like Johnson, Lacey made a good appearance and was committed.

On February 20, 1992, within a month of Pat Johnson's call and Liz Lacey's enlistment as another plaintiff, I called Eileen Wagner and Sylvia Clute, two lawyers in Richmond who were playing key *amicus* roles in the case there. South Carolina had no local women attorneys like these major players in Virginia who were fighting for women's rights at VMI. I also called Ellen Vargyas of the National Women's Law Center in Washington to ask about the *VMI* case. I wanted to know how to file a lawsuit that would have better results than what the DOJ's suit was having before the court in Roanoke. I also called Claudia Withers at the Women's Legal Defense Fund in Washington. In the early days I was throwing as broad a net as possible.

I called Nat Douglas at least five times between February 27 and May 14, 1992, to beg DOJ to take Pat's case in response to her own written request.

Johnson sent me a copy of her March 31, 1992, letter to Nat Douglas asking for help. Johnson's letter to Douglas included The Citadel's explanation that under Title IX, Johnson could enroll only in the Evening College. She could, however, transfer to The Citadel's engineering courses in the EC from Trident Tech through The Citadel's "2 | 2 program" for engineers after a couple of years. The director of the Evening College, Pat Ezell, stated that Johnson could spend the first two years at Trident Tech, then finish up at The Citadel EC.

During February and March 1992, DOJ continued to put off any decision whether to bring a lawsuit against The Citadel based on the letter it received from Pat Johnson. Johnson's letter, in fact, meant little more to them than the letters I had helped the two young black women send to DOJ nearly three years earlier.

VMI: Richmond 1992

Meanwhile, activity continued in VMI's declaratory action filed against DOJ on February 5, 1990. On April 8, 1992, I drove to Richmond for oral arguments on appeal and for the first time got to see DOJ and VMI lawyers go at it, this time Jessica Silver for Justice and Robert Patterson, senior partner at McGuire Woods Battle & Booth, for the Commonwealth and VMI Foundation. In April 1991, I had missed seeing Judith Keith in her losing argument for the Justice Department during the six-day trial on liability at the district court in Roanoke. Two months after that trial, Judge Kiser found no violation of the Fourteenth Amendment and ruled that "VMI truly marches to the beat of a different drum."

I heard that The Citadel's lead counsel, Dawes Cooke, was also present for the hearing and would be sitting in the courtroom as a guest of VMI. He was already preparing to defend The Citadel against any future attack launched like the one filed against VMI, even though I had not yet filed Johnson and Lacey's lawsuit and would not for another two months. Earlier in Charleston, Dawes knew that I was up to no good and asked me when I bumped into him on Broad Street when I was going to file a lawsuit.

I waited in a long line of VMI alumni for a seat in the gallery and pondered with some amusement about which side of the case I was supposed to be on. Cooke himself had no military experience, something he shared with many in leadership positions at The Citadel. I was an Army veteran and the descendant of dozens of Rebels from the Piedmont in South Carolina and others who rode with Nathan Bedford Forrest in Alabama and Mississippi. Cooke on one side of his family had plenty of distinguished Rebel officers, but he was also the great-great grandson of General George Gordon Meade, the Yankee victor at Gettysburg.

Dawes had been a philosophy major at the University of Virginia, so he knew Richmond. I caught a quick glimpse of him as he walked by in the company of eight or ten VMI administrators, all in U.S. Army uniforms with attached Virginia State VMI insignia.

Fifteen minutes later I got a seat to hear remaining parts of the VMI arguments, including Bobby Patterson's. The same arguments had been made successfully by Patterson in the district court in 1991 in Roanoke, namely, that

DOJ was the big bad government beating up on poor ole Virginny and states' rights—but this time, just states' rights to keep women out of public schools, not to own slaves. Patterson was an excellent lawyer with whom I enjoyed a cordial relation throughout the case. He told me he could work with me because I was a Southerner, regardless of our opposing views. Again, as with the best on each side, including Dawes, we were, after all, advocates of issues about which gentlemen—and gentlewomen—may disagree.

I left Richmond with a good sense of the kinds of arguments that would be made in the veterans' case at The Citadel. On the way out of town, I stopped by the Library of Virginia on East Broad Street to get a copy of a family plot of land deeded to a Norwegian ancestor, Telieff Alverson, on Reedy Branch in the Northern Neck, dated 1697, and to look for John Bennett Boddie's record of another distant ancestor who supposedly arrived in Jamestown prior to 1620. If the Citadel case had been decided along the lines of pure romance, I and others may have been among the many Southerners on its side.

God Bless the ACLU

By late spring 1992, it looked as if no one was willing to take on The Citadel. Even so, I continued to cultivate the local garden and turned again to several lawyers with whom I had worked before and who I thought just might be willing to take the case with me. None of the four or five I talked to was interested. Good lawyers who live to fight another day are understandably reluctant to get into a case guaranteed to ruin a law practice—for lack of income for many years to come and for the loss of a client base either as a result of reprisals or as a result of total commitment to one enormous file. Jim Blacksheer in Birmingham told me that civil rights lawyers, especially, have to have a fat cash reserve to last for the long haul since they get paid only at the end of the case, if they win at all.

Reluctantly, I began to look for out-of-state lawyers. I called Michael Olivas who had worked on the *VMI* case. Olivas was an extremely knowledgeable civil rights expert, but he could not put aside his primary obligations as a professor at the University of Houston Law Center. My next thought was to return to my Princeton friend Jeanette Kellogg Wotkyns to look for help among her out-of-state connections. Kellogg was still clerking for Judge Starr in Washington. She interviewed for a clerkship with Associate Judge Ruth Bader Ginsburg, but really didn't want to work in the Supreme Court, even though Ginsburg probably wanted to hire her. Since it is not smart to say no to an Associate Justice of the Supreme Court, Kellogg decided to hide her identity by getting married.

She simply changed her maiden name to her married name, lay low, and kept her disguise long enough to complete her clerkship with Starr. Surely, I thought, stealth-clerk Wotkyns would have other names of women lawyers in big firms who would want to take the veterans' case even if the attorneys at MoFo did not want to help the two young high school women in Charleston.

On May 6, 1992, Jeanette's contact, Madeline Collison in Denver, agreed to help. Company at last. It was a major psychological turning point in the case, but the plaintiffs still needed more muscle.

Armand Derfner then told me to call Steve Bates, ACLU director in Columbia.

"I don't want the ACLU in this," I told him. "You know what The Citadel will be able to say along that line. Never mind the fact that the cadets call the ACLU to represent them when The Citadel administration tells them they can no longer hang the Rebel flag in their rooms or play Dixie at parades. When the going gets tough, everyone calls the ACLU. But this is known only by the down-and-out, the poor, the desperate … you know, the huddled masses yearning to be free. The great irony of it all is that the ACLU is a lightning rod to white Southerners who, more than anyone, are fierce defenders of their individual liberties. But this has got to be a home-grown case, even if the women veterans we've got so far are both from out of state."

Nonetheless, I followed Armand's advice. Bates instructed me to send a letter addressed to him in Columbia, and he would forward the letter to Isabelle Pinzler in the Women's Rights Project of the ACLU in New York, the office Ginsburg had founded before going to the bench. After a few days Pinzler called me, and a union between the women veterans and the ACLU was formed.

On May 11, 1992, Pinzler, Collision, and I conferenced on the phone to set up the basic strategy of the case. It was clear from the start that Pinzler and the Women's Rights Project had the legal know-how and experience to represent the women. For the first time talk shifted to real "plaintiffs" and real "defendants."

I drafted the first complaint and modeled it on the DOJ complaint in *VMI* which Nat Douglas sent me. Pinzler responded to my draft complaint by ignoring it. On the phone she explained that the ACLU was used to drafting this kind of complaint themselves. She insisted that the experienced staff attorneys in New York handle the research and all the pleadings and briefs. My job would be to handle facts which the court would need to make a fact-intensive inquiry under *Hogan*.

This was hardly the way I wanted the case to be run. I had been through some of this with MoFo. I could dig for the facts all right, and even appreciated the Summary of the Supreme Court Reporter that began, "The Mississippi University for Women, a state-supported school in Alabama" and later pleadings that began, "Converse College, located in Columbia, South Carolina." But I wanted to be involved in every aspect from beginning to end, not to be just someone churning up facts. It was my baby, and I thought that outsiders would screw it up if left to their own devices. They knew nothing about the South and less about The Citadel and would make big errors without a local redneck with military experience directly involved in every phase, even in drafting the pleadings. At the same time, I could see the sense of what Pinzler had in mind. Let the ACLU do the drafting, if for no other reason than to keep them from walking away. Do what it takes to keep them in the case, I thought. I even thought I might exert more influence if I remained apart from the initial research and drafting and only critiqued the final drafts. So I convinced myself that I should leave that to the more experienced lawyers with all their resources. I really had no choice. After all, they, not I, would be advancing costs to run the case. I would remain local counsel who primarily dealt with facts, not the law and not the drafting. Such would remain my standard operating procedure after the real heavies at Shearman & Sterling joined the case.

A final complaint was hammered out by Isabelle and Joan Bertin, another civil rights expert at the ACLU and Columbia University. Although I objected and even considered Armand's idea of filing my own complaint along with Bertin's, Steve Bates eventually got me to agree to sign my name on Bertin's complaint as "Robert R. Black, Local Counsel, In Cooperation with the ACLU."

Bates further explained that the ACLU would require me to give a portion of any fees I might recover to the ACLU in order for them to advance costs in the case. At that time I had not even thought of getting fees, much less costs. I did not think I would be paid for my work because I was not aware of the statutory provision for attorney fees and costs in 42 U.S.C. Section 1988. I was a one-man, one-room firm without a secretary. The possibility of a salary was out of the question and was never raised. The ACLU, for a time, paid rent for an additional room at 23 Broad and sent boxes of computer equipment, which I never opened and eventually returned. It was an awkward marriage with the ACLU from the very start. Even so, my association with the ACLU, or dance with the devil as another attorney put it, was a great and highly productive experience. As it often does, the ACLU delivered when none other could or would.

The First Shot

Johnson and Lacey's complaint, *Johnson, et al. v. Jones*, was filed on June 11, 1992, after Pinzler and Bertin in New York, Collison, Darold Killmer, and Gilbert Roman in Denver, and I in Charleston signed off on it. When the case was filed, the ACLU sent out a four-page press release. The complaint was brought as a class action and filed on behalf of the individuals Johnson and Lacey and on behalf of those "similarly situated" in order to include women who were unnamed at the time but who would be able to join Johnson and Lacey in the VDP if the named plaintiffs prevailed. Jimmy Jones, in his official capacity as chairman of the Board of Visitors, was named as the first defendant on the caption of the case among the entire fifteen members of the board and select administrators simply because, under the Eleventh Amendment, a private citizen cannot directly sue an agency of the state. So from the start, the case against The Citadel was in a different configuration from that against VMI. In *VMI* the feds were able to use Title IV as well as the Fourteenth Amendment as a basis of their action, and they could directly name the state itself as a defendant.

Including women "similarly situated" also formed the basis for a motion for class action certification, although the defendants and the court, to some extent, considered other women to be sufficiently represented without class certification. In any event, despite several motions, class certification was never granted. It would never be granted in Faulkner's case either. The Citadel challenged the "numerosity" of veteran women wanting to go to the VDP as required for class certification, just as they later would challenge the "demand" of women who wanted to enter the Corps of Cadets.

I got Johnson and Lacey to be present at a press conference organized by the ACLU at the main gate at The Citadel right after the complaint was filed. Eugene Vasilew, president of the Charleston chapter of the ACLU, was there to introduce himself to Johnson and Lacey and to me.

This was the first time the press covered the story of identified women seeking admission to The Citadel. The questions and answers were predictable. Johnson did most of the talking. The event was completely ignored by the administration inside Bond Hall, about fifty yards away.

"Fuck you, bitch," a couple of cadets yelled from a car as the press conference was winding down. "You'll never get in." Cadets continued to drive through the gates, laughing, middle fingers poppin' as they sped away once they got beyond the cadet guard posted inside Lesesne Gate.

Both Johnson and Lacey were somewhat taken back. It was the first time they experienced what they realized was bound to be a major part of their lives from then on. Members of the press, if any heard it at all, chose not to report the incident, and Johnson, Lacey, and I did not draw it to their attention.

Lacey looked around. "Something bothers me about this place, Mr. Black," she said. "I keep seeing all these officers walking around on campus here. How did so many of them get such cushy orders teaching at The Citadel?"

Navy veterans Patricia Johnson and Elizabeth Lacey in front of The Citadel after filing their lawsuit in June 1992. Used with permission, Staff photo by Brad Nettles, *The Post and Courier*, June 12, 1992.

"It's not the real thing, Liz," I replied. "You're the real thing. That's why you've asked such an obvious question. They're SCUM — South Carolina Unorganized Militia — members of the faculty and administration. That's what they call themselves. I'm not making it up. When I taught here, that's what we all were called. Like the cadets themselves, most members of SCUM have never served their country in the armed forces, and they're certainly not in the U.S. military now." I went on to observe that how a nation treats its veterans is as telling of its character as how it treats women, children, and the elderly.

Angela Chapman

More of the real thing came the day after Johnson and Lacey filed suit. Another woman veteran called me to ask to join Johnson and Lacey in their suit against The Citadel. The plaintiffs amended their complaint on June 17, 1992, to add Angela Chapman.

Unlike Johnson and Lacey, Angela Chapman was married and was the mother of two small children and a teenage daughter. Chapman was not an active reservist in the Navy, although her husband was still on active duty at the Navy

Weapons Station located a few miles north of Charleston. Chapman had been trying to get into The Citadel since late 1991. She called me as soon as she read about Johnson and Lacey's press conference at The Citadel.

"They sent my application straight back to me," Chapman said. "I'm from California. I just don't understand you Southerners. I've taken all the prerequisite courses I can take at Trident Tech and now have to go to the day program at The Citadel to find the rest of the courses I need for my Electrical Engineering degree. But they won't let me because I'm a woman."

Chapman went on to explain that she could not go to the Evening College even if she wanted to. Her husband traveled out of state much of the time and she didn't have the money to hire baby sitters. The children were in school during the day, the only time she could go to class. If not allowed to attend classes during the day, she would have to give up her dream to be an engineer. Chapman's classic set of facts for women added what Johnson and Lacey's complaint lacked.

"How are your grades?" I asked.

"All A's at Trident, except for one B in English. I've got a 3.95 GPA," she replied.

What really upset Chapman was that she complained the previous December 1991, to the representative at the VA Hospital and asked him what the VA would do to help her. She could not imagine that the VA would sit by and allow a public military college to discriminate against veterans. She was a veteran of the Gulf War, honorably discharged after six years of active duty.

Chapman called the VA rep at the VA hospital, but he passed her off to the VA rep at The Citadel who told her over the phone that she would have to make application all over again to document that she had been discriminated against on the basis of her sex.

"I told him that was ridiculous—I won't waste my time anymore and do it all over again, so I threw away all my correspondence with The Citadel," she said.

Chapman later made full application and was flat-out rejected because of her sex. Laughing, she told me that at the time she was tutoring two of her daughter's friends in physics, both sophomores at The Citadel.

I pursued a line of inquiry with the VA to see where it stood on the issue of women at The Citadel. I called a member of The Citadel faculty to ask generally about active duty students in MECEP, the Marine Enlisted Commissioning Education Program, and ECP, the Navy's Enlisted Commissioning Program. I then called the VA rep at Trident Tech to hear the rule that directly affected Chapman's status with VEAP, the Veterans' Educational Assistance Program. Chapman could change colleges only three times, I was told. Any more college transfers and she lost her $300 month VEAP benefits entirely.

On October 23, 1992, I finally called The Citadel to speak to the VA representative. My questions about Chapman's status with the VA got nowhere.

"What are you hiding?" I asked him. "You're telling me that you can't talk to me about Chapman's application to The Citadel. I'm her lawyer, she's a taxpayer and an honorably discharged veteran, and you are a federal representative, not a Citadel employee. We have every right to talk to each other about why she can't get into The Citadel."

After I slammed the phone down, I immediately called again. This time, the VA rep said, "Mr. Black, I simply can't talk to you anymore. I can't talk to you about Ms. Chapman."

The president's assistant, a loyal alumnus, apparently took the phone from the VA rep at this point. Lewis Spearman informed me that I was violating clear rules of ethics to conduct discovery of a party to the case and that the VA rep refused to talk to me about anything regarding the case against The Citadel. He apparently knew, also, that I had recently visited members of the engineering faculty to do pretrial discovery, as I had with Brigadier General Meenaghan, and to talk to the Evening Engineering Program Coordinator.

"I don't want to talk to a party who can bind The Citadel or anyone employed by The Citadel about the case," I said. "I want to talk to a federal employee who happens only to have his desk next to yours at The Citadel, and I want to talk about VA procedures regarding applications to the day program. This is a proper and reasonable inquiry of a potential witness."

The president's assistant stated that he would talk to Dawes Cooke. He told me that he knew I had been snooping around the faculty and told me to stop making calls to The Citadel.

Confusion arising from this admonition not to talk to witnesses at The Citadel, even representatives of federal agencies, and an effort made by someone to keep me even from coming on the campus reached an early conclusion. Within minutes Cooke called to say that as much as he would like to tell his clients that I could not talk to non-binding parties, and as much as he would like to tell them also that they could stop me at the gate, we both knew that he could not tell them that. The Citadel, after all, was a public institution.

The First Hearing

During the summer of 1992, The Citadel hoped to piggy-back on the *VMI* case and simply copy the pleadings which had proved to be successful before Judge Kiser, wite-out "VMI" with correction fluid, and replace it with "The Citadel." They did so in the early days when claiming that The Citadel was like VMI. The claim gave them a "me-too" advantage before the Fourth Circuit. The Citadel made a few minor changes regarding the particular facts of the case without undermining its defense of the veterans' case as essentially a Corps of Cadets' case, and, handy-dandy, trotted them out at the preliminary hearing. But if *VMI* were ever a road map for The Citadel case, that road would later prove to be full of detours and dead ends.

On August 7, 1992, Johnson, Lacey, and Chapman had a very pleasant but quick conversation with Isabelle Pinzler regarding what would hopefully occur at the hearing. The Dean of Undergraduate Studies at The Citadel, Spike Metts, had earlier that morning filed his affidavit swearing that each woman "can enroll as a full-time student at Trident Technical College in the Fall 1992 sessions in the same courses for which each would have been academically eligible at The Citadel." A month earlier, I had to get an affidavit from one of the professors in physics at the College of Charleston to speak plainly about what little was available outside The Citadel—no mathematical physics, no research planning and only very seldom other necessary courses, such as electronic instrumentation, analytical mechanics, electricity and magnetism, and a laboratory in electron instrumentation.

At the first hearing, the three women veterans sat behind the rail separating the lawyers' tables from the audience. Journalists from the printed media were present. Television crews were required to wait outside the courthouse.

On the other side, for The Citadel, were nearly ten lawyers. Principals from the law firm McGuire Woods Battle & Booth from Richmond included Bobby Patterson whose firm now represented VMI, its Board and Superintendent, as well as intervenors VMI Foundation, Inc., and VMI Alumni Association. From a fax sent to me by Nat Douglas on December 3, 1990, I knew that McGuire Woods took the place of the Virginia Attorney General, Mary Sue Terry, who had represented the Commonwealth, VMI, its Board of Visitors, and the Superintendent. But in spite of the order signed by Judge Kiser on November 30, 1990, granting the AG's motion to withdraw, Governor Wilder refused to appoint special counsel to replace the AG because he thought such an appointment was a waste of state funds. Governor Wilder announced that VMI's all-male admissions policy served no legitimate public policy objective, a position at odds with the one McGuire Woods was taking. Also, a key point of strategy in the defense was that Patterson took the position that VMI was unique, while Governor Wilder said VMI was not unique. There could be no reconciling such a huge difference.

So this classic conflict of interest led to the appointment of Patterson as private attorney for VMI. A contrast with what was going on at the two state military colleges was clear. A difference of strategy and policy existed with regard to the positions taken by those charged with the duty to defend state laws. While Governor Wilder, who is African American, and the Virginia AG, a woman, refused to defend what they thought was an unconstitutional position taken by VMI, South Carolina Governor Carroll Campbell and AG Charles Condon both enthusiastically defended The Citadel.

It was clearly a religious issue for the Virginia law firm. The defense of The Citadel, in the eyes of the Richmond attorneys, was simply a necessary defense against what was seen to be a collateral attack against VMI as well as a direct attack on a brother military college. There would be no weak flank resulting from a loss in South Carolina to set a bad precedent in the Fourth Circuit. In this defense of the South, the exemplary military figure of VMI, Stonewall Jackson, was not about to be out maneuvered by the ACLU. The four six-pounder cannons in place on the VMI parade ground were ready to fire: Matthew, Mark, Luke, and John.

"Griffin Bell is here, Isabelle," I whispered. Sure enough, the former U.S. Attorney General himself had come to Charleston from the big law firm of King & Spaulding in Atlanta just as he had been in Roanoke for *VMI*. "We've seen the stuff they have written so far. It all looks like the stack that Tom Murray at Justice sent me in *VMI*," I said.

The Charleston courtroom, which Senior Judge C. Weston Houck, South Carolina District Court, used for the case, was the same in which *Briggs v. Elliott*, 98 F.Supp. 529 (E.D.S.C. 1951), 342 U.S. 350 (1952), was heard some 40 years before by Judge Waties Waring. It was the courtroom at the Four Corners of Law at Meeting and Broad Streets that Judge Houck used for most of his Charleston cases at the time. For his opinion in *Briggs* favoring integration of blacks with whites in public schools, Judge Waring was so unpopular in the Holy City that white citizens burned crosses in his yard and little white boys threw rocks at his house. Waring was forced to move to New York City. Parallel circumstances of women trying a lawsuit to join men at the public college on the Ashley River two miles north of the courthouse were plain as day, even though they were never acknowledged by most onlookers in town. The historical significance of the *Briggs* case itself was never felt strongly by Charlestonians. When Eliza Briggs died in New York in September 1998, *The Post and Courier* placed the notice of her death on page B6.

Judge Houck was a native of Florence, South Carolina, and a 1954 graduate of the University of North Carolina at Chapel Hill who served in the Judge Advocate General's Corps after being graduated from the University of South Carolina School of Law. He was appointed in 1979 by President Jimmy Carter. At the Judge's retirement party in Florence several years after the women's lawsuits ended, Senator Fritz Hollings described him as the best judge for the case. The Judge's full measure of devotion to the law in his ruling in the *Faulkner* case provoked bitter responses that still linger. In a letter to me dated October 8, 1999, Charleston attorney Arthur G. Howe observed,

> Not since the days of Judge Waties Waring has a Federal Judge been subjected to so much abuse. Yet, with patience and firmness he held to the facts and the law and was ultimately vindicated by the Supreme Court. No one involved demonstrated more courage than Judge Houck.…

District Court Judge C. Weston Houck who presided over the lawsuits filed by women veterans Patricia Johnson, Elizabeth Lacey, and Angela Chapman and by Shannon Faulkner and Nancy Mellette. Used with permission, Staff Photo, *The Post and Courier.*

It was bailiff John Fleming's strong voice that was used to announce that court was in session during *Briggs v. Elliott.* Sitting at the plaintiffs' table in that case was Thurgood Marshall. When Waring scheduled a hearing and Marshall appeared, the black community would say, "The lawyer's in town." But Judge Houck had no bailiff, and counsel before him were not so illustrious, in spite of Citadel honorary degrees to be bestowed on four of them later. Judge Houck used appropriated federal funds to pay an additional clerk to do legal research instead of having a bailiff. The judge would unceremoniously enter with the remark, "Please keep your seats." No one ever doubted who was in charge.

At the hearing, Pinzler's articulation of the women veterans' motion for a preliminary injunction turned on "irreparable harm" to the plaintiffs if they were not admitted and to the lack thereof to The Citadel if they were. For Chapman, particularly, if she did not get in the VDP right away, she would be forced to go to the College of Charleston for a physics degree and give up her ambition to major in electrical engineering. The women would also be stigmatized, in the minds of future employers, Pinzler argued, by their exclusion from day classes at The Citadel as their male counterparts moved more rapidly toward graduation and a job. Pinzler argued before Judge Houck that it was an absurdity "that somehow the mere presence of these three women in classes with cadets wearing uniforms is going to contaminate the atmosphere so badly that it will be irreparably harmed.

"They're eligible to fight for their country," Pinzler went on. "They're eligible to go to war and be wounded and taken prisoner, and even be killed, the whole nine yards, but they can't get into The Citadel. It's something that our Constitution takes very, very seriously."

Pinzler cited cases holding that any racial discrimination, which a defendant claimed to be necessary to further a compelling governmental interest, had to overcome the highest level of judicial review of "strict scrutiny." Classification by sex, however, had to meet a lower level of scrutiny, she said, one by which the defendants could claim their discrimination was substantially related to an important governmental interest.

Any other kind of discrimination against a class of people simply had to be such that the defendant could claim that there was a reasonable basis for the discrimination. Defendants usually failed on a strict scrutiny test and usually won on a rational basis test. The fight for women veterans would be up for grabs at the intermediate level but with a stretch toward the higher level.

In its pleadings, The Citadel claimed that its all-male education served an important governmental interest, then moved on to claim also that the diversity of educational opportunities which was created by its offering of an all-male education served South Carolina's interest. The Citadel wanted to move the inquiry out of *Hogan* and into the value of male-only education and a lack of demand for women in military colleges. The Citadel invariably used the term "single-sex" education instead of the more relevant term "male-only" education to cloud the real issue. Pinzler countered with the position that the value of male-only or single-sex education is irrelevant where there is unconstitutional discrimination. Plaintiffs, she said, were, therefore, in a win-win situation. Even if the court found value in an all-male education at

The Citadel that served an important South Carolina interest, where was the same for women? This would be the issue decided by the Fourth Circuit in the *VMI* case.

After Pinzler sat down, Dawes Cooke began by introducing all The Citadel dignitaries to the court, the president, General Watts, members of the Board of Visitors, and from McGuire Woods the lead attorneys in the *VMI* case, Robert Patterson, Bill Broaddus, and Bill Boland, another VMI alumnus, and Ann Marie Whittemore—who may strategically have been given the *VMI* file as ballast among the attorneys in the gender wars in both jurisdictions. Also, from King & Spaulding in Atlanta, Dawes introduced Bill Clineburg and former Attorney General of the United States Griffin Bell, whom Dawes always referred to as "Judge Bell." An observer might have thought that The Citadel hoped to make the courtroom of Eliza Briggs into the golf locker room at the County Club of South Carolina in Florence.

"And we submit that this case almost certainly will determine the fate of the Corps of Cadets at The Citadel," Cooke told the Court. "We think that if the Court were to adopt the plaintiffs' view, which is *per se* prohibition of state-supported, single-sex education, then that will have the necessary end result that there will be no more single-sex education in the entire country."

The Citadel wished to try the issue of value in male-only education in the context of the VDP. It hoped to preempt any future Corps of Cadets case with a win in the veterans' case based on the VMI record. Without citing one single case in support of its argument, it also was immediately taking a scare tactic to declare that getting rid of unconstitutional discrimination by a state meant that even private colleges could not continue to discriminate under the law. The Citadel hoped to strike fear in private single-sex colleges throughout the country with the warning that they would be next. The phrase "No state," which appears in Section 1 of the Fourteenth Amendment, was interpreted by The Citadel to mean "No person."

Later at Converse, The Citadel would continue to create fear that the all-women's private college would be forced to admit men if The Citadel were forced to admit women. The Citadel was aware that Title IX of the Education Amendments of 1972 permits private undergraduate colleges to maintain their admissions policy and still accept indirect benefits, such as tax-exempt status. Nonetheless, they persisted with the argument that Converse would have to admit men even after the Fourth Circuit had ruled that VMI could become a private college instead of admitting women. *The P & C* in an editorial on July 4, 1994, helped to perpetuate the argument.

At the hearing, The Citadel maintained that just three women sitting in classes with the male cadets would do irreparable, intangible harm to The

Citadel and prevent it from "creating stronger people and better educated people." Griffin Bell referred to the presence of women in the VDP as "gangrene." The danger for The Citadel defending against the women veterans was always that if they let three in, then there goes the neighborhood. Thus, following *VMI*, the issue initially identified by the parties as early as the veterans' case was whether South Carolina had an important state interest in offering men but not women the benefits of a liberal arts education in a military environment at The Citadel. What was at stake from the start was the value of male bonding and the benefits of Citadel networking—a palpable phenomenon—beyond graduation into professional life. No one at The Citadel wanted women to share the wealth that came with wearing the Ring. The Citadel made the VDP case a Corps of Cadets case from the start.

The Citadel was trying to force the issue in the district court which was on appeal to the Fourth Circuit in the *VMI* case. If the Fourth Circuit ruled that the all-male admissions policy at VMI was in violation of the Fourteenth Amendment—as indeed it did two months later—The Citadel could still claim that it was not like VMI because it had an Evening College which admitted women, among other things. But with a VDP hanging around its neck, The Citadel could not fashion itself in the image of VMI as a unique, pure all-male Corps of Cadets. The possibility of women being admitted to the veterans' program could create an "entangling" issue, as Judge Bell described it, that could prevent The Citadel from benefiting from the much-anticipated continued success by VMI to keep women away from male cadets.

Even if the Fourth Circuit ruled that VMI was not in violation of the Fourteenth Amendment, The Citadel would still have problems with women in the VDP—a Trojan horse inside Lesesne Gate filled with women to spill out and destroy the Corps within.

Griffin Bell seemed to qualify that route somewhat. For him, the Fourth Circuit was seen only as having a "percolating effect" as *VMI* worked its way to the U.S. Supreme Court. Bell got to the crux of the matter and spelled out what was going to happen to the Veterans Day Program in the very near future. It would be gutted by the Board of Visitors. It would be discontinued completely in order to prevent women from "lifting themselves up by their own bootstraps." Best to get rid of the Trojan horse altogether and not take chances.

Bell reasoned that VMI did not have the problem that The Citadel had through its VDP, a program that would have become entangled with The Citadel Corps of Cadets if VMI prevailed. So Bell looked to the future and warned the court, "If we lose the *VMI* case, I would say that The Citadel case was in bad shape, depending on what the court says. If we win, it still leaves this case," and by "this case" he meant the veteran women's case, a potential chain around the neck of the Corps and one that would necessarily distinguish it from any favorable decision VMI might soon enjoy. Time was of the essence. The VMI decision was due out any day and they were counting on winning and not taking any women prisoners.

Yet no one in the court room, other than The Citadel and VMI people, fully realized that Bell was telling the world that The Citadel was about to have its darkest hour and become the first and only state military college in American history to throw out military veterans.

The show was not completely over, however. It was time for more argument on the question of what public policy would be served by admitting the veteran women into the day program.

I got up to address the court in order to press the parallel between the struggle for racial equality in public schools in the South in the 1950s and 60s and the veteran women's struggle for equality now. I wanted to make a direct connection between The Citadel case as a civil rights case about sex discrimination and the historical race discrimination cases. I wanted to nudge intermediate scrutiny of sex discrimination cases as far toward the standard of strict scrutiny as possible. This connection to race was exactly what DOJ did not make in the *VMI* litigation. My personal experiences in Alabama prompted me to do so.

What jumped into my mind earlier in the day was an experience I had one midnight coming back from a party at the Mountain Brook Country Club in Birmingham to my parents' house on faculty row at Birmingham-Southern College. After being among a blazon of sweet beauty's best for most of the night, I stopped on Third Avenue to look at the back side of the statute of the goddess Electra standing tippy-toe on the top of the Alabama Power Company building. I always liked the view. I parked and got out. It was pitch black. Immediately, a swarm of policemen appeared out of nowhere, frisked me, and searched the car. Only weeks before, the nearby Sixteenth Avenue Baptist Church had been bombed and the four little girls murdered by the KKK. They were suspicious of everybody.

"One of my own colleges went coed not long ago," I said in addressing the court. "Pembroke College Oxford lost a 500-year tradition and happily so. We filed this case 29 years after George Wallace stood in the door of the University of Alabama. That bears on the emotions of this case. The word on the street is don't fix what is not broken. The bus in which Rosa Parks rode in Montgomery was never broken. This case is about equal opportunity in education."

Cooke immediately objected and said, "History may prove us wrong, but as of now the Supreme Court applies a different test for this kind of issue. This is not a race case."

After a recess, the Court denied the women veterans' motion and set a trial on the merits to begin November 9, 1992. The Board of Visitors voted to get rid of the Veterans Day Program the next month.

Johnson, Lacey, and Chapman came up to me after the hearing. "You know, these guys are pretty arrogant," Chapman said. "They stomped on our feelings."

"How's that?" I asked.

"Well, two of them, Jimmy Jones and another one, two of the most important guys on the Board of Visitors, I think, came up to Liz and me just a minute ago, and Jones asked if I was a housewife. He said, 'I got one of those at home.' They were saying that to put me down," Chapman continued. She was thoroughly disgusted. "Then on the way out the door, they said, 'Good-bye, girls.'"

The same stupid thing happened in the "Miss Mary" civil rights case in Gadsden, Alabama, in 1963, I told them, when white attorneys refused on cross examination to address Miss Mary Hamilton, a black woman, as anything other than "Mary." The case went to the Supreme Court where Hugo Black wrote an order to make them behave.

"Do you think those members of the Board were out of line, Liz?" I asked.

"They asked me if I was a secretary," she replied.

Call for Help

At the airport immediately following the hearing, while waiting to catch a flight back to New York, Pinzler confided that she was surprised. She thought we would have prevailed. Pinzler looked out the window of the airport lobby and watched a plane taxi down the runway.

"We're going to need a bigger boat," I said. "I guess that's what you're thinking."

"All I know is that I've got to go back to my Rolodex in my office and find a large enough firm to help us win this lawsuit," she said. "I was overwhelmed at the strength of the other side—ten lawyers. And mountains of retread *VMI* documents at the last minute before the hearing."

"I'm somewhat surprised to hear that the Women's Rights Project is not itself big enough to handle this case," I admitted. "But I'm not at all surprised we lost. But if you do look for help in New York, I have to insist that you do this for me: find a woman lawyer to help us, not a man. I want the lead attorney to be a woman from whatever big firm you find. She's got to be a woman to argue for women in this case. It just looks right, to the judge and to the people all over the country who will be watching this thing."

"I'll see what I can do," Pinzler replied. "There are a couple of firms. I'll ask the one that shows the greater interest when I call them Monday morning. Either one of them is good. I've had a few more conversations with one than with the other. I'll let you know."

Within days, by August 18, 1992, "Vile Val" Vojdik, as the cadets came to call her, Henry Weisburg, and the rest of the Shearman & Sterling troops would be in the case.

Sherman Returns to Charleston

William Tecumseh Sherman's scorched-earth march to the sea did not include Charleston, but the general's name—spelled close enough to the first name of the law firm—is still well remembered in the Holy City. "Sterling," the second name of the firm, only made matters worse by serving to remind the population of the silver their ancestors once hid in their back yards to keep it out of reach of the Yankees. The detachment of black Union soldiers which Major General Sherman dispatched to Charleston was received more kindly. Shearman & Sterling was a massive New York law firm with satellite offices all over the world. I was delighted with the willing response by Valorie J. Vojdik, a senior associate in the New York office who was to be the point-woman for the firm and thus the lead attorney of record to argue the case and be the principal attorney on all briefs and proceedings throughout the women veterans' and *Faulkner/Mellette* cases. To the cadets, she was "Vile Val," nearly as much a nightmare to The Citadel as Shannon Faulkner herself. In awarding attorney fees at the end of the *Faulkner* case, the court observed in its order of March 30, 1999, that "Vojdik demonstrated a grasp of courtroom procedure and evidentiary rules that surpassed most of the attorneys connected with this litigation, including those representing the defendants. In fact, Vojdik's continued savvy and persistence throughout the long course of this litigation leaves the court with the impression that she is a very skilled litigator possessing extraordinary ability...." In one of the lighter moments after a hearing, even the president of The Citadel kidded that he wished The Citadel had Val on its side.

The two senior partners, Henry Weisburg and Jonathan Greenblatt, were first-rate lawyers with international reputations. Greenblatt, however, did not take an active role in the case. The man in control of the money to advance the enormous costs of the case, after the ACLU took a back seat, was Henry. He was the ultimate shot-caller from beginning to end. And it was Henry who, as the highest ranking attorney from Shearman & Sterling, ushered the case to its completion after Val left the firm. In all proceedings, Henry was as nearly as ubiquitous a figure as Val. I was never privy to the inner-workings of the big firm, but it looked like Susan Schweiger and Tom Swift, assistant attorneys, were two of the main work horses writing the first drafts of numerous initial pleadings for Val whenever Val didn't draft them herself. Later, Jane Gordon and Mary Warren joined the team. It is unlikely, however, that many documents went out without Val both drafting and signing off on them. My own involvement was limited to a final review for some law, in rare cases, but mostly for factual matters which could be known only to one on the ground in Charleston.

Henry Weisburg, Esq., Partner, Shearman & Sterling, LLP. Used with permission, Shearman & Sterling LLP, October 24, 2011.

A total of 30 attorneys at Shearman & Sterling would come in and out of the case as it continued for the next six years. Some were members of what I affectionately described to Melinda as "the Children's Brigade," young lawyers learning the art of litigation in the firm's *pro bono* program which was one of the largest and best in the country. Seventy lawyers were on the other side from McGuire Woods, King & Spaulding, and, locally, Barnwell Whaley Patterson

& Helms—Dawes Cooke's firm—and the Hood Law Firm—Bobby Hood's firm. Plus 19 staff members for the plaintiffs and 93 for the defendants. That amounted to a total of about 100 lawyers and 112 members of their staff. And each side hired additional special counsel in Washington, D. C., to handle the U.S. Supreme Court pleadings as various occasions arose.

All along, the numbers of attorneys and staff members committed by DOJ in Washington was never a matter of public record, but their numbers—and costs—were no doubt also considerable.

I called co-counsel in Denver and gave them the news that Shearman & Sterling was in the case. Feiger, Collison, and Kramer nominally stayed on the pleadings for over a year before voluntarily removing themselves from the case.

After March 1993, when *Faulkner* was filed, more than 60 major memoranda and more than 30 motions and briefs would be filed by the plaintiffs in the district court, the Fourth Circuit, and the U.S. Supreme Court. And that does not count either the pleadings in the women veterans' case from June 1992, to December 1994, or those filed in the fight over attorney fees that lasted from September 1996, to June 1999. More than 200 depositions would be taken in the case, nearly 50 major briefs filed, and more than 50 days spent in court hearings. The docket sheet for *Johnson, Lacy, and Chapman* in the district court would contain 121 postings on 20 pages, while that for *Faulkner/Mellette* would contain 625 on 113 pages.

But these documents for the seven years from June 1992, to June 1999, do not count the pleadings filed by intervenor DOJ and defendants The Citadel and State of South Carolina after reporting requirements were ordered by the court. Those reports continued up to the dismissal of the case on March 28, 2002—thirteen years and more than $14 million after I read about Banzhaf in *The Birmingham News.*

Vets Routed

Shortly after Shearman & Sterling joined the plaintiffs' bar, the Board of Visitors voted on September 3, 1992, to close the Veterans Day Program to keep women out of daytime classes. The decision meant closing the VDP to the male veterans currently enrolled, as well as to any future male or female applicants. Upon motion by General Goodpaster, seconded by General Seignious, the Advisory Council to the BOV had cleared the way a day or two before. Cooke, Patterson, and Whittemore sat in on the special telephone meeting of the BOV at 4:30 p.m. Everybody was present except Governor Campbell, a named defendant, and *ex officio* member Barbara Nielsen, State Secretary of Education, the only woman on the board. She, however, never sat on the board. Her place was always taken by a male substitute.

On September 4, 1992, the court held that a resolution to moot the VDP was an inadequate basis at law on which to moot the case. Nonetheless, from the bench in oral arguments the court at that time provided The Citadel with a recipe to return shortly thereafter and renew its motion to moot.

By November 10, 1992, The Citadel did what it would take to move successfully to moot the case and came back with a second motion based on a fresh new resolution passed three days earlier. This time, while admitting no deficiency in its earlier resolution, but more by way of satisfying the court, the resolution of November 7, 1992, read, "That the September 3, 1992, Resolution is reaffirmed and the admission and attendance of civilian students to the Day Program shall be terminated permanently at the commencement of the 1993 spring semester"; and, further, that The Citadel seek "a permanent injunction prohibiting the admission of civilian students to the Day Program."

It took until September 20, 1993, before the district court would grant The Citadel's November 10, 1992, renewed motion to moot the women veterans' case and, after exhaustive briefs on appeal and in opposition in December 1993, and January 1994, another year went by before the Fourth Circuit affirmed the district court on December 5, 1994. The usual three-judge panel assigned to The Citadel case in the Fourth Circuit, Judges Hall, Niemeyer, and Hamilton, upheld Judge Houck in its unpublished *per curiam* decision, 42 F.3d 1385 (4th Cir. 1994).

Thus, a resolution to get rid of the veterans was finally passed "to avoid any risk of loss of its Title IX exemption" that allowed The Citadel to receive federal funds. No member of the BOV voted against it. The Citadel had at last fashioned itself in the image of VMI to be without an entangling program that would distinguish it from the much-anticipated continued success by VMI to keep women away from male cadets. The November 7, 1992, resolution sought "a permanent injunction prohibiting the admission of civilian students to the Day Program." Thus, the resolution sought to be over-inclusive and to reach far beyond the issues before the court in the veterans' lawsuit. *Johnson v. Jones*, 42 F.3d 1385 (4th Cir. 1994), was litigated for the purpose of gaining admission for women veterans to join male veterans in the Veterans Day Program at The Citadel. The final resolution, however, was worded to prohibit the admission of "[all—not just veterans] civilian students to the Day Program, [not just the Veterans Day Program]." The Citadel tried to preempt future efforts to admit non-cadets who were not veterans and to have the resolution apply to the entire day program attended by the cadets, not just to the Veterans Day Program.

Plaintiffs argued unsuccessfully on appeal that discrimination against women had not been eradicated by getting rid of the VDP. Furthermore, no administrative decision by a state agency such as the BOV would be binding to subsequent members. The VDP could be opened again by a simple vote of members of another BOV in later years. Thus, plaintiffs were entitled to relief "under any statement of facts," they argued.

Relying on *Palmer v. Thompson*, 403 U.S. 217 (1971), the district court ordered the case dismissed but retained jurisdiction in the event The Citadel did not live up to its end of the bargain.

The court's use of *Palmer* was taken up by The Citadel. *Palmer* was a 5–4 decision in which the Supreme Court found that equal protection was not violated when the city fathers in Jackson, Mississippi, voted to close all the city swimming pools rather than admit blacks.

As explained in a case five years later, *Washington v. Davis*, 426 U.S. 229 (1976), *Palmer* did not look into a facially neutral ordinance to determine whether the Jackson city fathers were motivated by racial considerations or whether they closed the pools because of bad motives. The *Palmer* court simply refused to look into the minds of the city fathers to infer discriminatory intent and ruled that they had a rational basis for closing the pools to save money and maintain peace.

The district court and, later on appeal, the Fourth Circuit did not give credence to the women veterans' argument that The Citadel closed the VDP because of an intent to discriminate against women, an element of analysis permitted in *Personnel Administrator of Massachusetts v. Feeney*, 442 U.S. 256 (1979), as well as *Washington v. Davis*, two applicable cases that followed *Palmer*. In *Feeney*, women plaintiffs claimed that a Massachusetts law giving preferential treatment to veterans seeking state civil service jobs favored males over females. Most vets are men and most non-vets are women, they argued; therefore, a law favoring employment of veterans discriminated against women. The *Feeney* court rejected this analysis and did not review the case under equal protection as a sex discrimination case, holding, instead, that the law had a rational basis. It was, of course, almost impossible for the women veterans in The Citadel case actually to prove at law that The Citadel meant to discriminate against them when they closed the VDP, although everyone in the world knew they did.

Palmer recognized that safety and costs did not permit a violation of the Equal Protection Clause but held, nonetheless, that the situation with the Jackson, Mississippi, swimming pools did not call for a *Plessy v. Ferguson* separate-but-equal analysis. After they were closed, there were no pools provided to either blacks or whites, so nothing was "separate" and nothing "equal" to compare. This logic in *Palmer* worked for The Citadel against Johnson, Lacey, and Chapman. It was used to close the Veterans Day Program at The Citadel in 1993 when The Citadel closed the program to both men and women. But cases applicable to facially neutral laws did not work to protect The Citadel from Faulkner's attack on a facially discriminatory admissions policy that excluded women in the Corps of Cadets. Faulkner did not have to prove that The Citadel intended to discriminate against women in its all-male admissions policy. Instead, The Citadel had to prove that its all-male Corps of Cadets served an important government purpose and that its admission policy was substantially related to achieving that purpose. In other words, The Citadel had to prove under an intermediate level of scrutiny, second only to a level of strict scrutiny given to racial discrimination, that its all-male admissions policy was substantially related to an important state purpose, a test under *Hogan* requiring The Citadel to prove an "exceedingly persuasive justification" for its all-male admissions policy.

Palmer v. Thompson was one of the worst cases the Supreme Court ever decided, but at least it was clear that the Veterans Day Program was closed under a constitutional analysis in context of racial discrimination, not gender discrimination. My analogy with George Wallace's school-house-door stand to keep blacks out of the University of Alabama, a point I made at the first hearing on the women veterans' case to which The Citadel so strongly objected, was accurate after all. The Citadel, in its gender discrimination case used a racial case to keep women out of the VDP.

The appellate court in *Johnson v. Jones* found the district court's reliance on *Palmer* inapposite. More significantly, it found the district court only dismissed the case as moot but did not in fact issue a permanent injunction based on a resolution willingly submitted by The Citadel "to keep its admissions door closed." "Nevertheless," the *per curiam* court wrote, "we agree with the district court that The Citadel has sufficiently demonstrated its determination to abolish the veterans program, therefore leaving the [1] reasonable expectation [2] that the challenged activity will not recur with respect to that program."[1]

In his concurring opinion in the Fourth Circuit's *per curiam* unpublished opinion, Judge Hamilton found the district court's order to be an exception to the mootness doctrine which was "anomalous." The only two-pronged exception, Judge Hamilton wrote, and the only way a court can retain jurisdiction after a case has been dismissed is "if the dispute is capable of repetition, yet escapes review," the same two prongs which the *per curiam* opinion "agree[d]" were the basis of the district court's order. Even so, Judge Hamilton's concurrence found that neither possibility existed in the lower court's order. Yet he alone addressed the issue whether the district court retained jurisdiction if The Citadel reneged on its resolution never to reopen the Veterans Day Program; no other members of the court joined in his concurring opinion.[2]

The resolution also provided that all of the 78 male veterans currently enrolled in the VDP would be allowed to finish all of their required courses for a degree in the Evening College or Trident Tech or the College of Charleston. In what may, to some, have appeared to be a violation of American Association of University Professors (AAUP) regulations, The Citadel presumed to be able to bestow a Citadel diploma on a male veteran who had spent more time elsewhere working toward his degree than at The Citadel. But even with the Ring on the end of the stick, most veterans felt betrayed.

In an effort to give a happy face to its announcement that the VDP was being canned, The Citadel asked Judge Houck for a private audience, with counsel for the plaintiffs in the gallery listening in. The judge politely declined, telling both sides that they must always proceed as directed by their clients and simply file any pleadings with the Clerk of Court, as usual.

It was a time of celebration for the Board of Visitors. What was in fact a termination was billed merely as "changes" in the day program. The Board of Visitors would do their own version of a rain dance in 1992, as the cadets would do when they got rid of Faulkner in 1995.

"Acting to protect its unique contributions to a diversified system of higher education and to prevent the loss of federal funds," the news release on September 3, 1992, read, "The Citadel Board of Visitors today announced certain changes in its Day Program.... Commencing with the 1993 Spring Semester, civilians will not be admitted to the Day Program."

The devil made 'em do it. "Having been put to an unfortunate and unnecessary choice by the ACLU," a later pleading on September 17 said, the BOV was forced to act. The Board of Visitors assumed an increasingly familiar indignant posture. "Plaintiffs' attempt to impugn the motives of the BOV constitutes a gratuitous, groundless, and offensive attack on individuals and an institution that are devoted to the achievement of laudable educational goals," the pleading stated.

Reacting to the BOV's treatment of some of their best students, the Faculty Council met on September 10, 1992, and voted 15 to 1 on a three-part resolution of its own. Central to their concern was an issue of national defense and economic prosperity. The nation needed engineers, and many of the engineers were the veterans whose careers were being destroyed or derailed by The Citadel. At that time, the council said, there were only about 240 cadets majoring in engineering, but a lion's share of the 78 vets were some of the best engineering students. The faculty, the one body which best knew how things stood at The Citadel, stated that it "deplores and opposes" the elimination of the VDP, that it "requests that The Citadel Board of Visitors honor the moral contract a college assumes when it admits a student."

Some at The Citadel also blamed Pat, Liz, and Angela for not backing off their constitutional rights and refusing to allow the VDP to stay open for men only—long enough to allow the 78 male veterans to finish their courses in the day program. Twenty-seven male veterans in the Veterans' Council sent a petition drafted by The Citadel to the three women. In response, on September 16 Pat, Liz, and Angela sent back a memo.

"Our permission was not required to close it," the women wrote, "and our permission is not required now to reopen it. Rather than take responsibility for their own action in closing the program, The Citadel seeks to shift the responsibility to us in an effort to pit veteran against veteran."

Not even The Citadel's offer to extend their stipulation to include just Pat, Liz, and Angela—but no other women in the future—tempted the women to sell out other women in the future and join the 78 male veterans to finish a degree in the Veterans Day Program.

On the day of the news release, September 3, I made one of my first long telephone calls to Val. By October 2 I had prepared a long memo for Henry and Val, just as I had for the League of Women Voters in 1989, and three days later I had a conference call with them and Isabelle to hear the strategy they advised for the future. Then, on October 10, 1992, I flew to meet with Val and Henry in New York. There I visited with an Army buddy from our days in the service in Korea in 1968. He lived in an eighteenth-century stone house along the Palisades on the east side of the Hudson River. It is marked by a brass plaque put there by the Daughters of the American Revolution to announce that Lafayette and Washington once marched troops along the back of the house. I thought of my ancestor whose unit, the 11th Virginia Regiment, was under the command of Lafayette at Valley Forge and who was captured at the Siege of Charleston in 1780. I always thought I had an advantage in dealing with The Citadel because I knew that the plaintiffs' ideals were more American. I knew that the equal protection clause in the Constitution was like the Golden Rule.

My own military record was brief. Although within days of being too old to be drafted—and notwithstanding the advice of the Selective Service that I would not be—I took a direct commission in the Infantry and Military Intelligence. I thought all Southerners should serve their country in the military. In August 1967, I left Trosly-Breuil, France, where I had been working for Jean Vanier at L'Arche, and went almost directly to Fort Benning in Georgia and, later, to Fort Holabird in Maryland where I got orders for MACV, Vietnam. From Baltimore, on two different occasions, I drove down to OPO at the Pentagon to request that my orders be changed. I opposed the Vietnam war. For my reluctance to go to Vietnam I could have been sent to Fort Leavenworth, but my orders were ultimately changed to Korea. There I briefed generals in I Corps, Camp Red Cloud, and along the Demilitarized Zone as a lieutenant in the Special Security Group, Assistant Chief of Staff for Intelligence, Department of the Army. The closest I got to Vietnam was playing golf in Hong Kong on "R & R" with Stanley Karnow, a well-respected journalist who covered the Vietnam war.

The male veterans who were thrown out of the VDP did not go quietly. They rallied in Byrd Hall shortly after the announcement to get rid of the VDP. Given permission to sit in on the meeting as long as I did not talk, I observed quietly from the back of the room as the men asked questions and Dean Spike Metts tried to answer them. Like the women vets, some of male vets appealed to a sense of fair play and recited their military contributions to the nation, all of which fell on deaf ears at The Citadel. After the meeting, two of the male veterans, Wesley Waters and Ted Blumstein, hired their own lawyer, Randy Horner.

I had already been in touch with Blumstein and Jerome Kinloch, another veteran, about serving as witnesses in the women's lawsuit and, more recently, about what to do about their own predicament after the VDP was closed. Long before the BOV destroyed the VDP, some of the male veterans had been fully prepared to testify that their female counterparts would not be a disrupting factor in the daytime classes. After the VDP was closed, however, they were reluctant to talk to me.

Waters and Blumstein filed their own suit for breach of contract on December 14, 1992. By January 27, 1993, the court set the first hearing on their case. Val, Isabelle, Henry, and I met briefly with their attorney before the hearing. The Court held that the male veterans' case was entirely separate from the ongoing female veterans' case of *Johnson v. Jones*, but the male veterans dropped their lawsuit in little more than a month since their issue would ultimately be resolved in the women veterans' case. I never claimed fees for the men's case, but I had to spend an enormous amount of time on it just to know significant collateral facts during the period of gathering witnesses for the *Johnson* trial, if indeed the women veterans' case itself were to survive as the case continued on appeal.

Veterans Day Program?
What Veterans Day Program?

By the spring of 2010, The Citadel reopened its daytime programs to all veterans—male and female, former members of the Corps and non-former members. Marketing the reopening of the VDP was conducted by The Citadel

Office of External Affairs which, on November 16, 2009, announced that The Citadel was "expanding its education program for veterans" to include all veterans, not just those veterans who were former members of the Corps of Cadets. The fictitious claim of "expanding" an existing education program for veterans in the Evening College allowed The Citadel to avoid a requirement to get approval of the state Commission of Higher Education for a new program. Instead of announcing that it is now reopening of the VDP to conform to the law—to apologize for its colossal mistake to close it in the first place—The Citadel put the ultimate spin on a completely disingenuous announcement:

> RECALLED TO DUTY: The Citadel Reactivates its Veteran Day Program. Charleston, SC, November, 2009—The Citadel today announced that it is expanding its education program for veterans of the military services. As done in the past, following periods of intense military service, The Citadel is recalling the non-cadet Veterans Day Program for undergraduate students.

Even more facetiously, another advertisement was pitched directly to veterans:

> The Citadel has long served the veterans of South Carolina with our undergraduate and graduate programs. And to help today's men and women, we have recalled to service our non-cadet Veterans Day Program.

But these ads, stone-cold silent about the complete history of the VDP, were not widely published. The latter ad mainly ran over Thanksgiving and Christmas, 2009, in *The Post and Courier* and two military newspapers, *The Fort Jackson Leader* and *The Boot*, as if The Citadel was embarrassed to draw attention to its prior actions taken against veterans. Ads were not run in other city newspapers, such as those in Greenville or Columbia. Since the ads—and articles, if any—in *The Post and Courier* slipped by unnoticed, plaintiffs and attorneys in the *Johnson* case did not know until July, 2011, that the VDP had been reinstated.

Eighteen years after the VDP was closed under court order, further debate over educational opportunities for hundreds of female as well as male veterans quietly came to an end. Judge Hamilton's final footnote in his concurrence in the 1994 opinion which put an end to the VDP elaborates on the effect on veterans during those years. The court's observation is perhaps ironical, since it may have been aware that one of the South Carolina District Court judges sitting in Charleston, Falcon Black Hawkins, Jr., was among 90 veterans in the VDP who made up more than a quarter of the Class of 1958:

> I am neither suggesting that the appellants would never be entitled to relief if the program were reinstated, nor that the principles of *res ju-*

dicata would bar their suit if the program were reinstated because a subsequent suit would have a different factual predicate, i.e., events occurring after the termination of the instant litigation, and be based on a claim that did not exist at the time of this suit since the appellants could not obtain the relief that they sought. *See, Meekings v. United Transp. Union*, 946 F.2d 1054, 1057–58. Rather, I merely emphasize that this particular case was properly dismissed as moot and there is no continuing jurisdiction in the district court.

Beaufort Bubble

I knew that there were still other women somewhere out there who wanted to join the Corps after Pat Johnson, Liz Lacey, and Angela Chapman filed their complaint to attend the VDP. Linda Meggett wrote an article for *The Post and Courier* on October 2, 1992, with the headline, "Ex-Citadel professor leads fight for co-ed." However, that would be the first and last time the editors of *The P & C* brought attention to the fact that a Charleston lawyer was involved in the case. The thinking was, probably, that if *The P & C* did not advertise the fact that I was local counsel, people would not know whom to contact without calling New York or Washington, D.C.

In spite of the black-out, a Navy veteran from Beaufort, South Carolina, called my office on November 8, 1992.

"We're having a hard time believing a military college would kick out its veteran students," he said. "I spent a career on the service and it just doesn't make any sense not to see that the Navy today has to include women if it's going to meet its quota of high-caliber people. You got to recruit men and women in every branch of the service to get the best. We own a communications company here in Beaufort. I see in today's *State* newspaper that Chernoff/Silver has been hired by The Citadel to do their PR. It's going to be a very high-profile case. I'm sure the media will be all over the place once Chernoff/Silver stirs things up. They're a very competent firm and represent some big clients in South Carolina."

Sometime during the case, a woman high up in Chernoff/Silver ad agency reluctantly called me to explain that she herself was not in favor of the commercial role her company was taking in promoting The Citadel side of the case.

The Navy officer followed with a fax on November 10, 1992. "What can I and my business partner—he's also retired Navy—do to help you in your lawsuit? This is the kind of *pro bono* work we enjoy," he wrote.

"Tell 'em to call a lawyer," I replied.

A few weeks later, on December 16, 1992, I was quoted by Tony Robertson of *The Charleston Chronicle*, the local black-owned and operated newspaper: "I just hope that my office gets hundreds of call from Charleston high school seniors who may be ready to go to college next year, so I can tell them that they have an opportunity that they never had before."

Robertson went on. "Black said he believes that the more female applicants to the college would likely help his court case in breaking the barriers to the veteran daytime program."

The Navy officer rang back from Beaufort around Christmas 1992, to say that he had a neighbor who knew a young woman who had indeed showed interest in going to The Citadel. He invited me down to meet her. "She always dreamed of going to The Citadel," he said.

I told him that I couldn't talk to the young woman at that time, but I gave him the names of Ray McClain and Sam Waters, two attorneys who had agreed to talk to her if she called them.

These conversations took place sometime in February and April 1993, but no application was forthcoming. A year later, on March 11, 1994, I made a call to the home number of the woman whom the Navy officer had identified. I was told the young woman simply had no further interest in The Citadel. But on April 11, 1994, a month before trial, a different story emerged. I then heard a more complete version of the story. I heard that the mother was afraid of losing her job if her daughter went forward with plans to make application to The Citadel. I immediately called the home again. The mother was anything but comfortable with my questions.

"Ma'am, I've just heard a rumor about what is going on down there. I'm very sorry, sorry for you, your husband, and mainly for your daughter. Is it true that your boss, a Citadel alumnus, has threatened to fire you if you let her make application to The Citadel?"

"No, Mr. Black, that's not the case. I've told you we just had a change of heart about it all, and that's the simple truth," she replied.

"There's no truth of losing your job if you let her go to The Citadel?"

"Not at all," she said.

"But I heard at one time she was so gung-ho," I said. "Your husband too. He was so proud of her for wanting to go to The Citadel. I heard he went around town bragging about her."

The mother of another would be first woman in the Corps of Cadets was silent, and we rang off after the short conversation. Here was a first-rate young woman, a senior at Beaufort High School in the top 10% of her class with a strong SAT score, a student leader already accepted at a good college. I suspected that there was nothing here but fear of reprisal, fear of The Citadel.

The Citadel in its deposition of Steve Bates on May 13, 1994, a few days before trial, tried to get collateral information about the family in Beaufort. Bates, the executive director of the ACLU, had also called the family to find out why the daughter had abandoned her aspirations of joining the Corps of Cadets.

"Her parents were concerned that their daughter's involvement in a lawsuit against The Citadel would result in the loss of their jobs," Bates said.

Rodrigo Diaz

On June 15, 1992, Ron Vergnolle, a Citadel alumnus of the Class of 1991, called me from Durham, North Carolina, to share his ideas about a research paper which he had written as a law student at Duke. I asked for a copy of the paper, but I preferred to have Vergnolle as a witness.

"From having been a cadet there, you might want to tell the court what you really know about The Citadel, what you learned about the way the place really runs," I said. Everything Vergnolle and I talked about would become a matter of public record at trial and in the deposition given by the former cadet.

The preceding April I had talked to two women members of the faculty who told me much of the substance of what would be Vergnolle's testimony. In their opinion, freshmen knobs were more sexually mature than upperclassmen at The Citadel, and cadets, after a short period of time in the Corps, learned to be disrespectful of women.

Vergnolle had a lifetime of social and business contacts at stake. He had been the top academic cadet his senior year. He was winner of the Star of the West Scholarship, The Citadel's top scholarship, a former Chairman of the Honor Committee, 2nd Battalion Academic Officer, President of the Honors Student Association, President of the Inns of Court, Member of the Race Relations Committee, and English major. His testimony would be critical. Ron Vergnolle was the first witness called to testify for the plaintiff at trial in May 1994.

Vergnolle was the only Citadel man out of 16,000 living alumni willing to testify to what the best at The Citadel really means. He was also the only alumnus I asked. I turned down one offer from a veteran. Also, after leaving a message, unreturned, at the Atlanta home of Pat Conroy in 1989, I did not press on and ask him to serve as a witness.

Vergnolle was from a strong Citadel family. His father and brother were graduates, and he spent five years at The Citadel Summer Camp for Boys before enrolling in the Corps of Cadets. His love of The Citadel was second to none. At trial he told the court what The Citadel meant to him.

"The most important thing The Citadel taught me was to stand up for what you believe in and to have the fortitude and the strength of mind to take on hard tasks and things that are difficult and do what you firmly believe. And that's the beauty of The Citadel."

He was Exhibit # 1 for why The Citadel needed to share the wealth. The facts at trial were never to be used to bash The Citadel—after all, the plaintiffs were trying to get in—but rather to show, often by contrast, its strengths from which women as well as men could benefit.

On direct examination, Sara Mandelbaum, who by then had taken over for Izabelle Pinzler for the ACLU, elicited testimony from Vergnolle that, after the freshman year,

> There is no real enforcement mechanism within the Corps of Cadets. There are always rules, and people could possibly be disciplined for not making their bed properly, but by and large, there's a whole group of cadets called senior privates and sophomore privates, and traditionally those people are given a greater extent of leeway. They are really not bothered.

This was a world apart from The Citadel defense line in which the Whole Man was a well-wrought product of four grueling years. This was the essential kind of testimony that Silver and Keith at DOJ did not have at the VMI trial in Roanoke. Vergnolle went on:

> After your freshman year, physical fitness fell off the deep end, so to speak. The only two times I ever was required to do anything physical was twice a year I had to take a PT test, and if I didn't pass the PT, I was required to attend what they call hog-jog.... No one was ever required to pass the test to graduate. I knew several cadets who never passed the test. I lived with a cadet who never finished two tests. He just went out there and walked the entire time.

As far as ROTC was concerned as an integral part of the Whole Man, Vergnolle testified that "it comprises a very insignificant part of your Citadel training unless you are going to go into the military. The military training that I received from ROTC had absolutely nothing to do with my Citadel education."

What was so telling was Vergnolle's statement to the court that, in his mind, the values of honor, discipline, and spirituality at The Citadel were not consistent with those conceived through the federal discipline of ROTC training. Honor and discipline in ROTC were "a part of the military creed, but they embody their own form" and take a "different form than The Citadel's form. It is a different hierarchy, a different system" in the federal military program, "a completely different process" from the one taught within The Citadel Corps of Cadets, Vergnolle testified. In ROTC "it's the United States government. And we learned—actually we learned a lot of things that would be counter-intuitive to what The Citadel would want to teach you. We learned about equal rights, quality, non-gender situations, how to deal with women in nonmilitary environments where those things wouldn't have been taught at The Citadel."

Mandelbaum asked him about women. What was he taught in the Corps of Cadets about women? He replied,

> Profanity is a part of the disciplinary process. Derogatory, racial terms, homosexual terms, sexual terms are used on a constant—I mean that is a part of the correction. When you make a mistake, you are either a fagot, a queer, weak, a woman, and then the terms just go right down into the gutter from there.

Significantly, Vergnolle said that the use of such language was absent at West Point when he visited the academy while he was a senior at The Citadel.

Calling a knob a woman was simply "a way of tearing a cadet down," Vergnolle said. He went on to say,

> I could not estimate the number. It occurred so frequently, it was an everyday part, every minute, every hour part of life there. And if the term "woman" was used, then that would be a welcome relief compared to the large majority of the terms you were called that were gutter slang for women. And it goes all the way down to the genitalia, and that's where the criticism was.

So Vergnolle's testimony was simply a public statement about what everyone always knew about The Citadel. It was just that Vergnolle was strong enough to talk about the bad as well as the good parts about The Citadel. He struck at the hypocrisy of The Citadel. The Citadel taught cadets to be deeply biased against women:

> Bigotry against women, homosexuals, and minorities exists, of course, in society as a whole. But at The Citadel, it is part and parcel of the cadet way of life. Though not officially condoned, such bigotry is tolerated by the administration, the Board of Visitors, and the alumni.

Testifying at trial about his personal experiences is "more like testifying for, not against, The Citadel," Vergnolle continued. "It's not just about women, but about the future of The Citadel if it's going to be a top notch school. I got an excellent education there."

Vergnolle acknowledged that The Citadel was much like a cult in which everyone protects each other and nobody would say anything that might hurt The Citadel.

And the big "secret" Vergnolle shared was that what really goes on inside has nothing to do with what they say goes on. There are two Citadels, he said. One in the daytime and one at night. They are completely different.

From Vergnolle's testimony, one could see that hypocrisy had a perfect nesting ground at The Citadel.

The Citadel did not cross examine Vergnolle on the stand. How would they, after all, get near a graduate who has just demonstrated the very best of The Citadel man, the very qualities which the current leadership there claimed to exist in all cadets? What would they ask Vergnolle on cross examination? Maybe, "Rodrigo Diaz, el Cid, will you please elaborate on what you meant when you testified that The Citadel teaches its graduates to stand up for what they believe in and to meet the world head on?"

Vergnolle represented what the Whole Man was intended to be. Vergnolle was a microcosm of the subplot of the trial itself, not whether one takes the right or wrong position but how he conducts himself in the fray, whether he intelligently acts from conviction and with decency and maturity.

For some, his observations about The Citadel were just not true. However, a 47-page document entitled "The Long Ago Memories of an Old F Troop Knob," dated October 22, 2010, and posted by alumnus Terry Kneen on The Citadel Class of 1970 Homepage corroborates much of what Vergnolle talks about.[3] This rare memoire is the only public non-fictional account of cadets' lives apart from Vergnolle's testimony and other published proceedings from lawsuits against The Citadel. It begins, "An outsider cannot begin to grasp what The Citadel is about."

Another former cadet was named by The Citadel in rebuttal. To the majority of alumni, however, Vergnolle's observations amounted to an account of cadet life that had already been presented in fiction through Pat Conroy's 1983 novel *The Lords of Discipline*. But Vergnolle's forum was a court of law, and The Citadel knew his voice could simply be denied by opposing testimony. In his novel, Conroy had control over the dissenting voices of his fictional characters and could weigh the balance in any direction his art took him, but Vergnolle could only present his factual side of the story. Vergnolle was a throwback to the grand old days of the old Citadel, before the intrusion of a corruption of barracks culture that persists even today.

Public Policy

At the end of the preliminary injunction hearing and before the veterans' case was mooted, the court directed both sides to offer testimony on public policy at a hearing on the merits, initially scheduled to begin on November 9, 1992. Any supporting testimony from any of the four military colleges recognized by the Pentagon, outside VMI and The Citadel, would therefore be crucial for the plaintiffs. I hoped to find a witness who could testify first-hand about the benefits which flowed both to the women who were admitted and to the college or university itself. Virginia Tech, I thought at the time, was within the state orbit of VMI and thus not worth trying for, and at the others, Texas A & M, North Georgia, and Norwich, my efforts failed. I later was told that evidence from Virginia Tech would have been supportive of the plaintiffs' case, if I had tried to seek it.

"Bud Watts is a very good friend of mine," Major General Thomas G. Darling at Texas A & M told me when I called him on the phone. "I would not dare take a position against him and his institution any more than he would do that kind of thing against me. What goes on there at The Citadel is the business of the people who run the place and the good people of State of South Carolina. I will tell you, though, that our top cadet a few years ago was a woman," he said and hung up.

At the same time, during August 13–18, 1992, I composed more letters seeking witnesses on public policy. Three-page letters went out by fax to General Norman Schwarzkopf in Tampa, Major General Tom Siegfried at Ft. Jackson, Colonel Mikolajcik, the commander at the local Air Force base, Admiral Kaup at the Charleston Naval Shipyard, and to Senator Fritz Hollings, Class of 1942, Charleston Mayor Joe Riley, Class of 1964, State Senator Arthur Ravenel, Jr., and North Charleston Mayor Bobby Kinard, Class of 1972.

I got nowhere with any of them. When I talked in person to Fritz walking out of McAllister Field House on The Citadel campus—he never slowed down— he expressed his sentiment for The Citadel remaining the way it was, but reluctantly acknowledged that equal protection of the law would probably require women to be admitted to the Corps. He also reminded me that he was actively sitting in the legislative branch of the federal government.

With Joe Riley I did not even get past a trusted aide. Bobby Kinard never called back. Later, after women prevailed, Fritz and Joe would claim they supported women at The Citadel at a great political price. And they would be right: had they been more forthcoming and actually served as witnesses, they would probably have lost their reelections. Ron Fulmer, the 1967 alumnus who fought against Sarah Manly's bill in the General Assembly, tried to unseat Riley almost solely on the limited stand Riley took in favor of women at The Citadel.

I was particularly fond of Admiral Stockdale, former President of The Citadel who was run off by the Board of Visitors in 1980 after only one year in office for trying to get rid of hazing. After he was released as a POW by North Vietnam, I sent him a copy of Boethius's *Consolation of Philosophy*. After my arrival at The Citadel, I responded to his request for junior faculty and TAC officers to spend nights in the barracks, a bad idea to the BOV which rejected it. The BOV reportedly were particularly incensed that Stockdale recognized in the fourth class system an echo of what he had dealt with in the Hanoi Hilton. His final reputation at The Citadel, according to Bland Mathis, Class of 1958, and beloved member of the English Department, was simply that he was "crazy" because of the changes he tried to make.

I called Stockdale's former aide-de-camp in Charleston for the admiral's address at the Hoover Institute at Stanford University so I could send him the letter. The aide cleared the air right away.

"He's probably not in favor of women being admitted to The Citadel," the aide said, much to my surprise. I was told that I was wasting my time to write the admiral. Worse yet, the admiral might end up testifying for The Citadel and would be able to say that he was asked to testify for the other side but decided instead to testify for The Citadel instead, the same way Professor Sandy Astin from UCLA would do for the plaintiffs. I never sent the letter.

It was a dead-end street trying to get active-duty officers to testify, and most retired officers as well. Yet some of the best evidence for the defendants in the VMI trial came from cross examination by VMI of West Point active-duty officer Colonel Talbot. And it all was simply a nicety that did not bother another star witness for The Citadel, Major General T. Eston Marchant, Commanding General of the South Carolina National Guard, whom I cross-examined at trial.

Antenor's Friends

In the spring of 1992, I asked five women who were teaching at The Citadel to testify for the women veterans, but only one, Jane Bishop, a Barnard College graduate in the history department, agreed to do so. The first woman ever tenured at The Citadel would have been the best witness, but she wanted nothing to do with the case. Another simply wanted to forget the experiences she had with cadets who left pornographic remarks on her office door and an administrator who did nothing about it. Another left The Citadel after being ridiculed in front of cadets by a male colleague on the faculty, and another would not even return phone calls.

Testifying for The Citadel were, among many others, Cynthia Tyson, President of Mary Baldwin College in Staunton, Virginia, Clauston Jenkins from St. Mary's Episcopal Junior College in Raleigh, North Carolina, and a couple of retired Army generals serving as college presidents, Sam Wilson at Hampden-Sydney, and John Ripley at Southern Seminary College in Buena Vista, Virginia. In-house experts in education included Professors Tom and Alice Mahan from The Citadel and Josiah Bunting, VMI Class of 1963.

On June 22, 1992, days after filing the veterans' complaint, I began to make telephone calls to the presidents of Princeton, Clemson, Winthrop, Sewanee, Davidson, and Washington and Lee. I was looking for witnesses who would testify from their own experiences at their own colleges and universities that becoming a coeducational university wasn't all that bad. Whether they were public or private institutions did not matter.

Both Sewanee and Davidson had become coeducational 20 years previously with great success. When I called both colleges, I began by reciting an expanded list of expert witnesses The Citadel had on the value of male-only or single-sex education—David Riesman, Elizabeth Fox-Genovese, and Richard Richardson were intended to make up for The Citadel's loss of Sandy Astin who was completely in the plaintiffs' corner by now. The Vice Chancellor of Sewanee, however, declined because he said the relation between Sewanee and the Episcopal Church dioceses in South Carolina was too strong to permit him to testify comfortably. Davidson's president declined because he just didn't want to get involved. These telephone calls and others, namely to the president of Washington and Lee, were in addition to letters of some length which I sent to the presidents of Winthrop and Clemson on June 23, 1992. I got to speak to only administrators in each office. The presidents themselves never returned my calls or responded to my letters. To Clemson's president I wrote again on August 25, 1992, laying out the issues as if the veteran women were trying to get in the Corps of Cadets. After all, consistent with The Citadel defense, most of the issues to be raised later in Faulkner's case had their first airing in the veterans' case:

> I still feel strongly that in order for the plaintiffs to prevail in this class action suit to admit women into the Veterans Day Program at The Citadel, facts that are common knowledge to everybody must be testimony from the witness stand or in deposition. Principal spokesmen from public colleges which were previously single-sex colleges in the state of South Carolina, Clemson and Winthrop, must speak out as to the success of coeducation at their own institutions. To remain silent about the suc-

cess of coeducation at their own state institutions, especially while experts from private colleges testify as to the success of single-sex education at their private colleges and public colleges, is to do a great disservice to women who seek an equal opportunity in higher education. Will you, therefore, please help by serving as an expert witness to the fact that your state institution has benefitted from its decision to become coeducational?

No dice. Also, to add some wisdom and spice to the roster of plaintiffs' witnesses, I called the president of the College of Charleston on December 17, 1992, but he politely refused. In spite of my interest only in hearing a story about successful coeducation at a sister college in town, the former appellate court judge looked at it from a trial lawyer's point of view. The Citadel lawyers, he surmised, would ask him: What do *you* know about The Citadel? The Citadel, on the other hand, on April 15, 1994, was able to name an alumnus among a list of 59 witnesses, John M. Palms, Class of 1958 and president of the University of South Carolina.

I had not run out of alma maters. I had been to seven colleges and taught at six others, so there were other fountains from which to drink. After calls to the dean and a few chairs scattered around Princeton, I was finally led to Bill Bowen, who had retired as president of the university and was then president of the Andrew Mellon Foundation. Bowen could tell, first-hand, Princeton's story of admitting women in 1969. What was a great surprise and real advantage to the plaintiffs was that so many facts and opinions about the matter at Princeton in those days were identical to the issues at trial and were recorded in detail, and Bowen was the scribe. The Citadel academic dean, General Meenaghan, was on record for finding similarities between The Citadel and Princeton. Bowen's lengthy depositions in New York at Shearman & Sterling in future months would, with Sandy Astin's, establish the most powerful educational testimony in the case.

"Today," I told Melinda, "I got the best expert witness in the entire case on either side. The president of Princeton, loaded with stacks of facts. There are reasons great colleges are great colleges. People. She flourishes, *sub numine deo.*"

By late August 1992, plaintiffs had responded to Judge Houck's directive to find expert rebuttal witnesses by September 3.

I knew that the plaintiffs' case would be greatly enhanced with powerful witnesses from the two South Carolina universities, Clemson and Winthrop. Winthrop from its founding in 1886 until 1974, had been all female. Since its founding as a military college for men in 1889, Clemson had maintained one of the greatest collegiate military histories in the country. More Army officers came out of Clemson in World War II than any other university except West Point and Texas A & M. In 1955, Clemson admitted women undergraduates and became a university which maintained its all-male Corps of Cadets until

1957. Until 1969, every male freshman and sophomore was required to take ROTC; two years later, ROTC was opened to women.

According to ROTC Headquarters in Fort Monroe, Virginia, there were, in addition to The Citadel and VMI, four other military colleges, Norwich University, VMI, The Citadel, and North Georgia College and State University, at which the U.S. Army ROTC Cadet Command had programs. Additionally, there were two universities—Texas A & M and Virginia Polytechnic Institute, now Virginia Tech—with a Corps of Cadets. Of the six military schools within the Association of Military Colleges and Schools at the time of litigation, only VMI and The Citadel had corps-only programs. The privileged status of these six institutions with regard to the commissioning dates of their graduates was taken away by the Pentagon in 1997.

Clemson still maintains the nucleus of its origin as a military college in its Fighting Tiger Battalion. The battalion is only a designation for its ROTC unit, however. It is not a Corps of Cadets. The Corps of Cadets at Clemson, however, may in the future be reinstituted to allow more students to live on campus. A dormitory for ROTC students already exists. Therefore, Clemson falls into a critical category all to itself. First, its history is similar to that of four of the six military colleges recognized by the Pentagon. Secondly, and more significantly, it is a South Carolina university that enlarged its mission to respond to all the people's needs, male and female, cadets and non-cadets.

At Clemson, as at every other university with an ROTC unit, only the ROTC battalion represents the military element in the university. At The Citadel, on the other hand, a cadet's structured life represented by the Corps remains, at best, interrelated and, at worst, confused with the true military component represented by the ROTC battalion. Both an ROTC battalion and a Corps of Cadets exist and every student is a member of each, but, as Vergnolle made clear, the ROTC Palmetto Battalion and the Corps of Cadets dwell far apart.

The Corps of Cadets at The Citadel exists for social, political, and economic purposes, for Westvaco, Wachovia Bank, Piggly Wiggly, and anywhere else the Ring gets an alumnus a job. ROTC exists for service to the country in the armed forces. Nonetheless, while the vast majority of students at The Citadel chooses not to take a commission after graduation, or is not offered a commission, it is still not uncommon for Citadel graduates to serve with distinction in the National Guard.

Put another way, the Corps alone is West Point—there is no ROTC unit there—but the Corps alone is not The Citadel. That and the fact that The Citadel is a public and not a private college are the two great facts that are sometimes not fully realized about The Citadel.

On November 3, 1992, I made my first trip to Clemson to see former president Robert C. Edwards, Mr. Clemson himself, affectionately known as "Royal Crown" or "R. C." His wife was with equal genuine affection known to the students as "Moon Pie." R. C. Edwards had a good reason to testify. He told me that his granddaughter, the apple of his eye, was a third-year student at South Carolina School of Law, and I assumed that she most likely gave her granddaddy his marching orders. A woman—wife, daughter, granddaughter, girlfriend—was never more than a step away throughout my search for witnesses among the men who could testify from important positions they held.

Edwards met me on the morning of November 4 in the motel room where I was staying near the campus. He had wanted to meet in an out-of-the-way secret spot, something that reminded me of my first meeting with one of the young women in high school at the King Street Library in Charleston.

Edwards was very straight-forward, but he limited his remarks strictly to telling only the "Clemson story," as he called it. He wanted to take no stand on the ultimate issue of whether The Citadel should admit women and offered only broad complementary observations about The Citadel. After all, together with several of the defendants' witnesses, he did hold an honorary degree from The Citadel.

"Of course, Clemson's better now than it was," Edwards said. "We changed our mission to become a comprehensive university and so we had to change our admission policy too. But you know The Citadel still has its own unique mission. The Board of Visitors at The Citadel has simply not changed its mission to include a wider-reaching student body, as we did at Clemson."

It began to look as if The Citadel lawyers could take this kind of testimony and run with it. I wasn't sure whether to use Edwards at all. But it looked better with his next brief observation.

"We just thought, frankly, that we could not serve the people of upper South Carolina the way we were going," Edwards added. "I can only tell the Clemson story."

"But," I said, "The Citadel, from what it claims its witnesses will say in their depositions—and we haven't taken them yet, so we really don't know—but The Citadel claims that former governors John West and Jim Edwards will say that South Carolina does indeed have a long-standing state policy of single-sex education in place."

After some hesitation, the former Clemson president said that he did not think Governor West and Governor Edwards would take the stand and testify that there ever existed a state policy in South Carolina before the VMI lawsuit. He did not think they would say that South Carolina ever had such a policy. "I don't know where they would find it, what they would point to," he said.

Bob Edward's deposition was admitted at trial in May 1994, but one of the best witnesses in the effort to get women in The Citadel was wrong about that one thing. John West and Jim Edwards would indeed later testify in depositions, also admitted at trial, that there had always been a state policy of single-sex education in South Carolina, one that existed before either the veteran women's or Faulkner's case was filed. By taking this position, they supplied The Citadel with necessary support in a losing effort to create a historical record that was lacking in the VMI suit. At that point in the case, The Citadel had to argue that it was not like VMI, and any proof of a prior existing state policy of single-sex education would do the trick, or so it thought.

Like Bob Edwards, Charles Vail, former president of Winthrop, was a man of great courage and integrity. Vail had been the principal player during the days when Winthrop admitted men to end a long-revered, all-women admission policy. He tirelessly went from one office to another in the State House and Senate to convince the politicians that a change at Winthrop was necessary for the college to better serve the state.

On September 24, 1992, I called Vail, who had retired and was living in Banner Elk, North Carolina, near the ski slopes. The Citadel had used documents from Winthrop to argue that men were admitted to Winthrop for quite a different reason from the one the veteran women were using in their case. The veteran women used the Winthrop story of coeducation to support a state policy of expansion of educational opportunities to all citizens in the state. To that extent, Winthrop had the same change in its mission that Bob Edwards relayed about Clemson. The women veteran plaintiffs argued that Winthrop's voluntary decision to admit males was constitutional because it was rationally related to achieving a legitimate goal. It was not simply a money-driven decision that benefited men in York County or a voluntary bid for more students throughout the state.

In his deposition on March 3, 1993, Vail said:

Winthrop had long been the state college for genteel young ladies in South Carolina. My main problem was to convince the male political forces that the future of Winthrop lay in becoming a total university, one which catered to all citizens of South Carolina and especially York County.... We had to change our mission. The very reason that Winthrop was made coeducational is the reason that I would say ... about The Citadel. That is, that a public institution, a public college, or university drawing funds from the general public assembly should not discriminate on its admission on any basis other than academic ability and preparation.

The Citadel's version of the history of Winthrop, however, was simply that the benefitted class—first women only, then women and men—profited from the admissions policy. Thus, The Citadel argued, the plaintiffs' version of the Winthrop story was constitutionally flawed under footnote 17 in *Hogan*.

For the plaintiffs, Charles Vail's story about admitting men into Winthrop was the same as Robert Edwards' about admitting women into Clemson. But through cross-examination, The Citadel intended to use the facts surrounding the admission of men into Winthrop to argue that the decision to go coed was no more than a voluntary act by the state legislature in order to meet a demand for greater educational opportunities for men. Thus, the issue of demand was grafted and infused into footnote 17 in *Hogan* by The Citadel. "Demand" is what women lacked at The Citadel—men demanded to go to Winthrop, The Citadel said, but women do not demand to go to The Citadel. Therefore, according to The Citadel, boldly adding language to the controlling Supreme Court case, the story of Winthrop was evidence of state policy and good precedent to keep women out of the Corps of Cadets.

South Carolina Commission on Women

One of the first clear pictures of the difficulty to get in-state witnesses emerged during the time I tried to get the director of the South Carolina Commission on Women (SCCW) to testify for the plaintiffs. On October 7, 1992, I called her to ask if her office could lend its weight to the side of the women veterans in their fight to get into The Citadel.

Her response was not only that she would welcome the opportunity to testify for Patricia and the other women, but also that her husband and she would like the opportunity to come to Charleston and meet with me. She said she had some ideas of her own.

But the director's plans for SCCW support of women collapsed shortly after I named her as a witness for the plaintiffs. Two weeks later, and before they drove to Charleston, her husband called to tell me about something that had come up since we talked in Charleston. The director herself did not even want to talk to me. She had to withdraw her offer to testify. She couldn't have anything more to do with the plaintiffs.

"Good gracious, why?" I asked. "We just got started. Her *amicus* brief would be crucial from another state entity separate from The Citadel. The state itself is not a defendant."

He calmly explained that his wife got a call from Governor Campbell's office. They got wind that she was willing to testify for the veteran women and that her office was drafting an *amicus* brief. They said to stop. Quit. Get out.

The state, of course, could use as an excuse for silencing the commission director the argument that it anticipated being named a defendant if and when the United States intervened. In Virginia the governor and state attorney general took one side of the case and the attorneys for VMI took another. State officials in South Carolina did not want to appear fractured in their full support of The Citadel, whether the United States ever sued South Carolina or not.

Plaintiffs were set back at the loss of such a strong witness. The Citadel sent out notices for the director's deposition on February 5, 1993, as if they were unaware that anything had ever happened. Subsequently, the matter was completely dropped and the director was never deposed.

Top Trainer and MacArthur Awards and NGC

In August 1992, I began to make inquiries of the Army ROTC program at The Citadel to see if the existence of an attached all-male Corps of Cadets did indeed result in a high quality ROTC unit. My discovery followed the initial brief inquiries made at North Georgia State during the time of the Manly bill in 1991. More to the legal point, I was looking for evidence of the performance of women in ROTC at other colleges. On September 22, 1992, I heard from Major Shepherd, Public Affairs Officer, ROTC Headquarters, Fort Monroe, Virginia, in response to my specific questions about the Top Trainer and the MacArthur awards. The Top Trainer Award was an annual award presented since 1988 to the best overall trained unit among the three categories of small, medium, and large units, nationwide. According to their size, the ROTC units competed with each other every summer at Fort Bragg. Only the contract ROTC students, that is, the best from each college, competed since they only were required to go to the summer camps in order to gain a commission upon graduation. The large ROTC unit at Campbell University in North Carolina, in the shadow of Fort Bragg, won the first two years, followed by North Georgia in 1990 and The Citadel in 1991.

Jack Muhlenbeck called me on February 25, 1993, to announce the winner of the MacArthur Award for the large category, Texas A & M, and to say that the Top Trainer Award was no longer given. I had earlier asked Major Shepherd for a comparison of the performances by cadets and ROTC units from The Citadel, VMI, Texas A & M, Virginia Tech, Norwich, and North Georgia. Shepherd replied with a little background information.

"All of these institutions are treated as military colleges for statistical purposes," he told me. "I averaged the grades given to the cadets from the six military colleges during the four years 1989–92 Top Trainer had been awarded. First was NGC with 66.2; second was Texas A & M with 49.3; third was The Citadel with 48.4; fourth was Norwich with 36.1; fifth was VPI or Virginia Tech with 35.6; and last, much to my surprise, was the venerable institute itself, VMI with 35.2."

What emerged from the Fort Monroe ROTC Command was a picture that could be used at trial. Not only were the best ROTC units coed, but also they were at colleges and universities that had a corps of cadets flourishing as only a part of a larger, non-cadet student body. The Citadel was just the biggest, not the best, ROTC unit in the country.

During January 1993, I renewed contact with Major Paul Kotakis at Fort Monroe for more follow-up information on how the Army ranked the various ROTC units in the country.

"Our best guys are not necessarily from The Citadel or VMI," Kotakis said. "They are from coed units like Texas A & M, this year at least."

"In 1991 NGC won," the officer at the Pentagon continued, "and one of the ranking female officers received the award on behalf of the University from General Colin Powell at a ceremony at the Pentagon. It was quite a show."

"Where did The Citadel place that year?" I asked.

"They were not high but were at least in the top ten. VMI did not even place in the top ten," he said. "Never has. Purdue won it in 1989, and they are not even one of the six military colleges outside the federal academies listed by the Pentagon.

"It's the quality of the students themselves that makes a good Army officer, not whether they are trained in an all-male, self-contained corps of cadets," he said.

Does the BOV at The Citadel know all this? I wondered. Did they do any research along these lines before just digging in to fight women in the name of leadership and military excellence? Would it have made any difference whatsoever to them one way or another?

"Is it true," I asked him, "that VMI once had as a condition to satisfy—in order to be graduated—a requirement that every graduate had to serve in the military, and that when the military refused to commission every VMI graduate, the folks in Virginia had to pay a visit to the Pentagon and beg that their graduates be taken?"

"I've heard that," the officer said. "It's true also that, in spite of the tremendous political pressure, we didn't relax our standards to take every VMI graduate. We still do not commission every VMI graduate who wants a commission. And we certainly don't take every Citadel man who wants one, either."

My own experiences while teaching at The Citadel bore that out. Two Army officers came to visit me in my office in 1981 in Capers Hall and asked if it were true that I was failing a senior who was supposed to receive a commission weeks later at graduation. When I told them that regrettably that was the case, they both smiled broadly. One said, "Great, now we don't have to offer him a commission."

The Citadel's own pleadings on November 17, 1992, dismissed the entire issue of the value of their commissioned graduates with a stunning admission, stating, "Defendants have no records of how many cadets sought or were offered commissions in the U.S. Armed Forces during the past five years. ..." They were not keeping track of those cadets who sought a commission but were denied by the military branches. The Citadel fell short in this instance of keeping good records of how well they perform as a military college. And spinning the issue to a positive turn, said, "Graduates of the Corps of Cadets have never been required by The Citadel to accept a commission if offered to them."

Nearly a year after my telephone conversation in August 1992, with Major General Tom Darling at Texas A & M, I turned back to North Georgia College. Some people in the ROTC program at North Georgia College were more than willing than others to help with facts about its Corps of Cadets and the enormous success the Corps enjoyed at the university. The retiring president at NGC was of little help. I called him on June 25, 1993, and got nowhere. But an administrator at NGC, Mark Cutright, saw an opportunity to publicize the strength of the program at NGC and answered all questions and furnished me with brochures and manuals.

A burr under The Citadel's and VMI's saddles was obviously that the coeducational Corps of Cadets at NGC was often superior in Top Trainer and MacArthur competitions. The story of a 1991 NGC graduate who held command positions during some of the Corps's most successful years was well known. Women became a part of the Corps at NGC even before women were admitted to West Point and Annapolis in 1976. NGC had a long record of success with women soldiers, although their numbers were small, about 5% of the total Corps. Like all previously all-male military colleges, NGC was different from The Citadel and VMI in that the Corps at NGC was only a part of a larger coeducational environment. As they did at Texas A & M, Norwich, and Virginia Tech, the cadets at NGC went to class in their uniforms with thousands of non-cadet students, but they had their separate lives as cadets and lived in the barracks together under a 24-hour military regime. The door that separated the men from the women cadets was unlocked in 1991. Incidents of sexual harassment were few.

I had been in touch with the director of public relations at NGC from the earliest days of the veteran women's case. I also had talked to Hugh Shott, II, former Vice President of Academic Affairs at NGC at the time women were

admitted into the Corps. Shott agreed to testify to the success of a coeducational
corps of cadets at a public college, and later in March 1993, gave a very useful deposition in Charleston. Hugh Shott, like Bill Bowen, Bob Edwards, and
Charles Vail, turned out to be a major witness from the upper ranks of university
administration.

The two people at NGC whom I especially wanted as witnesses, however, were
a former female cadet who had appeared with General Colin Powell in Washington, and Colonel Barkley, Commandant of the Corps of Cadets. Barkley
told me that he would gladly testify as to the facts that existed with regard to
women cadets under his command at NGC.

I called Colonel Barkley on February 2, 1993, to hear that, in his opinion,
many women do not have sufficient leadership skills, yet the military was the
only place women could get the kind of leadership experience necessary in
tough situations to break through the glass ceiling. This kind of factual testimony on leadership training would serve to contradict The Citadel's more narrow argument on teaching leadership skills exclusively adapted for men. In
fact, his point put The Citadel's on its ear. The Citadel's gimmick of a male-
only "adversative" concept of leadership conducive to hazing was as foreign to
NGC as it was to the federal service academies.

Major Cuyler McKnight came to NGC about the same time as Colonel
Barkley moved to a new assignment in New Jersey. I received notice of Barkley's
deposition in Dahlonega, Georgia, from Bill Clineburg at King & Spaulding,
but Shearman & Sterling did not. Depositions on the plaintiffs' side were set
by Shearman & Sterling. Clineburg, therefore, took the deposition without
opposing counsel present.

"I don't think he got much that will help his client," Barkley told me later.
"The Citadel's lawyer mainly asked a lot of questions about women's shoe sizes."
Plaintiffs let the deposition stand without objection.

McKnight was also willing to serve as a witness and quickly returned my
call. McKnight could now be the witness who could testify as to the actual
daily military activities in the Corps at NGC. But fear of The Citadel would apparently strike again. Major McKnight was directed by higher-ups at NGC to
cancel his plans to come to Charleston for his deposition.

It was clear to me that the very presence of a woman cadet as a witness, like
Melody Lutz, a retired Army officer, would completely undermine The Citadel's
defense based on the notion that women would ruin the traditions of the all-
male college and undermine military morale. Significantly, a woman from
NGC would be a cadet from a state military college, not a women cadet from
one of the federal academies, the mission of which The Citadel always declared
to be different from the mission at The Citadel.

I tried to reach NGC's 1991 top female cadet by her married name. On Monday, June 26, 1993, we chatted briefly about the case, and I set up a deposition. She had finished NGC and law school and was already working in a firm outside Atlanta. She did not take a commission and go into the Army. The former cadet was less than enthusiastic when I arrived at Clineburg's office at King & Spaulding in Atlanta for her deposition. Clineburg successfully neutralized her, and she let me know on the ride down on the elevator that she had had enough of the effort to get women in The Citadel. Another star witness refused to testify at trial.

First Defense

One of the early witnesses named by The Citadel was an adjunct professor at The Citadel who was the mother of a cadet. Other women witnesses for the defense included Citadel faculty member Alice Mahan, who was paid as an expert witness, another highly paid expert in women studies, Elizabeth Fox-Genovese, and women currently in the administration, staff or faculty, Angela Williams, Nurse Summerford in the Infirmary, Pat Ezell, director of the Evening College, and Celia Halford.

The adjunct teacher's deposition was January 20, 1993, from 10:00 a.m. until 1:00 p.m. Like the other depositions to date, it was prior to the time Faulkner filed her case, so it was conducted under the veteran women's suit. It got straight to the point of why mothers send their sons to The Citadel.

The deponent told Jane Gordon, the Shearman & Sterling attorney deposing her:

> What they did with my son in one year, after the freshman year, then four years at that school, I had not been able to do with having him for 18 years. He's my only child, so he got all my attention, all my energy, everything, and I wasn't able to do. That's why I love that school. I love that school. What they did with him I will be forever and ever grateful.
>
> If girls were in the classroom, it would create an atmosphere that would not be conducive to learning. Some guys in class with girls would be so afraid of making a mistake that they wouldn't speak up at all. They would have to be pretty dadgum sure they're going to make the right answer to show her up. I think a lot of guys just would not open their mouths rather than to be wrong in front of a girl.

When asked if she knew how many cadets left The Citadel as a result of hazing, she replied, "I think some pansies leave. I think some jocks who think

they deserve special treatment leave because they're just—they think they deserve special treatment and they didn't get it. Nobody is swooning over them."
The adjunct was an excellent teacher:

> They would rather have me than to have a man because I'm not
> totally at the bottom of the other side of the hill, you know, and those
> guys, they like signing up for my class, they enjoy signing up for my
> class. I'm not so old. I think if I had white hair and weighed 200
> pounds, but I think that the guys....
>
> When my son was there he heard a lot of the other cadets say, "Oh,
> get that cute teacher." It would make him real mad. I guess they signed
> up for my class because they thought I was attractive. Some would
> say, "It's sure nice looking at you instead of some pot-gutted old guy."
> They would say that on their anonymous teacher evaluations. Little com-
> ments like that.

She was too much for the witness stand. Like the name of another deponent who was an alumnus on the faculty, her name was quietly removed by the
defendants who initially put her on their witness list. Testimony on the value
of male-only education at The Citadel would have to wait until another day—
a day that never came.

The first deposition of an important alumnus on the faculty came the next
day. The second, after *Faulkner* was filed, came on May 7, 1993. Jane Gordon
deposed the professor to record the reason The Citadel exists:

> Q. What is the value of single-sex education?
>
> A. From what I've read and experienced, the value—a single-sex
> education allows a student to become more well-rounded, to find out
> who he or she is personally, socially, spiritually, physically, mentally
> during these very formative years between roughly 18 and 22.
>
> I raised cane in high school. I drank beer, I drank whiskey. I chased
> women, played sports and just had—I tried to kiss as many women as
> I could between the ages of 15 and 17. And I wanted to go to David-
> son or Sewanee. My grandfather graduated from Davidson, and I
> wanted to be a KA at Sewanee. I'm an Episcopalian. I wanted to go up
> there and drink beer because Sewanee is a great drinking place ... and
> my father said, "No. You have been a bad boy. You're going to The
> Citadel." By the time I graduated, I was the biggest hero I have ever
> been before or since. I was editor of the school newspaper. I was chair-
> man of the Honor Council. I was on the Round Table. I was on the
> Summerall Guards, a drill team. I was this, I was that. I had gold stars

for an A average, and I did just everything. I got the Algernon Sydney Sullivan Award. I was a hero. It turned me around. It does that. We now have become a Citadel family. The family believes in it because it changes people. That's the value of the single-gender. It wouldn't have happened if I'd gone to Clemson, Carolina, or Sewanee. I might have been a little more polished had I gone to Sewanee, don't know, or the University of Virginia, but The Citadel saved me from jail, I think.

In his deposition, the professor described part of his teaching method used with cadets:

> A. I can be risqué sometimes in class.
> Q. What do you mean by *risqué?*
> A. Just what we mean by *risqué*: allude to humorous sexual references and get their attention and laugh. I mean, if a pretty blonde—cadets look at blondes for some reason. A blonde woman can be very ugly, and she can walk outside a first-floor classroom to the bus stop, and they like—if she's got long hair, they'll all look at her. A woman much more beautiful with dark hair can walk by and they won't notice it. They just—it's frightening, and so I will mention their proclivities toward blondes, and they don't have taste and so forth.
> Q. What would you say?
> A. "All you guys ever think about is sex and beer, isn't it?" and they'll laugh.

The professor testified about his experience teaching undergraduate women at The Citadel:

> A. In summer school where the undergraduates are younger and in their adolescence, I have had experiences with women using their sexuality on me that graduate students wouldn't do.... The undergraduates sometimes play games with me, and I don't much like it.
> Q. Like what?
> A. Well, it's happened about three or four times. Back—I quit teaching summer school about five years ago. I just got tired of it and wanted to go off and write and travel in the summer. When I was teaching for 15 years and so on in summer school, it happened three or four times. After class an undergraduate woman, I don't know, 18 to 22 years old, would come up and say, "Professor, I don't understand why you marked this on the paper you just returned." I have cadets do this, too, and I say—my normal procedure is, "Well, give it here and let's look at it," and I'm willing to look at it. The class is over,

let's—"You got a few minutes?" "Yes." "Let's look at it." So I spread the paper out on the lectern, I move aside, and I point out this sentence. "This is a sentence fragment. Do you know what that is? It doesn't have a verb in it." You know, I go over things. Well, a coed student from time to time will lean on my elbow, put her nipple on me and just sort of lean into me and look very interested. Well, I know what she's doing. She knows what she's doing.

Q. What's she doing?

A. She's put an erogenous zone on me. She's touching me.

A fellow Citadel alumnus sent out a letter dated May 30, 1996, and later posted a note on a bulletin board at the Carolina Yacht Club encouraging the nomination of the deponent for president of The Citadel.

USPS

It was the fall of 1992. I looked out the window of my office, an office thought by some preservationists to be the same rooms where the first lawyer practiced in Charleston—the top floor of 23 Broad Street. The street below looked like the setting of a movie made sometime during the last 150 years. When I eventually moved out, the new owner of the building threw my shingle in the trash.

"There's a good man down there, a postman," I said to a friend standing beside me. "He told me a few days ago that some Citadel man called his supervisor at the Post Office to complain that the postman argued with him about whether the postman's two little girls had a right to go to The Citadel. The postman wasn't even the one who raised the subject. He was just disagreeing with The Citadel guy who said women shouldn't be admitted.

"Now here's an ordinary federal employee, a mail carrier, a black man who in civil service has been delivering mail door to door, office to office on Broad Street for I don't know how many years, and he stands up for his two little girls. A Citadel guy in the People's Building across the street calls his supervisor to get him into trouble. The mailman's a very reserved kind of guy, very friendly, even dignified. He could be in a movie as the mailman in Mayberry or Maysville. He stood up for his little girls. He's not an alumnus. He has no fear.

"I'd love to know if the supervisor himself is a Citadel man," I added. "I bet he is, or what is bonding for?"

PART II

Chapter 3

Dey Let De Lady In

1993: Si Bunting

By January 1993, The Citadel had named its experts in the women veterans' case, the principal of whom was Josiah "Si" Bunting, future president of VMI. The Citadel and VMI put forth Bunting as the best and brightest either could offer. A graduate of VMI and Rhodes Scholar at Christ Church Oxford whose roommate was teaching English Romantic literature at the College of Charleston, Bunting had won the *VMI* case before Judge Kiser, not single-handedly, but as their star witness on the issue of the value of male-only education. It was Bunting's testimony that women would be a "toxic virus" in the male Corps of Cadets at VMI and The Citadel.

I set Bunting's deposition for January 14, 1993, not in Lawrenceville, New Jersey, where Bunting was president of the prep school, but down the road at the Woodrow Wilson School in Princeton, affectionately called Woody Woo. It would be the first of two depositions by me and at least three by DOJ held in Washington and New York which I could not attend. His depositions were largely a play-back of his testimony at VMI except that he lacked familiarity with factual details at The Citadel.

Preparation for Bunting's deposition included a look at Henri Marrou's discussion of Spartan soldiers in his *History of Education in Antiquity*. Throughout the case I never opened the door to inquiries about homosexuality which Marrou discusses in context of a military education. I knew such testimony was an irrelevant play to the gallery. To my knowledge, there was no issue—apart from a phone call I received from a cadet during the veterans' case—at The Citadel like the one portrayed in Carson McCullers' *Reflections in a Golden Eye*.

There was, however, credible evidence that a gay bar on King Street was frequented by cadets who were homosexuals. In August 1994, Melinda took Susan Faludi on a field trip to the bar. Faludi subsequently reported what she saw in an article published on September 5, 1994, in *The New Yorker*, in which she made a connection between homophobia and hostility toward women at The Citadel.

The anonymous "Scarlet Pimpernel," who had a regular column in the cadet newspaper, *The Brigadier*, quickly seized on an opportunity to express his familiarity with the watering hole while jumping on Faulkner, as he would do repeatedly in other more tumescent issues of the cadet newspaper:

> It would seem that the LAND OF LOVE is full of many strange romances these days. EYESORE [Faludi] and WHALE-IN-PORT [Faulkner] appear to have danced the tango with some TREEHOUSE SNIPE SWINGERS. Hey boys, DUDE looks like a lady but you'd better not walk that way. Oh DIVINE BOVINE [Faulkner] how thou hath shamed me now.... Therefore, know ye BOVINE that our hate for thee is quite colorful and bound by the grey that thou shall never wear. 'Tis branded by a GOLDEN BAND [Citadel class ring] which shall never adorn your accursed finger. Thine only friend was once DONDICKLE [cadet Von Mickel], and now not even he will speak to the DEMIA DEMONS [the press] with his blasphemy.[1]

What did not appear in the article by Faludi was the substance of a call to me from Ed Rosenlieb of the FBI on the same night I was talking to the editors at *The New Yorker* on August 25, 1994, to verify the contents of Faludi's article. The FBI called my house to alert Shannon about a cadet who had threatened her with rape.

I gave detailed, limited facts only to Faludi, none privileged, about other general matters of safety and personal security, since I thought she might be the best conduit with the largest audience to tell the nation what was going on at The Citadel. Faludi's September 5, 1994, article followed almost exactly two years behind a critical view of the place written by Rick Reilly for *Sports Illustrated* on September 14, 1992. In a book published in 1999, Faludi also followed up on my conversations in 1992 with Mount Pleasant resident Michael Lake and his father, with whom I discussed hazing at The Citadel while looking for witnesses in the veterans' case. I also encouraged Faludi to talk to other women who had taught at The Citadel, notably two young women who were former professors, December Green and Karen Lazaro, concerning allegations of sexual harassment by cadets. Although discussed in general by Faludi, the particulars of those allegations were given to me in confidence on April 28 and 30, 1992.

Another writer and journalist, Catherine Manegold from the *The New York Times*, ignored me when she first arrived in town, but eventually she observed, "It looks like all roads lead to you. Will you talk to me?"

"Too late. It would take me a long time to tell you what I know about this case," I said. When I skimmed through the book she published two years before the case was closed, and saw her sources, I realized how difficult it was for an out-of-town observer from "Off," a derisive term used for anyone who was not born and reared in Charleston since 1690, to comprehend The Citadel.

In preparation for Si Bunting's deposition, I read everything I could find regarding his experience as a soldier and academic administrator. That included his book *Lions Head* about his experience as an officer in Vietnam, a book which was also read by Tom Swift who came down from Shearman & Sterling to help with Bunting's deposition. Bunting, after all, was presenting himself as the thing itself, exemplary of the "Citizen Soldier" in the *VMI* case and of the "Whole Man" in The Citadel case.

Bunting gave little attention to the federal academies except to say that in his expert opinion, VMI and The Citadel were superior to West Point, the Naval Academy, and the Air Force Academy precisely because all of them had admitted women. I ploughed into that. It was a lot of fun for both sides to discuss a wide-range of pedagogical issues. After a long day, Bill Broaddus from McGuire Woods who defended at the deposition remarked, "Now, that's the way a deposition should be run."

Part of the testimony of Bunting was also that the English all-male school system was exemplary for fashioning young boys into men. That is, his testimony covered not just those issues relating to coeducation in colleges, but also in secondary schools. The difference was critical since Faulkner's case never touched on coeducation below the undergraduate level at The Citadel. Ironically, several of the lawyers on the plaintiffs' side were themselves products of single-sex education in private colleges, myself included.

On March 18, 1993, I wrote my son's godfather, an artist in Oxford, for information on the recent decision to admit girls at Rugby School in Warwickshire, England, which is roughly equivalent to an American secondary school. A centuries-old tradition had been lost at Rugby at the same time the all-male traditions were coming to an end at most Oxford colleges.

"It is something of a puzzle to boys and girls when they are separated for the next three years to be re-united at 16," a Rugby brochure stated. Such a plain observation might serve as rebuttal testimony since it looked to the fact that wars are won by men and women at Bletchley Park, the secret code-breaking facility outside London during World War II, as much as by men alone on the playing fields of Eton.

More than a year later, on March 23, 1994, six weeks before trial, I wrote to congratulate the three newly appointed women heads of house at Oxford—Marilyn Butler, Rector of Exeter College, Averil Cameron, Warden of Keble College, and Jessica Rawson, Warden of Merton College. I wished to address what another Rhodes Scholar, Douglas Paschall, had described as Bunting's "patrician" attitude toward education.

"With this new bit of information about a changing Oxford," I wrote, "I hope to cross-examine Mr. Bunting, who looks to the English for guidance on how to run schools and colleges, to show that the times they are a-changing indeed."

I told them about Bunting's assertion that the previously all-male Oxford colleges had not all benefitted from admitting women, that the men had suffered as a result of women being admitted in Cambridge as well as Oxford after hundreds of years of all-male instruction. From Keble and Exeter colleges I received letters back declaring that they had not suffered at all. The Merton warden, Dame Jessica Rawson, was presumably too busy to bother to reply to something so silly. In January 1999, on a visit to Oxford, I talked in person to Warden Cameron about the limitations of Bunting's position.

After Bunting's January 1993, deposition, I had lunch at the Nassau Inn at Princeton with Professor Marvin Bressler whose 1980 research had been cited by VMI and The Citadel as being in support of keeping women out of the military colleges. Like Professor Sandy Astin and others whose true positions on male-only admissions policies had been twisted to support The Citadel's case, Bressler was amused at the audacity of the defense. He also was not surprised that Mary Sue Terry withdrew as Virginia's AG from the *VMI* case.

Judge Johnson and Comity

On February 18, 1993, The Citadel raised the issue of comity to argue that South Carolina's discrimination against women was lawful under a fundamental principal of our system of government. In doing so, The Citadel quoted Frank M. Johnson, Jr., the famous district court judge in Alabama who ordered an end to segregated buses in Montgomery, protected Freedom Riders, and opened Route 80 to Selma. Johnson's law school classmate, Alabama Governor George Wallace, once called Judge Johnson an "integrating, scalawagging, carpetbagging liar."

In a law review article, "The Role of the Federal Courts in Institutional Litigation," 32 Ala. L. Rev. 271, 273 (1981), the judge recognized that "because of principles of federalism and separation of powers," a "necessary first step" for federal courts in institutional litigation is to issue an "injunction to the responsible government officials, putting them on notice of their constitutional dereliction and leaving to them the responsibility of formulating and effectuating appropriate reforms." The Citadel, while earlier arguing that racial and sexual discrimination cases are entirely different, now looked to one of the South's most liberal jurist in the struggle for racial equality. Judge Johnson applied the *Brown v. Board of Education* decision to other racial situations. One of his first cases involved Rosa Parks. A United States marshal in Charleston, Fred Stroble, knew that I was from Alabama and showed me a copy of an editorial that ran in *The State* newspaper when Johnson died in August 1999, an event *The P & C* scarcely noticed.

Judge Johnson demonstrated the best in a federal courtroom, as Judge Houck would later. The tone of the times in the 1950s and 1960s when blacks were trying to get in public schools was absolutely relevant to the women's case. *Brown* and *Hogan* were controlling in *Faulkner*, yet even in *Brown*, equal protection for women was somewhat qualified. In a lecture to students of the Charleston School of Law at the Charleston Museum on March 14, 2011, Jack Greenberg, who was among Thurgood Marshall's staff of NAACP attorneys who tried *Brown*, observed that Oliver Brown's name was chosen out of alphabetical order ahead of Darlene Brown's to appear on the caption of the case solely because he was a man. Realistically, Greenberg said, they needed a man as the lead plaintiff. Greenberg, nonetheless, recognized that *Brown* would later play a role in "changing that sort of thing."

John, Samuel, Lemuel, and Robert Nesmith, the four brothers and personal bodyguards of the greatest South Carolinian, Francis Marion, the Swamp Fox, were not around on October 23, 1986, to help a man who shared their name. Filled with passionate intensity, a few cadets that night went forth to pluck bright honor from the pale-faced moon. After Kevin Nesmith, a black cadet, was hazed in his room in the middle of the night by five white cadets dressed in sheets, James E. Clyburn, then state Human Affairs Commissioner and later Majority Whip in the House of Representatives in Washington, was quoted as saying, "We're talking about The Citadel.... You're dealing with an entity where hazing is a way of life. The Human Affairs Commission is not here to say how a 'knob' should or should not be treated," only to help make sure that black and white cadets are treated the same.[2]

In his deposition on May 3, 1994, Major General Alex Grimsley, a native of Florence and longtime friend of the Houck family, gave the following response to my questions about how he, as president of The Citadel at the time, handled the 1986 Nesmith incident:

> Q. Yes, sir, what occurred?
> A. Well, there were five cadets who, after hours, that is evening hours, late one night, early morning sneaked into the black freshman cadet's room, and had a little paper cross which they burned. Did no physical harm to him. Their explanation was he was not a very good cadet. I think, based on the record, as far as performance of his du-

ties, and this was their role, or their means of getting him to shape up, as they termed it. It was discovered. He, obviously a youngster himself, who reported it, or the next morning it got to my attention. The biggest, because the intense interest on this from external sources, external to the college that is, what to do with the five cadets, should they be expelled or punished?

I punished them with the worst punishment, at least as of that time, that cadets had gotten, disciplinary punishment, without expelling them. I did not consider it an expulsion offense, my Board of Visitors backed me on that. That is a nutshell is what the matter was about.

Q. Did they go on to graduate, the five?

A. Yes.

Q. I'm just reminded of a movie, I think it was "A Few Good Men," Jack Nicholson had something of a plot like that. Did you ever see that movie?

A. No, I've never heard the title.

Later in the deposition, the general responded to another question:

Q. If women were admitted to the Corps, do you think they would become accepted over a period of time?

A. I do not.

"Unexampled Courage"

Isabelle Pinzler called me from New York on February 12, 1993. Before she could say a word, I boasted, "Isabelle, I think there is a possibility that a Beaufort girl may want to make application to The Citadel. Two Navy veterans told me about her. She's backed out but we're still hoping to hear from her again."

"It's already happened," Pinzler said. "A girl in Greenville has already applied to the Corps. I just got a call from Steve Bates. We have to move fast."

Pinzler made a good argument for us to get to the attorney representing Shannon Faulkner—Suzanne Coe—and convince her that the ACLU, Shearman, and I should be associated to represent her client. When I called Suzanne, I told her that we already had the veterans' case up and running in the district court in Charleston and that The Citadel had already made the issues relevant to her Corps of Cadets case front and center in our veterans' case. We both knew we could get a fair, unbiased hearing in either federal forum, Greenville or Charleston.

Within a few days, Shannon had associated Shearman & Sterling, me, and, with some concern, the ACLU.

Shortly after Coe recommended to Faulkner that she associate us, Faulkner appeared at my law office at 23 Broad Street in sweat pants, her parents beside her. Coe was not present. There were the usual cordial and curious exchanges.

I told her that my own feeling was that she would probably prevail under the existing law and, therefore, have a good chance of getting into the Corps. I said she would have the very best attorneys in the leading role of the big firm of Shearman & Sterling in the case. Everyone, I went on, would work hard to get her admitted. But, certainly, no promises of success. I added that if she did get in, other women would surely follow her lead, but unless we found another woman now, she would be alone.

I told her that The Citadel would fight her every inch of the way. They would be very hard on her personally. That would be their *modus operandi*. And the legal process would be difficult, too. I gave her the same terrifying introduction I gave Pat Johnson, Liz Lacy, and Angela Chapman the year before. I would give it again later to another woman who stepped forward for only a matter of days in August 1995.

I paused a bit, and asked, "Do you still want to go ahead?" Her parents said nothing and no glances were exchanged.

"Yes," she said.

There was nothing tentative in her voice. I left the conversation with an impression that would gradually develop into a conviction that I was in the company of the real thing. "Unexampled courage," as Waties Waring described the plaintiffs in *Briggs*.

Shannon Faulkner was born on January 20, 1975. She had just turned 18 years old, and was soon to be one of the youngest major civil rights plaintiffs in American history and the only young one to go it alone.

From March 3, 1993, the date of her amended complaint, to January 18, 1994, the day the Supreme Court lifted the stay to let her in the day program, the strategy in the *Faulkner* case was to get Shannon into the day program in the middle of the year as one step toward getting into the Corps the following August, and, by that later date, hopefully in the company of other women who would join the case.

It meant falling behind her age group, so that when she did get into the Corps, the cadre above her would be her peers in the same class of 1997. That was not good, but there was no way around it if she were to ease her way into the Corps. She remained at her parents' home in Easley, South Carolina, throughout the end of her senior year dealing with actual violence and the threat of violence as best as a teenager and her parents knew how. Initially, they knew nothing about the "Citadel family."

Shannon with her parents, Ed and Sandy Faulkner. Used with permission, Curtis Norman, August 11, 1995.

Supporters of The Citadel took their cars and did "donuts" in her front yard at any hour of the day or night. Ed Faulkner came to the living room window to discover a young woman writing obscenities on the side of the house. More than once he washed off "bitch," "whore," and other favorites from the side of the house, hoping that Shannon would not see the red stains on the white paint. Of course she did. Friends in the neighborhood, in town, in school, and in church kept their distance. Her high school principal never got over it. The Faulkners' close group of Carolina football fans who attended every game and sat in the same seats year after year was split as a result of the young woman who wanted in The Citadel. When my son John and I sat with Shannon in Ed and Sandy's vacant seats at the Alabama-South Carolina football game in the fall of 2010, however, all of that seemed to be put to the side as we watched Gamecock football rise against the Tide.

Coe insisted on drafting the initial complaint and faxed it to Val, Isabelle, and me on March 1, 1992. I consulted Armand Derfner, as usual. Coe correctly predicted that a motion for class action would never be granted anyway and so did not bother with it at the outset. As with the veterans' complaint, a decision was made not to ask for monetary damages. A judge, not a jury, would hear the case.

Faulkner's initial complaint, which was filed on March 2 had to be amended the next day. Attached was the veterans' motion for intervention, or in the alternative, for consolidation of their case with the new *Faulkner* case. Pat, Liz, and Angela were in full agreement to consolidate the two cases, and Judge Houck later consolidated them for purposes of discovery. A case which caught the attention of the nation and world in TV coverage, newspaper headlines and articles for over four years had begun in earnest.

"Gender Was Removed with Correction Fluid": Wite-Out

Nat Douglas called from DOJ on April 24, 1993, to ask if Faulkner would object to a motion by the United States to intervene as plaintiff in her case, but not the women veterans' case.

"I'm sure Shannon and everybody will be delighted to hear your decision," I told him. "But right now I can't do much good business. I'm glad you called, but you've caught up with Melinda and me at the Maternity Ward in St. Francis Hospital. I've got a phone with a very long extension cord in one hand and Master John Black in the other, with a somewhat shorter umbilical cord cut just minutes ago. Mother and baby are doing fine. Can you get in touch with Val and Henry on your own?"

The United States moved without objection to intervene on May 6, 1993. Now the parties were Faulkner as plaintiff against members of the Board of Visitors, the Governor, and various state office holders such as the Superintendent of Education and the Adjutant General, and the United States as plaintiff-intervenor against The Citadel and the State of South Carolina. The caption was wonderful to behold. "The State of South Carolina, Defendant," something only the federal government could do. It was a new ball game. Governor Campbell's office was right to see it coming.

The United States' complaint in intervention was filed on June 7, 1993. The state filed its answer on July 9, 1993. The first lawyer who made an appearance for the state at the first hearing, Wayne Rush, stepped aside on July 19 and Bobby Hood surfaced, to no one's surprise. Cooke and Hood had worked in tandem before when Hood had successfully defended the state in the Marc Buoniconti case that arose from a Citadel football game injury in October 1985. Both attorneys were being retained again—Cooke to defend the college, Hood, the state. Buoniconti's old helmet is in Cooke's office.

The Citadel immediately attacked Faulkner personally. Their entire defense from that time forward would be based on *ad hominem* attacks, ignoring all along her unexampled courage, but, instead, digging at peripheral issues and her physical appearance. "There is no place in our college for anyone cloaked in subterfuge by submitting altered documents to this institution," The Citadel PR man Rick Mill said in reference to the Wite-Out crisis. Shannon was under fire for having asked an official at her high school to remove with correction fluid—"Wite-Out"—references to her gender on her transcript as a part of her application for admission. There was no space to state an applicant's gender as either "male" or "female" on the application form itself. As Suzanne Coe reasonably observed, if The Citadel had asked Shannon for her gender and she lied, then it would have had an argument, but that was not what happened.

"The Citadel application," Shannon stated in an affidavit on May 27, 1993, after she filed suit, "does not inquire as to the gender of applicants or require them to provide a photograph. To insure that my application was considered on its merits, I asked my high school counselor to remove the description of gender from my transcript which my high school forwarded separately to The Citadel."

Shannon's application itself made no effort to hide her sex in the space where she wrote that she had played varsity softball, a uniquely girls' sport in South Carolina. Everyone other than those at The Citadel who worked in state college admissions offices knew that. The Citadel was just mad because nobody in admissions looked closely at the application. If they had read the application, they would have seen little pink ribbons all over it. Either that or they went berserk when they saw the 3.7 GPA and an SAT score with a comma in it and sent off an immediate acceptance, notwithstanding the usual practice of being wary of applicants with high marks. The average boy they got that year had a 2.5 GPA and a 967 SAT.

Strictly speaking, Shannon did not lie about her sex. Shannon was a kid having fun with a corrupt system when her school counselor took to the Wite-Out. With a little liquid paper her high school counselor, at her request, made her transcript consistent with her application and got rid of the question itself on the transcript. Shannon skirted the entire issue. By taking away the existence of the issue itself to conform with the application, she treated both males and females alike and anticipated exactly what the Board of Visitors would do six months later under the United States Supreme Court case *Palmer v. Thompson* when, with a little "Palmer paste," they rubbed out the entire Veterans Day Program to get rid of the sex of Johnson, Lacey, and Chapman. The Citadel attorneys got honorary degrees for that maneuver. In her own case Faulkner got pilloried.

Wally West, the director of admissions, sent Shannon a letter dated February 10, revoking her admission and cancelling her plans to tour the barracks the following week, and he sent another letter on the same day to Shannon's mother with a refund of the application fee just to be sure all the Faulkners got the point. But "Mr. Shannon Richey Faulkner" already had in hand a letter of acceptance dated January 22, 1993.

The Citadel's first defense against Faulkner was thus a moral one. They played the first round on their home court and talked about Citadel honor while playing with their own ball. To The Citadel, Faulkner's act was evidence of a moral failure to admit that she was a woman. To sympathetic women, it amounted to the same thing as not being able to pay their taxes if they checked "Female" on their IRS Form 1040. For most women everywhere, the indignation of the boys in the sandbox made for riotous good fun from the very start. The thrust of the joke was the kind that probably only women really know how to enjoy. The Citadel had rejected a high school honors student, member of the Beta Club, one of ten seniors selected by the faculty of her high school to its Hall of Fame, delegate to the National Youth Leadership Conference in Washington and to Palmetto Girls' State, a varsity athlete in basketball and softball, an active member of her church youth group, and the drum major in a band whose boys and girls marched to the same drum.

Sandra Fowler asked me to speak at the annual meeting of the Democratic Women of Charleston County the day after the *Faulkner* case was filed. Lucille Whipper was there to introduce new officers. Fowler circulated a very comical sketch of a little girl peeking out from behind a giant bottle of Liquid Paper, with a caption quoting a newspaper headline, "'Gender was removed with correction fluid,' say outraged Citadel officials."

The Strange Career of Violence

A basic routine military procedure is to tear down individual impulses in a cadet or recruit and to build the individual back up to be a part of a larger group. The purpose of all this is to teach cadets and recruits to follow orders, and, if they later join the civilian work force, to get to the job on time. They are taught to see themselves as part of a larger unit. The same humane principles are shared by anyone who understands his place in the natural world, as long as the more essential purposes of education, such as learning to think for oneself and nourishing a creative imagination, are not compromised. We are all part of a larger whole, men and women. But hazing perverts this pedagogical concept and corrupts any notion of egalitarianism. In the hands of inept tutors, knobs are purged of many ideals which they value prior to their arrival at The Citadel. In their place—through a process of arbitrary discipline which can easily amount to hazing—are put "heroic" and "honorable" virtues conceived and implemented by 19-year-old sophomore cadre members and other upperclassmen. Thus, a sense of honor at The Citadel is sometimes built upon the actions of teenage boys who, given free rein over other teenage boys, are prone to hazing. They strip the freshmen of what they learn at home among their family, relatives, friends, neighbors, church leaders, Boy Scout and civic leaders, teachers and coaches and often replace all of it with superficial and immature concepts. Since no outsider really knows what goes on at The Citadel, this procedure can easily calcify into "group think," a mafia-like code of silence, and ultimately, if hazing is added to the mix, mere thuggery. The argument that one has to have been a cadet to understand The Citadel was actually put forth, without success, as a defense throughout the case. The irony that anyone can make the same observation about any experience escapes a knob as he begins his chase after the Ring and the free lunch that comes with it. Even more ironical is that a cadet with such a point of view is the least likely to understand The Citadel and the process of indoctrination. During the entire course of litigation, no editorials or public discussion on the value of admitting women were written in the public or student press by any of the 2000 cadets. There was no controversy, no intellectual inquiry among the cadets. They took the side they were supposed to take.

Lafayette was 19 years old when he arrived in America to lead revolutionary troops, but teenagers on a tear at The Citadel are ridiculous. It is *Lord of the Flies* at The Citadel, not *The Lords of Discipline*. Currently, the local paper reports some, but not all, allegations of criminal conduct by cadets against other cadets on campus, but prior to Faulkner's lawsuit, such was typically not the case.

The history of hazing at The Citadel is exhaustive. Hazing is systemic, a problem born of failed leadership. It persists as a tradition which exists to get rid of students who are arbitrarily disfavored by others.[3] Hazing too often allows bad cadets to get rid of good ones, keeping the chaff and throwing away the wheat. The Citadel family and its powerful network includes many on graduation day who should not be among them and more who should. For fear of retaliation, those few cadets who report hazing are forced to drop out even if they want to stay. There is no such thing as a whistle blower who survives at The Citadel. Cadets who fall into line and bond together reap the benefits of

The Citadel network to gain employment in the private sector after graduation. The downside of that, of course, is that too often mediocre people end
up in important positions.

Academic standards alone rarely winnow out cadets. According to informal
records of F Company, a/k/a F Troop—which are inconsistent with The Citadel's
own records—of the 650 cadets who entered The Citadel in 1966, a little over
half, or 347, were graduated in the class of 1970.[4] The numbers, however, could
be typical of all classes. The self-described acts of hazing within F Troop during those years to reduce the ranks were committed at the pleasure of individuals at tax payers' expense.[5]

Evidence of the value of a Citadel education and the Whole Man was also
emerging in 1992 from the records of simple misdemeanors by Citadel cadets.
I was told on August 20, 1992, that arrests of Citadel cadets were being made
off campus for DUI, disorderly conduct, simple assault, public intoxication,
marijuana possession, underage drinking, and the like. This was a first, as
far as I knew. Previously, I thought no cadets were arrested on criminal
charges. A delinquent Citadel cadet, I thought, had been treated like a little
fish in a catch-and-release program. They were handed back to The Citadel
without any charges filed against them. Any punishment meted out by The
Citadel itself would be harsh enough, the thinking went. That is likely a part
of the reason why no lynching charges—far more serious than misdemeanors—were brought against Kevin Nesmith's tormenters in 1986: they just
had to walk tours. And, with no charges brought, delinquent cadets would
have no criminal record to impede their future professional progress after
graduation.

About a year later, charges were brought against two Citadel cadets for assault. The local news reported that on the night of October 7, 1993, two cadets
were at a bar while out of uniform, somewhat like the nude dancers. According to the paper, they had allegedly beat up a couple of knobs the night
before, or they went back to the barracks on the 7th and beat up about six
hapless knobs, just trying to see if the knobs could take it. Initial charges for
hazing were dropped because the existing South Carolina statute on hazing did
not apply to The Citadel. At any rate, the cadets got pretrial intervention in
their home towns.

Two freshman victims were the only two who reported the assault and battery, the only two out of the total six knobs that the upperclassmen allegedly
beat up. The two called the police. The father of one of them was quoted in
The P & C on December 18, 1993. He was furious at The Citadel. He criti-
cized the two different Citadels which Vergnolle talked about—the one by day
which you read about in the brochures, and the one by night where all the

"college plus" goes on. Voicing the same opinion as that of Representative Clyburn, the father said, "That whole incident is a normal occurrence down there," and further, "When you ... create monsters, that monster will strike." Two other, different cadets had, within a day or two earlier, beat up their knobs in a bet with each other to see whose knobs were tougher.

At least one Charleston City Councilman knew what was going on. Jerome Kinloch was quoted in *The Post and Courier* on October 13, 1993, that The Citadel administration was just "condoning this foolishness." He said, "These guys are clowns. They aren't real players. There's someone that looks off when problems happen. They don't want to control it. If it's not hazing, it's a racial incident. If it's not a racial incident, it's a shooting," Kinloch said.

The usual result followed. After the incident was known about, the administration pointed fingers at the kids and said, "We no longer tolerate that kind of behavior." The routine continues today.

Concurrent Resolution

> "Let me say this. When you're standing in the way of the tide, or if you are, as a member of the senate, one member can object to a bill put on the contested calendar and block its passage for some time. If you're the one brave soul willing to do that, the people behind whatever bill that is will very often do their best to make your life hell, and harass you in terms of calling you constantly, writing you letters, stopping you on the street, doing whatever needs to be done to neutralize your opposition, and that is something that The Citadel certainly has the strong ability to do."
>
> South Carolina Senator Holly Cork,
> Opposition to the Concurrent Resolution, May 6, 1994

Throughout April and May 1993, The Citadel was at its busiest, getting legislators in Columbia to draft a Concurrent Resolution to declare that South Carolina had always had a state policy of single-sex education and that such a public policy was in the state's interest. Voila! It was always there, and it just took the Fourth Circuit's ruling in the *VMI* case to discover it.

Without the existence of a state policy favoring single-sex education prior to litigation in the Faulkner lawsuit, the Fourth Circuit could find South Carolina in violation of the equal protection clause, as it did Virginia. The stakes, therefore, were extraordinarily high, and The Citadel needed to manufacture history in record time. Everyone in the state knew that South Carolina was no different from Virginia, in that neither had such a policy. Yet they, like R. C. Edwards at Clemson, could only look on with amazement as The Citadel once again demonstrated its power to control the General Assembly and political leaders, to create history, and so define the character of the good-ole-boy system.

House Resolution 4170, mimicked in shorter form by the Senate as S.763, was sponsored by Robert Sheheen, Speaker of the House to whom The Citadel had given an Honorary Doctor of Laws degree in 1986. The other five sponsors—Delleney, Fulmer, Harrison, McElveen, and McTeer—were all Citadel graduates of the classes of 1968, 1973, and 1974. Two were lawyers. Opposition was minimal.

The Concurrent Resolution was sent to the Senate by the House on a vote of 97 to 20 on May 12, 1993, with House Speaker David Wilkins, Representative James Hodges, and Representative Roger Young from Charleston voting in the affirmative. Wilkins would later serve as the United States Ambassador to Canada, Hodges would become governor, and Young would be elected by the state legislature to the Ninth Circuit Court. Most of the black members and women voted in the negative—four black women and seven black men and three white women.

The three white men to take a stand against the resolution—Herbert Kirsh, a Duke graduate, Tim Rogers, an attorney and former president of the Clemson student body, and Jimmy Bailey, a Charleston realtor and graduate of the University of South Carolina—were remarkable for their courage. One of those who voted in favor of the Concurrent Resolution was the representative from Florence, Dr. William S. (Billy) Houck, Jr., brother of Judge Houck.

On May 13, 1993, I attended the Senate subcommittee hearings held in Columbia on the Concurrent Resolution. Representative Sarah Manly and Candy Kern from the National Organization for Women (NOW) spoke in opposition to the resolution. The resolution itself had been drafted by Frank Mood, president of the Board of Visitors, and placed in the warm hands of members of the House and Senate to be passed immediately.

I spoke to a deaf, dumb, and blind legislative committee which showed only the top of their heads. I made noises about Clemson and Winthrop, about The Citadel's argument that admitting women to the Corps of Cadets would cost more than building a separate program for them elsewhere, and about how Title IX might arguably be a defense against admitting women, but that the Fourteenth Amendment was not. After a vote of 8 to 3 by members of the subcommittee in favor of the resolution, I faxed a report to Val in New York.

Senator Holly Cork couldn't stop it with a mere objection in the Senate. The Senate's most powerful member, Charleston's Senator Glenn McConnell, moved to suspend the provisions of a Senate rule that would have required a two-thirds vote to allow consideration on the Concurrent Resolution, since it had been untimely filed after May 1. The Concurrent Resolution was adopted by a margin of 29 to 14 on May 27, 1993.

Senator Cork, in her deposition on May 6, 1994, commented,

> If we were able to probe the hearts and minds of my colleagues in the General Assembly it might not have passed, but there is such a thing as political reality, and the alumni organization of The Citadel is very active, well financed, and is able to exercise some degree of intimidation on some of my colleagues, and even some of the strongest advocates for the single-gender status of The Citadel would admit to me privately that could they vote their conscience, they would have sided with me.

The Concurrent Resolution also made provisions for a committee of ten Citadel supporters to explore "alternatives" to admitting women to The Citadel, specifically to build a separate but equal military college for women, or, better, to put money toward establishing a military program at Columbia College and Converse College. Headed by Frank Mood, who was also the author of The Citadel's internal 1980 Mood Report, the Legislative Committee to Study Single-Gender Educational Opportunities for Women made its Report to the House within eight months, on January 11, 1994. The contents of the report were designed to support The Citadel defense as it prepared for trial the following May 1994. Again in January 1994, South Carolina state legislators and a legislative committee validated the alleged long-standing policy of single-sex education.

The Concurrent Resolution was one of the most absurd and public misrepresentations in the entire case. The brief rain dance in which The Citadel showed its remarkable power to fix a hole in its defense and prepare for trial had taken no more than a year. And most of this came during the spring of 1993 when the General Assembly was debating the proposed cut in funds for state higher education by $30 million.

Val and Sandy Beber had no trouble with the Concurrent Resolution. After two days of hearings prior to trial in May 1994, they showed that even according to the 1994 Legislative Manual, the Concurrent Resolution "does not have the force of law, as an Act or Joint resolution does." It only "records the sense of the two Houses." Even the legislative "investigation," with its staff of six Citadel alumni out of the ten total members, was hearsay. Concurrent resolutions were not used by the General Assembly to establish state policy but rather were used only to name highways and bridges and memorialize the dead. Thus, Citadel leadership helped with its own defeat. Bobby Hood admitted at the hearing that the state's purported single-sex policy was never written down prior to the post-litigation adoption in the concurrent resolution, and Frank Mood admitted that he went to Bob Sheheen to get the resolution drafted after the VMI decision.

The question again arose in everyone's mind. How can such a powerful body be so misdirected? Is this not more than simply good men who hold different rational opinions? And, after seeing state and Citadel leadership operate so narrowly toward such self-serving goals, what if, instead, it had directed its resources toward the common good?

August 12, 1993:
SRF Gets into the Day Program

The hearing on Faulkner's motions for a preliminary injunction and class certification was held on August 12, 1993. For two and a half hours the judge heard arguments on Faulkner's motions. The motion for class certification was denied, as Coe anticipated. But the other motion, the motion for a preliminary injunction to put Faulkner in the day program immediately, pending a trial on the merits on whether she should be admitted to the Corps of Cadets, took a lazy turn as the late afternoon stretched toward early evening.

Both sides droned on and on in a direction I could only guess would be toward an inevitable decision by the judge not to admit Faulkner without a trial on the merits. That's what he did with the women veterans. Affidavits were filed, certainly, and Faulkner even took the stand at the hearing, but the status quo is always hard to change. I quietly and purposefully wrote down the occasional word or phrase as the judge continued to lead up to his ruling.

Then I gradually began to listen a bit more closely. I was sitting along a row of seats under the portrait of Waties Waring, the Charleston judge who said "segregation is *per se* inequality" several years before *Brown*. Val, Henry, and Isabelle sat with Shannon at the table. I didn't dare look up but continued to doodle on the legal pad in front of me. Then I stopped. I could not believe my ears. I was listening to history.

Referring to *VMI I*, issued on October 5, 1992, and to a future trial on whether the Virginia Institute for Leadership at Mary Baldwin College was a suitable remedy—a trial that would not begin until February 1994—Judge Houck began:

> The Fourth Circuit Court of Appeals held that the admissions policy of VMI denied women equal protection of the law as guaranteed by the Fourteenth Amendment to the United States Constitution. It

did not, however, fashion a remedy. Instead, it remanded the case for the district court for it to do so....

I believe that Shannon Faulkner has been denied a constitutional right by not being admitted to The Citadel. I don't make that statement as a statement of the merits, but I make it based upon the decision in the Fourth Circuit. And if that case applies to this case, then she has been denied equal protection. She is not going to be granted equal protection by being admitted to the Day Program, but that's the only alternative we have.

We do not have any alternative available to us to provide her equal protection of the law. There is no other institution available that provides women the same rights that men have at The Citadel. And there is no structure under which she can be admitted to the full program, the Corps at The Citadel, at this time.

I think, therefore, that the irreparable harm that she will suffer if her constitutional rights are continued to be denied her far outweighs any irreparable harm The Citadel will sustain if she is admitted to the Day Program....

It is therefore the Order of the Court that the plaintiff Shannon Richey Faulkner be permitted by the defendants to enter their Day Program on August the 27th, 1993, and participate therein until further order of this Court or until some other policy of The Citadel, not challenged in this Court, requires that she no longer be permitted to be a student in the Day Program of The Citadel.

"Good gracious," I thought. I was silent as I peeked at Shannon and Val with wild surmise. "Good. So much for that. Just plain old clear legal precedent from VMI," I thought. "But, gosh, what courage to apply it."

Before adjourning, Judge Houck made a few observations of his own:

It's a hard question and got a lot of emotions and a lot of interest in it. And any time you have a case like that, it's—it's a hard case. You can't disassociate yourself from the reality of what you do. And this is an important motion. The plaintiffs feel that they're one hundred percent right and every Citadel graduate that I have ever talked to thinks that The Citadel is a hundred percent right. And it's hard when you have that strong emotion and long tradition to deal with the problems that change things. And I told my clerk, I said, you know, I said I was going out of the country come Monday. And he said, I can't think of anything better to do after you make a ruling like you made today.

On her way out of the courthouse Sandy Faulkner overheard Ms. Dorothy Washington, one of the African-American women who sold sweet-grass baskets on the steps of the courthouse, answer a tourist's question. In a distinctive Gullah voice she said, "Dey let de lady in."

An overnight brief was immediately prepared by Shearman associates in New York—who never slept—in preparation for the defendants' anticipated motion to the Fourth Circuit to stay Judge Houck's preliminary order enjoining The Citadel from admitting Faulkner into the day program. Faulkner herself stood by. It would not be the last time she would do so.

A stay was granted by Judges Niemeyer and Hamilton at the Fourth Circuit on August 16, 1993. Making a distinction between their ruling in *VMI I* and Judge Houck's ruling on the preliminary injunction, they wrote, "The public interest demands that resolution of an issue of such extraordinary complexity not be compressed into a proceeding solely to determine whether a stay is granted. We believe that maintenance of the status quo better serves this interest."

Judge K. K. Hall, however, dissented with the observation that the facts were "similar enough to those which we found unconstitutional in the *VMI* case." The court set oral arguments on an expedited schedule.

Chief Justice Rehnquist would not grant Faulkner's petition to lift the Fourth Circuit stay. Faulkner would not be able to attend classes at The Citadel and, instead, now would have to wait for the Fourth Circuit later in the fall to rule on The Citadel's appeal of the district court's August 12 order.

All, All Honorable Men

It was a glorious day, November 12, 1993. The four lawyers for The Citadel to receive doctoral degrees on Summerall Field at The Citadel at the Friday afternoon parade were Bell, Patterson, Whittemore, and Cooke. They had achieved dazzling success in the federal courts. They had made it impossible for veterans to attend the Veterans Day Program, they had convinced the Fourth Circuit to stay the district court order to admit Faulkner into the day program, and they had fought valiantly against the insidious ACLU, the oppressive federal government at the Department of Justice, women who hated men, and the powerful Yankees at Shearman & Sterling who hated Southern values and traditions. The sky was Citadel blue. It was Homecoming Weekend at The Citadel, and the big game against VMI was the next day. Even the game was tilted in favor of the home team since VMI did not play fifth-year seniors. That was a fact about the VMI football team that Si Bunting told my sons and me when we visited him on the VMI campus a few years after the case was over.

In typical fashion, The Citadel spokesman Rick Mill told Claudia Brinson, writing for *The State* newspaper in Columbia, November 12, 1993, that it was "the sheerest of coincidences" that The Citadel's legal defense team was being honored the day after Veterans Day for all they had accomplished as preeminent lawyers. They were not being honored for winning the *Johnson v. Jones* case, Mill implied. Everyone who didn't have Citadel sense knew differently. I expressed my outrage that The Citadel would pull such a stunt the day after Veterans Day when so many veterans, including the women veteran clients, had recently lost valuable educational opportunities at The Citadel. Did anyone even know it was the day after Veterans Day? Was this just more Citadel honor? I asked. "I think it's quite embarrassing and too much for veterans to stomach this gesture," I told Brinson. "It's more than ironical. It's disgraceful."

Chapter 4

Moses in the Neighborhood

1994: Moses in the Neighborhood— A Family at War

After the Fourth Circuit's stay of Judge Houck's order granting Faulkner's motion for a preliminary injunction, arguments on appeal were made in Richmond the following month. Like the district court, the appellate court had put the case on the fast track, knowing that the constitutional rights which Faulkner was asserting would be lost with too great a passing of time.

In the meanwhile, Faulkner enrolled at the University of South Carolina at Spartanburg, her mother's alma mater, and waited on standby to transfer to The Citadel to finish the second half of her freshman year if the stay were lifted. While going to school in Spartanburg, she lived with her parents and commuted to the extension campus.

Val argued brilliantly, as usual, on appeal in Richmond and prevailed. News came on November 18, 1993, that the Fourth Circuit had surprisingly affirmed the district court's August 12 order, thus putting Faulkner in the day program beginning in January 1994. This time, Judge Niemeyer sided with Judge Hall, who observed in his brief concurrence, "I question whether, under the Equal Protection Clause, a state can ever have a sufficiently important interest to justify expending public funds to maintain an institution that not only practices inequality, but celebrates it." Niemeyer's move to the majority at this point in The Citadel case and Rehnquist's move three years later in the *VMI* case were momentous shifts in the history of each.

Judge Hamilton's dissent was longer than the majority opinion. It was clear that he just didn't like Faulkner. He quoted Lincoln's Gettysburg Address and the Declaration of Independence to affirm that "all men are created equal," then ripped into Faulkner again on the Wite-Out issue for violating The Citadel's "strict code of honor" by "surreptitiously eliminating any reference to her gender on documents accompanying her application."

A few weeks later, on December 1, 1993, The Citadel asked for a rehearing *en banc*, that is, a request to go over it again with the all the circuit court judges participating this time. Specifically, The Citadel wanted to stress their sure bet, the value of single-sex education, in the context of The Citadel case.

But on January 6, 1994, the Fourth Circuit refused to hear the case *en banc*, a decision that effectively lifted the stay. Faulkner was in as far as the Fourth Circuit was concerned. Chief Judge Ervin and Judges Phillips, Murnaghan, Michael, and two South Carolina judges, Judges Wilkins and Russell, voted to join Judges Hall and Niemeyer against rehearing *en banc*. Virginia and South Carolina Judges Wilkinson, Luttig, and Williams disqualified themselves and did not vote. Virginia Judge Widener joined South Carolina Judge Hamilton and voted to rehear the case. These two judges at various times sat on the three-judge panel that initially heard the case, and both invariably sided with the status quo of their home states. I had earlier signed a motion to recuse Judge Hamilton which was denied.

On Wednesday, January 12, 1994, as Shannon Faulkner registered for classes, The Citadel petitioned Chief Justice Rehnquist to put the stay back in place and keep Faulkner out. In successfully getting the Chief Justice to place a temporary stay pending review by the full Court, Citadel lawyers especially trained to write pleadings addressed to the Supreme Court were called in. Charles J. Cooper and Vincent J. Colatriano at Shaw, Pittman, Potts & Trowbridge in Washington, D.C., put Justice Scalia's remarks on VMI, the "venerable institution," front and center "because an understanding of the *VMI* litigation is essential to grasp fully the dimension of the panel majority's error in this case."

On the next day, Thursday, January 13, the male cadets began classes without Faulkner who had to wait a week to hear from the Supreme Court. On Tuesday the 18th the Supreme Court lifted Rehnquist's temporary stay in *Jones v. Faulkner*, 114 S.Ct. 872 (1994). On Thursday, January 20, 1994, Shannon Faulkner began her first class, biology, in Duckett Hall at 8:00 a.m.

Faulkner began her momentous first day of classes on her 19th birthday. I had gone through her schedule of classes looking for any professors who I thought might be potential trouble-makers. I was comfortable with the list. The first assignment on Shannon's syllabus for English was to read Katherine Mansfield's "Miss Brill," a short story about a lady who has a foolish imagination and no real life.

In Charleston, it was too dangerous for her to live alone in a rented apartment in town, and no one wanted to room with her. I called the president of the College of Charleston who offered to let her live in the dorms there if any rooms were empty, but Shannon thought otherwise. Therefore, she and her parents decided to accept an invitation for Shannon to live with my family in our rather crowded household. She would not, of course, be allowed to live in The Citadel barracks with the Corps of Cadets.

Faulkner's room was made ready by Melinda. I refurbished an old chest of drawers. If Faulkner had a roommate at all during her freshman year, it was Spencer, a fifth grader at Porter Gaud School. The two girls with boys' names would live upstairs. Spencer Compton gave up her back bedroom to the only big sister she ever knew and moved into a smaller bedroom across the hall. Will and John were still babies and stayed downstairs with their parents. From her window over the back yard, Faulkner could hear the bugles sounding reveille and taps from across the Ashley River about a mile away over the PA system at The Citadel. Beginning the second semester of her freshman year in college and her first year at The Citadel, she had to adjust to a household with two little boys, Peasey and Joyful, with Spenceroo, Bradley the Big Guy, an 80 pound yellow lab, Chaser la Plume, a feral cat, and two lawyer parents. Also in the house was Ms. Rebecca White who came every weekday 8:00 a.m. to 6:00 p.m. to cook and baby-sit "her boys." Her picture with John at a house on Folly Beach remains a family favorite. Shannon would live as a member of the Black-Lucka-Compton household off and on for 18 months.

Charles Rittenberg, who lived nearby, came by to talk about Shannon's moving in. "It's like having Moses in the neighborhood," he said. The FBI advised Melinda to take the street address number "16" off the front door.

It was unrealistic not to expect the worst, and Faulkner probably always knew that she could face an ugly encounter if she ventured too far from the house at 16 Chadwick. That very thing happened when she briefly moved a few miles away to Folly Beach for part of the summer of 1995. No one there let her out of their sight.

Such an arrangement led to personal concerns I had for my family. On January 13, 1994, I wrote Dawes to object to what I thought was a cavalier and dismissive manner The Citadel was taking toward the harassment of Faulkner:

> As you know, Shannon will be living with Melinda and me, Melinda's ten-year-old daughter Spencer, our three-year-old son Will, and our eight-month-old son John. My thoughts therefore concern the safety of not only Shannon Faulkner, but also the safety of my wife and children.
>
> I would like to know who at The Citadel I can talk to directly and give timely information to, if need be, in the event of any act of hostility toward Faulkner or my family.... I am therefore writing to you as a father concerned with doing everything I can do to assure the safety of his family, not as one of Faulkner's lawyers.

William and John Black with Shannon Faulkner who lived with the Black-Lucka-Compton family in Charleston prior to her admission into The Citadel Corps of Cadets. Used with permission, Melinda Lucka, January 1994.

You may know also that I personally have experience with civil rights violence in Birmingham, Alabama. Arthur Shores's house was bombed only a few blocks from my house in College Hills. The Sixteenth Avenue Baptist Church was not too far away from where I lived. In high school I met with black young churchmen behind locked doors in Tuskegee so Bull Connor could not take our picture.

I cannot imagine why The Citadel does not, at its own insistence, want to talk to me and Melinda, given the history of harassment against Faulkner upstate and the broadly publicized incidents at The Citadel itself. Can we not agree that harassment is a serious issue when it concerns victims, potentially children, outside the gates as well as within the barracks?

In short, I think the best way to work together to avoid, not just to react to, a bad situation is to work quickly and directly with appropriate officials at The Citadel on a personal basis.... If anything happens to Faulkner or to my family, I will know that The Citadel did not do everything it could to prevent it.

The Citadel replied a week later, on January 20, 1994, with supplemental interrogatories and requests to produce:

Identify the following information relating to each act of violence, vandalism, or threat thereof directed to the plaintiff, any member of her family, any of her attorneys, or anyone acting on her behalf, which the plaintiff believes were or may have been a result of the plaintiff's efforts to attend The Citadel or any matter related to this action:
a) The date on which said act or threat occurred;
b) A description of said act or threat;
c) The name and jurisdiction of any law enforcement authorities to whom the act or threat was reported;
d) The name of the person who made the report to the law enforcement authorities;
e) The date on which the report was made to the law enforcement authority;
f) The name of the person who plaintiff believes committed the act or made the threat.

Shannon Faulkner with William Black. Used with permission, Melinda Lucka, January 1994.

Shannon Faulkner with John Black. Used with permission, Melinda Lucka, January 1994.

Shannon Faulkner, Spencer Compton, and William Black, Easley, SC. Photograph taken by Robert Black.

Shannon Faulkner with Melinda Lucka, Spencer Compton, William and John Black, Easley, SC. Photograph taken by Robert Black.

Melinda Lucka and Robert Black with Shannon Faulkner. Used with permission, Curtis Norman, August 11, 1995.

The Citadel's determination to stay all-male trumped all other issues. If The Citadel would not do everything it could to help commission female Army nurses after the Gulf War—as I would later come to find out—it certainly would not do anything it could just to help protect a couple of toddlers. To acknowledge the possibility of violence from cadets or alumni would be to compromise Citadel honor, the center-piece of its legal defense.

"You're out of luck, Peasey. You, too, Joyful. They won't work with me on this one," I told the little faces.

Robert with sons John and William Black in front of the entrance to The Citadel Museum on August 12, 1995, when Shannon Faulkner entered The Citadel as the first woman admitted to the Corps of Cadets. Used with permission, Melinda Lucka.

But somewhat like William Tell, I did get back to Dawes in a short note: "I know where they all live on campus. I used to live there too. If anything happens, I'm coming back for a visit. Laugh if you will."

First Blood

To: Robert Black, Attorney
RE: Shannon Faulkner

What a disgrace! Now a female is attending The Citadel. Do you feel you have accomplished all of life's best? Hope so—you worked at it hard and long enough.... One hundred fifty one years of military education for males only and this little witch wants to make public her wants and wishes along with getting her picture in the paper all for publicity.... I hope she is harassed, embarrassed and flunks out.... Sick. This means we can all break laws anytime we want to because our "constitutional rights" says its correct and we have the right. Get serious ... we could care less what Shannon wants, it's obvious she's a spoiled brat!

Thanks,

A Citadel Parent '93

[anonymous, postmarked Savannah, Georgia, January 24, 1994]

In preparation for SRF's first day as a student, I was given the names and home telephone numbers of U.S. marshals and FBI agents in the event of an emergency. DOJ was supposed to play an intermediate role with the office of the U.S. Attorney in South Carolina in Columbia to downplay the event, but the U.S. Attorney publicly announced that he had everything covered, that there would be no violence. Faulkner had hoped to slip in the side door of The Citadel unnoticed on the first day of classes, in the manner of Autherine Lucy, James Meredith, and the nine students at Central High School. By entering quietly she hoped not to put any bright ideas in the minds of defenders of the faith, but that hope was lost with the publicity given to the event by the U.S. Attorney.

Yet some of the U.S. marshals and FBI agents did not fully understand the possibility that not everybody connected with The Citadel was necessarily going to enthusiastically offer to bend over backwards for the woman who was going to change the place. Some U.S. marshals even advised Faulkner and me to make our first call in an emergency to The Citadel police. And then to call the Charleston police.

I could not imagine a greater waste of time. I had met the captain at The Citadel and knew he was a nice guy but, right or wrong, I thought that most of the other people in Security shared less of a concern about Faulkner's safety. And to call the Charleston Police Department was almost as much of a stretch. I had seen more than one Citadel license tag on the front of police cruisers, and even a decal on one window.

I could have been right in my assessment. At 10:00 p.m. on April 7, 1994, a woman living upstate called to alert me to the possible hostility that a Citadel security officer might have toward Shannon. She claimed that one of the security guards at The Citadel was openly bragging to her and his other neighbors that he could care less if Faulkner got hurt while attending The Citadel.

I had strong suspicions about the validity of the whole thing. As it turned out, the woman caller and the guard were in a personal quarrel, and the woman's call to me could have been a way of getting the guy in trouble.

Nonetheless, I dutifully called FBI agents Bill Zerillo and Israel Brookes, the chief U.S. marshal in South Carolina, in the U.S. marshal's office in Charleston. The information, name, and identity of The Citadel guard which the woman had given me was recorded. I was told on April 9 that the marshals had passed the information on to chief officer at The Citadel. On April 13 I called the woman to let her know what had transpired. She told me that she no longer wanted to get involved, yet I got another call from her on April 24. After that, I heard nothing more about "the bad cop" and had to conclude that a reputation needlessly may have been called into question.

Registration Day

In early December, Val had written Dawes to get everything ironed out in case Shannon was admitted in January. Dawes had written back to quote fees and tuition and to say that "if Ms. Faulkner intends to park a vehicle on The Citadel campus, she will be required to register her vehicle … and obtain a parking permit … as a part of the registration process." When she parked at her assigned parking lot for registration day only, she got a parking ticket from The Citadel police. The report in *The Post and Courier* hinted at the comedy of the event but, more, implied that breaking the law and breaking tradition was one and the same to a reckless Faulkner. And that was the nice part of the day.

Wednesday morning, January 12, continued with the press all over the place. Several of Faulkner's friends stayed at the Folly Beach house of Suzanne Coe's law partner the night before. I had called Pat Johnson to get her to join us and be visible that morning with Faulkner during the start of her registration process. Pat wore her U.S. Navy uniform.

Registration was at 10:00 a.m. in the small little office of Ron Gaskin, the registrar who was the only administrative official who handled the moment with grace.

"Who are all of these people?" Brigadier General Clifton Poole, the Vice President for Academic Affairs and Dean of the College at The Citadel, yelled

Shannon Faulkner walking to register as a daytime student at The Citadel, accompanied by attorneys Suzanne Coe, Valorie Vojdik, and Sara Mandelbaum. Used with permission, Curtis Norman, January 20, 1994.

to Lewis Spearman, President Watts's assistant, as the vice president came out of his office into a waiting room in Bond Hall. The vice president wanted to convey great indignation and to command authority at the same time. I jumped when I heard him yell.

Brigadier General Clifton Poole instructs Shannon Faulkner that she may have only a few people with her as she registers for classes as a daytime student at The Citadel. Used with permission, Curtis Norman, January 12, 1994.

The vice president immediately gave orders that were not exactly in keeping with the procedures thought to be worked out earlier between Val and Dawes. Registration was to be a procedural matter, not a legal matter, the vice president told Shannon. Not everybody could watch. Only two of Faulkner's lawyers could be in Gaskin's office to witness Faulkner's registration. Val would be one, of course. I deferred to Sara Mandelbaum. Coe stayed out, but Sandy and Ed Faulkner were given passes. Nat Douglas, who, as Dawes pointed out, did not represent Faulkner herself, was also allowed to put his toe in. In the registrar's small office, the vice president wanted to be sure there were few witnesses and no photographs à la MacArthur taking signatures of defeated Japanese on the deck of the USS Missouri. No cameras, no audio were allowed. History was in the unmaking.

Faulkner and her lawyers were instructed to mind their step while in Bond Hall and not talk to any Citadel employees. Bud Watts, the president of The Citadel, made it a priority to be out of town that day. The following week after

Faulkner began classes, Watts conveyed the same sentiment the vice president and some members of the BOV had expressed after SRF was admitted.

"We'll do what the courts say," Watts said. "Today proves The Citadel will comply with the law of the land. But that doesn't mean we are happy. We fully want our day in court."

A new kind of failure of leadership by the administration was thus fully in place, one that encouraged rebellion by the cadets and the creation of an alleged "hostile environment" in violation of Title IX of the Civil Rights Act that protects equal access to education. A cadet screamed and yelled outside Bond Hall as he angrily denounced Shannon when she began classes. No one who saw him could forget the anguish and pain the day had brought. The failure of the plaintiff to make a motion to the court to order The Citadel administration to refrain from making statements that could be construed by cadets as hostile and thus to encouraged them and others to resist Faulkner was perhaps a strategic error in the plaintiff's case. But, of course, it would have been a pointless motion, a violation of free speech, and would not have been granted. And what script would the Scarlet Pimpernel follow if it were granted?

"You mentioned that plaintiff's counsel wanted to discuss your concerns about harassment that Ms. Faulkner has experienced during the course of this litigation and might experience in the future," The Citadel attorney wrote on January 5. "If you have such concerns and feel that The Citadel is in a position to address them in some way, please let me know and I will pass your thoughts on to the appropriate officials."

A casual dismissal by The Citadel of actual and potential violence against Faulkner would eventually be translated into a serious subject directly addressed by the court. Meanwhile, animosity toward SRF continued to control the tempo of Faulkner's first days.

The vice president, the president's assistant, and the director of public relations were the three most passionate soldiers in the struggle against women. The president's assistant, Lewis Spearman, was always in the trenches and had been an observer and trusted counselor from the very outset. As a cadet at The Citadel, he was one of four battalion commanders in the Class of 1958, along with Bud Watts, who would become a Lieutenant General in the Air Force and the president of The Citadel. Jimmy Jones, who would become the chairman of the Board of Visitors and whose name appears in the caption of the case, *Faulkner v. Jones*, served as a company commander in Watts's battalion. John Palms, future president of the University of South Carolina and a named witness for the defense, was a company commander in another battalion. The Regimental Commander and later a Lieutenant General in the Army, Jack B. Farris, would play no role in the fight against women. In the college annual, *The Sphinx*, Farris was voted "Most Military," Watts was voted "Most Likely to Succeed/Most in the Know," Jones was voted "Biggest Politician," and Spearman "Best Personality."

As early as April 1993, a debate was set up by the ACLU and the political science department at the College of Charleston between speakers for the plaintiffs and for the defendants. Cooke and I spoke at the debate. The president's assistant was in the audience to track everything said about the plaintiff's position and even participated in the debate once it was opened to the audience. His comment was that there was no real live girl who complained about the VMI admission policy, but he might have been referring to Banzhaf's niece, not the high school girl who also wrote to DOJ.

The president's assistant (PA) was later deposed by Michael Maurer for DOJ during the remedy phase in 1997:

> Maurer: What are your duties and responsibilities as assistant to the president?
> President's Assistant: Basically to carry out any instructions from the president.
> Maurer: What specifically is your job description?
> PA: I think what I just said is essentially it. Carry out any instructions from the president.
> Maurer: Are there specific areas in which you have acted on the president's behalf?
> PA: Oh, yes. I think every time I have acted for the president has been in a specific area.
> Maurer: Would you describe for me what areas you have acted on the president's behalf?
> PA: I don't think it's possible for me to describe them all. It's been numerous.
> (Deposition, April 9, 1997, page 15)

> Maurer: Were you involved in the development of the assimilation plan in this case?
> PA: I don't know what you mean by development.
> Maurer: What don't you understand about the word "development"?
> PA: I don't understand what you mean by it.
> Maurer: Do you understand the word "development"?
> PA: I don't understand what development is, what development of a plan is, Mr. Maurer. You will need to explain that to me.
> Maurer: Unfortunately, I don't have a dictionary, but the word "development" usually refers to creating or designing.
> PA: Are you asking me did I create or design the assimilation plan?

Maurer: No, I am asking you, if you would pay attention to my questions, did you participate in the development—which is to say the creation of design—of the assimilation plan in this case?

PA: I did not participate in the creation of the assimilation plan in this case. I did not participate in the design of the assimilation plan in this case.

Maurer: Were aspects of that assimilation plan discussed in your presence?

PA: Yes.

Maurer: And by whom?

PA: By you and others.

Maurer: By me?

PA: Yes.

Maurer: When was that?

PA: In court.

(Deposition, April 9, 1997, pages 23, 24)

Maurer: Have you received any negative feedback about anything that you have done at The Citadel?

PA: Negative feedback from the president?

Maurer: From the president or anyone on his staff.

PA: Oh, sure. I receive negative feedback constantly.

Maurer: And what kind of negative feedback have you received?

PA: I've received negative feedback for the absence of publicity that we get out on what truly is happening at The Citadel as opposed to the slanted stories that go out. I receive constant negative feedback on the amount of time and money we are spending answering questions like you are asking me this afternoon. I receive negative feedback in regard to the dollars that are involved in this case. I receive negative feedback on why it is we are prolonging this thing as long as we are. I receive complaints constantly about what The Citadel is engaged in in connection with this litigation, and that has been predominantly the negative feedback I have received for the entire last four years....

Maurer: Have you received feedback from people suggesting to you that perhaps The Citadel should not have spent millions of dollars opposing the admission of women?

PA: Yes.

Maurer: And what have you done with that feedback?

PA: It depended on how that feedback came to me.

Maurer: Has that been communicated to you by anyone associated with The Citadel?

PA: By associated, you mean anyone at The Citadel, employed by The
Citadel, or a student at The Citadel?
Maurer: Associated in any way with The Citadel.
PA: You are associated in some way with The Citadel, so I would have
to answer that yes.
Maurer: How am I associated with The Citadel?
PA: You are constantly in court with it. You are constantly at The
Citadel.
(Deposition, April 9, 1997, pages 33, 34)

I made the point that the case lacked humor in a May 11, 1995, letter to
the editor in *The State*:

The Citadel's defense has its origins in medieval theology. Today, an-
tifeminism is being used by The Citadel to keep women out of the
Corps of Cadets.... On the shelf beside ancient and medieval authors
Lucretius, Ovid, Juvenal, St. Augustine, Jerome, Theophrastus, Walter Map, and Jean de Meun—all of whom wrote antifeminist literature—comfortably sit Citadel depositions and pleadings.

I observed in my letter that the theme of manliness corrupted by lust for
women is humorously portrayed in Richard de Bury's fourteenth-century *Philobilon* in which books themselves rail against women. The only argument against
women that The Citadel did not make was that the "biped beasts," as Richard
calls women—but not "toxic" or "gangrene"—did not like books and that
books did not like them.

According to a May 5, 1997, memorandum filed by The Citadel in response
to DOJ's motion to compel testimony from The Citadel during the fee fight,
"Any suggestion that the United States has not been provided every document
and every piece of information that it has sought would be absurd." More than
5000 pages of deposition testimony consumed over 150 hours of their time,
The Citadel claimed, not counting the 11,000 pages of documents copied for DOJ.

DOJ, to be sure it was getting as much as allowed under the rules, sent two
staff members from Washington to copy Citadel documents. They copied documents in Bond Hall for about two weeks. This memo from The Citadel came
nearly two years after the district court admonished The Citadel for not being
forthcoming in discovery on the assimilation plan to admit women.

On January 12, 1994, after Shannon registered at Bond Hall and headed
across campus toward the book store, a black middle-aged woman stepped out
of the kitchen of The Citadel Dining Hall on to the delivery ramp when she saw
the Faulkner entourage going by. Shannon was flanked by a team of her lawyers,

press, and cadets assigned to watch her every step. The woman yelled at the top of her voice, "Go, Shannon, Go!" She then smiled and went back to work.

The black kitchen staff at Central High School in Little Rock applauded when Minnijean Brown, one of the Little Rock Nine in 1957, dumped her bowl of chili on the head of a heckler. They expelled Minnijean for that. At Central, 17 black students were selected, nine participated in the effort to integrate, three were graduated.

Kick Off: January 20, 1994

The phone rang at 16 Chadwick Drive at 5:30 a.m. It was January 20, 1994, the day Shannon was to begin classes as a day student. I answered with a lot of disgust.

"Good morning. Good morning. I hope I didn't wake you. May I speak to Shannon Faulkner?" the voice said.

"Who is this?" I asked.

"This is the Critic." the voice said. I knew then that the call was coming from a local radio DJ on 96-WAVE-FM, the station which had been playing the Kinks's "Lola" with words to ridicule Faulkner. The Critic liked to sing,

"Here's a tall tale 'bout a woman's will.
She's a podunk chick from Powdersville.
Shan-non Faulk-ner,
On no, Shan-non Faulk-ner."

"We're live on the air," the Critic continued. May I speak to Miss Faulkner?"

"What?" I asked. "Why in the world are you calling at this time of morning?"

"We want to see that she's up and at 'em, just like the cadets at The Citadel. To see if she's ready to get goin' bright and early. Shannon's first day at The Citadel."

"Listen...." I was furious, partly because this was the only kind of coverage the local radio stations were willing to give Faulkner. No one wanted to do anything but taunt and laugh at her. Or to offer grave political and sociological observations on the destruction of Southern tradition. The talk shows of Dan Moon and Doug Donehue were two on which most guests aired such points of view. Terry Rickson's talk show on WTMA, on which I appeared on April 30, 1993, was later cancelled.

"Listen," I said. "It's too early to be calling here. Faulkner has her own phone upstairs. Call her at a decent hour. Get off her back. Give her a break. Leave her alone."

Later, on July 25, 1994, a Charleston lawyer called to tell me about an offensive song about Faulkner being played on the air. The song was an adaption of Eric Clapton's tune "Leila." The words were something like, "Shan-non, got me on my knees, Shan-non...."

I called the station attorney in Washington, D.C., and made arrangements to visit the station manager in Charleston. But as it turned out, the manager was the son of a woman from my home town, Sheffield, Alabama, who was a friend of my sister. What led to that discovery was a picture of Coach Paul "Bear" Bryant on the wall in the station manager's office.

"Good, another Alabama boy. Not a stupid local. Maybe we can resolve this thing reasonably," I thought to myself.

"I see you like Bear Bryant, too," I said. "Did you go to Alabama?"

"Sure did," he replied. An enlightened Alabama discussion ensued.

"No coach in the South," I said, "reminds you of a Confederate general like Bear Bryant, does he? I have a real weakness about that kind of crazy thinking. My favorite Confederate general is Nathan Bedford Forrest. No soft planter's son, but a real tough redneck who knew how to fight. Of course, he had nothing on Francis Marion, but that's another story. Southern writer and novelist Andrew Lytle used to tell the story about one of the few horses of Forrest's to survive after the war. It was so well trained that it charged a group of Memphis policemen in blue uniforms. The problem was that the noble steed was hitched to a milk wagon. The horse reminds me of our politicians who parade in a rebel colonel's grey uniform and say they'll never forget."

After that gentle prologue, the station manager kindly agreed to take the song off the air. We were Southerners whose South does not beat up on women.

"The Citadel Has Now Become a Household Word"

A reasonable suspicion was that The Citadel all along knew that they could not win a lawsuit to keep women out but simply needed the publicity. Medical University of South Carolina President James B. Edwards gave the publicity director of MUSC, Scott Regan, permission to consult for The Citadel.[1] In the spring and summer of 1994, Regan began working with The Citadel and the Association of Citadel Men to help promote The Citadel and to monitor a national television crew making a documentary on Faulkner, which the administration did not want to be made. Regan filed an affidavit dated May 10, 1994, in which he stated that during the week of April 25–29, "he was asked by officials of The Citadel to communicate with a video camera crew and producer of an ABC TV program called 'The Turning Point' because of a military assignment of The Citadel's Director of Public Relations." In a letter on November

21, 1994, I pointed out to The Citadel that a brochure prepared by Regan had not been produced in discovery. The extent of collaboration, if any, between MUSC and The Citadel was never fully made a part of the record.

For all colleges, any publicity is good publicity. Shannon was a dream come true for a college that needed to be put on the map, or at least back on the map—the world map—even if for all the wrong reasons. Playing against Shannon in the federal courts attracted more freshmen to The Citadel than a football game against Notre Dame in the Rose Bowl would have done. Ironically, a school girl with a noble cause did more to bring attention to The Citadel than anyone since Mark Clark, the famed Army general in World War II and Korea and president of The Citadel.

President Watt's report to The Citadel faculty and staff on January 25 completely missed the irony that most of the world was looking with amusement and slack-jawed incredulity at The Citadel's resistance to modernity. Yet Watts knew that all the attention was a good thing when it comes to freshman recruitment. Watts's "Update from the President on the Public Response to the First Female" was bursting with pride as it provided news on the public response to Faulkner's enrollment in day classes.

"There has been an overwhelming show of public support for The Citadel and our single-gender program," Lieutenant General Watts wrote, "since the events of the last two weeks have been played out through the nation's media...." He continued:

> Wednesday, January 12, when Shannon Faulkner registered for classes, there were 44 media representatives from 23 different organizations on campus that registered with our public relations office. Along with our local media, there were reporters from *The Washington Post, Chicago Tribune, USA Today*, Reuters News Service, UPI, Associated Press, and ABC and NBC network television.... There were also an unknown number of media that arrived late and did not register....
>
> Even more media were on campus after the U.S. Supreme Court lifted the stay granted to us from Chief Justice Rehnquist....
>
> The story was picked up on all the major wire services that feed information to newspapers, radio, and TV across the country, as well as international markets. I received a call from a supporter of the college on business in Australia that had just seen the story on TV there. We have received copies of stories run on the front page of newspapers across the nation such as *The Wall Street Journal, Chicago Tribune, USA Today, Charlotte Observer, The Atlanta Journal-Constitution, Miami Herald, and Los Angeles Times*.

> We have conducted live radio interviews with radio stations in Seattle, Atlanta, Charlotte, New York, Washington, Dallas, San Antonio, Baltimore, and at last count, more than 13 national radio networks. Some of the more familiar are the Pat Buchanan & Co. radio show, the Larry King radio show, College News Service, and MTV radio news. Requests continue to come into the college daily for information about The Citadel and interviews with Cadets and staff. My guidance is that we will accommodate every credible media organization that we can.
>
> We have received mail from across the country as well as faxes...."The Women in Support of The Citadel" group now has 1,500 members, has sold more than 10,000 "Save the Male" bumper stickers and pins, and has received letters of support and orders for bumper stickers from Alaska, Korea, Wisconsin, Pennsylvania, California, and Maryland. They also received mail from several female active duty military officers supporting our position....
>
> It is apparent that The Citadel has now become a household word. This is as a result of the professional atmosphere of all the staff, faculty, and Cadets to maintain our heads high and practice the very ideals we strive so hard to instill in the young men here....
>
> Claudius E. Bud Watts III, President

All this from a defendant who said that Faulkner applied to The Citadel just to get attention. About a plaintiff who would not promptly return a phone call from Attorney General Janet Reno or bother to be interviewed by the BBC: "I never heard of the BBC," Shannon said when she refused my request to come to the phone.

By June 18, 2000, The Citadel was setting enrollment records. "Interest in The Citadel has steadily rebounded over the last five years after a drop in 1996," wrote a reporter who was identified as one "of *The Post and Courier* staff." In her association with the college and newspaper, Charlene Gunnells has been both spokesperson for The Citadel and reporter for *The Post and Courier*. The admission of women is arguably the single most important factor in the ever-increasing popularity of The Citadel.[2]

Von Mickel the Great

Cadet Von Mickel, a black cadet from Charleston, happened to be walking in front of Bond Hall as Faulkner walked out after registering for classes as a daytime student. He wasn't walking in the gutter, so he was not a knob.

Faulkner was the kind of person who talked to everyone she met. So was Von Mickel.

"Hello," the cadet said. "Welcome to The Citadel."

"Why, thank you," Faulkner replied. "I'm Shannon Faulkner. Nice to meet you."

"I'm Cadet Von Mickel. I'm a second year cadet in Company M. Good luck."

The press caught the brief exchange and ran it on the national and local news. That little pleasantry between the black cadet and the woman, both victims of Southern heritage and tradition at The Citadel, would end up costing Von Mickel later in the barracks. Von Mickel was not as big as many of the other black cadets, many of whom were on varsity teams. He didn't play football or basketball. He was just an ordinary guy who was kind to Faulkner on her first day. For that reason, I needed him as a witness for trial.

I met Von Mickel in front of the Daniel Library at The Citadel on April 19, 1994. We talked from 4:00 p.m. to 5:45 p.m.

"My mother told me that I can't help you at the trial, Mr. Black," Von Mickel told me several months later when we met again outside The Citadel Library under one of the shade trees, not entirely in plain view but not hiding either.

"But you had a lot of courage to speak to Faulkner on that momentous day last January. All of you black cadets have courage just to be here. In fact, Shannon tells me that black cadets are the main ones who will talk to her. You and the black custodial staff in the physical plant. It's the silent treatment by the rest of the Corps, something outlawed at West Point. You know she appreciates what you guys are doing. Your day-to-day observations about the Corps will be dynamite."

"She says I have done enough. She's worried about me, afraid I might get hurt again."

"Again? Von Mickel, you're no coward. What happened?" I asked.

"Nothing really. I'm not too worried about it." Then he went on to tell me that some white cadets in his barracks started yelling at him after he spoke to Shannon. They told him he should have left her alone, but he told them it was none of their business what he did.

The white cadet who he said hit him in the gut was one of the guys yelling at the press in front of Stevens Barracks the day Shannon registered. But he said the cadet didn't get any demerits, nothing, no tours or punishment. Von Mickel said that he didn't hit him back, just protected himself.

"They said it was a fight that both of us caused," Von Mickel added. "Any rate, I can't testify for you. I'm sorry. It's like Berra Lee Byrd, I guess."

His last remark was chilling. Berra Lee Byrd was a black cadet who was shot on March 12, 1992, by a white cadet firing a 9mm pistol out the top-floor window of Murray Barracks. It was Corps Day and Byrd's company had just won

Citadel Cadet Von Mickel greets Shannon Faulkner after she registers on January 20, 1994, as the first women admitted to attend daytime classes with the all-male Corps of Cadets. Used with permission, Staff photo by Wade Spees, *The Post and Courier*, January 21, 1994.

a drilling competition. The student African American Society at The Citadel had recently gotten the administration to stop flying the Rebel flag and playing Dixie at parade and athletic events. After the shots were fired, The Citadel authorities did not order a lock-down or take any extraordinary measures to try to identify and arrest the assailant. The bullet penetrated Byrd's lung and passed out his back, missing his heart by a couple of inches.[3]

Byrd was blamed by some cadets for drawing attention, more bad press and bad things from outsiders who only wanted to bash The Citadel. Citadel authorities suspected that Byrd had been dating a white woman and in any case knew the identity of his own assailant. Bud Watts was quoted as suggesting that the shot might have come from duck hunters on the Ashley River.[4]

On August 28, 1992, I got Byrd's home phone number in Gaffney, South Carolina, from Herbert Frazier, the African-American reporter at *The News and Courier*. Frazier had warned me that Byrd probably did not want to talk about the shooting, that one rumor flying around was that Byrd got shot in a lover's quarrel, another that a janitor shot him over money.

Frazier was right. Byrd did not want to discuss the matter with me at all, so I followed Frazier's advice and went to *The News and Courier* archives to look at Frazier's filed reports among unedited hazing reports.

Four years after the shooting, after the FBI sent out 1500 letters to cadets, former cadet David Burdock finally identified his roommate George "Trip" Cormeny III as the man who shot Byrd. There was no proof that others might have known about the shooting, no proof that it was anything more than an accident. The Citadel family protected its integrity. "We pride ourselves on having a very close-knit group," Lieutenant General Watts said in a press conference after the shooting. The local press wrote that according to the Solicitor, several cadets at the time of the shooting knew that Cormeny had shot Byrd but none reported the incident.[5]

Cormeny and The Citadel became the victims that Byrd never was. According to newspaper accounts, Cormeny asked for the forgiveness of Byrd—and the Board of Visitors.[6] A former Assistant U.S. Attorney on the board called Cormeny a "man of integrity." "We don't sit in judgment," the chairman of the board said.

The board forgave him. Cormeny could now continue his studies in an Episcopal theological school. His roommate there later became The Citadel chaplain while Trip himself became pastoral assistant at a Charleston Episcopal church. The P & C pitched the story as one of mercy and forgiveness, two of the many virtues young leaders learn at The Citadel. It was a redemptive experience for both white cadets and the entire Citadel family.

Berra Lee Byrd was graduated on May 14, 1994, with his assailant who was unknown at the time.[7] Berra Lee Byrd lost his dream to enter the military. He later sued Cormeny and Burdock. Cormeny was indicted on October 9, 1996, by a Charleston County grand jury on two counts for possession of an unlawful weapon, one for having a weapon while under 21, and one for carrying a weapon in a public building. While he could have received up to seven years in jail, Cormeny was instead sentenced to spend 30 nights in the Charleston County Detention Center and ordered to tell inmates what he did. He was released during the daytime and required to do 400 hours of community service. Headlines in The P & C on October 25, 1997, read, "Ex-cadet Gets Jail in Shooting."[8] Burdock walked. Von Mickel's mother was right to keep her son out of harm's way.

The Ragadier

The budget for The Brigadier, the student paper for the Corps of Cadets, is approved by the administration. Once funded, the newspaper is protected under the free speech clause of the First Amendment. The Citadel administration would have had a very hard time suppressing anything the cadets

chose to write, since prior approval would usually amount to unconstitutional prior restraint. In some cases, however, sentences were blacked out in
the column by the Scarlet Pimpernel, as in the case of the issue which first
announced Faulkner's application to join the Class of 1997.[9] Even so, the
cadets' relentless attacks on Faulkner in *The Brigadier* created a moral issue, if
not a constitutional one, for lack of being viewpoint neutral. Although they probably had the right to publish their attacks, the attacks amounted to just one cheap
shot after another, unbefitting of a Citadel cadet.

The staff supervisor for the newspaper and a public relations officer for The Citadel
at the start of the case was a U.S. Marine. At some point during the case, he was
asked by Marine Headquarters at Quantico not to appear on television in his uniform when making public statements regarding The Citadel's position of opposing the admission of women. It presented the wrong image of a Marine.

In the 1994 April Fools edition of *The Brigadier*, published as *The Ragadier*,
the mysteries of menses and the ways of the "ACL-NOT A CLUE U" came to the
fore—easily the best pun in the case. And the editorial staff had had just about
enough of "LONG-HAIRED HIPPY FREAKS" who were the attorneys for
Faulkner. Editions of *The Brigadier* during the Faulkner years became collectors'
items as precious as the several versions of Citadel bumper stickers and the cof-
fee cups, hand bags, and T-shirts later manufactured by Converse to advertise
the South Carolina Institute for Leadership or SCIL program. Editorials, similar to the one on Susan Faludi's visit to the gay bar on King Street, routinely appeared in the column written by the Scarlet Pimpernel to ridicule SRF. As always,
capital letters—more than wit—were used as blunt instruments. The anonymous cadets who wrote in code for the initiates changed each year. Their identities were known only to a few, but rumor always served at The Citadel to
establish fact. In 1994, I was given the name of that year's Scarlet Pimpernel and
a key to bust the code.

What began as an inoffensive reference to "that cute LITTLE FAULKNER"
in the September, 3, 1993, edition of the student newspaper had become something more by the time Shannon was admitted to the day program in January
1994. Opposite "A Letter from the President" in which Lieutenant General
Watts provided The Citadel version of "where we stand regarding the public response to Shannon Faulkner now attending daytime classes," the January 22
edition reminded the cadets of the unholy alliance Faulkner had made with
the African-American cadet Von Mickel. Referring also to the challenge cadets
met in riding the life-size Coburg Dairy plastic cow on St. Andrews Boulevard,
cadets in the paper began to refer to Shannon as the "Divine Bovine" and
"Shrew," a step up from "Ms. Piggie" used in other editions:

The PIMP [Scarlet Pimpernel] doth long to tame the PLASTIC COW on this most wondrous of nights but it seems that we will have a live specimen, a home grown DAIRY QUEEN from the stables of Powdersville. Perhaps NON DICKLE will be the first to saddle up. He is the DIVINE BOVINE'S best friend after all.

For the front page of the April Fool's Day 1994, edition of *The Ragadier*, the editorial staff used some of their best material. Cadet Adam Reeder, investigative reporter, was "dispatched" to Shannon's home town to pose with two live "divine bovines" on Timbrook Plantation to give readers a sense of the real thing. The Coburg Dairy plastic cow would soon be replaced by Faulkner in the barracks, the paper surmised.

With the same dirk he used to deride the vice president as "Twinkle-twinkle, two-star fool," the Scarlet Pimpernel disclosed that The Citadel, in 1979–82, had employed a "psycho-pseudo" professor, now local counsel for Shannon Faulkner: "Get a real job and a real client before ye find thineself bankrupt and bouncing off the funny padded walls wearing a wraparound white jacket. But, again, BAA BAA BLACK, you were of that way whilst here at DICEL as a psycho pseudo-prof, hum?" DICEL was of course "El Cid," the cadet's affectionate name for The Citadel, or "Cidadel" as one of my students spelled it.

The cadet newspaper provided a cornucopia of proof of virtually everything childishly innocent yet seriously wrong with the Corps. At the same time, *The Brigadier* served a useful purpose to the administration, the Board of Visitors, the alumni, and—to what extent it was aware of the paper—the Charleston community. As in the case of the fringe element outside the walls of The Citadel over which The Citadel always said it had no control, the student paper operated to do the dirty little work of helping the administration and fellow cadets to wear Faulkner down. Keeping her constantly under pressure through humiliation and intimidation only increased the effects of isolation, the hissing and cursing in the hallways, and the silent treatment.

Had the case ever gone to trial on the value of a single-sex, all-male education, I was fully prepared to call as witnesses certain principals at The Citadel to describe to the court all acts of hazing that they personally took part in or witnessed during their own days as cadets at The Citadel. I was given the names of two officials who years ago as cadets had hazed knobs. Service of those sub poenas would have been explosive in ferreting out Citadel hypocrisy as no other event in the lawsuit. But it never happened. What was common knowledge to generations of Citadel men never made it to trial.

"Not an Inch"

The ordeal to create a normal collegiate experience for the first woman in the Corps of Cadets amounted to a subplot. The Citadel wanted her to have as little presence on campus as possible. So the fight began in August 1993, picked up again in January 1994, when SRF was ordered into day classes, and continued into August 1995, when she was ordered into the Corps. The Citadel tried to ignore her as a student on campus right up to the time she entered the Corps, at which time they gave her their full attention.

On January 26, 1994, Shannon made her case, the basic position of which was simply to have as normal a collegiate experience as possible.

The Citadel went through each request on February 17. Shannon could not join the Bulldog Orchestra because it was a part of the Regimental Band, strictly a cadet activity. She could audition to join The Citadel Players next year when a new production was offered. The Education Club no longer existed, so she obviously could not join that. And she could not be a student delegate to the State Student Legislature because it too was strictly a cadet activity.

"We do not believe Judge Houck's Order requires a change in the selection process of staff members or that non-cadets be selected for the editorial boards," The Citadel went on. "For obvious reasons, The Citadel cannot and will not allow Ms. Faulkner to participate in any activity except as ordered by the court."

On September 9, 1994, Faulkner filed a motion for clarification of the preliminary injunction order of August 17, 1993, to address what Shannon could and could not do while in the day program. The Citadel responded that it had endeavored in good faith "to treat Ms. Faulkner as a student rather than as a litigant," and "rather than avail herself of the benefits which The Citadel offers, Ms. Faulkner has chosen public confrontation with The Citadel by filing the instant motion." Faulkner, after all, loved publicity, they insisted.

The judge tended to disagree. At a hearing on September 23, 1994, the court made these observations of the spirit in which The Citadel had addressed a school girl's wishes:

> The Court: Mr. Cooke, all that may be in print and that may be the way it sounds, but when she lets you know that she wants to be a member of the staff of the yearbook, under the circumstances existing in the case, it's very easy for you to pick up the phone and call and find out what she wants and take care of it. You know that, I know that, and everybody in this courtroom knows it.
>
> And there is absolutely no reason whatsoever to go through what we are going through here today to get her on the staff of the year-

book. It is nothing but an effort to have confrontation with her and make her service on that staff unbearable if she ever finally gets on there. It is an insignificant thing that could have been taken care of very easily had you and your client in good faith wished for her to be on that staff.

Mr. Cooke: I understand, and I disagree, Your Honor.

The Court: You may disagree, but being associated with this case for many months, the trial and otherwise, I am convinced that you are wrong....

I've handled an awful lot of cases as a lawyer and a judge, and I think I know how easy it is to get something like this settled if you really want to settle it, and how easy it is to come into the court and stand on a privilege or whatever and make a big deal out of something that really doesn't need that much attention. And that's exactly what you have done. You have done it on every point right down the line. Not an inch do you give unless the court requires you to give it.

But the court again did not take the bait and issue an order. The Citadel would continue to be allowed to make such calls themselves.

Show Time

The calls I received from Citadel alumni after Faulkner got into the day program were a pleasant surprise. A doctor from Atlanta and a man from Nashville, both in the Class of 1965, called to offer help. One mentioned that he had two daughters. I was also happy to hear from an officer living in Towson, Maryland, Class of 1970. Direct encouragement from Citadel graduates was indeed extremely rare. But it did happen.

One of the clearest indications of Faulkner's determination to be accepted by her classmates in the Corps, to fit in and not complain in spite of their determination to see her fail, was the way she dealt with an invitation to be on the TV show *60 Minutes*. It is the ultimate response to her critics who said that she started the case just for media attention. Mike Wallace at CBS, through his agent Ty Kim, called me on February 18, 1994, to ask if Faulkner would agree to wear a secret recording device, to be bugged. She would wear a tiny TV camera to capture all of the hostile and obscene remarks made in passing by the cadets as she walked the halls on her way to class. Such remarks as "Go home, bitch" and "You don't belong" and worse. It would even capture the silent treatment.

It would be sensational journalism. Forty million viewers would see the Whole Man.

"She can wear it on her shirt or blouse so that no one will see it," he told me. "It's a tiny Japanese camera, state-of-the-art in clandestine surveillance."

But Shannon would have none of it.

"It's a great chance to prove to the world that you are in fact being hazed in a constant manner, something The Citadel is always able to say that we are just making up," I told her. "I think you should do it. It will reveal their malice and hypocrisy to the world. It also should be very funny."

But she would not put The Citadel in an unfavorable light.

"What do you owe them, Shannon?" I asked, waiving my hands in frustration. "They're making your life miserable—lying every day and getting away with denying that they are doing anything wrong at all. Taunting you to try to get you to isolate yourself even further by complaining. Let the country see who they really are."

It was too sneaky, she told me. She wanted to be able to join the Corps without having done anything that they might think was disloyal or a betrayal. The same reason she wouldn't snitch on them.

"If you caught all of that kind of stuff on camera, maybe it would put a stop to it," I continued to argue. "It's going to go on if you don't."

"Nope," she said.

"Shannon, help The Citadel get rid of the terrible stuff going on over there," I said. "Help them get rid of the bad and keep the good. Maybe the kind of exposure you and *60 Minutes* would make will lead to a change to put The Citadel back on course."

The irony was inescapable. It would be another year and a half before the press got the candid pictures of cadets as they truly were, as they were whooping it up and dancing in the rain after Faulkner quit. They, not pictures on *60 Minutes*, would be the enduring images that showed the true colors of the cadets. And they would unwittingly serve as an even more powerful record of The Citadel's treatment of women who do not know their place. A permanent record of bad manners—the ultimate corruption of Southern virtues.

"Surprise Attack"

"Faulkner launched a surprise attack on The Citadel, focusing on the manner in which Faulkner had allegedly been treated as a day student," defendants told the court at the February 11, 1994, hearing, and by the 23rd, they followed up with a letter to the judge:

At the hearing last Thursday the Plaintiffs charged the Defendants with participating in a conspiracy to drive Ms. Faulkner from The Citadel through a campaign of harassment. The Plaintiff gave the Defendants no notice of their claim. They have not made that claim in any document which they filed with the court or served upon the parties, and prior to Thursday's hearing they had identified no witnesses, documents, or other evidence to support the claim.

The Defendants regard this allegation as an extraordinarily grave matter. Aside from its possible relevance to the class certification issue ... it has already had a devastating impact on The Citadel's relations with the public to whom it is responsible.... [W]e respectfully request ... a full opportunity to conduct discovery upon this issue....

In fact, Faulkner had, on this one occasion, complained in confidence to the vice president about the Scarlet Pimpernel.[10] Word got to the student newspaper that she complained about being called a "bitch" and other such names. She had worked within the system and gone to the vice president, not Mike Wallace at *60 Minutes*. Val, at the hearing, said her complaint "demonstrates that The Citadel and its cadets are not exhibiting good faith in this litigation, good faith in the sense of trying to reach an expeditious resolution. This sort of harassment exemplifies the desire to run her out of The Citadel."

Shannon's silence about the silent treatment and every other act of harassment had allowed The Citadel to claim that it always treated Faulkner with courtesy. Because of her silence the administration could exploit the fundamental nature of young people trying to prove themselves to their peers. In the eyes of a fellow cadet, a complaint was not just a betrayal of the Corps but also an admission that she couldn't take it. This simple catch 22 elevated hazing to a pedagogical principle which was exploited by the cadre in charge of the Fourth Class System. But now The Citadel was given notice. Faulkner was being hazed. Out-of-state media gave it full coverage.

An article by a Citadel history professor in the October 1994, *South Carolina Historical Magazine*, published by the S.C. Historical Society, tracked the alliance among General Mark Clark, *The Brigadier*, and the *News and Courier* to keep blacks out of The Citadel in the 1950s. Integration, they thought, was a communist plot. Similar combined efforts were arguably made to resist women forty years later, although The Citadel administration, the student newspaper, and the op ed pages in the local press usually based their position on constitutional arguments, not on communism.

The court did not get into the exchange between Val and Dawes other than to observe that there seemed to be some harassment and that the harassment made it more likely that Faulkner would not stay the course. The court made a fair assumption that a lot of that harassment was coming from Citadel people and cadets.

When directly asked by the court if Citadel people opposed the plaintiff's motion for class certification in order to get rid of the case entirely if something should happen to Ms. Faulkner, The Citadel attorney responded:

> I would just say that if there is any doubt at all in the Court's mind about The Citadel's good faith, and Your Honor used the words "Citadel people," I challenge anybody to submit any evidence of any harassment that has emanated in any way from anybody that I represent in this case.

The Citadel's indignation grew as the vice president testified at the February 11, 1994, hearing, about just what could and could not be done to stop most of the 2000 boys from harassing one girl. He testified that he told Faulkner in his office that his hands were tied. He weighed the greater value of cadets' free speech over her personal concerns for her safety, which he implied were not serious:

> I told her very clearly twice that I would speak both to the editor of the paper and to the advisor of the paper. I told her I though it wouldn't do any good, but I told her I would do these things.... We do operate general control over the paper in terms of what is published. We certainly do not believe in censoring the paper. That's one thing Ms. Faulkner and I spoke about is freedom of the press, and free speech is something an institution of higher learning certainly has to hold dear and safeguard.... It's not just The Citadel. It's every school I know of. These people have a mind of their own and they have the Constitution to protect them.

The rationale that the First Amendment allows the creation of a hostile atmosphere, however, goes only so far. When the vice president was asked what he would do when cadets called Shannon a bitch and whore, he responded that all she had to do was point them out "and I'll take care of it." Shannon, however, saw no evidence of any change after her meeting.

The issue festered right up to the time of trial, although I tried to add a bit of humor to Shannon's predicament. In Shannon's deposition on April 25, 1994, the inquiry went like this:

> Q. Other than your attorneys, with whom have you discussed harassment that has been directed towards you since you've been at The Citadel?

A. Just the press after that court date.

Q. Have you talked about it to any other friends or friends of Mr. Black's or family members of Mr. Black?

A. Just his wife.

Q. Melinda?

A. Melinda Lucka

Q. She's not your attorney, is she?

A. No, sir.

Q. Can you think of anybody else?

A. No.

MR. BLACK: Will and John, ages three and one.

MR. COOKE: I'll get the deposition notices out.

MR. BLACK: Bradley is the yellow lab.

MR. COOKE: All right. Well, thanks, That's all I have.

MR. WEISBURG: We don't have any questions. Thank you.

(End of deposition)

After the trial several months later, in May 1994, a memorandum filed by The Citadel on June 10 in support for a mistrial included a personal statement to the court regarding what good boys the cadets were. The memorandum left out my own personal concerns about an atmosphere of hostility created by The Citadel against Faulkner, as recorded in the transcript:

> Mr. Black: May I just make a few comments?
>
> The Court: Sure.
>
> Mr. Black: I've worked personally with a number of young high school girls who want to go to The Citadel since 1989. I know two of them have dropped out because of fear of harassment. One is now waiting to hear the results of this case before she will step forward and make application.... Here is a civil rights case where for the first time— I don't know of any other civil rights case in which there was not an adult male. So surely part of the pressure that Ms. Faulkner is feeling is the kind of pressure that other high school seniors just don't know anything about and don't want to know. At any rate, if all African Americans had been children Shannon's age, where would they be now?

At this point in the case, the court must have sensed that Faulkner was never going to testify about how the cadets and administration were actually treating her day to day. The court would never hear it from the plaintiff and certainly never from the defendants. Therefore, the court would have to get any useful facts surrounding Shannon's treatment at The Citadel not as admissible evidence in the case but as information only. If rumors were flying, the court would not be the last to hear them.

The court turned not to the client but to the client's local counsel to rat out The Citadel:

> The Court: Tell me a little bit about that pressure. You live here in Charleston.
> Ms. Vojdik has talked about *The Brigadier*.… But what, in your observation, has taken place as far as harassment that you can report to the Court?
> Mr. Black: Well, again, the Court may know that Ms. Faulkner lives with my wife and our three children.
> The Court: I was aware of that. I think I read it in the newspaper. You never told me.
> Mr. Black: I have to concede that my wife, Melinda, may very well know much more than I do about her daily life. However, I will say that I did quiz her on the way to the College of Charleston game and The Citadel game last Thursday. Because I called Fred Stroble, United States marshal, as he invited me to do after we first came to register and then go to the first class, I think sometime the 18th of January.… Happily, by the way, cadets, everybody, were more interested in the game than they were in Shannon. So nothing happened. But in any event, my sense of … Citadel Security, their reply was that we cannot guarantee your safety. In effect, they said you will have a plain clothes man here, but, you know, there might be some things that happen. And then I said, wait a minute, and I called Ms. Vojdik later about this issue. I said to The Citadel, this is not my understanding, I'm unhappy with this situation.… We went on to The Citadel anyway.… Even though we knew there was some risk, that's the kind of risk that I don't want to happen anymore in the future.… Ms. Faulkner receives letters, very favorable, a big pile, and then the little pile unfavorable. It's the little pile that I ask her to give me every day of the unfavorable. So I do have those. The issue as far as harassment, which Ms. Vojdik addressed, again secondhand. Ms. Faulkner doesn't talk to me about this kind of thing, the words used and so forth. But I know from counsel and my wife that some obscene words have been yelled out. And I did get this as we crossed the parade ground to the McAllister Field House on the way to the game last Thursday. No surprise to me.
> The Court: Who was it coming from?
> Mr. Black: From cadets. Because one of the barracks is right by Duckett Hall, the entrance to Duckett Hall. So these gentlemen, none of whom

we know because none would come straight up to her and say these things, they always yell out the window, or going down the stairwell, they will hiss after they've passed. Nothing direct as far as I know. But, again, my information is secondhand, if not thirdhand....

The Court: You have a former relationship with The Citadel and are familiar with the procedures there at The Citadel. I think The Citadel, I guess the first thing you think about is discipline. And is it normal for cadets to be able to shout out of windows at The Citadel? Does that go unnoticed at The Citadel no matter what they say?

Mr. Black: I don't think—I don't ever remember it as a teacher there, any cadets yelling "bitch" at any other, at anybody else. But as far as, you know, "saddling up," I don't think any cadet is saddling up on any other cadet. If so, that's, you know, that's another issue.

The Court: I've observed cadets being interviewed by television on campus ... and I've seen the campus buildings in the background and the cadets in uniform ... and voicing displeasure with Ms. Faulkner being there and a desire that she not be there in the future ... and I just wondered if that was something The Citadel normally let cadets do? Do they normally permit them to comment on topics of current interest on television?

Mr. Black: Certainly not in my experience of being at The Citadel for three years. I think that strikes to the issue that I'm trying to make but a little bit more succinctly. I'm worried about the atmosphere of hostility created through this kind of slander in the student newspaper, through the obscenities being yelled out and so forth. This is not standard stuff. The answer is, no, I'm not aware of any other precedent of cadets going whole hog against any other cadet, or anybody else for that matter, as they are after this plaintiff. And that's what concerns me, and it's a genuine concern. The issue, and I talked to Nat Douglas yesterday in the Justice Department, is that we want to address this right now and get a hold on it. We don't want to say these are just boys, everything's going to be all right, and then later down the line have some nut do something that could have been prevented. It's this atmosphere of hostility that I'm concerned about and it's a genuine concern. And that's what I wanted to bring to the Court's attention.

Later in the proceeding, when Suzanne Coe offered to put Shannon on the stand to testify under oath about what kind of reception she was really getting at The Citadel, the Court explained why it refused to destroy any

Shannon Faulkner and local counsel Robert Black at the four corners of law, with St. Michael's Church in the background, prior to a hearing on the extent to which Faulkner would be allowed to participate in Citadel student life pending a final resolution of her case. Used with permission, Staff photo by Gabriel B. Tait, *The Post and Courier*, September 24, 1994.

hope that ever existed for Faulkner eventually to be an accepted member of the Corps:

> I don't want to put her in the position of pointing the finger at somebody else.... I don't want to put her in the position of being—I don't know what her name would be in *The Brigadier* if she did that. But I don't want to subject her to anymore criticism than she's already gotten. This is a legitimate inquiry that I made, and she didn't make it, and I made it for the reasons that—Ms. Vojdik advanced the thought, but it was something that was on my mind. And I believe I brought it up to Mr. Cooke when we discussed class certification earlier.

In spite of Faulkner's wanting to fit in as a rightful member of the Corps without complaining, on Monday, February 28, 1994, Faulkner's attorneys took the matter of verbal hazing to the attention of the Judge since it was such an egregious and persistent offense. This was going far beyond the silent treatment, The Citadel's official form of hazing. This was vocal and loud. The Citadel would never admit the catch 22 vise they always had Shannon in.

Faulkner was having trouble hearing anything in at least one of her classes because the cadets were yelling—and the teacher was unable or unwilling to stop them. After all of the Third Battalion, about 1200 male cadets, hissed at Faulkner standing to the side watching the parade on the previous Friday, her attorneys approached the court for an injunction directed at the administration which alone always could control that kind of organized hazing.

"We'll try to stop the yelling in class to keep you from hearing the teacher, Shannon," I told her, "but I'll have to tell you that maybe you shouldn't stand at the same little tree on the parade ground as they march back to their barracks after parade."

In a settlement that included Shannon giving the marching cadets more room, The Citadel was open to the idea of cracking down on the regiment if it ever hissed en masse at Faulkner again. No further pursuit was made for an injunction by the court along those lines, and the indication from the court was that none would be issued. Faulkner just had to stand away from her tree and, in all other contexts, hope for the best.

Yet the actions that transpired throughout this major aspect of Shannon Faulkner's case still stand as three pillars which support hazing as it persists at The Citadel today: first, acts of violence by cadets against other cadets are not attributable at law to The Citadel administration and Board of Visitors since cadets are not agents of the State; second, the cadets themselves, notably 19 year olds, are completely in charge of all that goes on in the barracks; and, third, Citadel honor prevents most youthful victims of hazing from ratting out their tormentors.

Letters

Word had gotten out about the kinds of letters Faulkner was receiving at 16 Chadwick Drive every day. Mary Jordan of *The Washington Post* and Claudia Brinson from *The State* in Columbia wanted to publish them, but they were often too obscene or threatening to be published. Another problem was that any news coverage of death threats, if any were ever directly made, would be seen by the FBI as simply an invitation to stir up more trouble and provoke copycats.

To my knowledge, no death threats were ever made against me or anyone else. If they existed, I had no personal knowledge of them. Shannon's account of a death threat against her parents shortly before and after she got into the Corps is a thoroughly credible account, but it is her own. Even so, the FBI's standard practice was not to make death threats public. To that extent, neither *The*

Washington Post nor *The State* got a story about Faulkner's mail. In the evenings on Chadwick Drive, Melinda would sometimes go up to Shannon's upstairs bedroom to sit with her and read the mail because Shannon did not want to read any hate mail alone. The little pile of hate mail I told the court about actually increased in size as the case progressed. Because the FBI never returned the threatening letters which I handed over to them, I began making copies before forwarding the hate mail to the FBI and simply let the stack grow. A few choice postcards I kept myself as they were addressed to me at 16 Chadwick Drive. The end result was that The Citadel was able, throughout litigation, to stick with its assertion that such matters were unproven or at least beyond their control. They denied creating a hostile environment or, if it did exist, that it contributed to hate mail from the public and "Citadel people." They claimed Faulkner was making it all up to get more publicity. Nonetheless, weekly attacks and derisive cartoons from The Citadel in *The Brigadier* remained hard to ignore—like an article in three long columns that filled half the 24" x 14" page on February 4, 1994, written by a very angry mother.

One of the most telling aspects of The Citadel's attitude toward Faulkner came by way of the U.S. Mail at the end of the case after Faulkner left The Citadel. Throughout the case, other letters with insufficient addresses were routed by both the U.S. and Citadel post offices to me to give to Shannon. "City Hall, Shannon Faulkner, Charleston, South Carolina" was enough. But in at least one instance the mail addressed to her as a member of the Corps was not forwarded to her at her home address in Easley, South Carolina. Instead, it was marked by the workers at The Citadel Post Office, "Address Unknown. Return to Sender," as if to punish both SRF and those still trying to correspond with the first woman admitted to the Corps of Cadets. After the letter was sent back to the young girl who had sent it from Birmingham, the father of the girl called me.

"I don't know why they didn't know her forwarding address. I guess she didn't leave one," he said.

"Of course, she left a forwarding address," I replied. "Even Martians know it. It's just that Citadel malice still will not allow that she ever existed."

Suffer Little Children

On March 16, 1994, an administrator called from Porter-Gaud School, an Episcopal Church school which my step-daughter Spencer was attending at the time.

"I'm so sorry about what happened this afternoon," a woman said. "We're so embarrassed. I'm afraid some of our students said ugly things to Miss

Faulkner when she came to pick up Spencer after school. I've talked to all of them about it. It won't happen again."

"Spencer and Shannon never mentioned it," I told her. "Spencer's classmates are only ten years old."

"Please tell Miss Faulkner that our children at Porter-Gaud know better," the woman continued. "We always treat everybody with respect, even if we disagree with them," she said, with slow emphasis on the trailing phrase.

"Why don't you call their parents and let them know what happened?" I asked.

"Oh, we don't have to do that. I don't think we need to do that," she replied. "I mean we won't let that kind of thing happen again. I've talked to all the children."

"It might let the parents know what kind of manners they really are teaching their kids at home," I said. "Of course that's what's really going on in reverse with the cadets themselves. Most of them never gave the role of women a second thought until they came to The Citadel."

Most churches in town never concerned themselves with the most widely publicized civil rights case in Charleston since *Briggs*. Few white ministers in Charleston bothered with the issue of equal rights for women any more than they did about those of blacks in the 1950s and 1960s. Most of their congregations, as well, acted as if the whole mess was just a legal matter and not a moral issue significant enough to take notice of. The only voice of support for Shannon I was aware of came from the members of St. Stephen's Episcopal Church, the only racially mixed church in the Holy City, and Morris Brown AME Church, a black church where Senator Robert Ford held a rally on August 28 after Shannon quit the Corps. The flyer handed out at the rally encouraged the community "to come out in support of Shannon Faulkner, the Harriet Tubman, Sojourner Truth, Mary McCloud-Bethune, Susan B. Anthony, and Rosa Parks of our time." Representative Lucille Whipper, Senator Holly Cork, and Senator Kay Patterson were scheduled to speak.

Shannon was a Methodist, but on one occasion she agreed to go with us to Grace Episcopal Church on Wentworth Street. That was before Spencer took the whole family from St. Stephens to Grace Church, known to some as a Citadel church.

Well, I'll be damned if they didn't shun her and give her the silent treatment at Grace Church. No one in the congregation spoke to one of the most recognizable faces in town. More to the point, some young punk devil even scowled at her as he was slouching back from the communion rail to his seat after taking Holy Communion. I was looking straight at him when he glared at Shannon.

I glanced at his feet.

A friend in the church told me years later that, in fact, one of the senior members at Grace Church said to my friend as they both saw Faulkner walking in the door that Sunday morning, "She shouldn't be here!" Faulkner did not ever go to church with us again.

First Remedial Plan

The Citadel submitted a revised list of witnesses and its first of several proposed remedial plans on April 1, 1994, as the court in February had ordered it to do. It was a thin, eight-page outline. For the moment, The Citadel hoped to comply with the court's order to furnish a plan with the casual observation, "Within sixty days of the court's determination of the liability issues, the Defendants will supplement this remedial plan by setting forth a specific proposed remedy that responds to the liability determination."

The remedial plan, therefore, submitted to the court on April Fool's Day was a few pages that told the court that it had no real intention of following its order to furnish a remedial plan prior to trial. Instead, The Citadel would tell the court that it would do what it wanted to do, not what the court ordered it to do. The Citadel would treat the trial as if it were bifurcated, first liability, then remedy, in the way The Citadel wanted it to be all along; then The Citadel would let the court know what it would do if it were found to violate the Constitution.

Its refusal to follow the court's order in no more than a cursory manner would have the operational effect, months later, of putting Faulkner in the Corps without a coherent plan of assimilation.

On April 8, Sandy Beber filed a motion for the United States to strike what little there was of The Citadel's remedial plan, to bar any other proposed plan, and wrote, "Defendants cloak their defiance of this Court's order in the guise of 'sound and responsible public policy considerations,' but however characterized, defendants have plainly failed to comply with their obligations.... It fails to specify a constitutional remedy." Beber again emphasized that it was a race against time. Everyone knew what The Citadel was up to.

Everyone knew that in order to attend fall classes, Shannon would have to be admitted by August 1994, and The Citadel would just somehow not have its remedial plan organized well enough by then for the court to review.

Big Dogs' Depositions

On April 14, 1994, I joined in the DOJ depositions set by Sandy Beber for members of the Board of Visitors. The board members were chosen by DOJ to depose without direct involvement by Shearman, mainly not to put more lawyers than absolutely necessary in a deposition, but I knew that anytime one of those guys talked, everyone should listen closely. The BOV was in fact the very center of all power at The Citadel. The BOV told the General Assembly what to do regarding all matters at The Citadel. The manufacturing of the Concurrent Resolution was evidence of that. The problem was to get members of the board to talk.

The depositions were held in Mark Clark Hall, just a few doors down from a recreation room where a senior cadet told me that The Citadel claimed that he had been caught with a janitor underneath a pool table. The cadet asked if I could represent him, but I could not. His overriding concern was not to give back his Citadel ring before they kicked him out.

The members of the BOV to be deposed included a few old soldiers, true enough, but not as many as there should have been. A strong reminder of a fundamental fact about The Citadel—that it is not really military—was the complete lack of military experience in many members of the Board of Visitors. In fact, because The Citadel was run as the private preserve of the board and alumni, what Voltaire said about the Holy Roman Empire could be said about The Citadel: that the Military College of South Carolina was neither military, nor a college, nor belonging to South Carolina. As alumni of The Citadel, members of the board were mostly business men. Several high-ranking military officers who were not alumni sat only on an Advisory Board, not on the board itself. I had seen a few real U.S. military lapel pins worn by members of the board, so not to be out-done, I wore my Army Commendation Medal, or ARCOM, lapel pin to one of the depositions. The ARCOM is not much compared to what many career service soldiers have, but I was proud of what little I did have. Neither the pin nor Beber's questions elicited any useful information about how the BOV really operated, however. A year or two after the case was over, I appreciated the humor of being anonymously invited to run for a position of the board, especially in light of my earlier role in removing the name of a nominee to the board.

But every member of the Board of Visitors knew one thing that many people did not fully understand, something that makes up The Citadel's chief service to the state and nation. The Citadel takes young boys who, in many instances, are at best very immature and at worse nearly juvenile delinquents and makes serviceable men of them. Men who will show up for work on time and do a job correctly, at times better than others. Networking as alumni does not explain all of The Citadel's success. Bonding as cadets is only part of the picture. Our case to get women admitted was no more than to let the same magic operate on girls of like disposition, but without a corruption of its best aspirations.

By April 22, 1994, I was preparing for the deposition of Colonel Roy Zinzer, Professor of Military Science and, as Commandant, the top active-duty man at The Citadel. It was at this deposition that plaintiff's counsel first heard of the request in 1991 by Brigadier General Julius Johnson at Fort Bragg for The Citadel to help address a "tremendous shortage" of Army nurses during the Gulf War. Zinzer's deposition was on the eve of more news that Texas A & M, with its coed ROTC unit within a surrounding non-cadet student body, had just won the prestigious MacArthur Award. The Citadel didn't even place or show. On May 6, 1994, the date of Colonel Zinzer's deposition, I had already talked to Lieutenant Colonel Donna Talbot at Fort Bragg about the MUSC nursing student enrolled as an ROTC cadet at The Citadel and received a memo from Fort Monroe to clear the way for the deposition with the office of Judge Advocate General's Corps or JAG. Lieutenant Colonel Talbot had taken the place of my initial contact, Major Karen Hazlett, at 1st Region ROTC Headquarters at Fort Bragg. I had assured her that I understood, as is the usual case when an active member of the armed forces testifies in a trial, that The Citadel Commandant did not speak for the United States. The JAG officer, Captain Allen Berger, not The Citadel's lawyer, accepted service of my subpoena for Zinzer's deposition. Off the record and before the deposition, the court reporter tried to identify who the lawyers were and what parties they represented. Even if none of the lawyers knew who was who, the court reported still had to make a clear record of the proceedings.

"Will you please identify yourselves for the record, starting with plaintiff's counsel?" the court reporter asked.

"I'm Sandy Beber for the United States."

"I'm Robert Black for the plaintiff Shannon Faulkner."

"We are Dawes Cooke and Lori Dandridge for The Citadel."

"I'm Allison Snead for the State of South Carolina."

"I'm Captain Berger. I'm representing the 18th Corps at Fort Bragg, here to observe on behalf of the JAG office in Fort Bragg. I'm here to represent the United States' interest of the United States Army."

Berger went on to say that he was not representing any party in the litigation and that it was his understanding that Sandy from DOJ would represent the interests of the United States while he was representing the specific interests of the Army.

"Whoa," I burst out. "You mean you expect Sandy here to defend Colonel Zinzer? She's here for the plaintiff-intervenor, not the defendant," I said.

It was the *Zentgraf* maneuver gone amuck.

"I was told by JAG that there would be an attorney from Justice here at the deposition," Berger replied. "Colonel Zinzer, as an active duty Army officer, is her client. Am I misinformed?" he asked.

"But not in this case," Beber chimed in. "You can defend the colonel, and I'll cross-examine him."

"Now this is a very screwy situation," I said. "Cross-over counsel. I know that the interests of the United States are not always the interests of Faulkner, but this is ridiculous."

Sandy Beber's letter to Clineburg on April 21, 1994, had in fact earlier hinted at similar confusion among DOJ counsel acting as defense of military personnel while being a plaintiff in the case. There on behalf of the Army, Air Force, and Coast Guard academies, she advised Clineburg that neither branch would search student files to satisfy Clineburg's request for production of documents, namely pregnancy statistics and the kind of information Clineburg wanted, apart from women's shoe sizes.

Dawes especially appreciated the curious set of circumstances which Colonel Zinzer's appearance presented. Other than the testimonies of Colonel Toffler's at West Point and Colonel Barkley's at North Georgia, which was given to Clineburg without any plaintiff's counsel present, this was the only instance of an active duty officer testifying in the case.

The confusion of who was on whose side ran into my law office. On more than one occasion, McGuire Woods in Richmond sent me a fax to ask about "our" case on which they thought I was co-counsel with them. I threw them away without reading them and let their office know they screwed up. Yet no degree of courtesy could guarantee honest professional relations at every turn. Some requests for production of documents were ignored. Requests which asked for documents regarding The Citadel's failed efforts to establish the academic and leadership fraternities Phi Beta Kappa and Omicron Delta Kappa chapters on campus and the refusal of invitations by notable speakers because The Citadel discriminated against women were never answered.

Hard Hats

Katherine Lee Brown, a high school student from Columbia, wrote the Director of Admissions at The Citadel on April 27, 1994. By certified mail, she asked for an application form and added, "Please expedite the sending of these materials and any other materials pertinent to my attending The Citadel this fall, and my joining its corps of cadets." Then she underlined the next sentence, "This letter is not an inquiry for information, but should be viewed by all as my formal first step in obtaining admission to The Citadel."

Bruce Smith from the Associated Press called the next day about Kat Brown. By then Kat had called me and sent a copy of the letter. Bruce wanted to get in touch with her for an interview. There was some question about whether Kat was a real applicant because she had not yet taken the SAT and filled out a complete application to The Citadel. The next day at noon, Kat and Shannon met in the living room at 16 Chadwick to discuss what it might be like to be the only women in the Corps. There they were given support by Margaret Fabri and another woman lawyer in Charleston.

Kat Brown never made it to the status of a potential cadet, nor did Pamela Jordan from Travelers Rest, South Carolina, who, with Brown, would nonetheless testify at trial a month later, along with Shannon.

Meanwhile, steel workers in Georgetown called to offer their support to Shannon. They still had not heard from her, much less gotten a requested autographed picture from her. It never appeared to be a trick or joke, so I tried to intercede with Shannon on their behalf. These were the kind of working men in the state who had probably watched Citadel graduates work their network of wearing the Ring while they had to bust it out by the sweat of their brow. But Shannon would not send them an autographed picture for their wall at the union hall.

So on April 26, 1994, I called Ed Faulkner to get him to pressure Shannon. "Just think," I said, "she's got a bunch of hard hats in Georgetown who love what she's doing so much that they have said that they will even get on a bus and come to Charleston to be in a parade in front of The Citadel gates. Now that's grass-roots if ever there was, and it adds a dimension to the case that other civil rights cases would love to have."

But that was not Shannon's style. She did not want to embarrass The Citadel.

Local Counsel as Witness

Melody Lutz called on March 23, 1994, about her testimony at the upcoming trial in May. The Citadel had named her as their own witness after her deposition in which The Citadel found enough to suspect that I was soliciting women to sue The Citadel, that I was "manufacturing evidence of demand," according to a pleading filed by The Citadel on May 5, 1994. I did not discuss her deposition while talking to Lutz and only explained to her that The Citadel had named her as one of its own witnesses.

The Citadel intended to use Lutz's testimony as a basis for dismissal on the grounds that Faulkner was just a pawn of her attorneys and the ACLU.

The Citadel also suspected me of being the primary cause for, if not the source of, applications and inquiries by women to the Corps. Letters produced by the admissions office in response to discovery by the plaintiff showed that young women as far away as military bases in Germany, high school age daughters of personnel based overseas, wanted to know about scholarships available and what it took to be admitted. In a May 5, 1994, Citadel pleading, which was calculated to prevent the court from giving the *Faulkner* case the status of a class action, The Citadel quoted my comment from *The Charleston Chronicle* in December 1992, in which I hoped that high school girls interested in going to The Citadel would call me.

Local counsel Robert Black standing by the side entrance at Lesesne Gate, The Citadel, September 1995. Used with permission, Curtis Norman.

On Friday afternoon, May 13, 1994, three days before trial on the following Monday morning, The Citadel filed a list of its 665 exhibits and 50 witnesses, eight of whom were expert witnesses, and supplemented its witness list by naming me as a witness to be called at trial. The Citadel announced that "Mr. Black will testify regarding any efforts on his part to identify and/or solicit women who may have an express interest in attending The Citadel."

The Citadel alleged that 45 young women who had made inquiries about admission to the Corps of Cadets within the last few days leading up to trial had been personally encouraged by me to do so. Out of the 45 inquiries for which The Citadel implied I was responsible, two were from women living overseas with military unit postal addresses. Thirty others were from young women living in states other than South Carolina. Six were from "College Day" inquiries completed on March 8, 1994, held in the Piedmont in the northern part of the state with addresses in Greer, Greenville, Traveler's Rest, and Fountain Inn, South Carolina. Another "College Day" card was dated March 1, 1994, from Ladson, near Charleston, and the four other letters were from Belton, McCormick, Huger, and Moncks Corner, all small towns in South Carolina.

I was not at all happy with my predicament and certainly did not want to testify. Everyone knew that no one person could possibly be responsible for a major civil rights case. In a panic prior to trial I called Armand. He was out of town. I then called Ray McClain. In a motion to strike my name from the witness list, McClain noted that The Citadel disclaimed any intention to seek to disqualify me as an attorney in the case, but McClain stated that "Black is plaintiff's only attorney in Charleston, and his disqualification would be a significant tactical advantage to defendants."

The motion McClain filed to keep me off the stand was heard on the morning the trial was to start. The judge brought McClain and Cooke to his chambers before 9:00 and told Cooke that he would not begin the trial with a lawyer's testimony. I was kept on stand-by but was never called to take the stand. Even so, the strategy worked. I was preoccupied with the possibility of being a witness and did not, therefore, completely concentrate on my role as an advocate. My job at trial was, as usual, to serve as the Passer of Notes to other attorneys and, more modestly, to examine Faulkner's witnesses Charles B. Vail, former president of Winthrop College, and Major General T. Eston Marchant, Adjutant General, South Carolina National Guard. Most of all, I was set to cross-examine Josiah Bunting, hero of Roanoke, if he were ever called to the stand by The Citadel. He was not, but I was more distracted than a cadet in a class full of women.

Chapter 5

The Trial and Right After

The Trial

On May 15, 1994, just days before the trial was to begin, I got a call from the mother of a young woman from Virginia who wanted to make application to her father's alma mater. The mother admired her husband's love of The Citadel and wanted their daughter to emulate his success as a member of the Class of 1967. After a lengthy conversation, the mother refused to let her daughter fight to get in. It again put the Faulkner family in perspective, including Mrs. Richey, Shannon's grandmother, who played a role of major support throughout. Sandy and Ed Faulkner bravely left their teenage daughter to live with strangers in a hostile environment.

The backdrop to The Citadel case was always VMI. Briefly put, in 1991 the district court in Roanoke found no Fourteenth Amendment violation in VMI's male-only admissions policy and allowed VMI to march on.[1] The Fourth Circuit ruled on October 5, 1992, in *VMI I* that VMI was in violation of the equal protection clause.[2] After the Fourth Circuit stayed its order on November 24, 1992, VMI petitioned the United States Supreme Court for *certiorari* on January 19, 1993, on the issue of whether the Fourth Circuit's remedial order for VMI to go private, to set up a parallel program for women, or to admit women was constitutional. The United States Supreme Court denied *certiorari* on May 24, 1993. This sent the case back down to Judge Jack Kiser in district court in Roanoke for trial beginning February 9, 1994, to find a remedy. It meant that in order to comply with the Constitution, VMI now would definitely have to come up with about $200 to $300 million dollars to become a private college, or that it would have to set up a successful women's military program through VWIL at Mary Baldwin, or that it would have to admit women. It quickly found a remedy in a parallel program for women at Mary Baldwin College (MBC). In *VMI II* in January 1995, the Fourth Circuit affirmed the district court finding and ruled that Virginia's parallel program at Mary Baldwin, VWIL, provided an adequate remedy.[3] Finally, the Supreme Court ruled to admit women on June 26, 1996, in *United States v. Virginia*, 518 U.S. 515, 116 S.Ct. 2264, 135 L.Ed.2d 735 (1996).

That a writ of *certiorari* was denied in *VMI I* was good news for Faulkner at The Citadel, even though she wanted only the last option and thought only it was constitutional. Only then would she be able to wear The Citadel ring. And while the Fourth Circuit in *VMI II* would on January 26, 1995, allow VMI to set up VWIL at Mary Baldwin—over notable dissenting opinions on October 5, 1995, by Judges Phillips and Motz not to rehear the case *en banc*—the Supreme Court would grant *certiorari* in *VMI II*, and Justice Ginsburg would write the final opinion to admit women into VMI on June 26, 1996.

Mainly, VMI won at trial on liability because DOJ was broadsided on the issue of the value of single-sex education, a superfluous issue in the *Faulkner* case. Nor, possibly, did the government cross examine the VMI witnesses well enough. Judge Kiser did find such a value in VMI, and the record in his court went up to the Fourth Circuit on an appeal that the DOJ barely decided to make. Faulkner's efforts to get into The Citadel were never so subject to failure as they were from her necessarily being tossed in the bag with the *VMI* case. Even though the findings in *VMI* were not all directly on the specific issues that would be heard by Judge Houck, Faulkner could not have had a worse set of Findings of Fact, which were never appealed, than those which were filed in the VMI trial. VMI also won at trial because they picked the right judge on a declaratory action and moved the case away from Alexandria, where it should have been, to more friendly turf in Roanoke.

VMI I was the only existing case from the Fourth Circuit which the district court in Charleston had for guidance. As Judge Houck noted in his order of July 22, 1994, admitting Faulkner to The Citadel, *VMI I* concluded that

> single-gender education, and VMI's program in particular, is justified by a legitimate and relevant institutional mission which favors neither sex; the introduction of women at VMI will materially alter the very program in which women seek to participate; and the Commonwealth of Virginia, despite its announced policy of diversity, has failed to articulate an important policy that substantially supports offering the unique benefits of a VMI-type of education to men and not to women.

In *VMI II* the Fourth Circuit found the parallel military program for women at MBC constitutionally acceptable. Thus, by January 1995, with the MBC program already accepted by the Fourth Circuit, The Citadel did not even try to set up a parallel program that was acceptable to the district court in South Carolina. They thought they had it made.

Yet, how could a parallel program ever have been created in the first place? *VMI I* on October 5, 1992, was a unanimous decision of 3–0, but *VMI II* on

January 26, 1995, after The Citadel case was well under way, contained a dissent by Judge J. Dickson Phillips which led on April 28, 1995, to another dissent by Judge Diana Gribbon Motz when the court refused to hear the case *en banc*. Judges Russell, Widener, Niemeyer, and Hamilton voted to let the case stand as it was decided by Judges Niemeyer, Hamilton, and Widener. Chief Judge Ervin and Judges Hall and Wilkins voted to hear the case *en banc*, and Judge Motz's separate dissent was joined by Judges Murnaghan and Michael.

The dissenting judges announced, in effect, that they had had enough of boys dreaming. Judge Motz wrote about VMI and MBC, "The proposed alternative program offers no remotely similar, let alone 'substantively comparable,' experience."

It followed that The Citadel and Converse were no more "substantively comparable" than VMI and MBC. The Citadel Board of Visitors should have admitted women on October 5, 1992, at the time of *VMI I*, and certainly by the time of *VMI II*. Instead, they waited for Justice Ginsburg to pick up on the language of Judges Phillips and Motz and write a United States Supreme Court decision that admitted women in VMI on June 26, 1996. But it was not until two days after the Supreme Court decision in *VMI* that The Citadel finally realized that they had to obey Judge Houck's order of August 5, 1994, and implement his order of July 22, 1994. And they did so without admitting it, instead admitting women under the ruse of a "voluntary" decision to do so.

Also on March 1, 1994, the day VMI released its remedy at MBC, Faulkner's attorneys met with Judge Houck in reference to summary judgment motions and the remedy trial set for May. Given the parameters already set by the Supreme Court in *Hogan* and the Fourth Circuit in *VMI I*, Judge Houck gave instructions for a bifurcated trial to be limited to two issues, justification and remedy.

First, how are facts in The Citadel case different from the facts that led to a Fourth Circuit finding that VMI violated the Fourteenth Amendment with its all-male admissions policy? Or, put another way, how is South Carolina different from Virginia when it comes to an existing state policy that supports substantially equal opportunities for women who seek a military college education? This the litigants and court called the issue of "justification" or the articulation of a policy in which South Carolina can justify the all-male admissions policy at The Citadel by articulating an important state policy or purpose that substantially supports the unique benefits of a Citadel-type education to men and not to women. Not since Martin Luther in the sixteenth century had the word "justification" been used in so religious a context.

Secondly, if South Carolina is not different from Virginia and is therefore bound by the law that controls VMI, how were they going to remedy the constitutional deficiency? What kind of parallel program for women in South Carolina exists—would be created—and where? Or would they have to admit women in the existing Corps of Cadets at The Citadel?

The issue of liability would thus be held in abeyance pending a final resolution in VMI or any further litigation in The Citadel case until after *VMI* was over. In other words, the issue of liability was already in the hands of the Supreme Court, put there by VMI, and litigants in South Carolina would just have to wait and see the results. For the present, the trial would go forward on the likelihood that The Citadel would, under the *VMI* ruling as it currently stood, also be found liable in the Fourth Circuit for a violation of the Fourteenth Amendment. The court hoped to try to save time and money under the principle of judicial economy. Even so, for trial at a later date, if necessary, Faulkner's attorneys preserved the issue of the value of single-sex, male-only education on which VMI prevailed before Judge Kiser and in the Fourth Circuit.

The Citadel, of course, wanted to try the issue of the value of male-only education at The Citadel before Judge Houck. Dawes wrote a letter on February 28, 1994, to ask the court to reconsider its decision following a conference call to require The Citadel to submit a remedial plan within the next few weeks. On March 8 each side argued over bifurcating the trial.

The court ruled against The Citadel and ordered a proposed remedy to be filed by April 1, 1994. Trial would begin May 16. Essential to the defendants' case was their effort to get the court in Charleston to see that the Fourth Circuit found a violation in the Commonwealth of Virginia, not in VMI itself: the violation found by the Fourth Circuit lay not in the exclusion of women from VMI, but rather in the Commonwealth's failure "to justify the absence of a comparable opportunity for women," as Dawes put it in a letter to the Judge on March 11, 1994. Again, the effort for The Citadel was to find a constitutional deficiency in women not having a parallel program. For Faulkner, the constitutional violation was simply that women were not allowed into The Citadel.

But in fact, if the Mary Baldwin parallel program had been ruled constitutional by the Supreme Court in June 1996, there would have been little chance of Faulkner's succeeding in making a distinction between VMI and The Citadel in order to return to a trial on liability, just as there was little chance of The Citadel's making a distinction between Mary Baldwin and Converse once the Supreme Court ruled the way it did. Faulkner never had a trial on liability and never got the chance to build a record from the ground up that showed that there was no value in male-only education at The Citadel. Yet it was within that issue that all the allegations and denials regarding hazing, male bonding, and the like were found. It was in Roanoke, not Charleston, where the more sensational issue of the value of single-sex education was tried and lost by DOJ.

The trial in Charleston, even with a real live girl, was left with the less sexy issues of justification and remedy.

As early as March 1993, more than a year prior to trial, more than 60 witnesses had been deposed in nearly 8000 pages of transcripts. Most were taken under the *Johnson* case before it was consolidated for discovery purposes with *Faulkner*.

Fact is that The Citadel knew that both of the issues set for trial were losers. South Carolina had no existing state policy of single-sex education in spite of the Concurrent Resolution passed by the General Assembly a year earlier, and the SCIL program at Converse was a joke.

Bobby Hood, writing for the state in a letter on March 22, 1994, allowed that The Citadel need not even offer "an all-female military-type institution to women." The Citadel would take a new tact in negotiating the waters around *VMI*. "Demand" led the way. Unlike Virginia, The Citadel argued, South Carolina has constitutional justifications for not having a women's Citadel. There was never any demand for one, and the state has too few educational resources to build one, Hood said. The Citadel's program was, nonetheless, "substantially similar to VMI's program," and not unique.

The Citadel never offered a study or report that assessed the demand among women for a Citadel education. There was no look at demand for a non-existing program, but only reliance on tradition and stereotypes. And, as the court again observed, The Citadel had not one case of legal precedent to support its central position.

Since demand was such a hot issue for The Citadel, I wrote a letter to Dawes on March 14, 1994, in which I complained that Wally West refused to give Shannon application forms for admission. Two young women had written directly to Shannon to ask her to get application forms from the director of admissions after one of the young women had earlier been denied an application form. During the first days of litigation, she had gone to The Citadel table during a College Fair in Greenville and been told that she could not have an application form because The Citadel was for men only.

"We are concerned," I wrote to Dawes, "that the position The Citadel is now taking with regard to providing application forms to women is further calculated to support its argument that there is no demand among women for admission to the Corps of Cadets."

West reportedly told Shannon to tell the young women to write him, and he alone would provide application forms to them.

In preparation for the trial in May, The Citadel submitted its list of 50 fact and expert witnesses on March 9, 1994, and supplemented it on April 15. The Citadel's pretrial Proposed Findings of Fact and Conclusions of Law were 165 pages long. DOJ's were 111 pages, and Faulkner's were somewhere in the middle.

While it appeared that The Citadel had one strike against it as it headed into trial during the spring of 1994—the Fourth Circuit, after all, had reversed Judge Kiser to find a Fourteenth Amendment violation—the court had also ruled that VMI still had three ways to remedy the violation. In reality, then, The Citadel was happy with the prospect of remaining all-male. The Citadel had only to come up with enough money to get Converse to set up a parallel program. Since his son was a cadet at VMI, Justice Thomas was going to recuse himself. A 4–4 split in the Supreme Court would permit the constitutionality of a parallel program to stand.

The Citadel thought that any South Carolina women's college would serve as the hostess of a parallel program if enough seed money and muscle were used to plant it. Even if Judge Houck were to rule that the parallel program at Converse was unconstitutional, Fourth Circuit precedent in *VMI* still would no doubt allow the State of South Carolina to create a parallel program at Converse in order to allow The Citadel to remain all-male.

A month and a half before trial, on March 30, 1994, The Citadel released its ten-page survey commissioned by the University of South Carolina Survey Research Laboratory to "determine the public's view" on the issue of women in The Citadel. The survey was intended to bolster the General Assembly's Legislative Committee report that appeared on January 11, 1994, and let the court know that the "public policy" among people in South Carolina was to leave The Citadel alone. It also was intended to off-set The Citadel faculty survey which indicated a preference to admit women into the Corps of Cadets. They surveyed 813 people over age 18. Sixty-two percent opposed women to be admitted to the Corps, and 38% were in favor of it. Yet, "the stark racial differences in opinion on this issue" were that 71% of whites were in favor of keeping The Citadel all male, but 62% of blacks were in favor of admitting women.

Using the three options given by the Fourth Circuit, the survey next claimed that 42% of the public thought The Citadel should go private in order to stay all-male, 29% thought women should be admitted to the Corps, and 26% voted to set up a parallel program. But, again, more blacks than whites voted in favor of admitting women to the Corps, 49% to 22%, and more women than men were in favor of women being allowed to join the Corps, 35% to 23%. More women than men, 47% to 39%, wanted The Citadel to go private to keep it all male.

The survey did not ask the question, "Is The Citadel public or private?" but it did report that three-quarters of those surveyed did not know how much state money went to private colleges and universities. It also was clear from the survey that if you were white and rich, you were more likely to have heard of the place.

The trial was procedurally uneventful, although the outcome itself was far from ordained for either supplicant. Much hung in the balance as some 28 witnesses took the stand, first for The Citadel for four days—Monday, May 16, through Thursday, May 19—then for Faulkner for five days—Friday, May 20, through Thursday, May 26. The court heard one more day of arguments on the 27th, then final closing arguments on June 16. From a fact-finder's point of view, the testimony was inordinately heavy on the side of expert testimony. The expert witnesses in fact were often dull, yet the issues at trial were not easily given to factual testimony. Justification and remedy, after all, are not as sexy as the value of single-sex education.

Since the court started with the remedy phase, The Citadel had the burden to prove that the SCIL program was constitutional. First up was Cadet Norman Paul Doucet, the top-ranked cadet who happened to be African American and, as The Citadel put it, a cadet who at one time had left The Citadel only to return and find himself in a celebrated position in the middle of a lawsuit. Doucet was conscripted to rebut the testimony of the plaintiff's witness Ron Vergnolle. After Val's and Mike Maurer's cross examination of Doucet, a parade of Citadel expert witnesses followed: Professor Elizabeth Fox-Genovese from Emory, Charleston attorney Ruth Williams Cupp, an alumna of Winthrop, Major General Eston Marchant of the South Carolina National Guard, former governors James B. Edwards and John C. West, BOV chairman Francis Palmer Mood, State Representative Paula Harper Bethea, Attorney Fernando Xavier Starks, General Robert E. Wagner, executive assistant to the president of Norfolk State University, President Peter Tislove Mitchell, president of Columbia College, Vice-President Thomas Rob McDaniel, the interim president of Converse, and Robert C. Gallager, the chairman—not the director—of the South Carolina Commission of Higher Education. None carried the day. Mitchell was not even a favorable witness for The Citadel.

By the end of the first week there was still time for the plaintiff to present a couple of her witnesses, Vergnolle first. Sara Mandelbaum did the direct examination on the first witness. Everyone listened closely. The defense team did not cross examine. On the following Monday, apart from Lieutenant General Watts who was called by the plaintiffs, Val and plaintiff's counsel began to call to the stand a line of experts and fact witnesses only now and then. Clifton Forbes Conrad, Professor of Higher Educational the University of Wisconsin, followed Vergnolle, then Bill Broaddus for The Citadel called their chief expert, Arizona Professor Richard C. Richardson, out of order, with the court's permission, before Val resumed the plaintiff's case with her direct examination of Watts. Then Wallace West from the Admissions Office, former Winthrop president Charles Vail, and Michael Scott Kimmel, Associate Professor of Sociology at SUNY, Stony Brook. Direct examination was conducted by Ms. Carstarphen from Shearman & Sterling, an attorney who must have spent only hours in Charleston. Michelle Fine, Professor of Social Psychology at CUNY, was another expert found by Sara to help establish the trial record. Then Marilyn Joan Haring, dean of the School of Education at Purdue, then Conrad, recalled by Sandy Beber, then my old telephone acquaintance from 1992, Alexander Astin from UCLA, and finally, the last expert, Patricia Barbara Campbell, director of a educational research firm in Massachusetts. Mary Warren, Vanessa Beaver, and Tom Swift, attorneys from Shearman, were fully involved in one way or another. Henry took his fair share of witnesses. Throughout, Val did a masterful job of handling most of the direct as Hood, Patterson, Boland, and Whittemore adroitly did most of the cross examination.

But the trial was not over yet. The plaintiff put up three women at the end of her case, Faulkner herself and two other young women who testified that they too would like to be able to join the Corps of Cadets. Whether bogus or not, the issue of demand had to be addressed. Pamela Jordan and Katherine Lee Brown testified briefly, in the middle of objections and discussions among the bar and bench.

The Citadel's defense strategy on demand was of course not a legal strategy at all, but simply a plain "sez-you" denial that women wanted to go to The Citadel. In cross-examination the dullness of expert witnesses' testimony gave way to The Citadel's failed effort to man-handle Faulkner, with a side swipe at local counsel:

> Hood: Ms. Faulkner, you want to go to a coed military college, The Citadel, and that's what you want in this case, period, correct?
> Faulkner: That's why I filed the lawsuit.
> Hood: You will not be happy going to a single-sex, all-female military college in South Carolina?
> Faulkner: I don't want a single-gender education....
> Hood: You know of two people in the courtroom that are friends of yours that want to go to The Citadel, as well?
> Faulkner: They're acquaintances. They are not friends as of yet.
> Hood: I see. And you have been looking, your attorney has been looking for how many years for someone else that would be interested in applying to The Citadel?
> Ms. Vojdik: Objection.
> The Court: Objection sustained, unless you can show she was with him when he was looking, otherwise it would be hearsay.
> Hood: What about you, have you been trying to find people to apply to The Citadel yourself, women?
> Faulkner: I haven't made a search or anything, no, sir.
> Hood: Have you made an effort to get and encourage others to apply?

Faulkner: Only when they ask me.
(Trial transcript, May 26, 1994, Vol. 18, pp. 33–34)

After the Trial

I did not fully realize until the death of Bill Kennedy, with whom I shared office space at 23 Broad Street, how much I counted on friends throughout the case. Kennedy was a Navy veteran who allowed free use of his copier "for the cause." A much closer friendship, one that continues today, was with United States marshal Fred Stroble. Stroble's first assignments in his illustrious career included protection of Judge W. Arthur Garrity in Boston and Judge Frank M. Johnson, Jr., in Montgomery. One of the surest anchors in town was Frank McCann, an attorney who donated and later loaned us money after he saw Melinda crying as she left the Broad Street post office with a stack of overdue bills in her hand. When we finally won, I forgot to repay him—but was gently reminded to do so. I relied on two bankers in town, one a Citadel alumnus. My own loan to an out-of-town friend after I won attorney fees was never repaid. Whenever I bumped into Arthur Howe at the post office, he always asked how the case was going. He sent me an encouraging letter that set the case in relief as only an established and well-respected Charleston attorney could. A Sewanee friend gave us a house on Martha's Vineyard for a summer vacation in 1994, and another Sewanee friend, David Norton, gave us free use of his house at Folly Beach for a week. Once a stranger stopped at an intersection downtown to yell out the window that he was proud of what we were doing. Yet in spite of support, I often shared Melinda's doubts about the wisdom of offending so many people and not providing for the family.

Within days after the trial and even before final arguments, The Citadel filed a motion for a mistrial on June 10, 1994, arguing that the court was unfair to exclude The Citadel's evidence on the value of single-sex education on the issue of justification while, as it alleged, admitting such evidence from Faulkner on the issue of remedy.

In denying The Citadel's motion, the court upheld its ruling that The Citadel's thin proposed remedy was inadequate, since the court found no evidence of justification for a state policy of single-sex education. Yet, after trial, The Citadel would not give up and, instead, moved on June 30, 1994, to reopen the record to admit the testimony of House Speaker Robert Sheheen. The resolution was a legitimate record of the legislature, Hood argued, and urged the Court to admit the Speaker's affidavit to "help the Court to understand the significance of the Concurrent Resolution being included in Amendment 169 to H. 3610," an appropriations bill. It needed to be in the record on appeal so Judges Hamilton, Niemeyer, and Widener could consider it, Hood said.

The Citadel also wanted to open the record to admit the affidavits of members of the Legislative Study Committee to Study Single Gender Educational Opportunities for Women. The six affiants swore incredulously to either of two statements, which I characterized as two types. Type A: "At no time was the purpose of mission of this Committee in any way related to The Citadel or an effort to provide a defense to The Citadel in the above-captioned case" (members Delleny, Fulmer, Bethea, and Lloyd); or, Type B: "The Committee did not consider its mission to be the development of a recommendation simply to provide an additional defense to the State of South Carolina and The Citadel in the above-captioned case" (members Mood and Starkes).

Things were getting curious and curiouser, especially in light of Virginia Crocker Lloyd's affidavit. Crocker Lloyd was clearly one of those in the House who had been misled by The Citadel's argument to think that the Concurrent Resolution was not a bill just to keep The Citadel all male. After all, Representative Crocker Lloyd ten years earlier, on January 10, 1984, had sponsored a bill of her own to admit women into The Citadel, H. 3254. That bill was shot down by The Citadel network before Sarah Manly sponsored her doomed bill in 1991. But The Citadel, in its June 10, 1994, motion for the Court to take judicial notice of the bills, used both failures to show, without a hint of good humor or irony, "that there has existed a policy of supporting single-gender education in South Carolina prior to the initiation of this lawsuit and prior to the VMI opinion."

Along with The Citadel's motion to reopen the record, the state filed copies of the Journal of the House of Representative for March 14, 1991, the day Manly addressed the House which subsequently voted to table her Amendment No. 169 to prohibit discrimination on the basis of sex in South Carolina public colleges and universities. According to The Citadel's way of thinking, Manly's statement on why her bill was voted down was simply evidence that a state policy was in existence. Manly said in the Journal:

> By far the greatest number of you have agreed with the rational premise that tax money should not be used to support discrimination, but then an interesting branching occurred. The quick response "of course I'll support that" would seem the logical next step after agreement with the premise, but I have been saddened by the few who have said "but I am afraid that I cannot vote with you." And then I've heard some really troubling admissions; "I work with a Citadel graduate,"

or "I have to go back to alumni meetings," or, lately, "I'm getting a lot of pressure from one or two or a half dozen people back home."

Yet another issue of "confusion and prejudice which precluded a fair and impartial ruling on the issues," as The Citadel argued in its motion for a mistrial, was particularly interesting: "The Court's statements regarding sexual harassment incidents are without any evidentiary basis and constitute a wholesale acceptance of the arguments of counsel at an earlier hearing."

The Citadel was again referring to reports of harassment made to the court during the first hearing after Faulkner filed her lawsuit.

"The Court has heard no *evidence*," Cooke wrote, "to support such claims and the criticism of The Citadel's institutional response suggests a prejudgment of The Citadel which is unwarranted and prejudicial on all issues" (emphasis in text). The Citadel wanted to maintain a clean stage on which it could later present the value of single-sex education, if it ever got the chance.

A few days later, on June 15, 1994, The Citadel filed a motion to strike the court's statements concerning sexual harassment on grounds that the court had heard no evidence on the issue. Furthermore, since for lack of evidence no sexual harassment ever occurred, according to The Citadel, The Citadel moved to rescind the court's order requiring The Citadel even to submit a plan to address claims of sexual harassment of Faulkner. The Citadel was bothering to come to court only to build a record on appeal for Judges Hamilton, Widener, and Niemeyer. And like the staff of *The Ragadier*, The Citadel was losing patience. It began to try the case in the media instead.

By June 25, 1994, nearly three months after the first proposed remedial plan, The Citadel filed its first submission of a post-trial remedial plan, a.k.a. contingency plan. Like the April 1 plan, this plan also was conspicuous for its brevity. The Citadel, one could tell from looking at the few pages submitted to the court, again had no intention of establishing a real remedial plan. It was not at all a systematic, coherent plan that would present in detail to the court what it planned to do in order to assimilate women into the Corps if such were a final order.

Since Faulkner was *per se* obviously quite sick for simply wanting to join the Corps of Cadets, The Citadel proposed to house her in the Infirmary along with other patients. As The Citadel saw it, not putting her in the barracks with the other cadets "will provide both Ms. Faulkner *and Cadets* a necessary measure of privacy and will minimize the opportunities for cross-sexual confrontations which may be perceived as sexual harassment" (emphasis in text). In fact, the barracks were off limits to SRF except for company formations and activities. No lock on the door. The door had to remain open at all time. At least three people must be present in the room at all times. One could only conclude from the June 25 plan that the remedial rules were more for the benefit of the male cadets than they were for Faulkner.

"Upon admission to the Corps of Cadets, Ms. Faulkner will receive the traditional 'knob' haircut," the proposed plan continued. But Shannon, for obvious reasons, was not to benefit from the much-celebrated bonding exercise of the "shirt tuck." For her uniform, "special tailoring will be made available to Ms. Faulkner as necessary."

Ten years later, the first female cadet to remain for a limited time in the Corps while pregnant—and who chose not to quit or take a leave of absence as she grew more and more pregnant—confided to me that in the initial months of her pregnancy she was denied proper maternity clothing by The Citadel.

Faulkner I, July 22, 1994: The Big Order

On July 22, 1994, Chief Judge C. Weston Houck issued his 42-page Findings of Fact, Conclusions of Law, and Order following the two-week trial in May and June. He ordered Shannon to be admitted into the Corps of Cadets in August, 1994, under conditions to be decided upon, and in the absence of an implemented remedial plan that adequately addressed its constitutional violation within a year, and to admit any other women who might apply for the school year beginning in August 1995. This case was referred to as *Faulkner I* and would be stayed by the Fourth Circuit until the Fourth Circuit issued *Faulkner II* on April 13, 1995, some three months after issuing its Order in *VMI II* on January 26, 1995.

Faulkner I was followed as quickly as possible by a hearing on August 1, 1994, on the practical issues of implementing Faulkner's admission, issues such as security to be provided by U.S. marshals, whether to have a lock on her door and a special escort, the length of her hair, and so forth. The district court issued a written order on August 5, 1994, embodying its rulings made from the bench on August 1.

The court found that one of The Citadel's chief cases, *Personnel Administrator of Massachusetts v. Feeney*, 442 U.S. 256 (1979), which requires the plaintiff to prove a discriminatory purpose as well as a discriminatory effect, was inapposite since *Feeney* involved a classification that was not facially discriminatory and *Faulkner* involved one that is. The court cited a long history of cases aligned against The Citadel: *Reed v. Reed*, 404 U.S. 71 (1971), *Craig v. Boren*, 429 U.S. 190 (1976), *Califano v. Goldfarb*, 430 U.S. 199 (1976), as well as *Hogan*.

Remedy was inexorably connected to the fact that, unlike *VMI*, the *Faulkner* case contained a real live plaintiff seeking admission only to The Citadel. Yet,

The Citadel's defense of a lack of demand was inadequate to defend against women recognized by the court who were similarly situated and who may be seeking admission in August 1995. Four such women did indeed step forward in 1996. In short, Faulkner alone was the driving force who made it possible for Mace, Lovetinska, Messer, and Mentavlos to enter the Corps in 1996. There is nothing "voluntary" in the court's language in *Faulkner I*, affirmed by the Fourth Circuit:

> At the very beginning of this order it was noted that the primary difference in this case and the one instituted by the United States against Virginia Military Institute is that we have a real, live plaintiff here who wants to be admitted to the Corps of Cadets whereas in *VMI* the Department of Justice was the only plaintiff. Because of that difference, the matter of remedy must be looked at from the standpoint of Faulkner and also from the standpoint of other women similarly situated who may seek to join the Corps of Cadets at some future date.... [A] plan that conforms with the Equal Protection Clause of the Fourteenth Amendment must be formulated, adopted, and implemented for the 1995–1996 school year. Otherwise, the court will have no alternative but to require the defendant to admit qualified women who apply in the future to the Corps of Cadets.

Dawes Cooke, Bobby Hood, John Douglas from the U.S. Attorney's Office in Charleston, and I were called to Judge Houck's chambers on Friday morning July 22, 1994, to be given the order by hand. After that, the Clerk of Court Judy McDowell, who was always mindful of the role of local counsel, would release it to the press. Was Faulkner in or out?

Susan Brown, the Judge's administrative assistant, passed out copies of the order. The attorneys took their copies and began to read. Brown later said to me, "I have never seen an attorney begin reading an order from the first page as you did. They always turn to the back first to read the conclusion and order."

I immediately called Shannon and Val with the good news and later in the day presented our side of the case on CBS Evening News, which was televised from the library at 23 Broad Street.

Citing major cases such as *Hogan* and *Missouri ex rel. Gaines v. Canada*, 305 U.S. 337 (1938) and the less well-know case of *McCabe v. Atchinson, T. & S.F. Ry. Co.*, 235 U.S. 151 (1914), among many others, the court's findings repudiated The Citadel's central argument that a lack of demand for an all-female college existed in South Carolina, even though the defense did not take into account the fact that Winthrop was not ever a military college as Clemson was: "There is no indication that single-sex education as such played any role in

Clemson becoming coeducational," and "The primary reason behind Winthrop University going coeducational was the desire of its Board of Trustees to better serve the educational needs of the citizens of South Carolina.... In fact, there is no indication that the need or value of single-sex education for women was even considered in the decision-making process."

The order also made short work of the true significance of the Concurrent Resolution: "The conclusion is inescapable that the Concurrent Resolution was prompted by this litigation and would not have been passed had it not been for this litigation and the Fourth Circuit's decision in *VMI*."

The order took notice of the recalcitrance of The Citadel in not producing a remedial plan. The Citadel "does not select any one remedy or even prioritize those suggested" by the Fourth Circuit in *VMI I*. Further delay by The Citadel was not an option: "From the day Judge Kiser filed his opinion to the day judgment became final, the *VMI* case consumed 21 days less than two years. It is a foregone conclusion that this case of Faulkner's will be pursued through every avenue of appeal available. If that process takes as much time as it did in *VMI*, a final judgment in this case will be rendered on June 29, 1996," the last day on which opinions would be published for that term of court. Judge Houck missed The Citadel's compliance by one day. Responding to the Supreme Court's final judgment in *VMI* on June 26, 1996, and in compliance with the district court and appellate court orders of 1994 and 1995, the Board of Visitors admitted women to the Corps of Cadets on June 28, 1996.

Finally, in noting that The Citadel had not followed the Fourth Circuit's three options suggested in *VMI I* nearly 21 months previously, on October 5, 1992, Judge Houck in *Faulkner I* made an assessment of the contentious litigation:

> To place the matter of remedy in proper perspective, the manner in which the case has been conducted should also be taken into consideration. The Citadel has made no secret of the fact that its primary goal in this case is to keep Faulkner out of the Corps of Cadets, and the State of South Carolina appears ready to give its support to that cause. Not once has a defendant done anything to indicate that it is sincerely concerned to any extent whatsoever about Faulkner's constitutional rights. The most revealing fact of all, however, is that the defendants have continued to defend this case at a cost of millions of dollars to the taxpayers of South Carolina when they do not have a single case to offer in support of their position that a lack of demand for single-sex education on the part of women justifies its providing such an education only for men.

The district court's order in *Faulkner I* on July 22, 1994, to admit Shannon to the Corps of Cadets in August 1994, and to pursue a remedial plan by the school year 1995–96, was stayed by the Fourth Circuit a few days later. With Judges Niemeyer and Hamilton voting to grant the stay, Judge K. K. Hall wrote in his dissent, "Justice delayed is justice denied." He continued as the only reliable voice in the Fourth Circuit:

> South Carolina stubbornly maintains that a system, proven by the nation's service academies to work, is unworkable. Meanwhile, as Faulkner views the drill field from afar, the state continues to deny its daughters the education that is rightfully theirs under the Constitution of the United States.
>
> That such a situation could be tolerated in the nineteenth century is not surprising, but we are about to embark on the twenty-first. In *Bradwell v. State*, the Supreme Court upheld a state's denial of a perfectly qualified woman's application to practice law. Mr. Justice Bradley, concurring, observed, "The natural timidity and delicacy which belongs to the female sex evidently unfits it for many of the occupations of civil life." Like many, if not most, prejudices about "the nature" of things, experience has put Mr. Justice Bradley's observation to rout. Someday, the spectacle of our handwriting over this case, whilst Ms. Faulkner's opportunity for a public education fritters away, will seem every bit as quaint as *Bradwell*.

A remedial "plan to plan" was subsequently filed by The Citadel on October 4, 1994, and was for its insufficient attention to detail again incapable of review by the court.

"Die Shannon"

Within days after the district court ordered Shannon to be admitted to the Corps, I got a call from one of the TV stations in town saying that there was a sign posted by The Citadel side of the Ashley River Bridge going out of the peninsula which read, "Die Shannon. Co. O."

I made an emergency call to Chief Greenberg. Greenberg and a sergeant got on the line.

"You got to do something about that sign, Chief," I said. "I just went over there after Nina Roffey at Channel 2 called me, and I took a picture of it. It says, 'Die Shannon. Co. O.' No kidding. Plain as day and in broad daylight. Nina says it's been up for a while."

The Chief asked what else I knew about the sign and stated that he had not seen any report of it from his officers or on TV. I was the first to complain.

"It looks like it was on one of Irv Condon's old portable signs used in advertising for his race for office," I said. "That's Charlie's brother, you know, but I know that Irv is certainly not the kind of guy to have anything to do with this mess. It looks like somebody, probably a cadet, just used the same letters Irv had for his sign and mixed them up to read, 'Die Shannon. Co. O.' I think I know the names of cadets who might know something about it."

Ann Fonda at Channel 2 called on July 27 to tell me that Channel 2 made a call to Dawes to tell him that a certain named member of H Company had left a message on the Channel 2 voice mail the night before to tell them that he was the one who put up the "Die Shannon" sign. Fonda then told me that Dawes, citing the confidentiality afforded students under FERPA, the Family Educational Rights and Privacy Act, or the Buckley Amendment, refused to tell them if there was even a cadet with that name in H Company at The Citadel. Fonda promised to investigate further.

Or it could have been another cadet who lived in Rifle Ridge Apartments in Spartanburg. He was the one Shannon thought trashed her car the night before she drove down to Charleston to enroll in January. They could have been in another company. The suspicion was that whoever put up the sign made it just a click or two off their own company to get the other guys in trouble. Part of bonding and The Citadel family. But it was too dangerous just to take such trouble-making to be a sign of plain mischief and not investigate to see if there was real evidence of a serious threat of life.

"So the guys are alumni, not cadets?" the Chief asked.

"No," I said, "one of them may have dropped out and now he's back in the Corps. That's about all I know. All hearsay, of course, but it's all I got now. You've got to act on this right away. Can you try to find out who put that sign up?"

"How can I protect her from something that hasn't happened?" the Chief asked. He was right about the law. Police are not compelled to do anything until a crime is committed.

"What?"

"How can I arrest anybody? Nobody has done anything to hurt her yet."

"Yet?" I yelled. "What do you mean by 'yet?' That's the whole point. If you don't do something and find out who it was—don't talk to the people over there—how can you say that you are protecting a citizen from harm?"

The Chief yelled back to tell me that without further evidence he could not under the law make an arrest of someone who just may or may not have threatened someone else's life.

"Well, you can at least look at the situation, can't you? You guys take these kinds of safety precautions every day, don't you? Even a threat of harm is an assault. And if they don't lie to you, you just have to call over there right now and find out who put up that sign. They can find out in ten minutes, if they don't know already. I can guarantee you that nothing like this at The Citadel goes on without somebody knowing about it within minutes. They just won't tell you if you are an outsider. But you got to make them tell you on this one. The old way of protecting one another over there has got to come to an end on this one, Chief."

"I'll get my deputy to call you if anything happens, but right now from what you have told me, we are not going to do anything," the Chief said and hung up.

I then prepared a subpoena for the manager at Channel 2 which aired a report on the death threat, and reviewed the TV broadcast which showed the sign before somebody drove by and saw it. At 9:00 a.m. I called Irv Condon's wife and asked her to take it down. It had been there for about twelve hours.

I wondered if it all was much ado about nothing. I knew that the police could use their resources as they saw fit. I let Agent Ed Rosenlieb and the FBI know what little I knew. It seemed like another one of those lose-lose situations The Citadel put the plaintiff in again. The more one looked into the facts, the more publicity generated by the media and the more nuts shaken from the tree.

Finally, it didn't matter much anyway. Whether I was right or wrong about a serious threat to life, the investigative authorities continued to dodge all questions. The Citadel Public Safety Office told me they were "working on it." The Citadel continued to protect the cadets the same way it always does, through FERPA. Someone said that the guy who put up the sign didn't even live in Charleston, and he was not a cadet.

The only thing I knew for sure was that nothing was ever done to find out who was responsible for the sign, and that alone spoke volumes about how safe Shannon Faulkner was in America's Friendliest City.

Bumper Stickers

While a struggle was going on among the attorneys responding to court orders, what caught the public's attention was The Citadel's intent, as the Charleston bumper stickers read, to "Shave Shannon's Head." I did not do much investigation into the source of these bumper stickers. The point was that The Citadel could have stopped them in their tracks if they had wanted to and as they did immediately after four women entered in 1996. The "NO [drawing of a woman]!" sticker which was displayed by the two cadets driving east on Interstate Highway 20 between Augusta and Columbia in November 2010, is, however, evidence of lingering resentment and hostility toward the presence of women admitted 15 years previously.

In August 1994, I drove around the peninsula to take random notice of the extent of hostility that many residents south of Broad Street were advertising toward Faulkner. My diary recorded the honor roll of the SOBs, as those living in that area of Charleston were sometimes called. A socially acceptable war cry of the oppressed and privileged majority, "Save the Males" was taken from bumper stickers in the *VMI* case to serve as the favorite here as well. "Shave Shannon's Head" could be seen well into the next millennium.[4]

A year later, on August 12, 1995, a woman prominent in The Citadel family was at Lesesne Gate, the main gate leading into The Citadel, passing out "Save the Males" bumper stickers to all the incoming cars of parents who were delivering their sons to begin their freshman year with a woman at The Citadel.

After Faulkner quit in 1995, some of the more expressive cars parked in front of the federal courthouse and in front of the grand homes on the battery joined the fun. One Isuzu Trooper was especially dressed out in full military battle gear for its owner: "Save the Males," "Males-1 Whale-0," "The Citadel Class of 1968," "The College of Charleston," "Episcopal," "Ducks Unlimited," "The Brigadier Club," "Ashley Hall," South Carolina tag JBR 440. Episcopal High School is a private Episcopal Church school in Alexandria, Virginia. Ashley Hall in Charleston is a private school for girls.

I did not have a camera to take a picture of the best fun-mobile, an old sedan usually parked on Broad Street, but I did get a few more. On a Ford Taurus with a peninsula "B" parking permit, "Males-1 Whale-0," "The Brigadier Club," "Clemson," "Delta, Delta, Delta," "Ashley Hall, Where Girls are Champions." And a very proud little red sportster and a big Lincoln with "Citadel Alumni" stickers along with "Shave Shannon's Head." Finally, a record of all the saints was too exhausting to compile, and I gave up.

Surprisingly enough, however, a shopkeeper at a shop downtown admitted that 25% of the profits of each T-shirt reading "1952 Bulldogs and One Bitch" went to the "Citadel legal defense fund." A friend bought the $15 T-shirt for me. The copyrighted artistic display on the front showed a group of male bulldogs in grey uniforms standing behind one female bulldog in a red dress with lipstick. This was the T-shirt that Shannon and Katherine "Kat" Brown autographed during the trial after their testimonies. On May 3, 1995, a woman delivered an embroidered version of The Citadel's "Bitch" T-shirt to me to give to Shannon. Dawes would later argue in court that Shannon's acceptance of it indicated that she really suffered no injury from being called ugly names, and even liked it.

Private contractors tapped into the passions of Citadel supporters. Renforte, Ltd., PO Box 666, in Mount Pleasant ran an ad in the paper, "We understand how you feel about Shannon Faulkner. Now you can wear your feelings on your chest." A Renforte T-shirt that showed a distraught Faulkner with "Go Girl" underneath cost $12 with shipping and handling.

I called a cadet in the barracks on Folly Beach to order a "Save the Male" decal, but my order was never filled.

The Citadel easily won the bumper sticker battle. The material was too good for the good ole boys not to score easy points with such odds in their favor. Yet the gals did try to make a decent showing. The retaliatory "I Support Shannon" bumper stickers were initially printed with small print at the bottom, "A.C.L.U. Women's Rights Division, New York, N.Y." Shannon was upset that the ACLU had tacked on its advertisement, and I dutifully trimmed off their ads from the few I had.

Yet even without the ACLU ad in fine print at the bottom, the "I Support Shannon" bumper sticker was still provocative enough around Charleston. With my three- and five-year-old sons in the back seat, and Ms. Rebecca White, their elderly baby-sitter, sitting in front, my car drew fire from two of the Holy City's bravest Citadel supporters as both cars stopped at a red light near MUSC. I was on my way to take Ms. White home after a long day.

The windows were down. "Look at that, would you?" the one riding shotgun muttered to the driver. "'I Support Shannon' on that asshole's car." Laughter. Their voices were loud enough to be heard by the little boys and Ms. White sitting just a few feet from their car window. "I wouldn't support that pig for shit," the citizen continued. More laughter as the car scratched off at the lightest shade of green.

I looked over at Ms. White who acted as if nothing happened. I looked back at the boys and saw that neither child was harmed and in fact were both strapped in their car seats.

"Rebecca, I suppose you're used to this kind of thing, but I apologize for all that." She was a black woman, born and reared in nearby McClellanville 75 years ago, and she was used to life in Charleston. But it was maddening for me to see that kind of trick pulled by deputized thugs in the presence of an elderly lady and two small children.

Hair

Riverdale, NY 10471
August 8, 1994
"You are a Wacko. Get the Hair ou[t] of your eyes and wake up! You are wrong and don't belong."

[Signed letter to Faulkner]

The summer of 1994 was the hair summer for Shannon just as the summer of 1995 was to be the weight summer. She either had too much hair or too much weight for The Citadel. Both fights, of course, took up way more energy than they were worth and wasted a lot of taxpayers' money. For the plaintiff, the hair war was a metaphor for not opening the gates to institutional and systematic brutality against Faulkner, and for the defendants it was a ruse to try to force the judge as well as the plaintiffs into untenable positions. For Faulkner herself, she implied that she could not care less, but she wanted to be the one to cut her own hair, if she were required to cut it at all.

The Whitmire Report on March 16, 1968, a report authorized by The Citadel, included no comment about the knob haircut simply because the issue did not exist for freshmen in those days. The next internal examination conducted by The Citadel twelve years later, the Mood Report on March 11, 1980, was critical of "instant traditions" and recognized that "All first classmen were against indignities, such as 'baldy' haircuts." It recommended action to "eliminate the requirement for a 'baldy' haircut for fourth classmen and substitute therefore a neat military haircut." By the time of the Lane Report another twelve years later on January 4, 1992, nothing had been done to curb instant traditions such as baldy or knob haircuts, sweat parties, excessive pushups, excessive rules designed to interfere with eating and sleeping, and the like.

Major General Grimsley, in his deposition, stated that shaving freshmen's heads "was not done when I was a cadet a long time ago," but now that it was one of the instant traditions, said, "I think it's expected, and I think that, in my judgment, I think it should continue."

Former Superintendent of the Naval Academy and witness for Faulkner, Admiral Lawrence acknowledged that during the Plebe Summer at Annapolis, only the male Naval midshipmen shaved their heads, then returned to a "conventional haircut conforming to Navy standards."

Same with the Air Force and even the Marines. On August 10, 1994, Jackie Hughes, an Air Force veteran from Mount Pleasant, South Carolina, sent me a copy of Army Regulation 670-1: "Female. Hair will be neatly groomed. Hair will not fall over the eyebrows or extend below the bottom edge of the collar." The difference was clear with regard to what men and women in the military did and what the boys at The Citadel did to manage their hair. On August 9, 1994, I called Major Barry Marks at the University of South Carolina AFROTC in reference to the haircut of Air Force women and got the regulations sent to me in a reply memo. Women were told not to shave their heads.

A chemistry professor at the College of Charleston offered to shave her own hair if Shannon wanted her to, just as a show of solidarity. It would be a good thing, the professor thought, for lots of women simply to shave their own hair to show The Citadel that their victim had the support of other women. A few days later, on August 8, another woman called with the same offer.

There was never any doubt to Val, Sandy, and me that shaving Shannon's hair was punitive, and should be resisted mightily. In the middle of one hearing, I raced home to get a picture from the WWII *U.S. Camera* photography book which included a French woman who had collaborated with the Nazis. Her head had been shaved after the liberation of Paris, and she was being taunted by female members of the Resistance.

The Citadel administration continued to insist that shaving Shannon's head was simply an act consistent with what was traditionally done to all male knobs. It was not to humiliate her, they said. It was simple goose-and-gander equal protection of the law.

On August 8, 1994, Val filed a memorandum in support of Sandy Beber's earlier motion on August 4 to reconsider the Court's August 1 permission for The Citadel to shave off Shannon's hair.

"Shaving Ms. Faulkner's Head Violates Her Rights Under the Fifth and Fourteenth Amendments," the argument went, and "Shaving Ms. Faulkner's Head Perpetuates The Citadel's Unlawful Discrimination Against Women."

The judge refused to convert his courtroom into a barber shop or beauty parlor and ruled that he would not order The Citadel either to shave or not to shave Shannon's hair. They could do anything along that line they wanted to.

The national press loved the story. I argued Shannon's case over the phone with Chief Gates, radio station KFI moderator Mark Germain, and sundry callers on a radio program on June 29, 1994, in Los Angeles. A professional hair dresser called to offer advice and no doubt draw publicity to his business.

The Citadel was really trying to set up the judge to show the Fourth Circuit and the world how victimized they were. The Citadel's capacity to whine was boundless, and they were inventive and resourceful in finding new avenues for complaint. They possibly never intended to give the public a picture of a woman treated the same as a man, since that would show that women could take it — and that "it" was never much at The Citadel since even women could take it — and at the same time, show how trivial the stuff of male bonding traditions really were. One of my first comments published by *The State* when the veteran women filed their complaint was, "The courts will have to decide whether male bonding or nurturing the male ethos is an important government interest worth taxpayers' support."[5]

On the other hand, the leadership at The Citadel simply wanted to do anything to humiliate this teenage girl. Armand Derfner, Terry Rickson, and Allan Holmes, who urged plaintiff's counsel to let The Citadel have at it, were probably right after all. Shannon should have insisted on having her hair shaved off. She herself could have played the role of victim, and at the same time it would have been a cheap and painless route toward achieving The Citadel notion of honor, unless of course they laughed at her nonetheless, and that very likely would have happened.

Sometime shortly after the Court's oral order at the August 1, 1994, hearing, The Citadel allowed itself to win the fight and decided not to shave Faulkner's hair in the same style of knob cut they gave the fourth class men.

Two years later, Lovetinska, Mentavlos, and Messer were reported to have complained precisely because The Citadel administration did not allow them to shave their heads. They got into trouble for hacking off their hair to try to fit in. The interim president was quoted in the local press in defense of the women's hair cut policy: "We worked very hard on our policy on female haircuts.... And we did not shave their heads because we thought it was humiliation."[6]

August 1, 1994, Order

At the hearing on August 1, the judge denied plaintiff's motion for the appointment of a special committee on sexual harassment, her motion for special escort services to and from the library, a lock on her door, and a request for a women's style military haircut. Apart from those issues, the August 1 hearing for the most part approved the conditions of Shannon's admission and rendered the July 22 order final. Those conditions would be reiterated and slightly expanded on four days later.

It was at the conference in the judge's chambers immediately after the August 1, 1994, hearing that The Citadel vice president again showed the intensity with which he detested Faulkner and her attorneys. It had not been fully measured even on registration day in January. The judge had directed all counsel from both sides to meet alone to sort out their differences following his August 1 order. The vice president came along and sat in one of the chairs lining the wall of the spacious conference room.

The issue I raised, which was not addressed in the order, was the presence of the "Save the Male" bumper stickers on cadets' cars parked on campus and the continued assault on Faulkner in *The Brigadier*. Dawes said that The Citadel could not legally require the cadets to take the bumper stickers off their cars.

"It's their privately owned vehicles. We can't tell them what stickers they can have on them," Dawes said. "These are free speech issues," he said.

"What if they had 'Die Shannon' on their bumper stickers instead of on a sign on a bridge?" I asked. "Apparently that's a joke no one at The Citadel takes seriously. Or what if the cadets had obscenities plastered on their windshields, the kinds of things they yell out the windows? I don't think *The Ragadier* does anything more than continue to fan the antifeminist fire either. Dawes, you can put an end to this hostile environment which the board and administration has helped to create if you want to."

"These are all free speech issues," the vice president interrupted. He was red in the face, as he usually was whenever he confronted SRF's attorneys. I knew that what was at stake behind the free speech issue was hazing, a primary weapon to get rid of Faulkner. I knew that The Citadel could lose in court, but it could win on campus and in the barracks by hazing Faulkner out of the Corps once she got in.

I could not run the risk of talking directly to the vice president. The judge had created a congenial atmosphere in which men of conflicting opinions could discuss their differences. However, the judge himself was not present in the room. So I pitched my remarks to Dawes as much as to the vice president.

"*The Brigadier* needs to give it a rest," I said. "They don't go after anybody else the way they go after Shannon."

"They deal with me the same way they deal with your client," the vice president shot back. "They call me, "Twinkle, Twinkle, One Star Fool.'"

"It's not the same thing," I said, "and we all know it. They may have the right to say all those stupid things about Shannon, but we're asking the cadets to be civil toward her. She can take the rough treatment if it's not personal hostility directed at her as a woman and her alone. She's by herself as the only woman. All that stuff leads to violence. That's the concern here. No violence could ever arise out of a senior administrator being called a one-star fool. That doesn't create a hostile atmosphere that breads violence. You're not treating her the same way you treat other cadets. No male cadet has ever had to put up with what you guys are dishing out on Faulkner. We're not even asking you to get them to stop giving her the silent treatment—we're not asking for the impossible. It's just not safe, as things stand now, the kind of hostile atmosphere those bumper stickers continue to create, and what *The Brigadier* continues to do to her. That's the kind of behavior that disturbs the peace, and it's unsafe for one woman victim in the midst of 2000 volatile young men and the hostile administrators running this case. We still have this funny feeling that you guys could put a quick end to cadets ridiculing her in the paper if you really wanted to."

Dawes told me, "You know it is impossible for the administration and the board to tell the cadets to like your client. They wouldn't listen to a word. That's ridiculous."

"I'm saying that the biggest reason the cadets don't like our client is that your clients, the board and administration, don't like her. Left alone, these young men, 95% of whom have grown up in coeducation environments in high school, would learn to accept women in the Corps. It's an old man's battle your clients are fighting, and it's not right to let the young cadets think that what they are doing will please their elders. Wait until they get out of The Citadel and meet the real world."

"Well, I can tell you this," the vice president said, furious by now from listening to my dribble, "the First Amendment is alive and well at The Citadel, and I am going to keep it that way." This was the vice president's favorite line when he lectured Shannon for her one complaint about the Scarlet Pimpernel and when he later took the stand on cross examination with Val.

When Nancy Mace, the Commandant's daughter, was admitted into the Corps in 1996, not only did the administration and *The Brigadier* resist attacking her and the three other women who entered, but also no new bumper stickers appeared. Truly vicious statements of disapproval eventually petered out. If a problem appeared, someone in the administration agreed to take care of it before it happened. Cadets continued to grumble, of course, and take their usual anonymous cheap shots, but such was bolstered more by the administration's public expression of preference for the old days than by an official creation of a classic hostile environment.

The Physical Examiners

On July 27, 1994, Dawes sent me a medical examination form for Shannon to have filled out by a physician. On August 9 he wrote to say that according to a letter dated the previous day by The Citadel physician, Faulkner's medical application was still incomplete. It lacked information on Shannon's knee, her body fat measurements, and a few other things such as notice of her blood type. Shannon also needed a brief examination by The Citadel head nurse. But The Citadel physician's letter also stated that according to the Manual of Standards of Medical Fitness (Army Regulations 40-501), the maximum weight for Shannon's height was 156 pounds. She was 39 pounds overweight.

Regardless of this early notice of what would be a big fight the following summer, in the summer of 1994 The Citadel paid attention to Faulkner's physical condition more in reference to her suspected bum knee than to her weight. In 1994 either The Citadel had not then felt desperate enough to make the argument that Faulkner was not eligible to enter the Corps because she was as overweight as some males who had been admitted—having routinely and arbitrarily waived the weight requirements every year for males of comparable height and weight—or they simply didn't think of such a losing argument. Or perhaps the BOV saw Faulkner's weight as an issue early on, but decided that nothing was going to get in the way of a winning season in football that requires the annual admission of a lot of fat bulldogs on the defensive line.

The first conspicuous challenge to Faulkner's physical condition was, therefore, with regard to the knee she banged up playing volleyball and softball for Wrenn High School in Easley. When the highly regarded Citadel physician made an issue of it in his August 8, 1994, letter and recommended a referral to an orthopedic specialist, I called the MUSC orthopedics department to find a surgeon who was not a Citadel graduate. I had rented the carriage house of the Citadel physician while teaching at The Citadel, and I myself had been a former patient of the orthopedic physician to whom The Citadel planned to send Faulkner for consultation. The referred physician was a loyal alumnus and also an excellent physician. Nonetheless, I directed my client elsewhere and set up an appointment for Faulkner with another well-respected orthopedic surgeon.

Dr. R. H. Gross, Department of Orthopedic Surgery at MUSC, examined Faulkner's knee on August 11, 1994, and in a letter which was totally without any hint of bias toward either party found her fit to endure the rigors of the fourth class system. "Fit for 4th class at The Citadel," it read.

Even so, the president's assistant accompanied Dawes for the deposition of The Citadel physician held after the hearing from 6:00–7:17 p.m. on August 10, 1994. Val asked him to leave because he was not a party and had no privilege to hear physical and medical facts about SRF. He left and heard nothing. The condition of a patient's health is a confidential matter between the physician, the patient, and her lawyer.

Nonetheless, in less than a year later, details of Faulkner's physical condition were made a part of the public domain by the public relations director at The Citadel, Terry Leedom. On August 4, 1995, plaintiff filed a motion to hold Terry Leedom in contempt of court. In its memorandum in support, with 14 attached exhibits gleaned from major news services all over the country, plaintiffs alleged that Leedom talked freely to the press about Faulkner's medical record in spite of the judge's orders sealing the record, as contained in both the physician's deposition and, later, the closed hearing in court, in which SRF's physical and medical condition was discussed.

Meanwhile, in a letter a couple of days later, on July 29, 1994, an angry alumnus from San Diego wrote "An Open Letter to Judge C. Weston Houck" in which he denounced Faulkner "who launched her effort with a lie." The letter became part of the record after Judge Houck introduced it in court. The alumnus identified himself as a member of the Class of 1943 and "District Director, District No. 18 (all states west of the Mississippi)." He wrote on official letterhead stationery of the Association of Citadel Men.

August 5, 1994, Judgment and Order

About this time, The Citadel had finally and reluctantly followed up on the production of the 45 letters from women produced prior to trial, and produced an additional 150 letters from young women who had made inquires about joining the Corps of Cadets.

One dated January 13, 1994, was sent from Buffalo on behalf of a couple's newly born baby daughters: "Kindly forward applications for admission to The Citadel for our daughters, Emily and Page, for entry to the classes of 2008 and 2011. Presumably by the time the millennium has passed, you will have entered the Twentieth Century, and we want to be sure that our children will be able to enjoy the advantages that a Citadel education affords, whatever they are." A copy was sent to Chief Justice Rehnquist.

A young woman named Rossella wrote from the ancient city of Pavia, the capital of the Lombard kings before the conquest of Charlemagne and site of Italy's most famous medieval university. The year before Columbus landed in the new world, a young and beautiful Beatrice d'Este, "donna beata," the future Duchess of Milan and half sister of Lucrezia Borgia, married Lodovico Sforza, Duke of Bari, in the Castello of Pavia. At her court and the court of Beatrice's sister Isabella d'Este, the very height and splendor of the Italian renaissance was realized in the lives of artists, poets, knights, and scholars—Ariosto and Bramante, Pistoja and Visconti, Galeazzo and Niccolo. Would "la prima donna del mondo," as Jacopo Caviceo described Isabella, whose portrait by Leonardo da Vinci hangs in the Louvre and for whom Michelangelo sculpted his lost Cupid, have been good enough to get in The Citadel? Even an imaginative letter of recommendation from the fairest and most perfect flower of womanhood which blossomed under the sunny skies of Virgil's land would not have done it for the modern-day Rossella.

Another letter from Oakland, California, birthplace of the Black Panthers, read, "Hi, my name is Candi. I was wondering if you can send me some information or brochure about The Citadel." Daisy and Roberta wrote from the Marshall Islands, and Selena from Nassau. The father of Tatiana wrote from Khartoum in the Sudan. But most of the inquiries were from young women from South Carolina. Many had prior military experience through JROTC. Others showed an interest in the military as a career. Several showed interest in engineering, premed, and pre-law. One drew a smiley face on her letter. It must have been a nightmare for anyone in The Citadel administration to read them, if they ever did.

Beside the name of "Robin" from Hannover, Germany, someone in The Citadel admissions office had placed a question mark to indicate another "Shannon" problem: was it a male or female? They were ready this time.

A letter from Chesapeake, Virginia, dated June 1, 1994, harkened back to the Wite-Out days of Faulkner's own application:

> I have received a copy of The Citadel catalog together with an admissions application form. Thank you. The form states that The Citadel "is a single gender" school. Notwithstanding same, item number 6 requires that applicants identify their gender, to wit: "male/female." Before submitting a completed application, the undersigned woman requests information concerning the current policy that controls the admission of women to The Citadel.

One letter from South Carolina, added, "Shannon inspired me." On a letter dated September 7, 1994, there was no return address on the letter itself, and The Citadel did not transfer the return address from the envelope when it produced the letter to the plaintiff. The plaintiff in that case could not trace the sender and get back in touch with her. From Gabriel, it read, "I love your college, and I would like to be a part of your tradition."

In its August 9, 1994, order, the court explained why it denied "extra protection" for Faulkner at the August 1 hearing:

> First, the court believes that The Citadel will exercise proper good faith in bringing Faulkner into the Corps of Cadets and, if given time, take all actions reasonably warranted to guarantee that she will be treated properly and not harmed or sexually harassed; and second, there is no evidence before the court to convince it that Faulkner, upon entry into the Corps, is in real danger of being sexually harassed or physically harmed.

Yet, in spite of its nominal wish for the best, the court was not in fact naive about what could happen to Faulkner once she got in the barracks:

> Until the passage of time draws a clearer picture of the situation, and how all players involved therein will act, prudence dictates that the court take steps of its own to insure the proper execution of its order. The court has, therefore, requested the United States Marshals Service to assist it by closely monitoring Faulkner's entry into the Corps of Cadets....
>
> So that the duties imposed on the Marshals Service herein can be properly carried out, the defendants are hereby required to give the Marshals Service complete access to the grounds and buildings at The Citadel at such time as they desire, to take no action to interfere with or impede to any extent whatsoever the activities of the Marshals Service undertaken in furtherance of this order and to fully cooperate with and assist said Service in those efforts.

Specifically, under the judge's directives, as implemented by Israel Brookes, this meant teams of two marshals, male and female, around the clock, 24 hours a day for the first two weeks. Brookes, like Fred Stroble, had seen it all. Everyone had great confidence in all of the marshals, including marshals Mitman and Zimmerman.

The Citadel's letter to the plaintiff on August 9, 1994, set out what Faulkner could and could not do as a cadet for the 1994–95 school year. She would be housed in the Infirmary. The area behind the Infirmary would be given additional lighting. The door at the end of the hall would be locked and fitted with panic hardware. The door leading from the ward outside would be locked also. The judge also wanted Faulkner to keep a horn or whistle in her room.

Thus, by sending in United States marshals to The Citadel, Judge Houck presumably knew that he could not order Faulkner into the Corps and leave her completely to The Citadel's care alone. Both in 1994 and in 1995 a reasonable effort was first made to protect her with the force of federal law—not with United States troops from the 101st Airborne, as at Central High School in Little Rock, but with United States marshals stationed at the headquarters of campus police.

The last time The Citadel had been occupied by federal troops were the years following the Civil War when the place was shut down and used as a federal garrison. What had historically been organized to put down slave revolts was later suppressed by Union troops. Now both plaintiff and defendants had images in their minds of social unrest during the era of racial integration. Some remembered the famous Norman Rockwell portrait that showed the little girl Ruby Bridges Hall being escorted into the William Frantz Elementary School in New Orleans. A requirement for intervention with federal force spoke volumes about the character of The Citadel. The Citadel was going to do everything it could to keep United States marshals off the campus.

This was a nightmare to The Citadel. It was a return to the 1960s and the need for a federal protective presence similar to that which was necessary in a culture of racial integration at the University of Alabama and Ole Miss. The Citadel's facade of law and order, of claims of patriotism, of service to the land of the free—all the superficial platitudes and hypocrisy of The Citadel were laid bare in the photographs of the United States marshals standing by Faulkner on campus to protect her from angry onlookers.

Like The Citadel's eviction of veterans, the court's ordering of United States marshals on campus was a severe blow to the prestige of The Citadel. Without federal marshals, however, The Citadel would have been lawless. The only thing worse for everybody would have been for her to be seriously injured or killed, shot accidentally from a window in one of the barracks the way Berra

Lee Byrd had been. The court knew that anything could happen when Faulkner enrolled into The Citadel. The court's careful preparations mirrored what was done at Clemson by the plaintiffs' witness, President R. C. Edwards, who told the story of how men and women of reason prepared for the arrival of women undergraduates in 1955 and its first black student Harvey Gantt in 1963. But Clemson was able to do both without intervention of the federal government. And at Clemson a "Welcome Coeds" sign was put up the day women entered.

Significantly, the two motions made by The Citadel which were pending after Faulkner quit in August 1995, were its renewed motions to isolate Faulkner by keeping her in I Company, not Band Company, and to remove the United States marshals from The Citadel campus.

The biggest welcome of all, literally, came to the coeds from the Clemson students (male). Sunday night the triangle was bare when faculty and staff went to bed. Monday morning it bore huge letters cut from cardboard cartons spelling out "Welcome coeds!" Mrs. Bolton and Miss Margaret Snyder are shown behind the signs with Mr. Bolton representing the men.

Clemson's male students welcome women to campus in January 1955, by displaying on Bowman Field huge cardboard letters spelling out "Welcome Coeds." Used with permission, Clemson University Department of Publications and Promotion and *Anderson Independent Mail,* January 1955.

Also, for the second time and without the defendants' attorneys present, pursuant to the directions of the court, Faulkner's attorneys met alone with the marshals in the Judge's chambers on August 10, 1994, regarding the safety of Faulkner.

In denying The Citadel's motion for a stay pending appeal to the Fourth Circuit of the district court's July 22 order, the district court order of August 5 took up the crux of The Citadel's case as it leaned on *VMI*:

> In its order of July 22, 1994, this court adopted a conclusion of the Fourth Circuit in *VMI* to the effect that "the introduction of women at VMI will materially alter the very program in which women seek to partake." The defendants rely on that finding and their assertion that the material alteration to The Citadel's program will be irreversible to support their argument that The Citadel will suffer irreparable damage if their motion to stay is not granted.
>
> There is nothing in the record that convinces this court that the admission of Faulkner to the Corps of Cadets under the circumstances settled in a hearing held on August 1, 1994, will cause The Citadel irreversible damage as the defendants claim.
>
> The fact that this court's oath of office requires it to "support and defend the Constitution of the United States against all enemies, foreign and domestic" emphasizes the preeminent role the founders of this country intended the Constitution of the United States to play in the lives of the citizens of this country. With due deference to the State of South Carolina, therefore, this court is forced to conclude that the interests of the public are best served by denying the motion the defendants make for a stay pending appeal.

The oath of office that he quoted was the same as that of Judge Waties Waring, a signed copy of which Fred Stroble showed me several years later.

On August 5, 1994, and again three days later, Bill Broaddus at McGuire Woods filed The Citadel's emergency motion and supplemental memorandum to stay Judge Houck's order pending appeal to the Fourth Circuit. This time, before the Fourth Circuit, The Citadel's motions were successful.

Thus, the excitement and apprehension that began on July 22 and August 5 with the district court's orders allowing Faulkner to enter the Corps ended on August 15, the day Faulkner was to enter the Corps, when the Fourth Circuit stayed the order. Faulkner would have to wait for full appellate review before she would be able to enter the Corps. Entrance into the Corps would now have to be in August 1995, at the earliest, or not at all.

ROTC Options

Even though Faulkner was not admitted to the Corps in 1994, she was still allowed to continue as a day student. To that extent an effort was made to get her into ROTC the same way the female MUSC student had been allowed to take ROTC at The Citadel.

Again, it all had to do with the military nature of the Citadel. Regardless of its limited military nature, The Citadel fought and won the battle to keep Faulkner out of an ROTC uniform.

I learned from Colonel Betta at The Citadel on September 30, 1994, that there were three programs for ROTC students. Most cadets just take ROTC classes because they have to in order to be graduated. They have no obligation to try to take a commission and serve their country after graduation, and the vast majority—a number that fluctuates between 60% and 80%—of the cadets spring for the option not to serve. But these students are not required to wear ROTC uniforms. The uniforms they wear during ROTC class are the uniforms of Citadel cadets. A second group is made up of juniors and seniors who, after two years of ROTC, commit themselves and sign contracts with a military branch. They have to wear U.S. military uniforms and are required to serve after graduation. A third group, which are also required to wear U.S. military uniforms, are students on scholarships who also have a military obligation after graduation, if indeed they are ultimately commissioned. This group enjoys the financial advantages of ROTC reserved for men at The Citadel. From Lieutenant Simmons, the JAG officer at ROTC Headquarters, I also got the impression on October 17, 1994, that Shannon was eligible for non-commitment ROTC the first two years, but that wearing a uniform was a local decision to be made by The Citadel.

The goal for Shannon was to participate in ROTC and to wear a U.S. military uniform while she was an ROTC student, just like thousands of other ROTC students do throughout America.

Wrangling continued with The Citadel as both sides filed "sez-you" pleadings in early September 1994, to ask the court to decide if Faulkner could join ROTC at The Citadel. It was one of The Citadel's most disingenuous of innumerable such moments throughout the case. The plaintiff alleged that "The Citadel's refusal to permit Ms. Faulkner to attend academic classes offered by its Department of Military Science violates the preliminary injunction." The Citadel responded that Faulkner

> did not attempt to register for any classes in the Departments of Military Science, Naval Science, or Aerospace Studies. In her brief, Ms.

Faulkner fails to distinguish between registering for courses in those military departments and participating in the Reserve Officers' Training Corps (ROTC) programs. Selection for participation in ROTC programs is made by the various branches of the Armed Services, not by The Citadel. In order for Ms. Faulkner to enroll in an ROTC program, she must apply to the branch of the Armed Services which sponsors the ROTC program that she desires. The Citadel has not prohibited any such application.

Therefore, because Faulkner made application to join ROTC through The Citadel and not through a particular branch of service, Faulkner was not allowed by The Citadel to join ROTC. The Citadel had earlier strongly objected to an ABC TV documentary to be aired on *Turning Point*, the one which MUSC employee Scott Regan monitored. A year in the making, it was directed by Elena Mannes and was to be moderated by Diane Sawyer, Peter Jennings, and Barbara Walters. The documentary was to include a view of Shannon reading a Pat Conroy book on the parade ground of Summerall Field. The Citadel was extremely adamant about not permitting the airing of any image of SRF on Summerall Field, much less one of her marching in an ROTC uniform. That image would remind the viewers that she was an American citizen on public property.

Sexual Harassment Handbook

On August 26, 1994, I reviewed a strange new document which Faulkner had brought home after she picked it up from the floor of one of her classrooms in Capers Hall. It had not been produced in response to plaintiff's request for production of documents. It just appeared, the way an earlier chiseled "Regulations" for Faulkner had appeared the day she got into the day program seven months earlier.

"Dawes," I asked over the phone, "what is this pamphlet that Faulkner found on the floor of one of her classrooms the other day? It's called *The Citadel Sexual Harassment Prevention: A Procedural Guide*. It's about eleven pages long. Shannon accidentally found it lying on the floor of one of her classrooms today."

Cooke replied that he would look into it and get right back to me. From what I could tell, *A Procedural Guide* was published by The Citadel but never distributed to Faulkner or the Court or to her lawyers or even to the press. *A Procedural Guide* on sexual discrimination was a list of procedures unapproved by the Court—and that was the point. The Citadel quietly issued in the midst of litigation what it on its own accord wanted to declare as sufficient rules to cover sexual discrimination—a conception The Citadel never really recognized as even existing on campus. As it first appeared in The Citadel's remedial plan of June 25, 1994, and became even clearer the following year, The Citadel felt it already had a sufficient sex discrimination policy in existing policies. "The Citadel Race Relations Advisory Committee" was simply re-designated as "The Citadel Human Affairs Committee" to deal with both race and sex discrimination. Apparently The Citadel had finally come to recognize a relation between racial and sex discrimination. "Cadets are expected to conduct themselves with dignity" was sufficient admonition, and what loose ends left hanging were covered by the Blue Book: "Cadets are forbidden to call from the windows of barracks."

For The Citadel there was no need to protect Faulkner with specific sex-discrimination rules, since The Citadel had perfectly good rules already in place against any kind of discrimination.

In a letter to Cooke on September 9, 1994, I wrote,

> It is also our contention that The Citadel remains in violation of its policies prohibiting sexual harassment. Specifically, we contend that The Citadel's very active support and encouragement since the 8/1/94 hearing of the publication of T-shirts, bumper stickers, and buttons, and its enrichment therefrom, is contrary to the observations of the Court and the sworn testimony offered by The Citadel during the 8/1/94 hearing, and, notably, in direct violation of both The Citadel's 1992 Blue Book Regulations, 114, a. (8), and The Citadel's *Sexual Harassment Prevention: A Practical Guide*, particularly those paragraphs that address a hostile environment and sexual harassment in form. Please let me know if the above-cited guide to sexual harassment is indeed a Citadel publication....
>
> Therefore, we would ask The Citadel, aggressively and in good faith, immediately to take whatever measures necessary to end the on-going sexual harassment of Shannon Faulkner.

The cadets had name tags on their uniforms, of course, but they would invariably cover them up to hide their identity when in direct confrontation with SRF.

The Citadel made its usual denial of any harassment of Faulkner but used the issue as leverage to get the plaintiffs to produce a letter from Steve Bates, director of the South Carolina ACLU, to Shannon. Furthermore, it wanted responses to its January 20, 1994, interrogatories and request of production of documents. Those were sent to me immediately following my letter of concern about my family's safety after Shannon moved in with my family.

In the meanwhile, The Citadel again wanted to "take a short deposition of Ms. Faulkner, limited to the issue of her allegations regarding sexual harassment." Another squeeze on Faulkner to try to make her rat on her classmates and poison the well, knowing all along that she could not expect to survive in the Corps as a rat. No cadet could. The Honor Code existed only to weed out individual enemies of particular cadets, not to enforce ethical rules of conduct throughout the Corps.

It was not until the remedial phase—after the June 16, 1995, version of its *Sexual Harassment Prevention: A Practical Guide*, and well after Faulkner left— that DOJ and Bernice Sandler hammered out a sexual discrimination policy with The Citadel. Sandler, with whom I had been in touch since June 29, 1992, helped draft Title IX of the Education Amendments of 1972.

Veterans Redux: Richmond 1994

During all the fuss over Faulkner's knee, her length of hair, and her desire to join the yearbook staff and band, the women veterans' appeal was moving forward on the Fourth Circuit calendar. On November 10, 1992, The Citadel renewed its September 4, 1992, motion to dismiss the veterans' case for mootness. The district court granted the motion by oral order about a year later on September 20, 1993. The veterans filed an appeal in a couple of days, and after another year, by September 29, 1994, arguments were set to be heard on the veterans' appeal of the district court's order to moot the veterans' case. By then, two years after joining the veterans' case, Shearman & Sterling had wiped its hands of the case and was content to spend its resources on SRF and let the ACLU and me waste our time on the veterans' appeal to the Fourth Circuit. DOJ had never sought to intervene in the veterans' case at all, so only Sara Mandelbaum for the ACLU and I pressed on with the appeal for Patricia, Liz, and Angela.

In Richmond, I sat at the table with Sara Mandelbaum and another ACLU attorney, Chris Hansen, whom I had not previously met. Sara explained that Hansen had dropped by Richmond for the hearing en route from a hearing in Illinois on *Brown v. Board of Education*. To my amazement, Hansen told me that some issues in *Brown* were still alive. Three Topeka attorneys, with the help of the ACLU, filed *Brown III* in 1978 to reopen issues still not fully resolved in *Brown I and II* in 1954 and 1955. *Brown III* would not be dismissed until 1998.

Sara and I had to divide up our time to make the plaintiffs' arguments to the three-panel court. None of the women veterans had come up from Charleston for the hearing.

Dawes began the oral arguments before the three-man panel. Sara spoke for about 20 minutes, returned to the appellants' table, and sat down. Then I began:

> May it please the court. The Citadel has succeeded in the lower court in making this veterans' case into a Corps of Cadets case. It did so in order to argue that there is a proper constitutional discrimination between military and civilian students in this case. In fact, there is instead unconstitutional discrimination between male and female students at The Citadel, or more precisely between male cadets and female veterans.
>
> Because the Board of Visitors had knowledge that the night program is inferior to the day program, it threw veterans out of the day program because of, not in spite of, the adverse effects on women. The board knowingly chose to adversely impact women veterans. The facts indicate a discriminatory purpose as the male cadets are given a superior daytime program and the female veterans have to take an inferior nighttime program.

It was a losing argument. Just as The Citadel used *Palmer* in the district court to moot the VDP, it now was successfully using both *Palmer* and *Feeney* on appeal, with *Los Angeles v. Davis*, 42 F.3d 1385 (4th Cir. 1994), as the *coup de grâce*. I was hammering away on two tangential cases. The Supreme Court in *Palmer* and *Feeney* ruled that for the government to be in violation of equal protection it must be because of a discriminatory purpose or intent, not in spite of a disproportional effect. The court found that there was no unconstitutional discrimination between men and women in the facts of *Feeney*, only permissible discrimination between men and women veterans. The impossible burden on the women veterans as plaintiffs was to prove that the Personnel Administrator impermissibly preferred male veterans over female veterans for state jobs.

"If The Citadel ran the Jackson, Mississippi, swimming pools in *Palmer*," I argued, "as it runs its day program in Patricia Johnson's case, the pools are now closed to male and female veterans, but it still remains filled with male-only cadets." The women veterans, I said, did not want admission into the Corps at The Citadel in order to wear the Ring as Shannon wants to do. The women veterans wanted only an education at The Citadel.

No one on the panel was listening, or so I thought. I droned on. "Our case is a case of discrimination between male and female students, not a case of discrimination between military and civilian students, or as The Citadel would have you believe, between students in the Corps, whom they call 'military' students, and veteran students, whom they call 'civilian' students."

At last, a question from the bench: "Mr. Black," Judge Niemeyer asked, "do you think this court can require South Carolina to establish a parallel program for women, substantively comparable to The Citadel, in order to satisfy the Fourteenth Amendment?"

I was completely knocked back by the question. It did not address the veterans' case at all, but I had kicked the hornets' nest. Judge Niemeyer was obviously picking up on my comparative remark about The Citadel's admissions policy in the Corps of Cadets. His question referred to the court's recent order permitting VMI to remain all male if Virginia could set up a parallel program at Mary Baldwin College. The judge was impatient and seemed clearly irritated that I would have indirectly brought in issues that the court had ruled upon already in VMI and that were not now before the court, even if I thought they were. Of course, I thought VMI and The Citadel had made the issues in *Johnson* inseparable from those in *Faulkner* from the very first day of Pat Johnson's case. But I had seriously breached court decorum.

"Your honor," I said, "I personally do not think that under *Hogan* you can use state funds to set up a parallel program and send the women of South Carolina to a military program set up instantaneously at a private woman's college and allow only men to continue to go to The Citadel. I personally do not see how such a place could ever be equal to The Citadel, and so women could never benefit from the powerful network of Citadel alumni."

"So you don't think this court has the authority to make such a ruling in your case?" Niemeyer asked.

"I don't think it can," I answered. "Not as I personally read *Hogan*, but of course I know that this court has done just that in *VMI* and that The Citadel would claim that it is just like VMI on those issues."

Judge Hamilton then made an observation regarding jurisdiction no longer belonging to the district court, and Judge K. K. Hall made another regarding Bob Jones University's loss of federal funds in a previous case. I walked around to the end of the table and sat down. I saw from the corner of my eye that Sara had jumped up and taken the podium again for the few remaining seconds left. Dawes Cooke was patiently waiting his time for rebuttal.

"Of course this court can do anything it wants regarding the establishment of a parallel program in this case," Sara said to Judge Niemeyer.

Good gracious, I thought. What is she doing? We discussed this prior to coming here to argue, just in case any judge wanted to get directly into issues more related to Faulkner than to Johnson. In Richmond on the veterans' case we were to stay away from Faulkner, but stand our ground if her issues arose. I had gotten myself in a pickle by picking a fight that was not the main event.

"This court can set up a parallel program in our case of *Faulkner v. Jones* consistent with its ruling in *VMI*," Sara stated to Niemeyer.

"You know your colleague stated just the opposite, do you not?" Niemeyer asked Sara.

"Yes, sir, I am aware of that," Sara replied.

"Are you saying that Mr. Black misspoke?" Judge Niemeyer asked.

"Yes, sir," Sara said, "Mr. Black misspoke. Thank you, your honor," she said and sat down.

So much for the only time the remedial phase of Faulkner was argued in the Fourth Circuit. So much for local counsel.

Of course, Dawes was delighted to see the plaintiff's side in such disarray. It's an opposing lawyer's dream, and he allowed the moment plenty of his own time on the clock to let it soak in. He slowly took the podium. He got up and then proceeded thoroughly to confuse me on another subject: whether the Navy "honored" The Citadel all-male admissions policy by not permitting women veterans to apply for the Navy's educational ECP program. According to what I understood from Mr. Clyde Losey at the office of the Chief of Naval Education and Training (CNET) in Pensacola, a qualified Navy veteran simply lists the three colleges he or she wants to attend and if admitted, the Navy sends them there, male or female. It was just that no Navy women to date had ever applied to the Veterans Day Program at The Citadel. There were no women Marines in the VDP because the application process for VDP worked in just the opposite direction. It was my understanding from Mr. Greg Shields at Quantico that the veteran must first get admitted, then the Marines would send the vet to the VDP—and The Citadel would never send an application form to a woman vet.

But my conflict with Dawes' remarks was the least of my worries. My position on Faulkner's case had just been undermined, to say the least, by ACLU co-counsel in oral arguments in the Fourth Circuit. I called Armand from a pay phone immediately after the hearing to be sure I had not gone crazy and missed the main point of our case, that SRF wanted in The Citadel, period. And, of course, I later reported to Val.

In a short order, on December 2, 1994, the Fourth Circuit upheld the district court and ruled that the veterans' suit was moot, based on a current administrative decision of the BOV which plaintiffs argued was anything but permanent. The court used not *Feeney* or *Palmer*, but *Los Angeles v. Davis*:

> Once The Citadel terminated the veterans program entirely and permanently, the relief for admission to it could not be granted, and with-

out a program, the discrimination claimed to exist in the admissions policy of the program also ended.

Jumping forward to 2010 when the VDP was reopened to all veterans, as far as one can determine from on-line data referenced and documents produced through a Freedom of Information request in August, 2011, the Board of Visitors made no formal decision to extend the Cadet Veteran Program of June 14, 2008, to all veterans. Rather, that decision was left to the administration, pursuant to the April 21, 2007, motion passed by the BOV. Minutes of the Board between the summer of 2008 and the fall 2009 simply indicate that marketing strategies were discussed as a run up to the announcement on November 16, 2009, "expanding" the VDP.

After the hearing in Richmond before the Fourth Circuit on the women veterans' case, I became wary of the potentially conflicting issues the ACLU was forced to deal with in all its civil rights cases throughout the country. And ever since my discussion of the *Zentgraf* case with Nat Douglas at DOJ, I had been wary of a separate agenda by the Department of Justice. The Deputy Solicitor General, Paul Bender, called Val, Henry, and me to Washington nine months after the hearing in Richmond, on June 1, 1995, to be sure the fed's case and Faulkner's were going along in tandem as each sought a writ of *certiorari* to the Supreme Court.

SCIL Announced

The state had earlier announced, on January 20, 1994, that its plan to study single-gender education included Columbia and Converse. Now, in June, The Citadel and state brought the two colleges in on their plan to let each know what they were thinking of doing to either one or both of the private women's colleges.

A principal administrator at Converse, Tom McDaniel, had testified at trial that Converse had no interest in developing a military program or starting a Corps of Cadets with a barracks life-style befitting a holistic, adversative military-style program like the one set up at Mary Baldwin for VMI. But the college quickly changed its tune when it saw the money.

On October 5, 1994, The Citadel came out with its plan to establish the South Carolina Women's Leadership Institute or WLI. WLI was soon renamed SCIL or South Carolina Institute for Leaders. The South Carolina equivalent was set up to be as much as possible like the Virginia Women's Institute for Leadership (VWIL) at Mary Baldwin. The South Carolina Women's Leadership

Institute (WLI), The Citadel proudly announced, would be a woman's military component located at either Columbia College in the state capital or Converse College in Spartanburg—they were not quite sure which one would be the lucky bachelorette—and would serve as a remedy to its violation of the Fourteenth Amendment, the long-awaited parallel program to the all-male Corps of Cadets at The Citadel. The Citadel Public Relations Office announced The Citadel Development Foundation's proposal to make a gift of $5 million to support WLI, the pay-off and seed money to get it started. Money was on the table. Now the only question was which woman's college could be bought?

Defendants at the same time filed with the court a supplement to the proposed remedies that they had filed on April 1 and October 4, 1994. In it they had to go with what little they had and stated, "WLI will be an integral part of the publically funded South Carolina educational system, but will not be restricted to a single campus or educational institution. Rather, it will provide scholarships to young women to use at any of a number of different programs."

The Converse College student newspaper, *The Conversationalist*, objected, claiming on November 2 that the WLI was developed by Elizabeth Fox-Genovese "without the knowledge or consent of Converse College." Provost McDaniel stressed that Converse had already turned down The Citadel twice and described a Citadel-type program at Converse as "problematic" and "not in Converse's mission."

Converse had a $19 million endowment but, of course, like Columbia College, used no existing military adversative educational method. Known for its curricula in art and music, Converse instead encouraged students, for example, to play the dozen Steinway pianos on campus. If they wanted interaction with men in a classroom setting, Converse women headed to nearby Wofford College or Wofford men came to them.

On June 14, 1994, Columbia College told the Legislative Study Committee that it was at least open to discussion regarding a compact arrangement with The Citadel, but the reasons for not establishing South Carolina Institute for Leadership (SCIL) in Columbia were many. Columbia College, after all, required first year students to attend chapel. Citadel knobs had to go through hell. A Methodist Church college, Columbia College require students to fulfill a religion requirement before graduation. The Citadel was a religion in itself. The $13 million endowment at Columbia did not come near the $86 million at The Citadel.

On the same October day that The Citadel announced the formation of SCIL, the nominal successor to WLI, Peter Mitchell, president of Columbia College, sent me a faxed copy of his "official statement" to the press, his "Response to the Remedial Proposed by The Citadel." He said plainly,

Columbia College was not consulted nor have we participated in any way in the drafting of The Citadel plan. We received a copy today.

The remedial plan in its current wording outlines provisions for admissions standards, curriculum requirements, and creates a Director for WLI who "will oversee applications, programs, and placement as well as establish standards for participation."

These provisions could be read to suggest what Columbia College's admissions standards and curriculum requirements shall be. Any such implication would be wholly unacceptable to Columbia College.

Columbia College will continue to pursue its unique mission and build upon being rated the fourth best regional liberal arts college in the South.

This is perhaps the only instance of a college making a completely unilateral effort to take over or commandeer another college for whatever purpose. Converse and Columbia College must have felt like they were about to embark on the ultimate blind date. The Citadel just did not have time to ring them on the phone to give them a heads up, as it earlier did with the General Assembly in creating the Concurrent Resolution.

A Quiet Place

In the fall of 1994, a woman professor at The Citadel had offered Faulkner a safe harbor in her office between classes, a place to come to between classes, a place to sit for a while and share the little, and sometimes big, things on her mind. She offered her a refuge, some peace and quiet and escape from the deafening silent treatment and muttered hazing remarks and hissing Shannon got routinely in the hall. In one class they not only hissed whenever she spoke, but also moved to the other side of the room. A counselor who worked in The Citadel Counseling Center told me privately years later that she saw Shannon only one time and that was when she was sent to the Infirmary on the day Shannon quit.

The front page of *The Brigadier* on November 4, 1994, announced the contents of the Scarlet Pimpernel's editorial: "The Pimp exposes the Capers Hall Triune." It was superficially the usual complaint about SRF getting special attention, but the cadet newspaper also raised the specter of administrative wrath. The professor, like Von Mickel, had broken the code not to talk to Faulkner or help her in any way. Cadets led the assault:

A great question hath caused the PIMP much ponderous thought. If the PIMP wore a dress to MINOR LALLY'S class would the PIMP get special attention as well? How interesting it is to hear the cries of discrimination against DECATS [cadets] at the hands of LALLY-GAG. It doth not surprise me that ye doth bite the hand that feeds ye for ye art such a TEMPERMENTAL K-9. Which shall it be ma'am, GENDER LOYALTY or the unemployment line?

Cadets writing for the student newspaper had nothing to fear from an attack on a female faculty member who treated Faulkner with simple kindness. Interestingly enough, *The Brigadier* never attacked other female faculty members who complained to the administration about sexual harassment by cadets. The reason cadets did not respond with equal contempt in the student newspaper to allegations of sexual harassment was possibly because the cadets were not aware of such allegations, since all evidence of such acts was either lost or misplaced.

Miss Gourdin

Miss Virginia Gourdin of Tradd Street, Charleston, wrote me on November 23, 1994, and on August 24, 1995, she sent me a package of information on the history of civil rights for women in South Carolina politics. She hailed from Huguenot stock in Kingstree, South Carolina. Her recitation of ancient issues in the Charleston mode would lead any reader to conclude that South Carolina women were a whole lot better people than South Carolina men. "Some people just don't know how to act," as my mother would say. In the bad ole days, the Nineteenth Amendment did not compel men to allow women to vote in the private Democratic Party primary elections, which, in those days, was the only election that mattered. Only in the public general elections could women vote. But in 1958, when Gourdin was first elected to the House of Representatives, "the men finally relented and let white women vote in their private party primary," Gourdin wrote. There was no such thing as a GOP primary then. The exclusion of black women went without notice.

"A woman was elected to the S.C. Senate as early as 1932, I think," Gourdin recollected, "and she, like the rest of us until 1970, had to swear she was a qualified male citizen to take her seat." She continued:

> The men in the legislature refused to let through any bill to amend the S.C. Constitution to conform with the Nineteenth Amendment. I was told in 1959 and 1961 that it was no use for me even to try for that; so I went ahead and swore twice that I was a man, as did the two other women in the House. The 121 men were afraid that, if they challenged

our oaths we'd go to the U.S. Supreme Court which might make them delete all other discrimination against women in the state's laws.

A change like that would change the law for jurors from "qualified male citizens" to "qualified citizens" and the lawyers, especially the criminal lawyers, apparently hated this: they would roll their eyes and whisper, "That would make us change our entire presentation."

So I introduced a bill, about 1959, to allow women on state jury panels. Robert McNair, who sat near me in the House for four years, never let my jury bill out of the Judiciary Committee, of which he was chairman.

At some point after I "retired" in 1962, they finally let women serve on state juries, a concession probably provoked by the threat of some female criminal to take her case to the Supreme Court as she had been denied a "jury of her peers."

According to Ms. Gourdin, Jean Toal, Chief Justice of the South Carolina Supreme Court, acknowledged privately to Gourdin in the spring of 1995 that Gourdin's effort to get women on the jury in South Carolina probably was a key factor that led to her appointment to the Supreme Court.

On March 13, 1994, about two months before the liability trial in Faulkner began, *The State* newspaper carried an article about Eulalie Chaffee Salley, the woman most responsible for getting the Nineteenth Amendment ratified in South Carolina. Salley first led women suffragists in a march through Aiken on January 26, 1917, a year after Congress passed the amendment giving women the right to vote.

Gourdin pointed out that the South Carolina Suffrage Bill, however, was not passed until 52 years later when it was signed into law by Governor Robert McNair in 1969. No state politician would dare touch the issue before then, Gourdin said. According to Gourdin, Salley finally told McNair that if he did not sign the bill, he could be forced from office "because he was elected illegally by women who did not have the right to vote." This was the real reason McNair hurried the bill to give women the right to vote in South Carolina, according to Gourdin.

Gourdin said that James F. Byrnes, FDR's right-hand man whose statue sits outside the courtroom where the *Faulkner* case was tried, even suggested that if the suffragists wanted to influence congressmen, "pretty women would doubtless have more influence upon them" than less attractive women.

Eighteen years after the *Faulkner* case was filed, South Carolina, with a population made up of 51.3% women, ranks last in the Union in the number of women in the state legislature. Although the state for the first time elected a woman as governor in 2010, no women occupy any of the 46 seats in the State

Virginia Gourdin, member of the House of Representatives from Charleston. Used with permission, Staff photograph, *The Post and Courier.*

Senate; and while in 2010, 10% of the 170 total State House members were women, none are now in 2011. Only three women have ever been elected to statewide office.

No women from South Carolina are in the U.S. House or Senate. Only one woman was ever elected to Congress in her own right.[7]

Few who looked in on the *Faulkner* case from a historical perspective had more personal experience of the struggle of women for civil rights than Virginia Gourdin. She concluded her letter with the observation,

> It is difficult to win any fight for women's rights in state courts—our only hope is from the federal court decisions.... Some women are happy to see Shannon fail to withstand the hatred of hundreds of bullies around her. But, I, too, am glad she left before they killed her (as they tried to kill the black cadets there). For two years I spent money calling SLED to give her physical protection, but somebody knew The Citadel administrators, not faculty, were encouraging the hatred and that the male S.C. legislature was passive; so U.S. marshals were fortunately brought in to cover the campus.

Chapter 6

Separate and Unequal

1995: "Die Nigr"

Bill Robinson of *The State* newspaper in Columbia called me on January 25, 1995, to inquire about the Scarlet Pimpernel and graffiti in the men's room at Mark Clark Hall.

"I don't know anything about any graffiti in Mark Clark Hall," I told Robinson. "I've heard of the graffiti only in Capers Hall—it said, 'Admit her and fuck her to death.' I told Susan Faludi and Val about it. It's been a couple of days, but I think they've got that one down by now."

Robinson also wanted to know about the "Die Nigr" sign that had been painted on The Citadel water tower on Martin Luther King Day. First it was "Die Shannon" on the Ashley River Bridge, a half mile from The Citadel, now "Die Nigr" on The Citadel water tower. Higher than the topmost parts of the barracks, the tower is the most conspicuous landmark at The Citadel and the first thing the eye beholds upon approaching the campus and even upon entering Charleston from Interstate Highway 26. The "Die Nigr" words had to share space with "The Citadel Bulldogs" which is permanently written on it, but somehow room was found. The "Die Nigr" sign was soon whitewashed over and nothing more was heard about it. No cadets were caught and punished. None were reported, and none turned themselves in.

"Duty is the Sublimest Word in the English Language," a quotation from General Robert E. Lee, and "A Cadet Does Not Lie, Cheat, or Steal, or Tolerate Those Who Do" are written on brass plaques at each main sally port of each of the barracks. The cadets going out to write "Die Nigr" would have seen both quotations as they exited the barracks to execute The Citadel night time Honor Code. For them a third plaque, one from Shakespeare, should be mounted at every sally port to quote Falstaff: "Honor is a mere scutcheon."

The "Die Nigr" boys at The Citadel, however, were not finished after decorating only the water tower. *The Brigadier* front page a few days later, on February 10, 1995, reported that a black sophomore cadet in E Company,

Echo Company, discovered "Die Nigr" written on the wall in his room above his light socket. It was Echo Company that Michael Maurer, attorney for DOJ, later questioned the vice president about after I drew Maurer's attention to the pride Echo Company took in its Nazi and KKK traditions. The photos of Echo Company in the school's *Sphinx* yearbook sent the usual wrong signals about the South with their abuse of the Rebel flag which hung side by side with their "Echo uber alles" motto. The company motto was still proudly hanging from company hand-painted signs at Homecoming 2010. In the 1958 *Sphinx* it was F Company, the "Kleen Kut Kompany" that displayed "KKK" along with the Rebel flag.

A day after the February 10 article in the student paper, another black freshman, a cadet in Romeo Company, quietly withdrew from The Citadel. He too had received his own bouquet of racial slurs in the usual anonymous letter, Citadel style.

The Citadel made a customary flourish of effete gestures which never rose to the level of rounding up the usual administrators. The administration went through its paces with the cadets. SLED and the FBI were called in. Watts marched the Corps to McAlister Hall and lectured them for 40 minutes, and all that. But Citadel honor held fast. The 2000 cadets again insulted General Lee and the South, and the administration—in the one place on earth where nothing ever happens that no one is completely unaware of—again wondered whatever they were going to do with such bad boys.

The next day, on the CBS Evening News, I gave a cheerful pitch that Faulkner would eventually prevail. I was getting too many clumps of fifteen-minute fame: bunches of CBS, ABC, NBC, CNN, local TV news, almost daily coverage on the radio, and national and international press all over the world. Most of the attention given to The Citadel that made it a household word, in Watts's phrase, applied also to Faulkner. Extensive, often front page, coverage and photographs in *The New York Times*, *The Wall Street Journal*, *The Atlanta Journal-Constitution*, *The Times* (London), *The Guardian* (Manchester), *The Independent* (U. K.), *Le Monde*, *Der Spiegel*, *Los Angeles Times*, *The Washington Post*, *The Boston Globe*, *The Globe and Mail* (Toronto), and *USA Today*, to name some of the most important. The Citadel hired a news service to send it all media production regarding the case. They presumably kept an enormous file on every article, editorial, and photograph on the case, but all documentation must not have ended up in the Citadel archives, as far as I could tell. I collected what I personally saw or was sent.

Friends returned from foreign countries with articles on the case in Germany and France and throughout Europe, Australia, and China. The Citadel was serving as a poster child to those who relished in the hypocrisy of America's calls for civil liberties in other lands while denying the same in its own. And they saw in the Southern drama of intolerance toward women a play-back of intolerance toward black Americans in the South 30 years previously.

Faulkner II, April 13, 1995

In its order of April 13, 1995, the Fourth Circuit wrote in reference to The Citadel's proposed plan to remedy its violation of the equal protection clause: "[I]f the plan is not court approved and implemented by the date in August 1995 when the Cadets are required to report, The Citadel must admit Shannon Faulkner to the Corps of Cadets as ordered by the district court." Thus, to recapitulate the bare bones of litigation, the district court's order of July 22, 1994, (*Faulkner I*), which was stayed, ordered Faulkner into the Corps of Cadets in 1994 and other women similarly situated in 1995. The Fourth Circuit's order of April 13, 1995, (*Faulkner II*) affirmed *Faulkner I*, ordering Faulkner into the Corps if no remedial plan at Converse were in place by August 1995. There was no express mention in *Faulkner II* of other women similarly situated being admitted with Faulkner, but the district court's order admitting them by 1995 was simply not modified by the Fourth Circuit to that extent. The Citadel refused to submit a remedial plan in time, so the district court enforced its July 22, 1994, order, *Faulkner I*, as modified by *Faulkner II*, and ordered Shannon into the Corps on August 12, 1995.

Thus, The Citadel did not "voluntarily" admit women in 1996. It was forced to admit women similarly situated in 1996 under the district court order of *Faulkner I*, affirmed by the Fourth Circuit in *Faulkner II*, just as it was forced to admit Faulkner alone in 1995. By January 1995, Shannon Faulkner had been in the day program at The Citadel as a non-cadet sitting side by side in class with the cadets for a full year. In the history of the case, The Citadel never submitted evidence of any harm done.

A crucial turn of events happened before *Faulkner II*. On January 26, 1995, the Fourth Circuit ruled in *VMI II* that the separate women's military program which Virginia set up at Mary Baldwin College was a constitutional option to avoid admitting women to VMI. Cadets at The Citadel greeted *VMI II* in *The Brigadier* on February 10 as welcomed news in a case that had "ruthlessly raged" for three years. "The Citadel will finally defeat Shannon Faulkner," the cadets wrote on the front page, since now VMI could establish a separate leadership program for women in spite of the arguments made by Vile Val, the ACL-Not-a-Clue-U, and Bla-Bla-Blacksheep or Bla-Bob-Blacksheep, the affectionate name given me by cadets when I taught there. My lambs had not forgotten me, but it was a bleak day for the plaintiff.

Oral arguments on *Faulkner II* came just four days after the Fourth Circuit issued its January 26, 1995, *VMI II* order. On April 13, 1995, the three-judge panel in the Fourth Circuit issued their ruling in *Faulkner II*. Judge Paul V. Niemeyer, a Reagan appointee to the district court in Maryland before he was appointed to the Fourth Circuit by George H. W. Bush, sat on both the *VMI* and *Citadel* panels. Judge Hiram H. Ward, a Nixon appointee from North Carolina, and Judge J. Dickson Phillips, a Carter appointee from North Carolina, made up the three-man *VMI* panel. Unlike the *VMI* panel, the *Citadel* panel included a native son. Judge Clyde Hamilton, also a George H. W. Bush appointee, was from South Carolina. From West Virginia, Judge K. K. Hall was appointed by President Ford. In affirming the district court order of July 22, 1994, that The Citadel was in violation of the Constitution, *Faulkner II* gave the first strong feeling that SRF might finally be admitted into the Corps. Of course, The Citadel could also go private or admit women without any more fuss, the two other choices allowed to remedy its constitutional violation, but the former was a serious option only to The Citadel and VMI loyalists who briefly tried to establish a failed Southern Military Institute.

Judge Hamilton looked outside the Record on Appeal to find newspapers critical of Faulkner and echoed the phrase used by Justice Scalia on VMI, "I cannot accept the majority's invitation to be a party to the destruction of a venerable institution."

The Citadel's July 26 motion for stay of *Faulkner I*, issued July 22, 1994, asked the court only "to stay that portion of its July 22, 1994, Order requiring the immediate admission of Shannon Richey Faulkner to [the] South Carolina Corps of Cadets, pending appeal." The Citadel did not seek to stay the effect of *Faulkner I* which pertained to the admission of women similarly situated the following year. Also, no objection was raised by The Citadel to the admission of other women, as well as Faulkner, during its voluminous production of documents in 1994 and 1995—documents that listed hundreds of names of women similarly situated who showed interest in the Corps. The Citadel came up with its resistance to other women only in the fight over attorney fees, and it continued the ruse when it "voluntarily" recognized all other women who all along were similarly situated with Faulkner. In its announcement on June 28, 1996, The Citadel never acknowledged court orders that Shannon Faulkner was ordered into the Corps by the district court, as affirmed by the Fourth Circuit. It acted with characteristic largess by reference only to the Supreme Court's order to admit women into VMI.

One ordinarily volunteers before having to do something. The Citadel volunteered to do something after it had been ordered to do it. But, of course, strictly speaking, the option to continue the fight against women still existed for The Citadel since the Supreme Court order was expressly directly only to VMI, and *Faulkner II* left open the specter of further litigation in district court.

Judge Hall concurred in *Faulkner II* for the same reasons Judges Motz and Phillips had dissented in the government's petition for a hearing before the full court in *VMI II*. The Fourth Circuit's decision in *Faulkner II* still did not, for Judge Hall, cure the unconstitutional remedy offered to The Citadel by Judges Niemeyer and Hamilton writing for the majority.

"I choose to write separately," Judge Hall said,

> because I am convinced that we have embarked on a path that will inevitably fall short of providing women their deserved equal access to important avenues of power and responsibility. We began this unfortunate journey in VMI when we promoted a means to an end—single gender education—to the status of an end in itself and avoided ascertaining, let alone analyzing, the true purpose behind the state's decision to keep women out of VMI. Though we correctly concluded that maintaining the status quo offended the Constitution, we failed to mandate VMI's integration—and thus we failed.

For Judge Hall, the only question that mattered was one the majority never asked: Why has the state decided to create or maintain this institution for the benefit of only one gender? Instead, Hall wrote, the court was constrained to ask a wholly irrelevant one: Does the state offer a substantively comparable educational option to the other gender?

Going on to quote the most obvious case throughout the VMI and Citadel litigations—the elephant in the courtrooms in Roanoke, Charleston, and Richmond—Judge Hall simply added his own observations to *Brown v. Board of Education* as they pertain to the Citadel case:

> "[T]he opportunity of an education ... where the state has undertaken to provide it, is a right which must be made available to all on equal terms.... Separate educational facilities are inherently unequal." In fact, though VMI, The Citadel, and their advocates have ceaselessly insisted that education is at the heart of this debate, I suspect that these cases have very little to do with education. They instead have very much to do with wealth, power, and the ability of those who have it to determine who will have it later. The daughters of Virginia and South Carolina have every right to insist that their tax dollars no longer be spent to support what amount to fraternal organizations whose initiates emerge as full-fledged members of an all-male aristocracy. Though our nation has, throughout its history, discounted the contributions and

wasted the abilities of the female half of its population, it cannot continue to do so. As we prepare, together, to face the twenty-first century, we simply cannot afford to preserve a relic of the nineteenth.

Judge Hall saw right through the good ole boys, as Justice Ginsburg would later. It was not simply to be presumed, however, even in 1994 or 1995, that The Citadel and State of South Carolina would automatically obey a federal court order. The Board of Visitors 30 years earlier hesitated at first to obey a directive from the Department of Education to integrate the Corps and admit African Americans. A letter from a state senator, as reported in *The News and Courier* on March 25, 1966, expressed the spirit of contempt and historical posture The Citadel then took with regard to federal interference in state affairs. Buddy Prioleau, the person to whom the letter was written, using Senate stationery, was also a named defendant in the women's lawsuits. In any event, an equally proud sense of state sovereignty governed the Board of Visitors in Faulkner's case. The governor at the time was Dick Riley, later Secretary of Education under President Clinton. The governor was having a tough time getting The Citadel BOV to comply with directives from the federal executive to admit blacks. Meanwhile, a state senator—and later in his political career a U.S. Congressman—wrote directly to Prioleau on the Board of Visitors:

"I was proud to read in the paper where you folks declined to 'sign up.' It's a hell of a come to pass when the Governor of South Carolina, in response to orders from a bunch of ass holes in the Department of Education 'to jump' says, 'how high.'"[1]

Demand

On May 25, 1995, The Citadel issued a "Progress Report on Recruitment Planning" that showed at a glance exactly how easy it was for The Citadel to reach out to young high school women who had indicated an interest in ROTC. The report was an astonishing admission of the ease with which The Citadel could recruit women if it really wanted to. It remains so today. And The Citadel really wanted to find young high school seniors who would go to the SCIL program at Converse. "Demand" was easily addressed in that context.

First, The Citadel got in touch with key ROTC officers in South Carolina "to begin identifying female members of the Junior ROTC units in South Carolina high schools." Those officers were Lieutenant Colonel Walter D. Brown, III, of the U.S. Army Columbia Recruiting Battalion and Captain Darrell E. Whitehurst, the Recruiting Company Commander of the U.S. Army Company located in Greenville.

Second, "Our preliminary plan is to arrange a visit with Colonel William Causey at Fort Bragg, NC, who is the 5th ROTC Region Commander, [an area which includes] most of South Carolina. The purpose of this meeting is to be briefed on all phases of the ROTC program including special emphasis on recruiting of college-bound women into the SCIL program."

Third, The Citadel planned luncheons for Junior ROTC students with the goal of identifying women to "become immediate prospects for the SCIL program."

Compared to The Citadel's efforts, my pathetic telephone calls in 1990 to guidance counselors and ROTC officers at high schools in Charleston looked ridiculous.

The next step in their plans to recruit high school women got serious:

> Arrangements have been discussed with the National Research Center for College and University Admissions in Kansas City, MO, to provide names and addresses, within five days, of all college-bound women in SC who have indicated an interest in pursuing an ROTC program in college for fall 1995. There are currently 8021 of these prospects in the NRCCUA [National Research Center for College and University Admissions] database. This number could easily be expanded to include students who indicated an interest in attending a private college, but who would now have some interest in an ROTC leadership program like SCIL.

The Citadel would call on the Computer Mailing Company in Kansas City to print letters, stuff them in envelopes, and mail them within five to seven days. Mailings to a minimum of 10,000 women would be made to include "a personalized direct mail letter to all SC fall 1995 college-bound women interested in ROTC to introduce the SCIL program and to provide a reply card."

The Citadel's argument that there was small demand among women for a military college education *per se* was thus set in sharp relief to its effort to find them. The same procedures could easily have been carried over to recruit women into the Corps of Cadets and establish a "critical mass" of 20% women cadets in the Corps in 1995 and certainly by 1996, but they were abandoned at the end of litigation. Nor are they in place today to recruit women into the Corps of Cadets.

With a token number of women comfortably socked away in SCIL, The Citadel turned back to the separate issue of establishing SCIL, but it purposefully never got an assimilation plan together in time.

State Senator

The plaintiffs had no insider in the General Assembly. The closest people on their side, apart from Representative Sarah Manly, were some of the black members of the legislature and Senator Holly Cork. Cork shared an office with Senator Arthur Ravenel, for whom she worked before taking the seat in Hilton Head vacated at her father's death. Cork was a strong Republican. At the same time, she was sensitive to women's issues in the state.

I called Cork to ask if she could get information about The Citadel Development Foundation and the costs which The Citadel and state had paid to date, September 1, 1993, on the defense of Johnson's and Faulkner's cases. She got nowhere with her inquiries. Ultimately, no one ever knew what exact amount The Citadel really received and spent to keep women out of the Corps.

On May 6, 1994, Holly Cork was deposed in Charleston. Cork's testimony was critical, perhaps for no other reason than she was able to testify as to the secrecy surrounding The Citadel in the General Assembly. She got into the case and became a strong voice in the Senate after she learned that The Citadel, to her surprise, was not a private college. Yet Cork was typical. She was not at all the only citizen and legislator in the state not to know much about The Citadel. Since it looked like a duck, marched and quacked, Cork and many others logically assumed the place was private.

On January 18, 1995, Senator Cork sent me a copy of a letter she sent to Lieutenant General Watts following his visit to the Senate floor for his inauguration as the new president of the state-owned college:

> Our chance meeting in the State House lobby prior to the Inauguration was surprisingly unfortunate. I had never met you before, and your response to my attempt to introduce myself was rude on your part and embarrassing on mine. Believe it or not, I introduced myself because I honestly did not know who you were and wanted to make the acquaintance of someone who seemed to be a dignitary. It was only when your name was announced during the procession that I learned your identify. I was shocked that someone of your stature showed such a lack of grace and inability to put politics aside.
>
> My position on whether The Citadel should remain a single-gender, public institution differs from yours, but up until now it has not tainted my view of the institution otherwise. Perhaps I should reconsider that attitude.
>
> Sincerely, Holly Cork.
> cc: Colonel Ben Legare.

Around March 17, 1995, Senator Cork sent an inquiry through an employee in the State Senate to The Citadel about how much money The Citadel was spending to defend its all-male admissions policy. From the very outset of the case, a few other members of the legislature had real concerns about how much money defending The Citadel against women would cost the taxpayers. Like the plaintiffs who looked to New York for the Women's Rights Project at the ACLU and, later, Shearman & Sterling, The Citadel looked to major out-of-state law firms. By December 9, 1992, the VP of Finance at The Citadel wrote to the Attorney General's office to request authorization to hire McGuire Woods Battle & Booth in Richmond and King & Spaulding in Atlanta.

"It is important to note," the registrar Colonel Lyons wrote, "that none of the costs associated with the use of these outside firms will be borne by appropriated funds. All such costs will be paid from unrestricted gifts to the college from outside sources."

After several unrecorded telephone conversations, the AG's office gave The Citadel administrator the green light to hire away. According to The Citadel's own Board of Visitors and the AG's office, it was perfectly OK for unrestricted funds from The Citadel Trust, Inc., to be used for legal instead of educational purposes. After all, as the VP of Finance explained to the AG's office in a letter dated December 15, 1992, "The use of these unrestricted funds to defray the attorney fees not otherwise covered by the college's Tort Liability policy through the State of South Carolina [Insurance Reserve Fund] has been approved by the Board of Visitors."

The Citadel was getting ready for a fight as early as the time when DOJ sent a letter of inquiry to VMI back in 1989. That was why they lobbied to get S.C. Code 59-121-55 amended on May 30, 1991. The emended statute allowed the BOV to transfer up to $20 million of non-state appropriated funds, which were intended to be used for scholarship and other college support purposes, to The Citadel Trust, Inc., the nonprofit eleemosynary corporation they set up pursuant to the same statute.

They knew all along that a legal fight would cost a lot of money and were determined even before Johnson sued them in 1992 to take every dollar they had out of any fund that existed for express educational purposes and put it in The Citadel Trust, Inc., to use to fund their defense. The Citadel knew it could always return to the General Assembly and get, from the taxpayers, money they needed for real educational purposes. It only had to figure out how to get taxpayers to pay to fight women, and it did.

They successfully got taxpayers to pay directly through the State Insurance Reserve Fund and indirectly through the additional appropriations of money they knew they would need to pay their attorneys after they had used money intended for scholarships and educational support. They took money out of

The Citadel Trust, Inc., as well as The Citadel Development Foundation or CDF that should have been used for teachers, students, and books. The CDF was a 501(c)3 entity founded in 1961 to raise money exclusively for educational purposes, but its funds were used to resist women.

That was why the registrar was happy to attach a copy of the new statute to his December 15, 1992, letter to the Attorney General's office. He also attached a copy of the document incorporating The Citadel Trust, Inc., which the Secretary of State signed a year earlier on December 13, 1991.

And they didn't want to have to request and report their payments to private counsel every time they got billed. Under the new statute, they did not have to do that either.

Senator Cork was perhaps the only suspicious member of twelve people on the Joint Legislative Study Committee to Study the Governance and Operation of Higher Education. When she wrote for information to the president's assistant, she was preparing for a speech she planned to give in Beaufort on Sunday, March 19, 1995. The president's assistant sent back his reply:

> The specific question ... requested that I answer is: "How much has The Citadel incurred for legal expenses, including attorney fees, court costs, and the like, without regard to the source of the funds, whether from state appropriations or private gifts, and without regard to who or what entity paid or is obligated to pay such expenses, whether public or private entities, and without regard to whether the expenses have been paid or charged and not paid, for the purpose of keeping women out of The Citadel?"

> The specific answer to that specific question is: "Nothing!" The Citadel has not engaged in the conduct described in the question. In fact, approximately 1600 women are currently enrolled and presently attending academic classes at The Citadel.

> The Citadel has been involved in litigation concerning the admissions policy of the Corps of Cadets in which The Citadel supports the efforts of this State to have the Federal Courts decree that the policy of the State of South Carolina to provide a freedom of choice to its citizens, both men and women, to select a single gender educational environment is constitutional. To date, the Federal Courts have been unanimous in so holding.

> I assume the request to me is a request for the expenses incurred in connection with the activities described in the immediate preceding paragraph. If I am incorrect, please advise. If the information described in this memorandum is correct, please advise.

I anticipate extensive time will be required to obtain and calculate the information I assume you desire. I will, therefore, appreciate your advice of whether your request is appropriate for state employees, on state time, and at state expense to render whatever services will be required to comply with the request, or whether such activities contravene the State Ethics Law.

The state senator sent a reply letter to the president's assistant by fax on March 20, 1995:

Dear Sir: I am in receipt of your memorandum dated March 17, 1995, and I note that although the cover sheet states it was sent by fax at 4:00 p.m. [Friday], the actual time of transmission was 5:04 p.m. I received your communication this morning [Monday], which should come as no surprise to you as I believe it was your intent to disregard my inquiry for as long as possible.

Your memorandum brings to a new height the level of arrogance I continue to experience in my communications with The Citadel. Your title indicates a graduate degree, so I assume you are not stupid. You knew the nature of the information ... requested of you on my behalf. If you are unwilling to provide it, simply say so.
Sincerely, Holly Cork.

SCWLA

Earlier in the case, Pat Conroy was quoted by *The Beaufort Gazette* for criticizing The Citadel for its "unconscionable bullying of Faulkner for two years." During that time, "not one women's group has come forward.... South Carolina must produce the most timid women in history," he observed.[2]

The South Carolina Women Lawyers Association (SCWLA) through the South Carolina Bar planned to sponsor an all-day Continuing Legal Education session on April 21, 1995, that included women judges from the Fourth Circuit, the South Carolina Supreme Court, and the South Carolina Court of Appeals, among other distinguished speakers. An initial announcement about the conference, however, did not include a topic that could be taken seriously. Instead, SCWLA announced that what women wore to court and how they projected their voice would be the issues taken up at the conference. On March 14, 1995, I wrote four of the members of the planning committee chosen at random:

Dear Selected Members of the Seminar Planning Committee: Your announcement of scheduled speakers on April 21, 1995, on the topic of "The Woman Advocate in South Carolina" leads me to ask if the case of *Shannon Faulkner v. The Citadel* will be ignored during the day-long session. As the local attorney for Faulkner, I am sometimes asked by out-of-state press and out-of-state bar members why no South Carolina women's organizations have shown any interest in giving support to Faulkner as she slugs it out toe-to-toe with the most powerful pound-for-pound group of men in South Carolina. You may know that many women of Virginia even picketed the State capital to admit women to the Corps of Cadets at VMI.

The South Carolina Commission on Women has not been heard on the case, so the public presumption must be that it is opposed to women being admitted to all public colleges in South Carolina. The South Carolina Women Lawyers Association has not been heard on the case, so the public presumption of it must be the same.

Justice O'Connor in a controlling case, *Mississippi University for Women v. Hogan* (1982), cites a case your members may already know about, *Bradwell v. Illinois* (1853), in which the U.S. Supreme Court held that women were unfit for the practice of law, that "nature, reason, and experience" and "the peculiar characteristics, destiny, and mission of women" rightly excluded women from the practice of law which requires a "firmness" found only in the "sterner sex."

That's funny now, but it's not that funny when one sees that South Carolina was the last state to put women on the jury, that the first women legislators in South Carolina had to swear allegiance to a state constitution that said they were all male — the list goes on, of course — and that the *Faulkner* case is the only major civil rights case in American history without an adult male as a plaintiff.

The point is, now that women — and more importantly, women lawyers — are organized, why are they meeting on April 21st to talk about clothing and effective use of the voice instead of helping other women win their freedom?

It all reminds me of the *Harvard Lampoon* issue years ago spoofing *Cosmopolitan* magazine. One humorous article was entitled, "How to Decorate Your Uterine Wall."

Three days later, one of the women reminded me why my older sister took so long to get dressed for a date:

I am independently responding to your letter because I believe that you intended your letter to be a positive prod for visible support for your client. Your letter, however, demonstrates an absolute lack of awareness, or to use a much battered term, a lack of sensitivity, to the very issues faced by women and, in particular, women attorneys. I was appalled that you dare chide us for presenting speakers on clothing and the effective use of voice "instead of helping other women win their freedom." Mr. Black, I am a litigator and if I fail to be attune to jurors' sensitivities to the way women present themselves in the courtroom, it will have a direct effect on my effectiveness and my ability to successfully represent my client. These are not issues of fluff as you have implied. All one has to do is watch the nightly news and get the latest fashion critique of Marsha Clark [in the O. J. Simpson trial] to know these are issues of which we are forced to be aware. Furthermore, by your characterization you have chosen to trivialize the entire subject of distinct issues faced by women attorneys.

Can't live with or without 'em, I thought. But my comments were premature outside the context of SCWLA. During the following May and June, women's groups would take strong public positions opposing the $3.4 million appropriation which the budget conference committee agreed on May 19, 1995, to recommend to the General Assembly to implement SCIL. A news release announced that on May 30, 1995, "a coalition of statewide and local civic organizations" met on the State House steps in Columbia to voice their objection and to serve members of the legislature with a two-page written appeal. Among those who participated were representatives from the American Association of University Women, the League of Women Voters, NOW, the South Carolina Federation of Business and Professional Women, Democratic Women of Greenville County, South Carolina Women's Political Caucus, Project COED (Citizens Organized to End Discrimination), and 52 Percent.

But even so, five years later, on September 21, 2000, at the Women's Studies Program: Distinguished Speakers Series in Charleston, not a word was spoken about the veteran women's and the *Faulkner/Mellette* lawsuits. The program was sponsored by the SCWLA. *Eslinger v. Thomas*, 476 F.2d 225 (4th Cir. 1973), a suit to get women pages in the South Carolina Senate, got all the attention. It was noted that while Eslinger herself never became a page, she opened the door for others.

April 7, 1995

April 7, 1995, was a pivotal day in the history of the case. On that Friday afternoon, a high school girl in her junior year in Pennsylvania, called about her interest in going to The Citadel on a Navy ROTC scholarship. I thought she would continue where others dropped off.

But the usual turn of events followed after I talked frankly about what Shannon's situation had been like so far.

"She gets hate mail?" the young woman's mother asked.

"Well, yes, but Shannon also gets letters telling her to go for it," I said. "I just have to be frank with you. I don't want to run your daughter off. I hope she pursues her goal, her dream even, if this is what she wants."

"We'll get back in touch soon. We'll have to think about everything and let her make up her own mind," she replied.

The next few days I set about getting enough material together from Lieutenant Simmons at CNET and from The Citadel NROTC. The young woman had an explicit interest in making the Navy a career after college, but she was ultimately unwilling to deal with everything Shannon dealt with on a daily basis.

Also on April 7, 1995, The Citadel was busy quietly making the necessary arrangements to try to establish a women's program, SCIL, at Converse, which would be "substantively comparable" to the Corps of Cadets at The Citadel. Richard Rieger, the Executive Director of The Citadel Development Foundation, and Jimmy Jones, the Chairman of the BOV, sent a letter to attorney Sam Applegate at the law firm of Haynsworth, Marion McKay & Guerard in Charleston. Applegate, a former chairman of the S.C. Health and Environmental Control Commission, was the attorney hired by the state, without notice to plaintiffs, to negotiate a deal between The Citadel and George Dean Johnson, Chairman of the Board of Trustees at Converse. The letter signed by Jones and Rieger assured Applegate that a week later "I," apparently meaning Jones and Rieger together, "will deliver a check to you in the amount of $5,000,000 on the account of The Citadel Development Foundation at Wachovia Bank of South Carolina. I trust this is satisfactory evidence of the good faith and intention of The Citadel and The Citadel Development Foundation to meet this obligation."

Applegate flew to meet with Johnson at his home in Florida on April 7, 1995. Johnson, a classmate of Applegate's at South Carolina School of Law and a classmate of mine for a year at Sewanee, had been a groomsman in Applegate's wedding. After the meeting with Applegate, Johnson agreed to accept $3.4 million in the future from the state ($2 million for one-time capital appropriations, plus $1.4 million each year for seven years after The Citadel's obligation ceased) and $5 million up front from The Citadel, with an additional $1.6 million to be paid by The Citadel in eight quarterly installments, for a total of $11.4 million. The Citadel's lobbyists in Columbia worked to be sure the state coughed up the money.

Roll call at the BOV's telephone conference on April 7, 1995, to approve the hand-out to Converse read like a who's who in the Palmetto State. Voting for it were William Sansom, Edward Croft, Jr., Roddey Dowd, Sr., Eugene Figg, Jr., Frederick Harris, III, Cantey Higdon, Francis Hipp, Edwin Latimer, Richard MacMillan, Bettis Rainsford, Robert Russell, James Self, Howard Suitt, Anderson Warlick, Tucker Weston, and Michael Wilson. The three who voted against the motion were not even identified in the BOV's April 7 minutes. Watts then promised $1.5 million to Converse directly from The Citadel's unrestricted funds, and Michael Wilson amended his motion to allow The Citadel to provide $1.5 million and the CDF to provide the remaining $3.5 million, with the exact terms of the agreement to be taken up on April 22, 1995.

The exact terms, however, were not contained in the April 22 minutes which made only passing reference to the 3.5/1.5 split. After reporting a market value of nearly $75 million for CDF in securities at Wachovia, equally little space was given in the minutes to voice a regret that "The Citadel Scholars Scholarship was not being used to attract the best qualified students" and to an expenditure of "$5,000 to send The Citadel cheerleaders to compete in national competition in Orlando, Florida." According to the BOV's minutes for April 7, 1995, participants in the conference call also took up the delicate issue of a forfeiture clause for the $5 million given in advance of the initiation of SCIL. "It was explained," presumably by Dawes who was in attendance, "that the only grounds for reimbursement by Converse would be action by Converse which would disqualify the program."

In other words, the BOV agreed that the suitor could beg and scheme and shell out big money, but if anything happened that led to a failure to consummate the affair, the object of desire still got to keep all the money which The Citadel gave her. No prenuptial here. If SCIL failed to make it through the courts and was ultimately ruled to be unconstitutional, Converse still got to keep the $5 million which CDF advanced to The Citadel, even if there were a pull-out clause to allow the state itself not to finalize contributions to the scheme if the Supreme Court ordered women into VMI. The understanding with The Citadel was orchestrated by Johnson, a consummate business man who had made a fortune from Blockbuster video stores and various other enterprises. Pandarus himself could not have struck a better deal for Criseyde.

At Johnson's insistence, Converse would remain in full control of SCIL, and the state and The Citadel would have no authority to influence the operation of Converse as a private college. Converse, The Citadel claimed, would never be under the Commission on Higher Education. In return, all Converse had to do was to guarantee just four years of SCIL to the students entering in August 1995. An agreement roughly outlining the terms between The Citadel and the CDF was signed June 24, 1995, to allow The Citadel to repay $1.5 million beginning December 31, 1995, to the CDF which had advanced the entire sum of $5 million to The Citadel to give to Converse on June 14, 1995.

To repay the CDF and its attorney fees, which by that time had amounted to nearly $3 million, The Citadel, by the end of the year, sold most of the 80,000 shares of stock worth $2 million given to The Citadel by Ted Turner whose three sons were graduates. Under Turner's gift, The Citadel received $1 million each year for five years beginning in 1994, with the remaining $20 million placed in a charitable trust until Turner's death.

But, again, the state itself did not have to deliver on its promise to give money to Converse if the courts did not approve SCIL. Senate debates that followed on May 4 dealt with that. As recorded in the Senate Journal, May 4, 1995, Amendment 192A to Part 1B, Section 18A, regarding the June 5, 1995, Agreement between Converse and the General Assembly, the $1.4 million to be appropriated was to be "allocated to The Citadel" for SCIL only "when a female leadership program has been approved as in compliance with the federal district court order." Another section added that "No funds may be expended if the Fourth Circuit Court of Appeals renders a decision which would prevent the establishment of the Women's Leadership Program." Another section covered the possibility of a Supreme Court ruling in *VMI*, stating that the Converse deal "shall be void and of no effect if the United States Supreme Court issues a ruling which reverses the holding" in the *VMI* case. Even so, Converse would, under the worst scenario, get to keep at least the up-front cash of $5 million from the CDF.

A Program Agreement between The Citadel and Converse was signed by Watts, Jones, Sandra Thomas, and George Dean Johnson in June, and a separate Agreement between Converse and the state by Condon, Thomas, and Johnson. The memo in support of their July 10 motion, signed by Condon for South Carolina, again summarized the money that would be flowing into the program from four different broad avenues and boasted a favorable comparison with the support the State of Virginia was giving to VWIL. In Virginia, Mary Baldwin would get only the interest on a $5 million endowment set up for start-up costs at the private women's college until 2000. No initial outright gift was made to Mary Baldwin by the Commonwealth or VMI. Instead, all monies were contingent upon court approval of the parallel program. But, according to the memo, South Carolina, better than Virginia, knew how to treat a lady:

> In VMI, the Commonwealth of Virginia agreed to support VWIL financially with a per-student payment equal to the per-student payment made to VMI. State funding was contingent on plan approval by the Court of Appeals. South Carolina's financial commitment to SCIL

exceeds Virginia's commitment to VWIL. South Carolina has agreed
to pay [1] annual program operating expenses up to $1.4 million, in-
cluding a per-student payment equal to that paid by The Citadel, and
to make a [2] one-time capital appropriation of $2 million. [3] As for
start-up funding, Converse has received $5,000,000 in unrestricted
funds from The Citadel for use in the SCIL program. In addition, [4]
The Citadel has agreed to advance the per capita payment for up to 40
SCIL students for the first academic year of the program (beginning
in fall 1995) regardless of whether the Court has approved the program by then.

What Condon neglected to add was that Converse's obligation to operate
SCIL was not only conditional but also, as plaintiffs argued, unlawful. The
Citadel agreed to pay Converse an additional $1.6 million in quarterly install-
ments of $200,000 for two consecutive years, but in this case only if there were
a final, non-appealable court order approving the Converse proposal. Receipt
of an additional $1.4 million in funds by the state was to continue the quar-
terly payments for seven consecutive quarters after The Citadel's obligation
ceased. Converse did not even have to operate SCIL if any future money dried
up from the state or if The Citadel defaulted on payments. The state was not
obligated to pay its $3.4 million or The Citadel its extra $1.6 million if the
Fourth Circuit and the Supreme Court did not finally approve the program. Converse had no obligation to operate SCIL if Charlie Condon, the Attorney General, was not authorized to enter the June 5, 1995, agreement with Converse
or if Converse ever became a public college under the Commission on Higher
Education.

There was no provision by the state or by The Citadel to maintain funding
of SCIL in the future. The four-year limitation in the agreements provided
only for a quicky, a four-year stand. Sandra Thomas had repeatedly said that
Converse would not continue SCIL if the $3.4 million in state funds were not
made available or if the Court did not approve the program. Neither the legislation adopted by the General Assembly nor the contract between Converse
and The Citadel guaranteed the additional $1.4 million necessary for SCIL to
exist in the future.

It was just all too contingent to be legal, the plaintiffs said, too contingent
on future court rulings, on future funding, on the authority of the Attorney
General, on Citadel performance, on formula funding by the General Assembly, and on absolute control by Converse. Even precisely following the money
was nearly impossible. Yet as late as January 1996, months before *VMI* was decided, a state senator who would later be appointed to direct the South Car-

olina Lottery urged his fellow senators to go ahead and release $1.4 million to Converse because the state had a moral obligation and duty to fulfill to Converse.

So SCIL failed. After the Supreme Court ruled in *VMI*, Converse never got the $3.4 million from the State or the extra $1.6 million from The Citadel, even though it got to keep the $5 million from the CDF. It, therefore, got to move its books from red to black ink. It built a new fitness center and made renovations on its gymnasium, theater, and some of the dormitories. It bought new computers and, at best, disappointed dozens of young women who thought they were in SCIL for the long haul. By the end of the four-year run of SCIL, Converse was spending only about 6% of its endowment on a simple leadership program, the residue of SCIL which initially had more military components. Well over 60% of the women did not see the end of a proposed four-year stint in SCIL. After SCIL folded, The Citadel looked to taxpayers to pay for educational needs on which their own millions from CDF could have been spent.

Converse Faculty

"Hello, may I speak to Mr. Robert Black, please? This is Sandra Thomas in Spartanburg, president of Converse College."

Thomas was calling me at home on Sunday evening to get me to address the Converse faculty the next morning, Monday, May 1, 1995. May Day is traditionally a day when young ladies dance around a pole. That day, a special faculty meeting was to convene to address the issue of establishing the SCIL program for The Citadel.

"I've tried to reach Miss Val Vojdik, but she is in New York and cannot come, so I'm hopeful that you can come. We want you to address the plaintiff's side of the lawsuit that has been filed against The Citadel and how it might affect Converse should we establish the SCIL program here."

"You mean there will be no one from the other side, from The Citadel, to present their side of the story?" I asked.

"Attorney Anne Marie Whittemore has also been invited, but there will not be a debate between the two of you. You will address the faculty alone, as she has done," she replied.

In an April 26, 1995, note to Sandra Thomas marked "PERSONAL AND CONFIDENTIAL—NO COPIES," Don Keel wrote that Sam Applegate said all was going well with the government and the Attorney General to get $1.4 million and $5 million from State, but not an additional $5 million from CDF. According to the note, Converse apparently wanted a total of $10 million from CDF initially and $1.4 million from State annually. "Between CDF and State, we are looking at $17 million over the first five years ($5 million from the CDF, $5 million from the State, and $7 million in operating funds over five years)," the note said.

Unknown to Val and Henry at central command at Shearman & Sterling in New York at the time, and to me, such was the background for my visit to speak to the faculty four days later.

Without faculty approval of SCIL, the note claimed that George Dean Johnson said "that we cannot submit the budget (which will be public on Monday) until and unless the faculty is on board. Thus, we are between a rock and a hard place."

Thomas had to get the faculty to accept the deal before Johnson would go forward. They had only 18 hours to get this done. In spite of Don Keel's confidential note on the 26th, key members of the faculty certainly knew the details and all must have known that big money was on its way.

The April 26, 1995, note advised Thomas herself to act thoroughly convinced of the propriety of their actions so that other colleges, both public and private, will think that Converse has taken tax dollars that should rightly go to them, "that we took money that was rightfully ours."

Shortly before walking into the faculty meeting the next morning in Spartanburg, I saw Whittemore, but only at a distance. She asked Thomas a few questions about something and ducked back up a flight of stairs.

"I see Anne Marie is here, working away, as you told me," I said. "You seem busy. I have a feeling that I am wasting my time, that the SCIL program is already a done deal."

My indecorous remark went unnoticed. My inquiry about the life-sized statues of Athena and Diana in the main entrance of the building also was ignored. No one I talked to knew exactly which statue was which goddess. It was going to be a day of war or wisdom, hunting or chastity, that's all I knew.

I was led into a room adjacent to the classroom where the faculty was meeting. A bit later I was introduced by Thomas, who promptly departed, giving everyone the clear signal that she herself was not interested in a word I had to say.

Converse lawyer Ken Darr and the college provost Thomas McDaniel sat among the faculty. I had talked to each of them on the phone during the past year. McDaniel asked me to characterize the defense's argument that private women's colleges would be in danger if The Citadel were forced to admit women. Ken Darr followed up on a brief summary about what *Grove City College v. Bell*, 465 U.S. 555 (1984) meant to Converse. *Grove City* concerned Title IX of the Education Amendments of 1972 which forbids sex discrimination at colleges and universities that receive federal funds. *Grove City* ruled that institution-wide Title IX coverage is not triggered by receipt of federal funds by just one unit. The court applied Title IX restrictions to financial aid offices through which students receive federally funded scholarships, but not to the college as a whole. So Converse thought that it could be just a little bit pregnant and could continue to take direct federal funding even if it could not take federal scholarship money without compliance with Title IX. The private women's college thought that it could continue to discriminate against men in its admissions policy. What money it lost in federally funded scholarships it could simply get from the state and Citadel. Converse never wanted to make any deal with The Citadel that would risk its women-only admissions policy.

"But Congress returned to that issue in the Civil Rights Restoration Act of 1987 to override *Grove City* and render exactly that kind of partial compliance with Title IX unacceptable," I said. I never knew, however, if my understanding of *Grove City* and the overriding Act made a difference to the debate.

The faculty had been set up like stooges, an old administrative trick. It is always sad, as my father used to tell me, to see faculty forums gathered together by highly paid college administrators who are just using the timid little souls to bless decisions already made. But in this case, the faculty was as hungry for food money as were the administrators. The fix was definitely in.

"Let me first say," I began, "that I am here as one of you. I am really first a teacher and then a lawyer. I got into law because affirmative action knocked me out of teaching. White males just were not in fashion anymore when I began my teaching career in English literature. I got in this case because my client wanted to go to a public college. I got in because of my own interest in education. This is a case about education as much as it is about networking and women's rights. I think you all know that. Converse is a private college, so you are aware that Title IX permits you to maintain your single-sex admissions policy. And you are well aware that South Carolina hovers at the bottom in education when it comes to measurements like the SAT and ACT test scores. So I would like you to keep the backdrop of public education, and particularly the education of women in the state, in your minds as I talk a little bit about what's going on at The Citadel.

"Shannon Faulkner wants to go to a public college that is a military college that has kept women out for nearly 150 years. You no doubt have been told that The Citadel can continue to keep women out if you at Converse will only let them set up a parallel military program for women on your campus, far away from The Citadel. I am here to tell you that that will never happen anyway. Even if you do take the $5 million and sell yourselves out and turn your back on the women of this state. And by taking the money you might, ironically, even become a state actor, exactly what you're trying to avoid because that possibly will tighten control by governmental agencies like the Commission on Higher Education.

"Even if you do set up a SCIL program, you are going to lose in the long run. I don't know what the attorneys for the state and The Citadel have told you, but the Fourth Circuit ruling that a parallel program is constitutional is not going to stand. It won't stand at Mary Baldwin and it won't stand here. The United States Supreme Court will reverse the Fourth Circuit on the parallel program, I'd venture to guess. So don't just think about the money. Think about the prestige of Converse, not The Citadel. Think about your independence and what this college has meant to women in this state for so long. I used to visit Converse as an undergraduate. It's a great college. Don't wake up tomorrow morning and wish you had not gone to bed with the boys at The Citadel. Don't identify yourselves as that kind of place. This case is no less than a battle for the virtue of this college."

It was a floor show, so I trotted out an old joke. A cartoon along the same lines would run in the May 17, 1995, issue of the student newspaper, *The Conversationalist*. "It's like the joke about the lady who was asked if she would sleep with the man when he offered her $10. She said, absolutely not and began to walk away. He asked her if she would get in bed for $5 million. She thought about it and said OK. Then he said, well, I've changed my mind. I can give you only $10, after all. You may know the rest. She was very indignant and said, 'What kind of a lady do you think I am?' To which he replied, 'We know what kind of lady you are. We're just haggling about the price.'"

About that time, a voice interrupted me from the back of the room. An administrative plant, as I later found out, was sitting on the last row and up to now had been reading a newspaper to purposefully send a signal, as Thomas did, that he too had no interest in what I was saying. Now he had a juicy moral posture to base it on.

"I wish to take exception to that kind of language here, Mr. Black, and ask that you refrain from speaking to this audience in such a manner," the man said.

"You clearly are not a full-time teacher, are you?" I replied. "I mean you aren't an academic like the rest of the people here, are you?"

Nearly everyone in the room laughed out loud. The man sat expressionless and did not answer. I had taken a chance and luckily hit the mark. The guy was another lawyer who held an occasional part-time job at the college. Years later he was identified to me by one of his colleagues as a man who had something of a reputation for ignoring restricted parking signs on campus.

"We'll take a vote," I said without waiting for the man to answer. "Before I go on, let me see who in the faculty is offended by my language. If they are, I will speak less forcefully to you and not exactly tell it like it is. But I know that as an academic myself, you want to hear me talk straight. No pulling punches that some folks might be used to as lawyers. You're in a different setting now, my friend. We're talking English here."

The faculty voted by a show of hands to allow me to continue to curse and tell dirty jokes. The pious critic on the back row was routed. But in spite of any sense of personal vindication, the day would be won by The Citadel. When I returned to Charleston, I called back to find out that the faculty voted by a healthy margin to take the $5 million from The Citadel and run. Their jobs at a college which was going down the drain financially and drawing from its endowment to survive were saved. By July 17, 1995, The Citadel had identified 50 women who had shown interest in SCIL. But the dean of the College of Arts and Sciences at Converse voted against having SCIL at the college. Dean Jo Ann Lever believed that people would perceive the SCIL program as a discrimination against women.

"Something You Can See"

On May 1, 1995, the same day the Converse faculty voted to take what money it could, the South Carolina Senate surprisingly voted not to give The Citadel $1.2 million of tuition grant money. Senators Ernie Passailaigue and Glenn McConnell from Charleston had worked hard with Representatives Harry Hallman, Yancey McGill, and Billy O'Dell to take that money away from South Carolina students who needed it to attend state-wide colleges in order to give it to Converse to support The Citadel's cause. According to news reports, Senator Passailaigue even stated that it was "mean-spirited" not to give the $1.2 million to help The Citadel.[3] On May 4, 1995, I traveled to Columbia to observe the South Carolina Senate in action as it debated S-763. The debate was over whether to appropriate some $1 million to $3 million to Converse to supplement annually The Citadel Development Foundation's own $5 million for the initial establishment of the SCIL program. Plaintiffs argued that the effort was in complete violation of the statutes governing the Commission on Higher Education (CHE). Fred Sheheen also pointed this out to me as we talked outside the Senate chambers. As director of CHE, Fred Sheheen, as well as his staff, had been a constant source of educational data since 1989 while putting the case together. A man of remarkable integrity, he put his career on the line by putting his office, a state agency, on record in support of admitting women into the Corps of Cadets. His was the only state entity that supported the plaintiffs. His stance on the admission of women would later partly account for his removal from office.[4]

Senator Cork spotted me in the gallery and sent a message up by a runner to help me keep track of what was going on. She and the black senators, including Senator Glover, did what they could do. One or two white senators, such as Senator Land, spoke up to say, much to my surprise, that the General Assembly may as well let Faulkner in The Citadel since she was going to get in sooner or later, that the federal government would not tolerate such a violation of the Fourteenth Amendment.

Senator Maggie Glover spoke briefly in favor of admitting women. But it was Senator Kay Patterson, the black male senator from Richland County, who gave one of the best speeches that anyone who talked about the case ever gave in the entire debate of the issues. Representative Canty would later give a similar speech at Lesesne Gate.

In his deposition, given later, Senator Patterson repeated his speech to the Senate. He could not recall any time in which The Citadel failed to get anything it wanted from the General Assembly:

> Whenever The Citadel wants to lobby, they generally wind up getting whatever they ask for, and it's due to their board and their lobbyists and their Citadel connections. Through their network, if they put in a request of the General Assembly, it just about automatically goes through, just about. There'll be some discussion, but it's no real meaningful discussion; just a matter of people getting up stating their views. But it's a foregone conclusion that when this request comes forward, it's going.

The Citadel network is "something you can see," he went on. "You can see it at receptions.... All those board members we elect and put on The Citadel board, plus their lobbyists, plus their president, you know. And you put all that together, you have a hell of a force to reckon with."

Like Frederick Douglass, who was the only person who knew all along what the Civil War was all about, Patterson made the simple eloquent argument that Faulkner's effort on behalf of all women to join society was not basically different from that of his own people in their own continuing effort. He ended with the remark, "Let the little girl in," a non-deprecating reminder that the fight was indeed being conducted not so much by a woman as by one teenage "little girl." I later got Patterson to agree to testify at the remedial phase of the case if that phase had ever gone to trial.

NAACP and Shouting Billboard

There were few blacks in *Faulkner v. Jones*. No black attorneys that I knew of, no black plaintiffs or judges. And there were few black men and women in the South Carolina General Assembly. Like Patterson, Representative Ralph W. Canty brought the real thing to the fight.

For the most part, blacks like Nelson Rivers, who was reared in the shadow of The Citadel before becoming president of the NAACP in Atlanta, sat back and watched with amusement as the good ole boys fought girls at The Citadel. Most blacks in Charleston probably saw the whole mess in a light incomprehensible to whites, if they bothered with it at all. Elwood Watson, commentator in *The Charleston Chronicle*, wrote that Faulkner's opponents were attempting to make her the "Negro" of the 1990s, and he recognized the importance of a critical mass in a civil rights struggle by declaring that the main reason for Shannon Faulkner's failure was due to the lack of peers needed to serve as support groups.

On May 21, 1995, Alexia Niketas called me about staging a rally at Lesesne Gate on behalf of Shannon by the Women Against Rape.

"The rally will be attended by Dr. James L. Felder, the Executive Director of the South Carolina Conference of Branches, NAACP, and Representative Ralph W. Canty, the black representative from up state," Niketas said, "so if you want to come, there will be more people than just us there. The women in 52 Percent are also going to rally." As far as I knew, Shannon did not participate.

According to his news release from his hometown in Sumter, Canty charged that

> the tragic standoff which has evolved out of the refusal of The Citadel to admit Shannon Faulkner threatens the constitutional progress which South Carolina has made during the last fifty years.
>
> For me it was race. I was not allowed to attend certain public schools in the state of South Carolina solely because of my race. Today, for Shannon Faulkner, it is gender.

Canty's deep voice and sonorous tone of a Baptist preacher brought all the complex legal issues down to earth. He shot down the soaring corruption of the concept of the Whole Man, the adversative system, the Honor System, and every bit of phoniness that anchored The Citadel's defense. The case was about unconstitutional discrimination.

Canty described the program which The Citadel and General Assembly set up at Converse as

> morally grotesque and constitutionally untenable. It is not the sort of honest proposal which responsible and well-meaning Americans make in the Twentieth Century. It is also a billboard shouting our implacable backwardness to the world.
>
> We also now have — once again — a South Carolina legislature appropriating public money, and South Carolina governors signing into law, actions by our state government whose sole purpose is to keep a citizen for South Carolina out of an educational institution of South Carolina for discriminatory reasons. Forty years after *Brown v. The Board of Education* our public monies — contributed by men and women alike — are actually being used in extensive legal actions to keep half of the population of South Carolina from attending one of our more prominent state educational institutions....
>
> The Citadel does not belong to men.... What corruption has fallen upon the moral values of The Citadel? I would have thought that The Citadel would conduct itself in these modern times as a beacon for constitutional progress, as a magnet for socially progressive thought and morals, and that her sons would have been thoroughly educated year after year, decade after decade, to throw away the hatreds and the venomous divisions of the past — that they would have entered the world of adults, not considering themselves exclusive of anyone, and would have conducted themselves thereafter in a charitable, just, and open way.... Clearly, there is something very amiss in what is being taught about civic responsibility and about constitutional principles at The Citadel of today.

Representative Canty closed his speech with his intention to propose an amendment to the state appropriation bill to establish a commission to "review the moral values and the constitutional teachings" at The Citadel. Unlike the May 1993, Legislative Study Committee to figure out how best to keep women out of The Citadel, Canty's commission would not contain a majority of Citadel alumni. And he hoped that from the labor of such a commission, Citadel graduates "will go forth" into society and "will not divide and damage it any longer."

What To Do with the Girls

"Is that lesbian Hillary Clinton—and all the feminists—paying you or pushing you to pull off this deal with the Citadel—why should people pay extra to have feminine accouterments added to convenience *your* living at the Citadel?"

[Unsigned letter to Shannon, February 10, 1994]

"I hope you have to use the men's toilet."

[Unsigned letter to Shannon, January 20, 1994]

Hearings on The Citadel plan for assimilation of women into the Corps of Cadets, as the plaintiff would have it, went in tandem with plans for SCIL at Converse, as The Citadel would have it. The June 6, 1995, hearing on the 51st anniversary of D-Day, however, was not given to The Citadel's parallel program at Converse, but rather to the prospect of what to do with Faulkner if she were ordered into The Citadel Corps of Cadets. The hearing took up The Citadel's repeated efforts to isolate Faulkner from the rest of the Corps and put her in a permanent state of what could be called constructive XMD. Being on XMD was a status no knob ever wanted to be on, since the rest of the Corps would always think a knob in the Infirmary on XMD was feigning sickness or injury just to escape the rigors of the Fourth Class System. But The Citadel planned to do just that by kindly—"there's not a mean-spirited atom to that proposal," The Citadel insisted—excusing Shannon from all the stress of the Fourth Class System, especially the stress caused by the adversarial system and the "dangers of cross-sexual confrontations." Equal treatment, The Citadel argued, might easily be misinterpreted as sexual harassment by those who don't understand The Citadel. "Cross-sexual confrontations" meant hazing.

In 1994, the court would have allowed Shannon to live in the barracks, treating her as male cadets are treated and thus giving her equal protection under the law. But Shannon herself would have chosen to live in the Infirmary, if the Fourth Circuit had not stayed Judge Houck's order. Now, in 1995, the court's position was again that it would treat Shannon the same as male cadets, but this time Shannon wanted to live in Band Company, not the Infirmary.

Cooke's argument was, "I don't believe that the appropriate starting point in a constitutional analysis is to say that all treatment must be identical," to which the court responded that it did not say all conditions must be identical. We start off with them being equal, and we adjust them when we are convinced that acknowledged differences between the sexes dictate the same, the court said.

Val and Sandy Beber agreed at the hearing, with one point of emphasis. Val reminded the court that the valedictorian at West Point at that time was a woman, and she was able to withstand the stress of a federal service academy. Shannon wanted to be treated the same way the men were treated—adversative system and all—even though the academies did not use a so-called "adversative" system in which, The Citadel argued, only males could succeed. The academies taught leadership through what was called a "positive" system.

Then Val again addressed the big issue, one of the major issues that lay behind the entire litigation: the failure of leadership in the administration.

> We would accept one modification at this point in time, not because Shannon is a woman, not because there are differences between men and women, but because of the hostile environment that the defendants have permitted and that they refused to correct.... In this situation, we're not talking about pure coeducation where you have many women and men admitted on an equal basis with an administration that is willing to take a positive leadership role.

Without using the words and phrases in open court that consistently have been tolerated by The Citadel administration, Val referred, by way of example, to its tolerance toward cadets' use of "derogatory terms toward women to refer to washing the quad, to refer to one's hat." These references, as I told her before the hearing, were terms for "douching the quad" and "cunt cap."

So with that kind of leadership routinely tolerant of that kind of language, Val asked the court to modify The Citadel's assimilation plan to allow only eight to ten cadets to be in charge of Shannon's discipline within the Fourth Class System.

"We would be willing to reconsider that if at a point in time it's been demonstrated by their actions that they are willing to take charge of their cadets ... and if their leadership were committed to women being there," Val said.

The Citadel conveyed the usual indignation at The Citadel being perceived to be without clothes and tried to weigh in with Cadet Doucet's testimony at trial describing what a wonderful place The Citadel was. The court had no interest in hearing from either side on that issue again and simply acknowledged that there was a substantial amount of evidence to support the plaintiff's conclusion that The Citadel was not committed to accepting Shannon as a full partner in the Corps of Cadets.

At the hearing on the following day, June 7, 1995, the court determined that because The Citadel's contingency plan had come in at the very last moment, the defendants would bear the primary burden of assuring that the discovery process went smoothly. The court had only weeks to try the viability of the SCIL parallel program, as ordered, if possible, by the appellate court in *Faulkner II*, and The Citadel and Converse held all the documents.

At the same time, the court knew that there was no way for the case to be tried fairly within the time frame that The Citadel had created, the hole it had put itself in. By dragging its feet, The Citadel was defaulting by not producing a remedy in time to have a trial to see if it were constitutional. The Citadel's flimsy proposed remedial plans had been stacking up on the runway like airplanes in a fog: April 1, 1994; June 27, 1994; October 4, 1994; and still nothing the plaintiffs could conduct discovery on. During all this time, the plaintiff's own versions were trying to keep pace.

On June 1 The Citadel filed a plan for assimilation that put Shannon in the Infirmary pursuant to the agreement the previous June—the constructive XMD billeting. But in 1995, in her desire to live in Band Company she would have a lock on the door (twelve years before all Citadel cadets got them) and a guard posted at the entrance to the hallway leading to her room; her door would remain open and unlocked when she had visitors; she would be subject to Army physical fitness, height and weight standards; her hair would be worn above the collar; and "shirt tuck will not be required."

The Citadel agreed to have a special chain of command assigned to her, but it still insisted that she be denied the adversative system. And they alone would handle any complaints of sexual harassment, notwithstanding the Court's post-trial order of August 1994. Attached was a 24-hour schedule that included 20 minutes for lunch, 1220–1240.

And another thing outlined in the plan: "Ms. Faulkner has been provided with the appropriate medical forms, but she has declined to return them as required. Ms. Faulkner will not be admitted on August 12 unless all required medical information has been provided and her medical eligibility for admission has been determined in accordance with the regulations of The Citadel."

A few days later, on June 5, Charlie Condon filed a proposed remedial plan that looked at the other side of the coin and put Shannon in SCIL. Two days later Dawes chose to file a supplemental memorandum to explain that "The Citadel's program is gender-based," and that Shannon would be accommodated in a way that makes The Citadel's male-based "educational experience make sense." In this perfectly serious four-page memorandum, The Citadel held that "A superficial notion of equality [for women] ignores this experience [for men]."

At the June 7, 1995, hearing, Charlie Condon asked the Court for two or three more weeks—right up to days before classes were to start—to get another plan together "to see how things are going" and declared that the State of South Carolina, Faulkner, and the Justice Department would all be satisfied with the Converse parallel program whenever it did finally take shape.

Court orders of June 1 and June 6 to come up with a plan to put Shannon in the barracks were reluctantly complied with by The Citadel on June 16, 1995. The Citadel did all it could to deal with this toxic element in the barracks. She would not, after all, be put in the Infirmary and certainly not in Band Company where she wanted to be. She would instead be pitched into I Company, Number 3 Barracks, 3rd Division, Room 3344. I or India Company was the old company of Jimmy Jones, chairman of the Board of Visitors. Anything to keep her out of Band Company. On each side she would have members of the cadre in her direct chain of command. To satisfy some of the concerns of DOJ, The Citadel allowed her to have a window covering to block the view of peeping Toms and to have her own bathroom. To reinforce its basic position that exposure to the "adversative aspects of the Fourth Class System" was not good for her, The Citadel would assign a barracks guard to monitor traffic on the gallery outside her room.

Since the last thing The Citadel wanted was for the cadets to see Faulkner as a person and to succeed in anything "adversative," she would not be allowed to "join the male freshmen in the freshmen squad room prior to formations" or "participate in clean-up details or other activities in the barracks requiring entry into the rooms of other cadets." The list of restrictions went on and on. The handling of a bomb was not conducted with greater care. "No visitor shall enter Ms. Faulkner's room unless at least two people in addition to Ms. Faulkner are present. The wooden door to Ms. Faulkner's room will remain fully open throughout the time of any visit by male visitors."

In response to arguments by the plaintiff, the plan on June 16, 1995, attached an updated *Sexual Harassment Prevention: A Practical Guide.* As in the policy found by Shannon on the floor of Bond Hall the previous year, The Citadel was defiant in its position that no new or modified version of its existing policy on sexual harassment was needed with the entry of Faulkner into the Corps. What already existed in The Citadel Regulations was sufficient. "No change in the Regulations is required in order to effectuate The Citadel's policy against sexual harassment. The manner in which Regulations are enforced is an integral part of the cadet system, and will not be altered." This was General Poole's position and he was going to stick with it.

The June 16 plan to incorporate Faulkner into the Corps became one of the defendants' most hypocritical documents filed in the case:

> The following types of conduct are prohibited within the Corps of
> Cadets and will be specifically prohibited as to Ms. Faulkner unless

otherwise directed by the Court: Use of derogatory nicknames for her … Statements that Ms. Faulkner is not capable of performing up to standards … Expressions of opinion that she should not be in the Corps of Cadets at The Citadel … Statements regarding her state of physical conditioning … Statements regarding her physical appearance … Use of derogatory comments towards her.

By early August, plaintiff would allege that The Citadel public relations director Terry Leedom violated not only the judge's order sealing Shannon's medical records but also The Citadel's June 16 plan in his attacks on Faulkner during the following weeks. Further, no such plan would be complete without instructions for a young cadet wanting desperately to fit in: "Ms. Faulkner shall be required to report all incidents or complaints of sexual harassment immediately." This rather than nip them in the bud.

The Court Pays a Visit

On June 17, 1995, Judge Houck wanted to visit Mary Baldwin College (MBC) in Stanton, Virginia, and Converse in Spartanburg in quick succession. The Virginia Women's Institute for Leadership (VWIL) at Mary Baldwin and the South Carolina Institute for Leadership (SCIL) were themselves physical subjects of discovery.

On June 27, 1995, the same entourage that would follow Judge Houck at Converse a week later—attorneys, college officials, and members of the press—followed his path as he was escorted through the women's college looking at sites relevant to the establishment of the VWIL.

The display was idiotic and embarrassing. There they were at Mary Baldwin, trying not to laugh, trying to convince the Judge that the moon was blue cheese. You would have thought that some adult would have finally said, "Hey, look, we're grownups—let's be honest: this place is no more like VMI than a New Guinea cargo cult air strip is like LaGuardia. Can't you just give us a little bit of money for trying?"

Sandra Thomas was particularly proud to welcome the Judge as the court made an Elizabethan progress to inspect Converse on July 3, 1995. By the Judge's directive, the court was in session in exactly the same manner as if the proceedings were being conducted in the courtroom in Charleston. A court reporter was present and there were many jesters around. As at MBC, the judge let the college officials do the talking and only asked questions whenever he wanted to. Even though it was the court's inspection, and not that of the plaintiff's or defendants', attorneys still were able to ask questions and see and hear what the Judge saw and heard, even if they had to run to catch up as he walked from place to place and, more importantly, even if Thomas tried to ignore them to focus only on the Judge.

Thomas kept saying that everything was "good to go," a phrase nearly as tiresome as The Citadel's "set for success" and "meet the challenge." Like MBC the week before, Converse was putting its shop goods in the window and the sales pitch was on.

I would later be offered an invitation to stay as a guest in the house of an Episcopal priest and his wife in Spartanburg during depositions at Converse. I had not seen my friend from Camp McDowell in Alabama in 40 years. But when I called to confirm the invitation, the good preacher's wife let me know in retrospect that it was somewhat awkward to have me stay there. She had been talking to some of the parishioners. I and my New York, Washington, and ACLU buddies were, after all, on the wrong side. That was the oldest friendship I lost during the case.

Chapter 7

Honor and Good Sense

Mt. Pleasant, SC 29464
August 24, 1995

Mr. Robert Black
23 Broad Street
Charleston, SC 29401

Dear Mr. Black,

I am not sure whether you saw this article [Cal Thomas, "For Shannon the Point was Politics," *The Post and Courier*] in yesterday's paper so I decided to send it to you. I think it hits the nail on the head!

I also saw your interview on television the other morning wherein you stated that you (attorneys) "could not keep up with Shannon." If that is the case, I would suggest ambulance chasing.

Sincerely,
[signed]

The Battle of Obesity

Mostly children of privilege at the time leading up to the Civil War, the cadets of the Military College of South Carolina were among those who fired the first shot on Fort Sumter. The shot went unanswered as the Star of the West sailed away. The Union vessel simply departed the scene and left the war to start in earnest a short time later at St. Augustine where hostile shots were fired from both sides for the first time, according to a National Park ranger at the fort.

In the Daniels Library at The Citadel there are three gigantic paintings of the Corps of Cadets' involvement in the Civil War. By far the largest framed pictures are in the main library—they dominate the Reading Room. Next to the one that portrays the firing on Fort Sumter, depictions of two lesser known events hang high on the wall. They are "The Cadet Company" fought under General Wade Hampton at Louisa Court House, Virginia, on June 11, 1864 and "The Battle of State Cadets," a fight with some of Sherman's marauding troops at Tullifinny Creek, near Pocataligo, South Carolina, on December 6 or 9, 1864, under Major J. B. White, the fifth superintendent at The Citadel. These skirmishes, perhaps as much as the attack on Fort Sumter, are what many Citadel cadets look to with pride. The pike on the regimental colors for the Palmetto Brigade carries a half-dozen or so streamers for engagements such as those with the Star of the West on January 9, 1861; at Wappoo Cut in November 1861; on James Island in June 1862 and 1864; in Charleston and Vicinity from July to October 1863; and at the Battle of Tullifinny Creek in December 1864.

While it is true that the Corps of Cadets at the Arsenal in Columbia and The Citadel in Charleston were used to keep down slave uprisings prior to the Civil War, that part of their service to the South was considered to be of the same kind as shuttling Yankees to POW camps. But the skirmish at Tullifinny Creek included the Corps of Cadets at The Citadel—the Palmetto Brigade—as a fighting unit in and of itself.

The hot heads from The Citadel and Charleston got the South into the Civil War, but they did not do most of the fighting. Most had to be left to other Southerners, one of whom was my great-grandfather John Franklin Marion Foster from Spartanburg and Clinton, South Carolina. I suppose it was Dawes' great-grandfather, the Yankee General Meade, who personally shot and wounded great-granddaddy Foster in the Peach Orchard on July 2, 1863, at Gettysburg. As a private in Company I, 3rd South Carolina Infantry, McLaws Division, Kershaw's Brigade, John Franklin Marion Foster fought at First Manassas, Seven Pines, Seven Days, Peninsula Campaign, Savage Station, Malvern Hill, Harper's Ferry, Sharpsburg, Fredericksburg, Chancellorsville, Gettysburg (WIA), and Knoxville (WIA) where he was captured. That could be more battles from one upstate rank-and-file redneck than all of those in which 209 Citadel cadets fought during the Civil War, including the nine insignificant scuffles in which the cadets fought as a unit in the Battalion of State Cadets from 1861–1865. According to General Watts in his Forward to the 1991 reprint of John Peyre Thomas' *History of the South Carolina Military Academy* published in 1893, "Graduates led and died in such Civil War battles as First and Second Manassas, in the West at Shiloh, then at Sharpsburg in Maryland, as well as the Wilderness, Seven Pines, and Gettysburg."

According to a lecture by Professor Kyle Sinisi, a VMI graduate teaching at The Citadel in 2010, and several published accounts of cadets in the war, approximately 209 of 224 Citadel graduates served throughout the war, but only

20% as rank-and-file soldiers. Of the total number there were 44 KIA, 94 WIA, 6 captured, and 12 died of wounds or disease. According to Professor Sinisi in his lecture in an auditorium two doors down from where Shannon registered for classes at The Citadel, at their last battle at Tullifinny Creek the Cadets were joined by a unit of seasoned veterans, possibly from the 3rd South Carolina Infantry. But great-granddaddy Foster, by then a POW in Rock Island, Illinois, would not have been with his old regiment fighting the Yankees side by side with Citadel cadets, those soldiers in Company I with Citadel-sounding names like Byrd, Beasley, Canady, Ferguson, Gordon, Holland, Hollingsworth, Hanby, Hipps, Huckabee, Langston, Lyles, McKelvy, Meeks, McDowell, Owens, and Oxner, and on down to Zeigler. Although he did not live to fight at Tullifinny Creek, Colonel James D. Nance, their commanding officer, was a Citadel graduate and lawyer from Newberry who was killed seven months earlier in Virginia at the Battle of the Wilderness.[1]

But now as the hot sun ground into July and the terrible Charleston trilogy of humidity, insects, and people began to lay on, The Citadel was about to fight its first great battle since the Battle of Tullifinny Creek. Second only to their destruction of the Veterans Day Program, it would be their finest hour. And this time shots would be fired from both directions. I talked to Shannon on July 1, 1995, regarding The Citadel's discovery requests for her medical reports for which The Citadel had begun to clamor. She was overweight. The Battle of Obesity was about to begin.

It would soon be over, however, because plenty of evidence showed that The Citadel applied its height and weight requirements for admission arbitrarily. The Citadel wanted to deal with Faulkner in a strict and unequal way that it never dealt with men.

The Citadel's obesity defense made a renewed showing in 1995, but this time with an urgency and newness which it did not have the previous summer. Plaintiff's lawyers were caught off guard as they fine-tuned Faulkner's admission to the Corps, dealing with the minor issue of being sure her knee was OK, for her own good. A doctor at Oakwood Orthopaedic Clinic on June 13, 1995, examined her again, as Dr. Gross did in 1994, and found no reason why she should not be able to participate in the Fourth Class System.

The only remaining issues in the side skirmishes in 1995 seemed to be limited to her being allowed to join the band and to be billeted with Band Company. Dawes sent me a letter on June 7, 1995, directing me to call the president's assistant to arrange an audition.

But the real fight, as the plaintiff and world soon discovered, turned out to be over Faulkner's weight. The Citadel planned to make it as public as Public Relations Director Terry Leedom possibly could. Giving up on the district court and operation of law, the spokesman for The Citadel would again take its case directly to the streets.

The Citadel never appealed the court's finding in its order of July 22, 1994, that Faulkner met all the requirements for admission, a finding that became the law of the case. Moreover, the court found at the hearings on July 25 and 26, 1995, that on August 11, 1994, The Citadel stated that in spite of the fact that they contended that Faulkner's weight permitted The Citadel to deny her admission to the Corps in 1994, The Citadel chose to waive any health requirement that they thought Faulkner might not meet that would keep her out of the Corps. Even the president gave his word on it. Lieutenant General Watts had agreed to waive any physical problems and deficiencies, particularly Faulkner's weight, and let her join the Corps.

About the August 11, 1994, waiver, the court concluded at the July 25 and 26, 1995, hearings that "to come in at the last minute and to say that she doesn't have the right to rely on it and to insist that she reduce her weight some 15 or 20 pounds I think is not only unlawful, it's unconscionable."

Besides, the facts weighed more heavily in Faulkner's favor in August 1995, when she weighed 189 pounds, than they did in August 1994, when she weighed 198 pounds. Since May 3, 1993, when she weighed 150 pounds at her first deposition two months after filing suit, Shannon had gained nearly 50 pounds in a year. The monumental stress was obvious to the world, and it would continue to be revealed.

The entire record of all *in-camera* proceedings held on the matter, after appropriate redaction of the names and other identifying information of non-parties, was unsealed by order of the district court on August 25, 1995. The court held that the public's right to access weighed in favor of unsealing the hearings, and that information about Faulkner's height and weight was "not of such a stigmatizing nature that it deserves a high level of privacy." Besides, as alleged in plaintiff's motion of August 4, Terry Leedom had already violated the court's order and told the press gathered at Broad and Meeting Streets that Shannon was overweight.

The Citadel requirement to pass the physical training test was to do 45 pushups in 2 minutes, 55 sit-ups in 2 minutes, and to run 2 miles in 16 minutes. The test was seen by many cadets as a joke, as Vergnolle testified in his deposition. The unlucky got caught cutting corners. Many cadets did not even take it. Out of the 1886 cadets enrolled during the first semester of the academic year 1992–93, 143 football players and 33 cross country runners were excused from taking the physical fitness test. Of those remaining who took the test, 10%, or 176, failed. The second semester was worse. Out of the 1844 cadets in the Corps, 159 athletes were excused, and 15%, or 254, failed. The only encouragement to pass the test was to get out of having to take Fitness Training three times a week as required by the Commandant in a memo dated July 31, 1992.

Unlike VMI, The Citadel had no requirement to pass the physical fitness test in order to be graduated, even though all cadets had gone through four years of ROTC. One had only to look around at the hoards of chubby business majors each spring on graduation day to tell how seriously The Citadel took physical training. Just by looking around at all of the cadets marching at a Friday afternoon parade, anyone could tell that plenty of good ole boys had trouble fitting in their uniforms.

After the *Faulkner* case, alumni grew sensitive to the issue and, according to one female cadet who helped me find a parking space during Homecoming 2010, cadets—male and female—who are overweight are not allowed to park cars or walk across the stage at graduation. They are kept out of sight.

The plaintiffs and defendants renewed their skirmishes on the fussy side issues relative to admission, which had begun the previous year and continued from June into early August 1995. By then, however, defendants produced a stack of documents dealing with Faulkner's weight.

For the entire month of July the plaintiffs tried to find out what parallel plan existed at Converse in preparation for trial, and the defendants tried to find out how much Faulkner weighed. The plaintiffs never found out because SCIL was not even a coherent plan on paper, much less an existing program. The defendants found out what Shannon weighed and posted it on a bumper sticker: "Congratulations! It's a Girl. 186 Pounds. 6 Ounces." Seven of them appeared almost immediately after August 9, one on an old black Crown Victoria with S.C. tag HXF 124 parked, as if abandoned, in front of 13 Broad Street at 4:30 p.m., just a few doors from my office. The valiant efforts by both sides provided great entertainment for people all over the world.

Bobby Hood announced to the court that the defendants had subpoenaed Shannon's medical records from her pediatrician in Greenville. Plaintiff's attorneys complained that they got no notice of the subpoena.

Of course, without notice, the plaintiffs would have no opportunity to object. Marie Antoinette in giving birth to a child had more medical privacy than Faulkner. The intended long-range effect was to create a chilling effect on all other women who dared to make application to the Corps.

But the disclosure of Shannon's personal medical history served as a stage to demonstrate how each team of lawyers conducted themselves at trial on every little issue and how suspicious they were of each other. An allegation by the plaintiffs' lawyers *in camera* before the judge that Bobby Patterson allowed the news media to look over his shoulder as he reviewed the records was for the defendants "but another instance of reckless and unfounded accusations against The Citadel, the State of South Carolina, and its attorneys," as Patterson said in an affidavit.

Two days of hearings *in camera* were held on July 25 and 26, 1995, to argue over Faulkner's physical fitness to join the Corps. Reciting the arguments, Val's memorandum on August 6, 1995, in opposition to The Citadel's motion to the Fourth Circuit for a stay pending appeal, was a masterpiece. The usual fare of Citadel hypocrisy and malice, in its effort to use Shannon's weight to try to keep her out of The Citadel, brought out the very best in everyone on Faulkner's side, especially Sandy Beber and Val. The battle was never over proving that she was overweight and didn't meet the physical requirements for admission. Nor did the battle consist of arguments that the requirements were exact criteria for being healthy and hardy. The Citadel had already conceded in 1994 that she would be admitted anyway, and everyone, including Shannon herself, knew she was still overweight in 1995. The judge said it was obvious that Shannon was overweight. Some then assumed that she therefore must be unfit to be a cadet, regardless of how well she carried her weight. Instead, the battle, as always, was over how The Citadel treated her application for admission, whether they were treating her the same way they treated male applicants.

Val wrote,

> The Citadel is increasingly desperate to keep Shannon Faulkner from becoming a cadet. In this effort, The Citadel has practiced delay, discovery abuse, leaks to the press of materials ordered to be sealed by the district court, and overall disregard for the Constitutional rights of Ms. Faulkner and the women of South Carolina.
>
> Now, having lost every other argument and faced with Ms. Faulkner's imminent entry into the Corps of Cadets, The Citadel is pursuing an ugly and specious attack on Ms. Faulkner's medical fitness.

Yet to prove that it was business as usual for The Citadel, plaintiffs had to dig for the medical records of male cadets who were found to be physically deficient yet given waivers to be admitted into the Corps. That was the one clear way to demonstrate The Citadel's uneven playing field it had created for Shannon. If Shannon were overweight, the record showed clearly that numerous male cadets who were admitted were even more overweight. Bubba was fat.

As it played out, there was no objective standard to apply in the process of making a physical evaluation of male cadets. There was no Citadel "policy" on physical fitness any more than there was a state "policy" on single-sex education.

A so-called Citadel "policy" of waiving those up to 20 pounds overweight was not enforced. "It's nothing—it's not a cut-and-dry thing, you know. It's a guts—it's a guide," is how The Citadel physician described the process of making physical evaluations for admissions of male cadets at the hearing on August 11, 1994. And at his deposition The Citadel physician admitted that evaluations were not based on objective, fixed criteria. They were subjective: "It's just a gut call."

That subjective standard especially applied to athletes. The Citadel automatically accepted all athletes as being fit, even walk-ons, and had no independent determination as to whether they were physically fit for the Fourth Class System. No effort was made to determine whether the excess weight was fat or muscle.

According to medical records, one football player who was 55 pounds overweight was told that he had to lose 30 pounds before being admitted, and even then he was still 20 pounds over Army regulations.

On July 17, 1995, the Dean of Enrollment Services was compelled to write a letter to Faulkner, addressed to 16 Chadwick Drive, rejecting her application for admission to the Corps because she was 68 inches high and weighed 194, when under the Army regulations she could weigh no more than 154 pounds, or no more than 174 under The Citadel "20 pound leeway."

In an undated affidavit in July 1995, The Citadel physician stated that for purposes of admission, U.S. Army regulations were only a beginning point. The Citadel had, since 1987, allowed cadets who were 20 pounds overweight to enter the Corps. In his June 27, 1995, letter to Faulkner, The Citadel physician had told her that she was 21 pounds overweight.

"I am of the opinion that Ms. Faulkner should be rejected as an applicant for admission to The Citadel because of her physical condition, i.e. her records indicate that she is physically unqualified and will face a substantial increased risk of health problems," the physician warned. Maybe she could be admitted by a body fat measurement, he continued—if she passed that test—but she had only until July 15.

The Citadel was so concerned about Shannon's health that they required Ed Faulkner to sign an affidavit in the event she got in. On July 23, 1995, Ed and Sandy swore they knew the physical risks their daughter was taking by being overweight.

The Citadel called on its heavy reserves for further testimony at the July hearings. The vice president and nurse would take the stand, but if they lost this round, they would have their final triumph only days later. The Citadel does indeed exempt its football players, if not all other athletes, from its physical fitness guidelines, the vice president testified, because it needs large and bulky players to compete with other NCAA teams. The Athletic Director simply provides the vice president with a statement that the football players have a "far superior state of physical condition of the average cadet." If they do not meet The Citadel height and weight standards, their coach gives them the standard PT test and the Athletic Director, not The Citadel doctor, "makes a determination as to the physical condition of the athlete," the vice president said.

Yet Val and Sandy uncovered layers of Citadel records to show that not all athletes were inherently fit. A recent walk-on football player who was 50 pounds overweight was found by The Citadel physician to be "terribly out of shape." The doctor recommended a medical discharge. The cadet was allowed to stay, however, and the policy of rejecting such applicants was not followed. Instead, the cadet was excused from cadet physical training and continued to play football even though the doctor said that "he simply can't do even minimal exercise."

Val then proceeded to admit into evidence a long series of medical records of male cadets who were admitted even though they, like Faulkner, were not athletes but were overweight for their relative heights. In 1993 The Citadel admitted a general's son who was 57 pounds overweight. Another was 44 pounds over; another whose body fat measured 28% was allowed in if he reduced down to 30 pounds overweight; another was 27 pounds overweight; another was 42 pounds over the mark; another, 28 pounds over; another, 91 pounds overweight, but The Citadel would have admitted him if he lost 50 pounds by August, just as they would have admitted another male set to enter the Corps with Shannon if he lost 34 pounds in six weeks; and, typically, at least three others were noted by The Citadel to be overweight, but their medical records were unavailable to establish exactly how much over weight they were.

Just as significantly, evidence showed that The Citadel identified only one male cadet, the cadet who was 44 pounds overweight, and asked his parents to sign the kind of waiver Ed and Sandy Faulkner were later asked to sign for Shannon.

For Shannon, on the other hand, it was still decided that she could not weigh more than 20 pounds over Army regulations and that it was "medically impossible," as the doctor said, for her to lose that kind of weight in such a short period of time.

Val dug deeper as the hearing continued. Everyone but The Citadel was embarrassed. The resounding question again surfaced: How could love for one's nourishing mother lead men into such folly? The court, in its order on July 26 found the case of one cadet "so ridiculous, [it was] almost unbelievable." He weighed 265 pounds, putting him 79 pounds over Army regulations, but still not heavy enough for his own bumper sticker.

July 24, 1995, Order

> "Each morning when the sun comes up there's a horse race in South
> Carolina between Arrogance and Ignorance. If you look up in the sky
> during the day from anywhere in the State you can see 'em runnin'.
> Sometimes as the sun sets, Arrogance wins and sometimes Ignorance.
> Sometimes it's a dead heat."
>
> Anonymous

As in many other civil rights cases, the real cost of litigation of The Citadel
case lay not only in the millions of dollars spent but also in the divisiveness
and ill will it created among fellow citizens and, even more, the neglect of
greater issues in education, health, the environment, and the economy. To that
extent, July and August 1995, were months of feasting for arrogance and ignorance.

The Fourth Circuit and the district court found that The Citadel defendants were on notice to present a remedial plan as early as October 1992 (after
VMI), then again in November 1993, and again in February 1994. Yet the
Proposed Remedial Plan setting out SCIL was not filed until June 5, 1995,
and amendments came along even later on June 12 and 16. VWIL, on the
other hand, was filed by VMI in September 1993, giving the plaintiffs seven
months for discovery prior to approval by the Virginia district court on April
29, 1994, and for implementation more than a year later during the 1995–96
school year.

As directed by the court, plaintiffs dropped everything to make it in time
for trial. They served their initial discovery requests two days after the parallel program at Converse was filed.

A total of some 215 depositions were conducted in the *Faulkner* case and in
related issues from the veterans' case. Most were held in Charleston, but others were held in Virginia, New York, New Jersey, North Carolina, Georgia, Arizona, California, Colorado, Illinois, Florida, Washington state, and Washington,
D.C. In the four-year period between September 1992, and August 1996, I attended some 66 depositions, about 30% of the total. I recruited approximately
70% of the total number of witnesses named in court pleadings for trial in
May 1994, but most of the plaintiff's witnesses who actually testified were experts I did not recruit.

By June 5, 1995, The Citadel had produced 13,000 Bates stamped sheets
of paper.

The deposition schedule for Shearman attorneys and Val, who had left Shearman toward the end of litigation, was packed throughout July 1995, with 15
depositions of as many of the Converse College personnel as they could iden-

tify. I sat in on most of them. Toward the end of July 1995, alone, plaintiffs were running 14 sessions of depositions of eight Converse witnesses.

By July 31, 1995, after the court ruled on July 24 to admit Faulkner into the Corps, The Citadel complained that Faulkner and DOJ together had made over 224 Requests for Production of Documents. Nearly 75 more depositions followed in October and November in preparation for the remedial trial that never happened, but I conducted or attended only seven of those.

The court's historical July 24, 1995, order did not recapitulate its explicit order of July 22, 1994, *Faulkner I*, to integrate the Corps. Its language, "And It Is So Ordered," operated by reference to the April 13, 1995, *Faulkner II*, order by the Fourth Circuit, and thereby ordered the first woman into the Corps of Cadets in the Military College of South Carolina. The district court order did not, for a second time, have to order that Faulkner be admitted since its first order to do just that the previous year, on July 22, 1994, had been upheld with modifications by the Fourth Circuit on April 13, 1995. Thus, the district court on July 24, 1995, only found that The Citadel and state did not meet a deadline set by the Fourth Circuit and thus did not satisfy the modifying requirements made by the Fourth Circuit.

On July 24, 1995, the district court found that the defendants deliberately withheld the important role of Sam Applegate, an influential attorney who was hired without notice to the plaintiffs to represent South Carolina in contract negotiations among Converse, The Citadel, and state. The court went on to characterize the conduct of The Citadel in discovery on SCIL:

> When South Carolina's Proposed Remedial Plan was filed on June 5, 1995, and the court began searching on June 7, 1995, for a way to consider approval and implementation of the same before August 12, 1995 [when classes started], it knew that such a goal would be difficult, if not impossible, to obtain. With the assurances made by the defendants that they would waive some objections and make a good faith effort to accelerate the discovery process, it seemed possible. In hindsight, it probably was possible. The problem is, the defendants have not done what they said they would. Instead of speeding the discovery process up, they have slowed it down.
>
> Instead of being open and fair as they promised, it has been business as usual for the defendants. They have failed to respond properly to discovery requests in violation of the rules of this court, and they have made legitimate objections to discovery that seem to serve little or no useful purpose for them but delay the completion of discovery significantly. In short, they have continued to make the plain-

tiffs dig for every piece of information they get. As a result, the case is not even near being in a position to try at this time. The parties need at least several more months to prepare. The court, therefore, reluctantly concludes that it cannot consider the issues relating to the approval and implementation of South Carolina's Proposed Remedial Plan prior to August 12, 1995. The parties shall have until October 15, 1995, to complete discovery with the trial of all outstanding issues to commence on November 6, 1995.

Death Row

On July 28, The Citadel made an emergency appeal of the district court's July 26 order denying their motion to keep Shannon out because of her weight. When that motion was denied on August 9, 1995, by Judge Hall, with a concurrence of Judge Niemeyer, Judge Hamilton filed a dissenting opinion warning that Faulkner did not fill out a complete medical history in her application for admission. "I assume those waiving this requirement are prepared to accept the responsibility and consequences of Faulkner's suffering a serious injury if, in fact, she is not physically fit and qualified to undertake the rigorous training program of the Corps of Cadets," he wrote.

On August 3, 1995, both DOJ and Faulkner's attorneys filed memoranda in opposition to The Citadels' motion for recall and stay of the Fourth Circuit's June 5, 1995, mandate pending the filing of a petition for writ of *certiorari* from the April 13 order. It was denied five days later. Again, Judge Hamilton dissented. The court was "trashing" century-old benefits of single-sex, holistic education. What Scalia said about "venerable" VMI went for The Citadel too, even though VMI was ruled by Judge Kiser and affirmed by the Fourth Circuit to be "unique." Shortly afterwards, Judge Hamilton filed yet another lengthy dissent decrying the operation of the court's April 13 order to put Faulkner in the Corps by default without a hearing on the merits.[2]

As ordered by the Fourth Circuit, the plaintiffs responded by August 4 to The Citadel's request for a stay. As of August 7, however, no action had been taken by the Fourth Circuit. The time constraints on The Citadel were obvious. So with August 12 just around the corner, on August 7 The Citadel had both appeals working at the same time—to the Fourth Circuit and, in anticipation of a lack of success there, to the Chief Justice of the United States Supreme Court. Charles Cooper of the Washington, D.C., firm, Shaw, Pittman, Potts & Trowbridge handled all the specialized procedures in filing the timely pleadings in the Supreme Court for The Citadel. On August 7, The Citadel had already lodged with the Supreme Court its application to the Chief Justice for a stay of the district court order of July 24, 1995, pending the filing of a petition for writ of *certiorari* to the Fourth Circuit. When the Fourth Circuit denied The Citadel's motion for recall and stay of its June 5 mandate on August 8, Cooper simply wrote to William Suter, Clerk of the Supreme Court, and asserted that the application on the 7th "should be considered to have been filed with the Court as of yesterday evening."

On August 8, 1995, the plaintiffs wrote a letter to Chief Justice Rehnquist objecting to this simultaneous whammy amounting to a virtual *ex parte* proceeding. When Henry and Val wrote the letter, the Fourth Circuit had not even ruled yet, but The Citadel's further appeal had already been prepared and sent to the Supreme Court, thus denying the plaintiffs an opportunity to respond.

By Friday, August 11, 1995, Chief Justice Rehnquist had denied The Citadel's application for a stay. In a letter sent later on the same day, Cooper asked the Clerk to "renew" the application to Justice Scalia, but Justice Scalia took no action. Faulkner was, therefore, admitted into the Corps, this time without a stay. Photographs taken by Charleston photographers Curtis Norman and Roger Cureton ran in newspapers and television all over the world to record the celebration by Team Faulkner at a carriage house downtown.

Valorie K. Vojdik, Shannon Faulkner, and Robert Black upon news that Faulkner would be the first woman to be admitted into The Citadel Corps of Cadets. Used with permission, Staff photo by Roger Cureton, *The Post and Courier*, August 12, 1995.

Band Company

Shannon—Next time audition on the skin flute.

[Anonymous letter, postmarked Kansas City, MO, July 18, 1995]

The first order of business for Ed Faulkner, as he discussed with the press after the July 24 order, was physical training with his daughter. Dana Nettles, who lived down the road from 16 Chadwick said years later that Shannon used to drop by during breaks while running in the neighborhood. Now Shannon was at home in Easley with her mother and father.

On Thursday, August 3, 1995, Ed Faulkner said that he and Shannon were running every morning to get ready for the PT test when she reported to The Citadel. Shannon was running in a rubber sweat suit in the early morning before it got too hot. Ed was confident that she would be able to pass the test, even though he had not yet put a stopwatch on her. She was the kind of young woman who carried her weight well, like her father.

What amounted to an in-house devilish little PT test existed at the foot of the stairs to the second floor at 16 Chadwick. To keep baby John from climbing the steps, the gate across the steps had a latch which could only be reached during the descent from the second floor by leaning over the gate at the bottom of the last step. Spencer jumped over it. Shannon handled it with ease. Melinda removed it in less than a day.

The ordeal of trying to get Shannon in Band Company began in June 1994, and lasted for more than a year. Getting her in Band Company was important because Band Company could serve as a relatively safe harbor since it contained few, if any, "hard-corps" misogynists. It offered some sense of safety as close as possible to that provided by the presence of another woman cadet. The Citadel's strategy to get rid of Shannon by isolating her to wear her down as quickly as possible would, of course, be weakened if she were to room in Band Company. Band Company had the reputation of not caring much about all the military matters that went on at The Citadel. The members of Band Company pretty much kept to themselves. They weren't eggheads, but they liked to play music and have a good time together, sometimes in the cadets' secret hideout under Padgett-Thomas Barracks where the booze was kept. Band Company was relatively bully-free and had no "high and tights" on military contract eager to show that they were tougher than other cadets.

Getting her in Band Company was related to the issue of Faulkner's participation in extracurricular activities while waiting for full admission into the Corps. Shannon still wanted to play in the orchestra, join the student legislature, and work on the yearbook staff. At Wrenn High School she had played the flute, tuba, the baritone, and the xylophone in the band. On Friday, August 11, 1995, the judge heard four hours of The Citadel's arguments why Shannon should not be allowed to have a room in Band Company, even though she was continuing to audition as a member of the band, having failed the first time. Part of the testimony included factual evidence of males being accepted into Band Company even though they had failed initial tests in playing their instruments.

Security

Columbia, SC 29223
February 16, 1994

Miss Shannon Faulkner
The Citadel
Charleston, SC 29409

Dear Miss Faulkner,

I am not a Citadel graduate, but I am a native South Carolinian. I greatly appreciate the traditions and the values that The Citadel represents and have high regard for cadets there. There is no question about the value of single-gender schools, especially where military training is involved.

Therefore, it distresses me to no end to see these values trampled upon in pursuit of "equal rights" and in order to be "politically correct." I, of course, do not [know] what your true motives are, but I can only feel that they are an attempt to draw attention and publicity to yourself. That being the case, I truly wish you all the ill can befall a person of such selfish motivation. You do not belong there and I hope that the brief time that you do spen[d] there will be some of the most miserable of your life.

Most sincerely,
[signed]

You are a sick Bitch—Just to be a Teacher you could have went anywhere—they should beat the Hell out of you.

[Anonymous letter to SRF, January 24, 1994, Harrisburg, PA]

All I can say is I hope those guys make your life a living Hell.

[Anonymous letter to SRF, February 16, 1994,
Suburban, MD MSC208]

Matters of security were never taken lightly, even in the most absurd circumstances. During a Continuing Legal Education meeting in Columbia sometime right after Shannon filed her lawsuit, Judge Houck was one of several other judges who were speaking. As the judge went into the auditorium at the Law School, I noticed a man, about 40–45 years old, dressed all in black, as if he were a country music star. He had a menacing look, and he stared right at me. Inside the Law School auditorium he sat right up front on the first row and asked Judge Houck some questions that everyone thought way out of line for a federal judge to address. They were aggressive, rhetorical questions. Onlookers rolled their eyes and let it pass as just another eccentric lawyer.

The judge took it all in stride. But as the audience left, I noticed the man staring at the judge this time. A real jerk, I thought, and let it pass as bad manners, at least until I got back to Charleston where I was told that they stopped the same man on Interstate Highway 26 driving from Columbia to Charleston. And the picture on his driver's license showed him dressed in an old Citadel uniform. Whether it was his own, or a borrowed one, I never found out.

After FBI agent Bill Zerillo called me from the U.S. marshal's office and I relayed Zerillo's concerns for Shannon's safety to Sandy and Ed in Easley, some members of The Citadel faculty gave me their own impression or sense of security at The Citadel. I carried their concerns to the meeting which Judge Houck called at 11:00 a.m. on August 9, 1995, to talk about security. The preceding year, on August 10, 1994, before the Fourth Circuit placed a stay on the district court's order to allow Faulkner to enter the Corps, Faulkner's attorneys had met alone with the United States marshals in the Judge's chambers to discuss her safety. Now we met again, but this time the Judge met with us. Initially, the meeting included Dawes and Colonel Bingham from Citadel Security. Later, only Shannon, Ed Faulkner, U.S. marshals Israel Brooks, Bill Zerillo, and Ed Mitman, along with Shannon's lawyers were present. It was an extraordinary example of the nature of the case.

Zerillo outlined the security measures to be taken from the time Shannon drove through the gate to the times throughout the following weeks or months she lived in the barracks. There would be no campus police giving Shannon a parking ticket this time. In her room, Shannon would have an electronic device which was connected to the United States marshals stationed in The Citadel Security Office by Lesesne Gate, some 200 yards from her room on the third floor of Law Barracks. Tapes from the 24-hour camera outside the door to her room would be kept for seven days. Two marshals would make hourly checks but make no direct contact beyond a debriefing with Shannon at the end of the day that would be sent to the court.

To see her room, the Judge then moved the security meeting from a conference room in the courthouse to The Citadel campus itself. He had earlier, on July 12, conducted discovery at The Citadel in the same manner he did at Mary Baldwin and Converse. The Judge, Val, Sara, Henry, and I listened intently to the marshal as he recited the security procedures in place at Faulkner's room. A lot of the security precautions were ironed out the previous year. Unlike the door of any other cadet's room, Shannon's door would have a lock. She would also have a whistle. The camera outside her door at that time was without accompanying sound. To have sound was still a legal issue being argued over in other cases around the country. Meanwhile, one of Charlie Condon's assistants in the AG office was reportedly busy drafting a memo opposing any use of a listening device outside Shannon's room. The concern ostensibly was that cadets may be caught for other kinds of violations, their constitutional liberties violated by Big Brother. Zerillo's effort to protect Shannon was that much more impeded.

As we left Shannon's barracks, news from the Fourth Circuit arrived. The Citadel's motion for a stay based on the issue of Faulkner's weight was denied. Faulkner had cleared the last barrier to be admitted into the Corps of Cadets.

In its decision the previous year to post U.S. marshals at The Citadel, the court expressed an optimistic view that The Citadel would exercise good faith in bringing Faulkner into the Corps of Cadets. The court believed in August 1994, and also in August 1995, that The Citadel would, on its own, in time, take whatever actions that were reasonably required to guarantee that the first woman in the Corps would be treated properly under the law and not harmed or harassed. To a degree, I shared that wishful thinking.

The facts, however, turned out to be quite different. After The Citadel's initial phases of resistance, the persistent harassment, and the legal phase itself, the procedure was to get rid of her the moment she set foot in the barracks. More precisely, it was to complete the job on campus after wearing her down with harassment during the legal phase that lasted a year and a half. To get rid of her, they would need total isolation. Thus, the second most important motion, filed after its motion to the Fourth Circuit and Supreme Court to grant a stay, was The Citadel's motion for clarification or modification of the district court's August 10, 1995, order. In its motion on August 14, 1995, The Citadel complained about entry by the U.S. marshals into the barracks where

Faulkner lived, about the marshals' entry into classroom buildings where Faulkner took classes, and about the daily briefings the court had ordered the marshals to receive from Faulkner.

The Citadel claimed:

> The omnipresence of federal marshals, assigned exclusively to protect Ms. Faulkner, will inevitably deprive her of the Fourth Class experience. Their presence will necessarily chill the conduct and experience for other cadets. The Corps of Cadets is designed to be operated mostly by cadets. It is inconceivable that these cadets could go about their business of learning and practicing to be leaders, unaffected by the presence of federal marshals.... The presence of the marshals is tantamount to an indictment of the Corps which has engaged in no conduct that warrants this measure.

To bolster their argument that Faulkner should be isolated from the marshals, The Citadel argued further—again, with a straight face—that the marshals' presence in the barracks and academic buildings would deprive Shannon of the Fourth Class experience "and hold her apart from her peers." Daily oral debriefings by the marshals would even constitute *ex parte* communications with the court since the court may have to rule on subjects covered in the debriefings, they said.

Melinda Lucka with Shannon Faulkner as she prepares to enroll in the Corps of Cadets. Used with permission, Curtis Norman. August 12, 1995.

Brigadier General Poole filed a supporting affidavit in which he expressed indignation at the very idea that Shannon needed protection by an outside force appointed by the court. Presence of U.S. marshals would be disruptive to the leadership responsibilities of the other cadets and set Faulkner "apart from the other Fourth classmen."

United States marshals escort Shannon Faulkner to report to The Citadel as the first woman to enroll in The Citadel Corps of Cadets. Used with permission, Curtis Norman, August 12, 1995.

Beginning and End

On August 2, 1995, The Citadel sent Faulkner a collection of materials that was given to all incoming freshmen. The materials included a schedule of events for Saturday and Sunday, the 12th and 13th. Dawes conveyed Poole's encouragement to Shannon to report two days late, on Monday, August 14, to avoid excessive media coverage, and, "for security reasons," not to sleep in the barracks until the training cadre arrived the same day. Evidently, The Citadel did, after all, fear for Shannon's safety. It also just did not want any photographs of her among her peers.

The Citadel's letter also included a letter from Bruce and Betsy Byford, "Vice Chairpersons" of the illusive CFA or Citadel Family Association. Since parents at every campus are reluctant to leave their babies behind, the CFA schedule included observing the Swearing-in Ceremony on Summerall Field on Monday at 6:00 p.m.

A more interesting CFA letter dated July 1995, was hand-delivered to me from Dawes's office on August 9, 1995. That letter included the CFA's "Citadel Knob's List of Most Needed Items." The list contained items that were "highly recommended by previous knob moms," items such as Skin So Soft to keep gnats away, nail polish remover for removing lacquer on brass, large can of Brasso (not the small can), Bar Keepers Friend for polishing brass, two large cans of black shoe polish, two bottles of shoe sole dressing, one can of Pledge or Endust, and on and on through 21 items.

Surprisingly, the list also contained one collective item, wherever and however it might express itself during a cadet's time at The Citadel: "Pencils, pens, staples, stapler, paper clips."

This was the kind of inside information that was essential for a knob to succeed at The Citadel, and the Faulkners were just now being let in on what small items would loom large in the life of a knob. Those "most needed items" were the nail in the horse's shoe, and SRF didn't know about them until it was too late to go out and buy them. An invitation to participate in the full activities of the CFA had remained out of reach for Sandy and Ed Faulkner until the very moment Shannon was to report—and would remain so. They simply were not welcome to fraternize with The Citadel family.

All Alone

Shannon Faulkner:
I truly feel sorry for you! A typical, unattractive (female) feminist, having to impose yourself upon an all-male college, just to get some attention from the opposite sex.
How sad!

[signed]
January 21, 1994

If the greatest failure in the case was that no other woman joined SRF as she entered the Corps, the next greatest was to leave her alone once she got in. Yet such concerns were perhaps not as dominant as they should have been since SRF was always her own woman and everything she ever did was on the basis of her own decisions. Faulkner was as tough as they come and absolutely beautiful for her convictions.

The most common cliché and the centerpiece of all pedagogical principles at The Citadel, the one every president always preaches on the first day he addresses the Corps, is that no one makes it alone. "You've got to learn to help your fellow knob, and your fellow knob has got to learn to help you," knobs are told. "You as a class, not as an individual, make it, if you're going to make it at all." All Citadel men know that as if it is carved in stone. However, The Citadel would betray this fundamental principle to get rid of Shannon.

This is the point Susan Faludi made in an op-ed piece for *The New York Times* on August 23, 1995, after Faulkner's fall. Shannon left The Citadel observing what every Citadel knob and alumnus completely understands—"maybe it would have been different if there had been other women with me." Networking is what The Citadel is all about. That and promptly getting to the job that networking provides.

"As I heard that remark," Faludi wrote, "it occurred to me that she had received a Citadel education after all. She had grasped the only aspect of The Citadel teachings that really matters: there is strength in numbers; solidarity counts."

Shannon was not allowed to join Band Company while she continued to audition. On the following Sunday, August 13, 1995, when Faulkner reported to I Company to begin her knob year, her loneliness was palpable. Even someone standing right beside her—which never happened anyway—in the barracks quad, with its distinctive red and white checkered markings, could not have relieved her loneliness. Photographs in the media throughout the world caught her sense of isolation. Without one friend among other male knobs or another woman with her, she was an untouchable. India Company—as the letter "I" is expanded to "India" in the military alphabet—was an appropriate name for her company. She was set up for failure, and everyone at The Citadel knew it. Why then let her go forward? Why then did she go forward on her own? What stuff did she have that others did not? And did her lawyers fail her after all?

On the same day and at the same approximate hour, another young woman was safely beginning her own college career as a freshman a few miles away at another state institution, Trident Technical College in North Charleston. By her own account, Nancy Mace was intensely following the news of Shannon's ordeal.

Sandy and Ed Faulkner sat with Shannon throughout the morning orientation at Mark Clark Hall. Right next to Mark Clark Hall stood The Citadel Chapel. "Remember Now Thy Creator In The Days Of Thy Youth," the passage from Ecclesiastes, was inscribed over the door. No one came up to talk to them. The Citadel's official blue and white "Save the Male" bumper stickers, which were handed out at Lesesne Gate as Faulkner and her parents drove in earlier that morning, effectively gave all parents written instructions to ignore the Faulkners. There were no Von Mickels among the parents. Sandy

An isolated Faulkner is allowed with supervision to inspect her room in Law Barracks, The Citadel, August 9, 1995, in the event she is admitted into the Corps of Cadets and permitted to live in the barracks. Used with permission, Staff photo by Wade Spees, *The Post and Courier*, August 10, 1995.

and Ed later found out that there was a reception earlier that morning for all new cadets and their parents at the Alumni Hall. The Faulkners were not invited.

"Cancer to This Institution"

As a part of the 1980 Mood Report, letters from George McF. Mood, Jr., MD, were attached. Since 1968, Dr. Mood had been The Citadel surgeon. As is the case with all Citadel physicians, Dr. Mood was in charge of the cadets' health and general physical well-being. Although most of the reforms called for by Admiral Stockdale, who commissioned the Mood Report, were ignored by the Board of Visitors, Dr. Mood still had his say. In letters written in 1978, 1979, and 1980, Dr. Mood took the board to task for its insistence that physical and mental abuse of freshmen by sophomores somehow created a Whole Man who was superior to the graduates of other military colleges and everyone else in America. The war with the board over hazing cost Stockdale his job, and like Stockdale, Dr. Mood was also no doubt regarded as someone who simply did not understand the character-building virtues at The Citadel.

While teaching at The Citadel, I noticed that a lot of freshmen dozed off in class. I thought I needed to find some new beatitudes to keep them awake, until I read Dr. Mood's letters.

On January 23, 1980, Dr. Mood wrote,

> Over the past twelve years I have been recurrently shocked by the abuses of what is called the Fourth Class System. This Fourth Class System defies definition, is not systematic, and its so-called tradition is extracted from the experiences of the preceding one or two years.... It appears to me that the Fourth Class System is, at the present time, a license to harass Fourth Classmen, thereby getting revenge for the harassment experienced by the upperclassmen during the previous one or two years....
>
> Every year I cringe when August rolls around, knowing we will have numerous freshmen leaving The Citadel with nothing good to say about the school: a bad taste in their mouth. Some parents are indignant and threaten libel suits. Some are disgusted that their sons "couldn't take it." Neither one of these attitudes is of any positive value to The Citadel or to these dropouts. They will remember and be reminded that they quit and their entire future may be tainted by this memory.

Dr. Mood then discusses the "abuse of power by cadremen" who make knobs do excessive pushups in hot showers or in rain gear, called "sweat parties." Furthermore,

> Another little trick was brought about by the limitation on the number of pushups that could be imposed upon a Fourth Classman who is required to temporarily hold his body and arms in a semi-pushup position until his muscles fatigue and cause him to collapse. He is usually then brought to the Infirmary on a stretcher.

Addressing the key point about hazing and the entire Citadel pedagogical theory, Dr. Mood continued:

> When these infractions occur, information given to me by the Fourth Classman is confidential and of course can only be used with his permission in order to bring a complaint against the upperclassman. Should this be done, it is tantamount to his withdrawing from the

school since he would be ostracized not only by the upperclassmen but by his own classmates.

It was a perfectly conceived construct, one that Judge Houck acknowledged in commenting on Shannon's own desire to fit in and any knob's reluctance to rat out his tormentors. The very strength of a corrupt system lies in the refusal of its victims to do anything about it. Dr. Mood continued,

> How should we cure these ills? And why don't we cure them? To answer the second question first, I suppose it is because we dislike ruffling the feathers of the Corps which, after all, is supposed to cure its own ills. I suppose that cure by Presidential decree might be unpopular, but I know of no better way.... I suppose that the system is supposed to be a method of training; however, it has become very insidiously a punitive system.

Then Dr. Mood hit close on the mark: "I agree that the Corps should be in charge of training, but certainly not in charge of punishment. This charge takes a very mature adult to accomplish with any degree of value. Punishment by a peer only leads to revenge."

Dr. Mood again got to the point about the end result of hazing: "I sincerely believe that The Citadel is an outstanding college and that we do graduate outstanding patriots and leaders, but I also feel that we lose many good men by attrition."

Dr. Mood addressed his memo of September 19, 1979, to Colonel Harvey Dick, Commandant of the Corps of Cadets. Colonel Dick would become one of the members on the Board of Visitors in the *Faulkner* litigation. Dr. Mood recognized "the fact that there is very little you can do directly to change this situation."

To be made XMD meant to be excused from duty for a medical reason. Dr. Mood continued,

> There is a definite desire by some freshmen not to be made XMD, not even to be at Sick Call, and definitely not to be admitted to the hospital. The reason given has been that the cadre, or certain members thereof, seem to resent their using the Medical Services unless there is something that is visibly ailing the cadet. Also, it appears that when the freshman leaves the hospital and comes off XMD status, he is apparently "racked" even more vigorously or more frequently in order to make up for the time he was hospitalized or on XMD status....

During the previous year, in 1978, Dr. Mood had filed another report and acknowledged that within The Citadel administrative structure as it was organized, the Commandant himself, then Colonel John Gibler, could do little to stop the infractions, assuming that it would ever want to. "I realize that this type of memorandum is of very little value for investigation; therefore, I submit it to you only for information." The administrative divide between "investigation" and "information" provided the perfect cover for abuse. Dr. Mood sent a copy of his September 14, 1978, memo to Major General Grimsley.

Dr. Mood was particularly critical of a failure to protect the health and safety of freshman:

> Freshmen are afraid to divulge names of upperclassmen who harass them. They are well aware that they will be put in double jeopardy. I, therefore, advise them that their names will not be used in my reports to you.... There have been instances in several companies, particularly F and N, where the status of XMD was completely ignored. In two instances, fourth classmen were made company runners when they reported being XMD. In another instance, a fourth classman who had intestinal bleeding was being kept XMD until studies could be completed to rule out bleeding ulcer or tumor. This cadet was mentally harassed to the point that he hyperventilated and was brought into the infirmary unconscious.... I am very sorry I cannot be more definite. I am also sorry I cannot offer any cure for the abuses of which I complain. I do feel that the fourth class system is quite easily abused and that it is a cancer to this institution and is undoubtedly the cause of 90 percent of our attrition rate.

It was Dr. Mood's report that Admiral Stockdale used as a basis for his proposed reforms of the Fourth Class System. The Board of Visitors rejected the proposal and fired Stockdale.

When The Citadel asked Ed Faulkner to sign an affidavit stating that he and Sandy knew that because of Shannon's physical condition she "will face a substantially increased risk of health problems," the parents did not know the risk would come from physical and psychological stress in the form of being forced to eat too much spaghetti. The cadre supervising Faulkner's departure did not use pushups or racking. That was a method of corps cleansing preferred by cadets in the Mood Report.

All eyes in the Long Grey Line now turned to the present members of the cadre to perform as well. No words of instructions were necessary. Since starving freshman at mess had by then been outlawed, at least ostensibly, the cadre turned to another device. They simply reversed the traditional deprivation of food during mess when freshmen were not allowed to eat and, instead, forced Faulkner to eat too much in order to make her sick. It worked as well as anything Dr. Mood had ever seen. Even so, it was not the food itself that made her sick. It was a staple diet of malice toward Faulkner like none other The Citadel has ever dished out before or since.

Forced feeding in the mess hall was never a subject of concern during litigation. A member of cadre in an adjacent company, Kilo Company, told me that there would have been no way for India Company cadre to force Faulkner to eat too much. "She was always surrounded by United States marshals," he said. Such was one version of the event, even though the marshals under court orders remained at all times in security headquarters by Lesesne Gate, unless called upon in an emergency. Shannon never called them and neither did The Citadel.

"Honor and Good Sense"

> "You cannot tell from appearances how things will go. Sometimes imagination makes things out far worse than they are; yet without imagination not much can be done.... Never give in. Never give in. Never, never, never, never—in nothing, great or small, large or petty —never give in, except to convictions of honor and good sense."

Winston Churchill to boys at Harrow School, October 29, 1941

Most of the cadre during Faulkner's knob year were sophomores and members of the freshman class of 1994. According to a demographic survey commissioned by The Citadel and completed by UCLA, the 1994 freshman class at The Citadel included 90% whites, 5% African Americans, and 3% Asians. Fifty-two percent described themselves as conservative, 7% as far right, 34% as middle of the road, and 6% as liberal. Forty-five percent were born-again Christians. The objective which was rated most essential for cadets in the future, for 84% of them, was raising a family. The lowest, 4%, was creating artistic work.

The average high temperature during the first week of cadre in 1995 was 99 degrees Fahrenheit; with the Charleston humidity, the real index was merciless. According to The Citadel, about 24 male knobs dropped out during this Hell Week.

On Tuesday, August 15, 1995, I got word from Henry in New York that Shannon was admitted into The Citadel Infirmary and then to Roper Hospital for heat exhaustion. Knowing that The Citadel nurse would not give me any information, and being unwilling to let her know that I had not yet heard directly from my own client, I was at a loss for further information. Then I got a call from Roper Hospital.

"Mr. Black, it is the policy of this hospital not to release any information about the patients admitted here. The press has called to ask how your client is doing, and what she's doing here. I just wanted you to know that we are not telling them anything."

"Thank you," I replied. "I'm glad you have that policy. How is Shannon doing?"

"She's OK. She just needs rest. It's obviously been terribly stressful for her, I guess."

"What do you mean? Has she told you anything in particular?" I asked.

"Only that she was made to eat a whole plate of spaghetti in less than a minute, then drink a lot of liquids, that kind of thing. So she threw up and she's still suffering from symptoms of digestive disorder."

"They do that to the knobs at mess," I said. "But with her, probably with relish."

Tom Chandler, who had written all of the government's appellate court briefs, called later the same day, Tuesday, to ask if Shannon were well. Word of her demise had already reached the national media and was playing in Washington. Through Wednesday, Shannon remained in the Infirmary.

On Thursday morning, August 17, 1995, I called Ed Faulkner to ask what was going on behind the news media reports about Shannon's health. Ed replied that Shannon was doing well enough, although she was under a lot of stress. No mention of wanting to go home.

Then Henry called me later on Thursday. He told me that Shannon wanted to quit.

"She never talked to me about it," I said. "She never told me she wanted to go home. The only guy I've been in contact with is the Methodist chaplain who says he sees her every day. He came last night to get an iron Shannon wanted and told us that she was OK in spite of all the media reports. I told him to tell her to be sure to unplug it when she's finished. She's forgotten to do that here at the house.

"I've stayed away from her precisely because I thought she wouldn't want me to intervene, you know, no matter what they throw at her. She never wanted us to get in the way of whatever she set out to do.

"But I have to admit that I trusted them. What a fool. I trusted them even though I knew they hated her," I said.

I immediately called The Citadel Infirmary.

"She's not to be disturbed," The Citadel nurse replied. The nurse told me that Shannon had given her explicit instructions not to let anyone, including me or Val, to speak to her. She was not taking visitors, I was told.

After the case was over there was a great dispute over whether Shannon told the nurse not to let Val and me talk to her and whether the nurse refused to let Shannon make calls from the Infirmary. Headlines in *The P & C* on August

26 read, "Nurse Says Faulkner Owes Apology" for being critical on "Prime Time Live" of the treatment she got from The Citadel in the Infirmary.

I decided not to go over to the Infirmary and not to continue to try to talk to Shannon—one of the biggest mistakes I made in the case.

I called The Citadel physician but got no information about Shannon's medical condition, whether it was serious nervous exhaustion or heat exhaustion, easily potentially fatal. And no one from The Citadel ever called me to enlist my help with my client, an obvious thing to do if they seriously had her health and safety in mind. They could have called Melinda, her surrogate mother in town for a year and a half. They could have treated her equally as they do male cadets.

Years after the case was over, I would refuse to allow the former Citadel nurse, then in a new job, to assist in a colonoscopy performed on me by my physician who was Bobby Hood's Kappa Alpha fraternity brother and roommate at Sewanee. A perfect metaphor for my position at the end of the case.

Praying and Dancing

Dawes sent all of Faulkner's lawyers a fax around high noon on August 17, 1995, that read, "You may contact Ms. Faulkner at the following address: MSC 2344, The Citadel Station, 171 Moultrie Street, Charleston, SC 29409. Should you need any additional information, please do not hesitate to call me."

Henry called first thing the next morning, Friday, August 18, 1995, to tell me what the world knew. Suzanne Coe was at the Infirmary with Ed and Shannon's brother Todd trying to help Shannon.

I put in a call to Ed Faulkner's shop in Easley. Mr. Faulkner, the grandfather, told me that they were all down in Charleston. Same report from Suzanne's office.

I did not do anything until an hour or so later. I continued to hang on the false notion that The Citadel would not so brutally assault Shannon in plain view enough to actually force her out. Then I went to Mount Pleasant to see Murray Thompson, MD, to line up a visit by Shannon in the event I was able to get through to see her and talk The Citadel administration into letting her be evaluated by a neutral physician, something Shannon always insisted on. Thompson was a pediatrician who also specialized in young adults. I was able to get him to be on stand-by in his office if and when I could get to Shannon. I was sure that if I could get Shannon to get in the car with me to go see Thompson, then she would be able to get some distance, literally, from the anxiety of the moment and with Thompson's help, friendly professional help, be able to make up her mind in a reasonable way about whether to quit or try again to stay. It would be up to her when she was thinking straight, I thought.

I never got to make my proposal to The Citadel or to Shannon to see Dr. Thompson. In fact, I never even got to talk to Shannon or Ed or Suzanne. I made another call to the Infirmary, but again the call was not accepted. I did not know whether one more lawyer would make matters better or worse. Suzanne had always been the lawyer closest to Shannon.

Ed Faulkner, in an affidavit dated September 12, 1995, recounted the events on August 18, 1995:

> I have never, in the twenty years I have raised Shannon, seen her as emotional and irrational as on that day. She was hysterical, said she could not take the pain of her stomach and stress anymore and wanted to come home.
>
> General Poole kept coming in and asking, "What are you going to do?" to us all. We would respond that we were talking and needed time. Shannon asked him, in my presence, if she could have a medical leave to consult another doctor about the pain in her stomach and stress. General Poole told her this was not possible. When he had been in the room about 45 minutes with Shannon, the provost pulled me aside and told me Shannon had 15 minutes to make a "final" decision to stay or go. He told me that if she was not in "formation" in 15 minutes, she would have to withdraw. At this point, Shannon was so upset that I was powerless to do anything about it.
>
> During the approximate 45-minute session we had with Shannon, we tried to get her other counsel on the phone and let her know how everyone was behind her. When the nurse, who testified against Shannon in court, learned that we were using the phone, she sent someone in to take it out of the wall to further cut Shannon off. I was in disbelief at the pettiness.
>
> When our 15 minutes were up, Shannon was still hysterical. There was no way she could be in formation. General Poole came in the room and asked for either an immediate decision or for Shannon to go to formation immediately. That was when Shannon told them she desired to withdraw.
>
> During this entire process, a massive press entourage was gathered outside the Infirmary, in Shannon's direct view. She would look out the window and cry, holding her stomach.

But Ed Faulkner was no match for the vice president. The brigadier general relentlessly pressed Faulkner for a decision in the Infirmary. Suzanne was no match either. Shannon needed her immediate health and safety risks to be addressed before she could make a rational decision to leave or stay. No serious military operation outside of combat would have put emergency care for troops subordinate to routine drill formations. But, for The Citadel, this was more serious than Tullifinny Creek.

As soon as Shannon recovered and returned to her company, we then could have asked the court to have an emergency hearing to air all the facts of what went on with the hazing and forced feeding in the mess hall. Faulkner's traumatic illness at the time could well have been life-threatening.

Years later, Shannon emphasized the significance of the threat against her parents' lives just before she entered the Corps as the reason for her quitting, but between August 12 and the 18, the hostile atmosphere that built up over the past 30 months took a severe toll.

The Citadel lost no time in refuting Ed Faulkner's affidavit of September 12. On September 29, 1995, The Citadel filed affidavits of several cadets, the nurse, and the vice president. In its reply memorandum in opposition to The Citadel's motion to dismiss Faulkner, The Citadel wrote,

"Despite the best efforts of The Citadel to assure her success as a cadet, she voluntarily withdrew from The Citadel on August 18, 1995." Then it added in a footnote:

"The Citadel implemented both the letter and the spirit of the orders of the courts regarding the admission and assimilation of Ms. Faulkner into the Corps of Cadets. The Citadel did everything possible, within the constraints of the courts' orders, to afford Ms. Faulkner every opportunity to succeed in the Corps of Cadets."

An affidavit by Shannon's company commander in India Company was attached:

"I received sensitivity training," the cadet said. Cognizant of the "battle" to be fought and won, he assured cadets in her company that the "battle concerning Ms. Faulkner is not with her personality.... I told them that The Citadel is about obeying the laws, about duty, integrity, and honor."

He later visited Shannon in the Infirmary. "I asked her if she would like for the two of us to pray about her decision, and she said that she would. I did pray out loud, and at the end she thanked me," he wrote.

When Shannon left the Infirmary and returned to her room in India Company, she was upset to discover that the cadets in her company had already cleared her personal belongings out of her chest of drawers and completely emptied her room of all her other belongings and happily packed them into her suitcases.

The cadet wrote in his affidavit, "After everything was packed, several cadets helped carry her boxes down to the van on the quadrangle and load them for her.... Ms. Faulkner has made public statements in which she questioned the sincerity of the cadets who worked with her during her stay at The Citadel."

The cadet describes the exit by saying, "When she finished her press conference, she and her father and brother got into the colonel's jeep and left the campus."

Another cadet supported The Citadel's memorandum with an attached affidavit. Like his classmate, the cadet had sensitivity training by The Citadel to deal with Faulkner. As Shannon's squad leader, he would have been sitting at or near her table in the mess hall in the hostile atmosphere in which cohorts forced her to eat too much. He would have had authority to stop the forced feeding and resulting physical injury that only added to the existing emotional injury. The cadet wrote, "I escorted Ms. Faulkner to the Infirmary after she became ill at lunch."

When the cadet saw Shannon in the Infirmary talking to the vice president, "she was kneeling down on the floor, crying and holding her stomach.... Ms. Faulkner asked to speak with General Poole privately, and she and her father then had a private conversation with the general."

The Citadel filed affidavits the following month declaring that Faulkner gave the staff instructions not to accept phone calls from Val or me. Shannon said that never happened. The affidavits of the vice president and nurse were simply wrong, she said. Instead, The Citadel administration's strategy of keeping her in total isolation had continued beyond the barracks and into the Infirmary itself.

According to the head nurse, the chaplain, who was the only life-line I had with Shannon during her few days in the Corps, visited Shannon daily.

"On Thursday Shannon went to Roper Hospital for tests," the head nurse stated, and on Friday, August 20, 1995, "The Citadel physician told her that there was medically no reason for her not to go back to the barracks."

On Friday morning, the head nurse declared that she helped Shannon call her mother on the phone to ask her father to come get her.

"Throughout the time waiting for Shannon's father," the nurse stated, "we talked at length. None of it was about The Citadel or the lawsuit, except that Shannon told me that she would not talk to Val Vojdik or Robert Black or any of the other lawyers other than Suzanne Coe if they called."

When Coe arrived she asked the physician to put Shannon on medical leave, but according to the nurse, "The doctor said that a medical leave was not appropriate.... Nobody ever said anything about wanting to get a second medical opinion."

Then the vice president arrived and the head nurse escorted him to Shannon's room.

"When we got there," the nurse wrote, "Shannon was crouched on the floor and her father was standing over to the side. Shannon told General Poole that she wanted to talk to him privately, without Ms. Coe or her father or brother. General Poole said he would talk with her and her father, but not her alone."

The Citadel head nurse returned at the end of her affidavit to explain the business about Shannon's use of the phone in the Infirmary. Her recollection of the facts are somewhat different from Ed Faulkner's account of having the phone taken away from Shannon:

> I had put a telephone call in Shannon's room on Friday morning when she wanted to call her mother. Later, Ms. Coe and Mr. Faulkner. I observed that they had the telephone on Shannon's bed. The receiver was off the hook, and Shannon was visibly upset. I told Ms. Coe that I would have to remove the telephone, and I did return to the room and remove the telephone a few minutes later. Other telephones were available elsewhere in the Infirmary.

The vice president's affidavit was filed so fast that the copy I received was not notarized. It consisted of quotations from Ed Faulkner and Suzanne Coe as it described events on Friday, August 18, 1995. Thus the affidavit of one of the cadet's began with meeting Faulkner on "Saturday, August 14, 1995," and the vice president's ended with sending her packing on "Friday, August 18, 1995," but The Citadel was counting only the sunny hours.

The vice president wrote, "Ms. Faulkner was in her room, and I was told that she had issued instructions that she would not speak with anyone other than Suzanne Coe and her parents. She explicitly stated that she would not take calls from either her attorneys Val Vojdik or Robert Black."

The vice president gave Shannon two choices, but not among them was an immediate trip to the ER, or a medical leave of absence with the option of returning in a few days, or the option of getting a second opinion at that time from someone other than The Citadel doctor. Shannon had already missed one of the most sacred times at The Citadel, Hell Week. To what extent other cadets had missed parts of Hell Week, or been given temporary medical discharges, would presumably have been a part of the record at an emergency hearing if one had ever been sought or granted. The medical reports of males in the Infirmary and the medical concessions they were afforded would probably have shown the same lack of equal treatment as the medical reports of overweight males did just days previously. Everyone, especially on The Citadel side, knew that it would have taken months of discovery to discover exceptions to the primacy of Hell Week, just as it had taken months to get at the truth about the importance of cadets' weight and physical training requirements.

"Time passed," the vice president wrote, "and by 1545 I had heard nothing from Mr. Faulkner or Shannon Faulkner as to whether she was going to go back to the barracks or was going to go home."

The vice president then stepped into the nurse's office and called for Ed Faulkner:

> When Mr. Faulkner came to the office, I told him that Shannon had missed all the cadet training for the entire week and there was only one more training day left for the Cadre week. If Shannon was going to participate in any training at all during Cadre week it was necessary for her to return to the barracks prior to retreat formation on that day, which was Friday, August 18."

The vice president gave a different account of Ed Faulkner's request for more time for Shannon to make a decision: "He asked me how long he could have, and I said 'Will 4:15 be sufficient?' He said, 'What time is it now?' and I said, 'It is approximately 5 minutes 'til 4,' and he said 'fine.' "

After quoting Ed, the vice president then quoted Suzanne Coe as she came out of Faulkner's room. His affidavit reads like an ideal pleading on the egalitarian principles on which the defendants argued their case:

> Suzanne Coe came out and began saying how unfair she thought it was that Shannon was deciding to leave and how unfair she thought it was of The Citadel to treat her as we would treat any other cadet. She said to me, "Shannon is not like just any male cadet who's been here before and she should be given special consideration." I said, "What kind of consideration are you speaking of?" and Ms. Coe stated that she thought Shannon should have just different consideration because she is a woman.

The vice president added, "I told Ms. Coe that I needed to converse with Ms. Faulkner's father. I said, 'Mr. Faulkner, it is after 4:15 and if Shannon's going to go back to the barracks by retreat formation, I have to have a decision now.' "

Her father, brother, and Coe, according to the vice president, then encouraged Shannon to go back to the barracks, but "Shannon doubled over even more and even went down on her knees on the floor. She was slightly gagging at this time, crying and saying, 'I do not want to go back to the barracks.' "

All the affidavit lacked was leadership, but for the vice president, the nightmare was about over:

> I said to Shannon, "Your father's indicated your decision is, you want to go back to the barracks, so you need to accompany the cadet, who is your squad sergeant, back to the barracks at this time." Shannon looked at me and she said, "Sir, can I speak to you privately?" I said,

"Ms. Faulkner, I do not think I can allow myself to speak with you privately, but I will be glad to speak with you if you will allow your father to be present during the conversation."

The vice president's account continues with Shannon asking "from her knees" for a medical discharge instead of dismissal from the Corps:

> I responded to her by saying that our doctor had given her extensive testing and found nothing wrong with her, and as far as he could tell she was fit for duty and should return to the barracks. I also told her that I was not a medical doctor, and therefore I could not grant a medical discharge. At no time did she, her father, or Ms. Coe say anything in my presence about wanting to seek a second medical opinion.

What the vice president should have said was, "I understand. Take a temporary excused absence to see a private physician. We have treated you more harshly than any cadet in the 150 year history of The Citadel."

So the first woman ever admitted was summarily dismissed from the South Carolina Corps of Cadets. By her own insistence, she would leave by the front door and pack her own baggage and leave.

"I told her that we could have her things packed for her, but she wanted to do it herself," the vice president testified. "I also offered to take her out the back door of the Infirmary in order to avoid the press, but she said that she would go out the front door."

Sometime after all of this, I drove to the Infirmary and parked by the tennis courts as the news crews were milling about the front door. I went in and talked to the nurse. The place looked empty.

"I think she's gone," the nurse said nonchalantly as she pretended to continue with more urgent matters. "She's no longer in the Infirmary. She's checked out. I'm sorry. Did you miss her?"

As I walked out the door of the Infirmary, from across the street, I saw Shannon at a distance surrounded by TV cameras and the press. Melinda arrived about that time and stood with me to watch the feeding. We could do nothing to stop it. A local reporter left a pride of Citadel men including the vice president and public relations director who were standing nearby. Melinda saw him give a thumbs-up sign to his crew as he returned to the truck.

"Oh, they got her," Melinda said. "It just makes good sense to give in now."

Melinda left and tearfully got back in her car and drove away. Shannon left with her father, brother, and Suzanne for Greenville. I never talked to them. I stayed to watch the cadets dance and sing in the rain.

After The Citadel filed a motion on August 24 to dismiss Faulkner's lawsuit, Suzanne Coe on September 13 filed a memo in opposition. Attached to the memo was the affidavit from Ed Faulkner and one from Shannon in which she stated, "I withdrew due to the severe stress from the situation." She continued:

> I asked General Poole if I could have a medical discharge to see another doctor and seek another medical opinion (beside the opinion of The Citadel physician, who testified against me even being there and submitted an affidavit attempting to block my admission). General Poole told me that this was not an option.

Shannon went on to say that she attributed the stress that led to her departure to her role as the only woman at The Citadel. She noted that The Citadel re-admits male cadets who have left under far less strenuous circumstances.

"If other women were present at The Citadel, I would definitely consider re-applying to finish my degree at The Citadel.... I fought for the right to be treated equally," she said.

Henry, Val, and I did not sign Suzanne's memo, and Shannon had already fired the ACLU on July 25, 1995, the same day *USA Weekend* published her personal account of the hatred she had received from The Citadel and its supporters.

But could the court hold an emergency hearing every day, as it most certainly would have to? The court had already declared that it would not micromanage The Citadel, and The Citadel had indicated at almost every turn that it was above the law. The Citadel would also have continued to use FERPA in discovery and protracted hearings to protect male cadets from any allegations of wrong-doing. A new investigation of The Citadel by the Department of Education under the Clery Act, 20 U.S.C. 1092(f), for alleged aggravated assaults against Faulkner would probably not have been made since DOJ was already a party in ongoing litigation. If Faulkner had returned to formation on August 18, more United States marshals and even federal troops might have been needed to protect her throughout the year, and even they, given the central role of the cadre and administrative intent, would not have been able to protect her.

When Faulkner was at The Citadel, there was no one and no office in place to deal with women in the Corps, no women's dean, no women's counselors, no one but the most vocal opponents of Shannon. Alone and in trouble with her cadre, Shannon could look to only the most hostile witnesses for the defense during the course of her lawsuit for help.

As a matter of record, no Citadel cadet was ever disciplined for any act of violence or harassment against Shannon Faulkner during the entire two and a half years of litigation of her case from January 1993, when she made application to the Corps, to August 1995, when she dropped out. No administrator was fired. No member of the BOV resigned.

Faulkner's demise was, of course, embraced by a majority of South Carolinians. *The P & C* included reports of cadets celebrating their momentous victory with bouquets of push-ups, yells, cheers, whoops, taunts, laughs, sighs, grins, jumps, and slides across the quadrangle on mattresses taken from their beds. *The Post and Courier* photographers Wade Spees and Mic Smith again showed the Whole Man to all the world.

The Citadel cheerfully explained the dancing and singing as the usual kind of celebration by cadets who are extremely happy when the regularly scheduled Friday afternoon parade is cancelled because of rain. Like the ceremony conferring honorary degrees on defense lawyers who got rid of veterans in 1993, the rain dance after getting rid of Faulkner two years later was purely coincidental, The Citadel maintained. Friday formation had been cancelled. The joyful outburst had nothing to do with Faulkner, they said. Faulkner, after all, never existed.

Cadets gloat over successfully hazing Faulkner out of the Corps of Cadets on August 18, 1995, within days after her admission as the first woman in the Corps of Cadets. Used with permission, Staff photo by Mic Smith, *The Post and Courier*, August 19, 1995.

"Courtesy, Respect, and Dignity"

Bud Watts had sent faxes to the staff and faculty on the day Shannon registered for classes boasting of "the professional atmosphere of all the staff, faculty, and Cadets to maintain our heads high and practice the very ideals we strive so hard to instill in the young men here."

On August 31, 1995, Ben Legare faxed a memorandum from Bond Hall to key state legislators:

> Television coverage and newspaper accounts of events surrounding Ms. Faulkner's stay and departure from The Citadel have resulted in some criticism of our cadets for their brief display of happiness that the Corps of Cadets remained all male following her withdrawal. The juxtaposition of photographs and events create a great misperception of the facts surrounding Ms. Faulkner's stay at The Citadel.
>
> Ms. Faulkner was treated with courtesy, respect, and dignity while she participated in cadet activities associated with her week at The Citadel. While she was on campus, Ms. Faulkner spent less than a day going through in-processing before being admitted to the Infirmary. During that time she was treated very professionally by all cadets and staff with whom she associated....
>
> All of us at The Citadel appreciate your support during the 1995 Legislative session. The Citadel Board of Visitors and the Alumni who feel so strongly about preserving single-gender education are aware of that support....

To Ben Legare's memorandum was attached six editorials. Fox-Genovese in *The Wall Street Journal* effectively said "I-told-you-so" and predicted that all women's colleges would fall if VMI and The Citadel lost in the Supreme Court. Others merely joined the cadets to cheer in the rain, but the best were predictably from the newspaper that gave the BOV, administration, alumni, and cadets the most help all along.

The lead editorial in *The P & C* on the day after Faulkner quit crowed loudly over the folly of a "forced admission" of Faulkner into the Corps of Cadets. Now there was every reason to believe that SCIL would measure up to VWIL and all-male state supported education would be preserved. Judge Hamilton was right, even though he did not correctly anticipate forced feeding as the cause of injury to an overweight Faulkner. Now, the editorial stated, the public deserved to have access to Shannon's medical history, including all the testimony of July 25 and 26, so that it can "know the truth about this high-profile case." When the judge unsealed the record, however, The Citadel got more on its plate than it wanted the public to see.

A follow-up editorial sent to members of the legislature took up Pat Conroy's letter to the editorial staff of *The Post and Courier* on August 27, 1995. Conroy had told *The Washington Post* in a previous conversation that "The Corps of Cadets could run Arnold Schwarzenegger out in two days." In his letter published in *The P & C*, Conroy hit hard on a key issue. "The kid never had a chance," he wrote, "and I lacked the courage to tell her so."

This, of course, did not fit with the prevailing summary of why Faulkner quit. The Citadel all along claimed that no woman can take the tough adversative treatment in the Corps, but Conroy made the more telling point that no man can either, if his classmates do not want him to.

So the myth was born that The Citadel fought against SRF only because she personally was unfit, not that it fought against her because she was a woman. Faulkner herself just couldn't hack it, the myth allowed, but a woman with the right stuff could. The Citadel would bury its ugly past with a view toward the future. While Shannon Faulkner and all women similarly situated would later win the battle to get women in The Citadel, loyal supporters would forever protect The Citadel by continuing to preserve the myth. SRF said that things might have turned out differently if she had had the company of other women. The Citadel, however, continues to say that things might have turned out differently if only a stronger woman had been the first to be admitted into the Corps. By completely buying into The Citadel's myth and thus denigrating Faulkner's real success for lasting as long as she did, loyal supporters of The Citadel continue to do a disservice to the advancement of equal rights for all women.

A radio talk show in Charleston on the same day especially condemned those who, they claimed, should have taken better care of Faulkner. Poole was not to blame, the moderator asserted. "Houck and Black should have known what would happen," a caller said. "They're both locals who know The Citadel." A few weeks later, Oprah Winfrey would pick up on the same theme to hint at expanding blame to Faulkner's attorneys who may not have had her best interests in mind.

A vendor at a downtown bar frequented by cadets, Big John's, sold T-shirts on the day Shannon quit: "No all-you-can-eat buffet in the mess hall." Eventually, more Citadel bumper stickers attacking the young girl from Powdersville collected on cars like charms on a bracelet. "Males 1, Whale 0" and "The Whale Has Beached. Aug. 19, 1995. Go Citadel" appeared. "Shave Shannon's Head" remained the moral equivalent to "Native."

Banzhaf faxed me a Herblock cartoon that ran in *The Washington Post* depicting two characters' reaction to the cadets rejoicing in the rain after Shannon left the Corps. One character said to the other, "What I'm wondering after this performance—what kind of *man* would want to get in there?" Bob Rae, premier of Ontario, Canada, at the time and John Black's godfather, called to express his dismay.

Faulkner's reasons for dropping out remain her own, of course, but what does remain certain to everyone is that Citadel versions of why Faulkner quit the Corps have been told and retold with the same ill feelings that have existed since 1995.

On the evening of the first day after Faulkner quit, I got reports of two of the other 25–30 knobs who had dropped out as of August 18. Their names were available to Citadel alumni on the internet.

The sister of a cadet in India Company called from Jacksonville to tell me that her brother had moved in with her and was now getting counseling to deal with his experiences at The Citadel. Another older sister of a knob called me the same day to say that her brother had just called her to say that he was going to jump off the top floor of one of the barracks if she didn't come get him immediately. She would not give me the name of her brother or tell me which company he was in because she swore that she would tell no one. A boy her brother knew at Goose Creek High School was an upperclassman who hated his guts and was doing everything to get rid of him.

Chapter 8

Mellette Steps In and Out

Saved by a Citadel Family

"Bob—call Suzanne at her office—there's another young woman! A DY-NAMO!!!! (Daughter of an alum and sister of a senior cadet) She's in a military high school now—a student.) I've gone to Harris Teeter."

So read Melinda's note announcing the appearance of Nancy Mellette. I got the first call from Johnson, Lacy, and Chapman; Faulkner first called Suzanne whom Isabelle Pinzler told me to call; and now Suzanne first heard from Mrs. Mellette and Malissa Burnette, an attorney in Columbia and family friend of the Mellette's. After hearing from Burnette, Val reconvened Team Faulkner and Suzanne, Henry, and I met at Oak Ridge Military Academy (ORMA) in Guilford County, North Carolina, where we were introduced to Nancy, her parents, and Burnette. Nancy was finishing her senior year in 1995–96 and wanted to begin classes at The Citadel in the fall of 1996, so she had standing to intervene. Her father attended The Citadel, and her brother was then a senior at The Citadel.

Not everyone was happy with the news. The President of South Carolina Sportsmen's Coalition wrote in *Carolina Outdoor News* in November 1995, "As a graduate of The Citadel, I have followed with some interest the Shannon Faulkner story. When she punched out early, the Dyke department of the ACLU must have worked overtime to find a replacement candidate. But, find one they did...."

After The Citadel filed its motion to dismiss Faulkner's lawsuit, on August 31 Nancy Mellette filed her motion to intervene and to renew the plaintiff's motion to certify class action. A hearing was set for October 3, 1995, at which time the court granted Mellette leave to intervene, denied her motion for class certification, and dismissed Faulkner as a plaintiff in the lawsuit. A trial on SCIL was rescheduled from November 13 to December 4. Shannon herself was not present. Mellette, along with her mother, was introduced to the court.

The court told Mellette that if she wanted to intervene she would have to use Val and Shearman as her attorneys. Val would be in charge.

Nothing changed as *Mellette* went forward, except I did not attend as many depositions. I kept getting copies of all pleadings from both sides, kept putting time in the case, but later took off for several weeks to look for a job in Denver. I fully anticipated that I would have to move out of state after the case.

I had also been invited by Becky Hoover Herrnstein of the Women's Studies program at the University of Akron to speak at the law school on October 5, 1995, two days after Judge Houck allowed Mellette to intervene in the case. My audience at the law school included a professor who challenged me for soliciting clients and pushing Faulkner into failure.

Herrnstein would later discuss my role in the case in a law review article, "Shannon Faulkner and The Citadel: The Effects of Using Litigation as an Instrument of Social Reform," 5 CIRCLE Bu. W. J. L. & Soc. Pol. 4 (1997). Whether the code of professional responsibility governing attorneys should be expanded to include a broader concept of informed consent was the topic for debate. Should lawyers disclose their own private political beliefs and ideological bent when they take on a client in a civil rights case?

I realized that I had been invited to Akron to explain what Shannon meant when she discussed the case on the Oprah Winfrey television show on September 7, 1995:

> Winfrey: The 2½ years of preparation and the lawsuits and fighting to get in there—do you think that you were used in any way by attorneys or people who had other interests, other than your own?
> Faulkner: I am becoming aware of a lot of things that I was disillusioned about.... I—I'm starting to realize that they—a lot of people didn't care specifically about what was best for me....
> Winfrey: And how does that feel to you?
> Faulkner: It hurts me now.

I never saw the Oprah television show, but I always presumed that Shannon was referring to false friendships from strangers, such as those she moved in with briefly on Folly Beach, and not to her lawyers. I never took it as criticism directed at me personally, or at Melinda, or at any of her other lawyers. The Blacks remain friends with the Faulkners, stay in touch, and occasionally talk on the phone.

While I was talking to a group at the law school in Akron, one of the professors brought me the news that the Supreme Court had granted *certiorari* in the *VMI* case to hear questions on both liability and remedy. Oral arguments were set for January 17, 1996, a time when I had appointments, through Jeanette Kellogg Wotkyns, to interview for a job in Denver.

That a writ of *certiorari* was granted in VMI, of course, changed everything back in Charleston. Even though Justice Thomas would recuse himself because his son went to VMI—after his high school years at St. Paul's as a classmate of Dawes Cooke—it was still possible for the court to render a split 4–4 decision. In such a worst-case scenario, MBC could have its VWIL for VMI and Converse could have its SCIL for The Citadel.

June 26, 1996

The United States Constitution recognizes more similarities among people of different races, sexes, religions, and national origins than differences that would justify discrimination. In the VMI and Citadel cases, the plaintiffs pushed the similarities in the sexes, and the defendants pushed their differences. Regardless of what value single-sex education may have in primary and secondary education, the Supreme Court ultimately agreed with the plaintiffs that the value of a males-only military education in a public college is not as important as the interest the state has in admitting women as well as men to all public colleges.

On July 10, 1995, Val filed Faulkner's Petition for a Writ of Certiorari, asking the court to require The Citadel at the highest level of scrutiny "to prove that the continued exclusion of women from The Citadel is narrowly tailored to meet a compelling government interest." On October 16, 1995, the Supreme Court dismissed Faulkner's petition for *certiorari* as moot and refused to allow Mellette to intervene in the *VMI* case. At the same time, it agreed to address the legal standard of strict scrutiny which DOJ, in its brief in *VMI* on November 16, 1995, encouraged the Supreme Court to substitute for the "intermediate" level of scrutiny for gender discrimination cases. On November 16, 1995, Val filed an *amicus* brief for the *VMI* case, conceding that *VMI* had controlling authority in The Citadel case and that The Citadel case could not be tried under a standard not yet announced by the court.

Thus, while the Fourth Circuit could hook up MBC with VMI and Converse with The Citadel, their coupling still could not make it past review of a majority of the Supreme Court. Like a house mother on a party weekend, Ginsburg was not fooled for one minute by either cute couple and knew exactly what they were up to.

Much to Justice Scalia's consternation, Chief Justice Rehnquist changed his initial vote in conference to write a concurrence. Justice Scalia dissented, so the message which a unanimous court sent on behalf of blacks in public schools in the Warren court in *Brown* was denied to women in *VMI*.

Within two days of Justice Ginsburg's opinion, The Citadel admitted all women similarly situated to Faulkner and Mellette. The Board acted on June 28, Carolina Day, a day commemorating General Moultrie's victory at Fort Sullivan in 1776 and Danger Thomson's beating back the British at Breach Inlet to prevent a flanking assault on Sullivan's Island just across the Cooper River from Charleston. Now, unless The Citadel wanted to go to trial and argue that it was unique and not like VMI, it was stuck with the Supreme Court *VMI* precedent. Nonetheless, The Citadel appealed the district court's order the following month, on August 14, 1996, which enjoined The Citadel from continuing its all-male admissions policy. The Citadel claimed such an order was moot and argued that it had voluntarily admitted women. While the Fourth Circuit did hold, on February 2, 1998, that there was no evidence on the record that The Citadel would ever revert to an all-male admissions policy or even that SCIL was not inadequate, it ruled against The Citadel and affirmed the most important orders of Judge Houck's which The Citadel had appealed. Those were the orders of July 22, 1994, and July 24, 1995 — the two orders compelling The Citadel to admit Faulkner and similarly situated women in the Corps.

Therefore, when the BOV boasted that it voluntarily admitted women in 1996, it would within weeks appeal the very orders requiring them to do so in 1994 and 1995.

The fact is, had Johnson, Lacy, Chapman, Faulkner, and Mellette not filed their suits and brought all issues to bear between 1992 and 1996, The Citadel could have continued the fight after *VMI* was decided. Yet even the BOV knew that the chances of putting up sufficient evidence in a trial to show that its SCIL program met constitutional muster were virtually *nil* after the Supreme Court found VWIL unconstitutional.

Some loyalists actually praised the BOV for acting quickly to admit women. They ignored the fact that the Fourth Circuit held that The Citadel should have seen it coming after *Mississippi University for Women v. Hogan* in 1982. It took the BOV 14 years after *Hogan*, not two days after *VMI*, to obey the law. That's longer than it took The Citadel to obey the law after *Brown* and admit the first African American, a mere 12 years.

Also on June 28, the president of the Board of Visitors, Jimmy Jones, quietly signed the last of 14 out of a total of 36 all-male scholarships which were executed between the time Faulkner filed suit and the time the board admitted women. Nearly 40% of the all-male scholarships, therefore, were executed during the historical days at The Citadel when it was litigating the question whether women would be allowed to enter the Corps.

VMI never had a Shannon Faulkner at its door. To give time for VMI to come to grips with real live women, DOJ agreed to let VMI start admitting women a year later, in the fall 1997. For The Citadel, however, the historical background was different. On July 2, 1996, nearly a year after Shannon quit, Mellette received the same acceptance letter sent to Nancy Mace, Petra

Lovetinska, Kim Messer, and Jeanie Mentavlos by the acting director of admissions at The Citadel. Mentavlos was an unknown at that time. Another letter went out to a young woman in Kentucky who did not show up.

By August 1996, when Messer, Mace, Mentavlos, and Lovetinska entered The Citadel, Mellette had already accepted admission to the United States Military Academy Preparatory School (USMAPS) in Fort Monmouth, New Jersey. If she did well, she would have an inside track into West Point the following year. She acknowledged that if she were admitted to West Point in 1997, she would probably go there, and that would remove her as a plaintiff-intervenor.

"Let Us Now Praise Famous Men"

The reaction to Faulkner did not stop with her failure to endure the wrath of the Corps. It continued in the form of praise of a job well done by The Citadel. On July 7, 1996, the Sixth Sunday after Pentecost, the downtown Episcopal cathedral and seat of the Bishop of South Carolina, held a big to-do to mark with solemnity and grace the end of The Citadel as they knew it. "Let us now praise famous men" was read with tears and bag-pipes. The dean of the cathedral based his sermon on Hebrews 11:8, "By faith Abraham obeyed," and vowed that The Citadel would obey the law. In attendance was the suffragan bishop, a Citadel graduate, but he did not preach the sermon.

The dean's "Independence Sunday Sermon" was titled, "Tradition, Liberty, and the Witness of The Citadel." It never mentioned a lack of Christian charity toward the teenage girl whom Citadel men had bullied for so long or the invaluable contribution to higher education and the professional and economic life of the Lowcountry and the nation that future women graduates of The Citadel might make. Instead, the verbiage was more like that of the cadet cadre who, in their affidavits, served as sensitivity-trained myrmidons during Faulkner's final days in the Infirmary.

"The Citadel, like this nation on the occasion of Independence Day, has ever rededicated itself to the precepts of honor and duty in the face of any and all challenge; and its Board of Visitors has now done so again in the face of unsought change imposed upon it," the dean declared.

It remains to be seen, he went on, if the admission is just a fad:

> But what is already sure and certain is that in the face of loss and tragedy in times past—in America, in the South—the losers have often proved to be not just martyrs but, by the Grace of God, the most loyal and stalwart champions of all that was and is and ever will be

true and good and beautiful.... Yes, The Citadel may never seem quite the same again, but those who continue even now steadfast in its furtherance may prove its most faithful champions. No, it won't have an all-male Corps of Cadets, but it will have its even more essential precepts of Honor and Duty and Liberty.

The world needs more men like Citadel men, the dean said, and he concluded his sermon with praise for men who "are occasionally wrong and always willing to admit it. In short, the world needs leaders. So it has in the past, so may The Citadel continue in its tradition of training leaders to defend the Liberty of our Nation and to witness to that faith which otherwise is so endangered in our Nation."

I missed the sermon but heard about it, and on August 15, 1996, called the office of the dean to get a copy. A secretary answered. She was not like the bishops' young secretary in Birmingham who typed the letter to Martin Luther King.

The lady told me that she was very upset about women getting into The Citadel. What the dean said in his sermon was benign, she said. She would have been more forceful if she had been preaching, she said. The secretary identified herself—she would not give me her first name—as the mother and wife of a Citadel graduate who proudly wore a Citadel "sweetheart ring," as she called it.

"Ma'am, you are the problem," I said. "All-male public college education is not all there is about the case," I said. "It's about opportunities. And it's not just whether The Citadel resisted women—it's about *how* they resisted women. They lead a malicious, brutal attack on one teenage girl."

In a letter to the editor in April 1996, a couple of months before the *VMI* decision, a lady praised the participation of Citadel cadet bagpipers who participated in the installation of the suffragan bishop in March. The *P & C* routinely prints such letters in praise of Citadel men whose manners toward women are gracious as long as the women know their place.

"Every day," she wrote,

> you read and hear of the violence committed by young people, yet recognition is often lacking when that particular age group of citizens does do something good and right. It is unfortunate that the general public has little opportunity to see or read about the positive behavior and contribution of young people and especially about the members of the Corps of Cadets.
>
> It is my hope that those who have seen the negative reports generated in response to The Citadel's stand to remain a haven for single-gender education will realize that there is a fine group of young men who

do benefit from that particular environment and who do positively contribute to our community. We would be much poorer without them.

The secretary kindly mailed me a copy of the dean's sermon on the same day I talked to her. The dean and I had overlapping academic careers at Sewanee, Toronto, and Oxford. I refrained from writing him a personal note about his sermon that I had never read such a load of horse shit in my life.

DOJ Assimilation Plans

The last published case that wraps everything up appears under the caption *United States v. Jones*, 136 F.3d 342 (4th Cir. 1998). After Mellette's motion to intervene was granted on October 3, 1995, Mellette became a party to the pleadings and discovery pertaining to the assimilation of women in accordance with the court order of August 14, 1996. Until her case was mooted on February 11, 1998, Mellette was thus a party to the periodic status reports ordered to be filed by The Citadel in the district court. Those quarterly status reports to DOJ, with copies to Mellette's attorneys, began in October 1997. They continued with modifications for nearly three and a half years until the case was dismissed by Judge Houck on March 28, 2002, under an agreed order by DOJ—the last plaintiff left in the case—and The Citadel. I continued to get copies until the bitter end.

Specifically, as Val stated in her December 18, 1996, letter to the district court, Mellette remained a party because she had to respond to The Citadel's standing claim at that time in the Fourth Circuit that "nothing has surfaced which would indicate a problem requiring the intervention of federal courts" and "there is nothing to suggest that The Citadel has set about its new course with anything but the utmost good faith."

On July 27, 1995, the BOV approved a plan for assimilating women into the Fourth Class system for 1996–97. The vice president, Brigadier General Poole, now the interim president after Lieutenant General Watts left, later described the plan as little more than an "operational or tactical plan to deal with the immediate situation." Even as late as August 14, 1996, the court, observing that The Citadel's plan was still only an outline of something to plan in the future, held that SCIL did not conform to the equal protection clause and ordered The Citadel to "adopt a policy that requires the admission of women to the Corps of Cadets on terms constitutionally equal to those applied to men."

For years, since *Hogan* in 1982 and even since being served notice in 1988 that the VMI admission policy was under constitutional scrutiny by the Justice

Department, The Citadel made no plans to assimilate women into the Corps. Even ten months after the Supreme Court ruled in *VMI*, and eight months after four women began the second wave of women's admissions, the question still remained: What is The Citadel going to do to assimilate women over the long-haul?

There was method in the madness. The over-all strategy of The Citadel prior to the ruling was, of course, to keep women out altogether. The cynical view was that after the admission of women, it shifted to a strategy to keep the numbers down. In 2010 a male cadet told me that all but one female cadet in his brigade were on athletic scholarships. A quieter hostile environment, albeit not nearly as hostile as that in which Faulkner lived, would be maintained at a sufficient level to keep The Citadel the kind of college that women would not want to attend. To their credit, Nancy Mace and Petra Lovetinska endured a residue of hostility that existed after SRF's departure, but a plentiful reserve supply knocked out Kim Messer and Jeanie Mentavlos.

The Citadel attracted only 20 women to enroll in the fall of 1997, the year after Messer and Mentavlos left. VMI attracted 30 women, largely because VMI at the same time wisely admitted two women transfer cadets from the New Mexico Military Institute, an old and prestigious junior college, and eight upperclass female exchange cadets from Texas A & M and Norwich.

Approximately $14 million were spent to keep women out of The Citadel. A mere pittance of that figure, but an undetermined amount less than a million, was spent to prepare for them. On September 30, 1996, the interim president made a typical request for $67,000 in special funding to Fred Carter, Budget and Control Board, for two "female latrines" in Barracks Number 2 and 5, Padgett-Thomas and the new Watts barrack, respectively. It was that time of the litigation in which The Citadel became grouchy over what VMI called "potty parity."

As early as January 1996, before the Supreme Court ruled in *VMI*, The Citadel was ignoring the possibility of having to adapt the barracks to accommodate women. Holly Cork sent me a fax on March 26, 1996, showing that the same faithful Citadel alumni and servants of The Citadel who fought so hard to pass the Concurrent Resolution in May 1993, sponsored a notorious bill, S. 963. The bill proposed to increase by $10 million the maximum principal amount of revenue bonds authorized under S.C. Code of Laws 59-122-20 to give The Citadel $35 million to spend at its discretion on refurbishing existing barracks and building new ones. But no accommodations were in the blueprints for women. Senators Passailaigue, McConnell, McGill, O'Dell, Richter, Short, and Rose let The Citadel act as if it could simply ignore the future needs of women cadets and carry on with architectural plans for male-only barracks. The Citadel would have to go back to the drafting board when women were admitted the following June, but they knew it would never have to allow for many.

Mike Maurer for DOJ argued mightily to try to get The Citadel to spend at least as much money on the assimilation of women into the Corps as it did on SCIL at Converse. According to The Citadel, the cost would be about $4.5 million over the next three years, but The Citadel claimed to have only about half the necessary money. The interim president reported in the newspaper that The Citadel had a $400,000 loan from the state for assimilation and had plans to request another $737,000. Maurer wanted more, but, as always, Judge Houck refused to micromanage The Citadel in ordering a certain figure to be spent on assimilation.

The women who entered in 1996 were not as welcomed as the men. Even if a totally hostile environment did not exist as it did for Faulkner for a year and a half, most of the defenders against Shannon were still in charge, and all publicly declared that they wished for the good old days. The interim president, as quoted in *The Atlanta Journal-Constitution* on August 4, 1996, said he had

> difficulty embracing the Board of Visitors' statement that it will "enthusiastically" accept applications from women.
>
> We realistically accept the situation. We are not morose and hanging our head. But we are not enthusiastic.
>
> I do not think there is anybody on the board or on senior staff who does not want the school to be single-gender. But it is now the law of the land. We are now going to do the best we can to educate men and women.

Si Bunting would continue to make the same gigantic mistake in leadership and poison the well as late as June 14, 1998, when he told the National Press Club in Washington that he maintained his opinion that women were a disruptive influence at VMI. Neither he nor Poole, the top officers at their respective academies, was following orders. That kind of failure of leadership in the civilian sector, of course, is what precisely separates The Citadel and VMI from real leadership at the federal military academies.

By May 19, 1997, The Citadel had expanded its assimilation plan from 53 issues to a 79-point plan orchestrated by DOJ. This new plan was shaped by the hazing experiences of Kim Messer and Jeanie Mentavlos. The Citadel's 1997 plan capitulated on most of DOJ attorney Michael Maurer's demands and included new positions for a female dean of women, a female recruitment officer, and a female assistant commandant of cadets.

Issues No. 31 and 32 in the July 27, 1996, assimilation plan took up the cultural problem of dealing with women cadets:

The Art of Good Taste will be re-printed in the future to include customs, courtesies, and manners that apply to female cadets as well as male cadets. The Citadel and the Department of Cadet Activities will revise its current lesson plan on etiquette briefings to include the addition of females into the Corps.

Another fax on August 31, 1996, went out to Henry, Val, and Mike Maurer as I reacted, or overreacted, to an article in *The Post and Courier*. I wrote in reference to The Citadel's student activities director known as Miss Manners who declared that she would simply continue to teach etiquette to female military cadets pretty much the same way she teaches it to female civilians. "They will learn to wear two hats," Miss Manners was quoted as saying, "as the woman, girlfriend or wife, and as the official military officer, and to act according to the situation. I don't think that good manners ever change," she continued. "I still think women like the door opened. It has nothing to do with him thinking that I can't open my own door. It looks good and it feels good."

I wrote in a fax to Shearman:

I have already heard comments from local women that the article about the survival of "etiquette" at El Cid "makes your blood boil." It seems to me that we either need very quickly to put Miss Manners out of a job continuing sexist stereotypes (called "Southern manners") or get the boys to teach manners in the classic true tradition of western civilization defined oh so long ago as magnanimity, virtue, largess, *areté* and *paideia*, and all the other good things that Si Bunting misrepresented and that cadets hear in their humanities classes, or should. Whatever the study of manners includes, it should not be superficial and concern merely opening the door for someone or helping a lady out of the car (my favorite). The point is: there is already a Mr. and Ms. Manners at The Citadel and he or she is called a cadet's professor.

It seriously puts the women cadets in an impossible position of, again, wanting to fit in, yet being discriminated against in a subtle, most serious way.... I think Judge Houck's order speaks directly to this point, quoting *Louisiana v. United States*, 380 U.S. 145 (1965), to "eliminate [so far as possible] the discriminatory effects of the past." The days of Miss Manners are gone.

I hoped to address the principal issue we had all been fighting against for so long, the defining characteristic of the Whole Man: that chivalry and gentility exist toward women only as long as women know their place. But if women get out of line at The Citadel, Pow!

Issue No. 38 of the assimilation plan revived the confused language of "adversative" versus "positive" method of the Fourth Class System. Lieutenant General Watts had testified in his deposition on January 5, 1993, in the women veterans' case that he did not know the meaning of the term "adversative" education and had only heard it in "court briefs." A letter from Dawes to Val a couple of days later acknowledged that Watts "expressed some uncertainty as to what you were trying to ask him" on another issue in the Johnson case, so Dawes had to write to explain what Watts really meant to say in his deposition. General Goodpaster testified in his deposition on May 4, 1994, that The Citadel had abandoned the negative type of military training used at VMI for the "positive leadership training" used at the federal service academies. But now that the case was over, under Issue No. 38 of the assimilation plan, women at The Citadel would receive a failed method of "adversative" leadership.

In late July 1996, as in the previous year, I was told by a deep-throat caller that the proposed Citadel committee dealing with sexual harassment in the assimilation plan did not include any faculty members. Only a brief outline of a sexual harassment policy to which the committee would refer was attached to the assimilation plan of July 27. The two-and-a-half page EEOC definition of sexual harassment and the two-and-a-half page policy on cultural, racial, and religious discrimination—Issue No. 12 in the plan—were both lumped together in the Blue Book. Together they gave the intended impression that The Citadel administration alone would deal with sexual harassment ("grabbing, bumping, pinching") in the same manner it would deal with escorting ("A male cadet may offer his arm to a lady when walking conditions warrant. A woman cadet may take the arm of a gentleman under similar conditions").

Even though the new plan shed the pretense of First Amendment protection and ostensibly prohibited the creation of a hostile environment as a category of harassment, everyone knew that a sexual harassment committee must not be packed with the usual cadets and administrators organized in a Citadel-style honor council to mete out Citadel-style justice. I sent a list to DOJ of people on the faculty who I thought might be willing to serve on a new committee.

"A woman cadet should be able to make a complaint of sexual harassment to the new committee which would then operate consistent with the laws of South Carolina or the Code of Military Justice," I wrote in a letter to DOJ on July 17, 1996. And, further,

That is, The Citadel must not be able to police itself with regard to sexual harassment with reference to only in-house rules of "honor," as it does now.

To that extent, The Citadel must be forced to waive its exemption under the S.C. Code on hazing and allow Citadel cadets to be prosecuted under the S.C. hazing statute that pertains to all other S.C. colleges.

In a July 17, 1996, letter to DOJ, I again addressed the persistent major problem looming as August approached. The administration in place at The Citadel would be made up of exactly the same men who failed Faulkner. Forgetting that Ross Barnett, not Orval Faubus, was the governor of Mississippi, I wrote, "The interim president greeting women knobs would be like George Wallace greeting Autherine Lucy or Faubus greeting James Meredith. No matter how hard we work to put a viable plan in place, if it's managed by the interim president, his assistant, the PR director, and former president (who only moves to the Business Administration department), it will fail."

Half of the four women entering the next month were gone by Thanksgiving.

Also, in a memo on August 17, 1996, I discussed the local lay of the land with regard to sentiments about cadets getting pregnant. Following Issue No. 36 in the July 27, 1996, assimilation plan, that issue would be fully addressed in later publications, but the plaintiffs wanted both male and female cadet-parents to be responsible parents.

"Whatever the policy is," I wrote, "we can't let stud cadets simply get women cadets pregnant and get them out of the Corps. The putative fathers have to take time out to demonstrate custodial responsibility too. This is popular now that dead-beat dads are being identified. Of local note is a 'Wanted' poster in the James Island Post Office here in Charleston that identifies a 'Dead-Beat Dad,' who owes over $100,000 in child support, as a 'Citadel Grad.'"

Messer and Mentavlos

After the Supreme Court's *VMI* decision on June 26, 1996, the district court realized the urgency of having Mellette's lawyers make direct contact with the four women who had been admitted by The Citadel to begin the fall term. If they were to have any chance of success, the thinking went, they would need to be in touch with Shannon's lawyers who knew better than anyone exactly what they were getting into. The court instructed The Citadel to furnish Val, Henry, DOJ, and me with the names of the four women about to join the Corps. The court dictated the substance of a letter to be sent to entering women and instructed us to call the women to answer any questions they may have about their own plans to attend The Citadel. Now familiar with the ways of The Citadel, plaintiff's counsel shared the hope that the demise of Faulkner would not be repeated by those coming immediately after her.

The Citadel was able to avoid giving us advanced notice of Mentavlos' admission, but I got her address and tried, without success, to get in touch with her father who was a Secret Service agent. My calls to Messer at her home in North Carolina also went unanswered. Both Mentavlos and Messer hired other counsel after they were hazed, within a short time after they were admitted, but by then it was too late for any attorney to protect them physically and emotionally.

It was Val's job to call Lovetinska in Washington, D.C., where Petra's father worked as a driver for the Czech embassy. According to an article in The P & C, The Citadel admissions office also supplied Citadel alumnus Tony Motley with Lovetinska's name. Motley visited her and her parents to convince her to come to The Citadel.[1] The Citadel routinely uses the Family Educational Rights and Privacy Act (FERPA) to protect information pertaining to students when it wishes to hide something from the public or opposing counsel. Faulkner's attorneys had numerous hearings to enforce discovery to get The Citadel to release the names of women applicants. But with regard to furnishing Lovetinska's name to Motley, one of their own, an exception to FERPA was made.

Motley was a former ambassador to Brazil and assistant secretary of state under President Reagan. He launched a fund-raiser to cover the cost of tuition, nearly $15,000, for Petra to begin her first year at The Citadel. More than 80% of the contributors were Citadel alumni. Motley did not pay all of Lovetinska's tuition himself, as Pat Conroy did Faulkner's after she left The Citadel, but nonetheless, both deliberate acts of kindness represent The Citadel man as he should be known.

Motley's generosity had an ugly side to it, however. In her deposition on April 17, 1997, in support of her petition for attorney fees, Val Vojdik discussed her effort to fulfill the court's directions to get in touch with the four women about to enter the Corps in August 1996. Ken Woodington, attorney in the Office of the Attorney General asked her about threats she had received during the case:

Woodington: What kind of threats did you receive?
Vojdik: Tony Motley.
Woodington: Who is Tony Motley?
Vojdik: He is the alumni from the Citadel who helped organize Petra Lovetinska, and from some unknown anonymous person in the Washington, D.C. area.
Woodington: What did Motley do?

Vojdik: Threaten me on the phone.

Woodington: By saying what?

Vojdik: If you try to contact Petra, I will cause you trouble and you know I can.

Woodington: This is after *VMI*, after the Supreme Court decided *VMI*?

Vojdik: Yes, Christmas Eve, this year.

When I called the Maces, I knew nothing of the family or the father's eventual plan to return to The Citadel as the new Commandant a few months later. I was only responding to the directions of the Court to get in touch and offer help if needed.

"Why wouldn't you let Nancy join Shannon if Nancy really wanted to start her freshman year there?" I asked Mrs. Mace.

"Oh, no," she replied. "We have too much respect for The Citadel."

In a letter to the editor on August 22, 1996, Anne J. Mace, Ed.D., took umbrage at the very idea that one of The Citadel's own would ever need help from Faulkner's lawyers. While expressing concern that her daughter's name was now in the public domain, she expressed outrage at the "glaring inaccuracy" at the newspaper's reporting, even if its usual coverage was "precise." She was at the same time purposefully drawing early notice to arguments The Citadel would later make to get out of paying attorney fees:

> I must strenuously object to a reference made in the August 13 *Post and Courier*. An article by Sybil Fix referred to "Citadel officials and attorneys for women seeking admission to the military college." Robert Black and Val Vojdik do not represent anyone in our family. In fact, of the two women *The Post and Courier* has reported that these lawyers represent, one dropped out of The Citadel and the other has indicated that she will attend the West Point prep school. It seems patently obvious, therefore, that Mr. Black and Ms. Vojdik represent no female currently identified as planning to attend the school. They certainly do not represent anyone in our family.

Even the hard times necessary to make it happen were not acknowledged. In a simple observation that separates the world of civil rights pioneers such as Foster, Gantt, and Faulkner from the world of those who follow, the first woman transfer student to be graduated from the Corps told *The Post and Courier* four years later on her wedding day to another former cadet in The Citadel chapel, "I didn't make The Citadel go female. I sometimes had a difficult time understanding why they blamed us."

The history of women in the Corps of Cadets did not begin on June 28, 1996, yet for all good Citadel families, Shannon never existed. The caption behind Shannon's name on the lawsuit, "individually and on behalf of all others similarly situated," meant nothing to them. Certainly, in their minds, Shannon personally deserved no credit for making it possible for other women to join the Corps. And no thanks to the Constitution, the rule of law in the district court, the Fourth Circuit, and the United States Supreme Court. Instead, in a letter to the editor of *The Post and Courier* on May 24, 1999, Nancy's mother wrote from the Commandant's Quarters to give thanks to The Citadel people who made it all possible:

> Like most significant accomplishments, Nancy's graduation was not achieved alone. Change is never easy and for traditional institutions, it is an especially difficult process. Without the devotion, support and dedication of many people—classmates, faculty, administration, staff, friends, and mentors—her journey along the "road less traveled" would not have been possible.

Of course, she was correct, but the irony that no one is able to make it alone was missed.

Two months after Mace was graduated, a classmate of her father's from Nashville, Tandy Rice, at Top Billing, Inc., served as Mace's literary agent. When I called Rice in 1991 to tell him that I had heard he had a daughter who might want to join the Corps, he set me straight. Rice was not about to put his daughter in the position that Sandy and Ed Faulkner would later put theirs.

In a book "for young readers," Mace's encounters with unhappy male cadets were celebrated as superior to what Faulkner had to endure, although the name Shannon Faulkner is not mentioned in the book. I never knew what role, if any, was played by The Citadel toward publication of the book. I did hear a rumor that the book was written during visits to her parents' house, the Commandant's Quarters on The Citadel campus. Bruce Williams, Vice President for Communications at The Citadel, warmly praised her efforts to tell her story which Rice described to the newspaper as a "story of triumph involving great people and a great institution." The irony escaped The Citadel spokesman that only six years earlier The Citadel had characterized similar arrangements made on a world-wide stage on behalf of Shannon as clear evidence of a publicity hound. By 2001 Nancy Mace had enlisted Mary Jane Ross, a former English teacher in California, to help write the book, and the rest is Citadel history.

Because Mace, the Commandant's daughter, unfairly goes out of her way in the appendix of her book to taunt Messer and Mentavlos as "babies" and "a bunch of you know whats, wusses. Whah, whah, whah, I want to go home, whah, whah, whah," it is perhaps appropriate to recognize that when Faulkner entered the Corps, the one with the right stuff who could have joined her that first year was playing it safe at Trident Tech.

And if she had really wanted to go the The Citadel and not team up with Faulkner but remain anonymous and out of harm's way, she could at least have written a letter to DOJ, objecting to the male-only admissions policy at The Citadel. That's what Banzhaf said an anonymous high school girl did to get the ball rolling against VMI in 1989.

A few years later at Barnes & Noble I saw a stack of Nancy's books sitting alongside a smaller stack of *To Kill and Mockingbird*, *The Adventures of Huckleberry Finn*, and *The Catcher in the Rye*. No one behind the counter knew why these four great works of American literature shared the same table for required summer reading at Wando High School, so I did some discovery.

"It's just assigned reading, that's all I know," a lady in the Wando High School principal's office told me on the phone.

"Isn't Wando where Nancy's mother, Dr. Anne Mace, works?" I asked. "Isn't she a doctor in education, an administrator at Wando?"

"Why, yes."

"A good way to boost sales. Christine de Pisan and Marie de France would be proud," I laughed.

More than any other standard today, the claim that Faulkner was not an appropriate candidate to integrate The Citadel indicates one's support of everything wrong with The Citadel. As a piece of propaganda, the co-authored book written by Mace and Ross implies that The Citadel, once again, did not treat SRF with singular brutality. The book, written with the steady hand of The Citadel, implies that Nancy Mace had to deal with even more emotional stress than SRF had to deal with, that Mace made it because she had the right stuff and Shannon did not. Only the affidavits filed by The Citadel vice president and the head nurse in September 1995, were more quickly published to establish The Citadel version of subsequent events that took place after Faulkner was dismissed and forced to quit. Mace's "groundbreaking predecessor" in her book was the first black admitted to the Corps, not the first woman, another admission by The Citadel of the basic analogy between sex and race discrimination. That analogy went back to my confrontation with Dawes at the first hearing on the Johnson case in 1992.

Yet the *VMI* case history shows exactly what debt the first female graduate from the Corps of Cadets owes to the first woman to be admitted. Mace owes everything to Faulkner. If SRF had not been admitted in 1995, The Citadel would have been in the same posture as VMI was in 1996 and would have sought and been given the same one-year delay to admit women which DOJ gave to VMI. Nancy Mace, a year behind already as she transferred into The

Citadel her sophomore year in 1996, would not have been admitted to The Citadel had she tried to go through her knob year as a junior in 1997—notwithstanding any observations to the contrary made by Judge Hamilton.

I lined up on November 9, 2001, with others at the Alumni Center Gift Shop to get a copy signed by the author who asked to whom I would like it dedicated. "For Val, Henry, and Bob," I replied. Nancy signed it and added what she always wrote for everyone, "O Citadel, we sing thy fame," the first line from the Alma Mater. She was familiar with the music. She had played clarinet in Band Company.

After the four women enrolled in the Corps in August 1996, the hostile environment during Faulkner's days had to go further underground and behind the doors of the barracks to get at the unprotected Kim Messer and Jeanie Mentavlos. Much like SRF, they were just good ole girls who didn't know their place. They were summarily hazed out. Of the two women who survived, one virtually had diplomatic immunity and the other was, quite simply, the Commandant's daughter.

I scrambled to the Alumni House on Saturday afternoon, December 14, 1996, to hear the interim president say, "We see smoke, and if there is smoke we need to know if there is fire." Through all the smoke, of course, one could see that the experiences of Messer and Mentavlos would only mirror those of Faulkner's.

A month after The Citadel Council commended the Board of Visitors and the interim president for their handling of The Citadel's transition from male-only to coeducation, the two women alleged that they had been routinely hazed and sexually assaulted, hit with the butt of a rifle, shoved against the wall, humped while standing in formation, and, without an invitation to display a knob ritual, set on fire with lighter fluid. For Faulkner and her lawyers, it was a look at what would have been, what would have followed on the cadre's menu after a plate full of spaghetti, if she had only stuck around. Or it could have even been worse for the first woman, as Shannon in her own account has claimed.

FERPA again protected the complete disclosure of all the names of the cadets and even the offenses which they allegedly committed. According to the press, The Citadel's internal investigation of some 36 or 38 charges against 14 or 15 cadets led to one dismissal from the Corps, nine punishments, and one exoneration. The particular disposition of all matters in general, even those of a potential criminal nature, was simply none of the public's business, The Citadel said. On March 11, 1997, the interim president described The Citadel's action as being "faithful to our charge. There is nothing further we can do."

The Citadel's treatment of Mentavlos and Messer completely exonerates Faulkner. It took more than a few days for The Citadel to get rid of them because they had not been the first, and they had not been around for a year and a half to draw fire.

Messer's statement printed in *The Post and Courier* on January 13, 1997, included an observation that could have come straight from one of Faulkner's pleadings filed in court, and probably did: "I believe that when the criminal investigations are complete and the entire truth is known, it will be shown that The Citadel's administration either knew, or should have known, long before 13 December 1996, of the complete failure of its command structure."

The State Law Enforcement Division's eight-inch thick report into possible violations of the state anti-hazing law went to Charleston County prosecutor in June 1997. No criminal charges were ever brought against any of the male cadets.

Like Messer, Mentavlos mainly complained of the hostile environment created by The Citadel family. In a statement printed in the press, she replayed the facts in *Faulkner* to write,

> My family and I sincerely thank Judge C. Weston Houck and Chief Deputy Bill Zerillo of the United States Marshals Service for taking the time to listen to our concerns and discuss strong security measures. However, no amount of security measures can now make hundreds of cadets, the alumni, the administration and (Citadel spokesman Terry Leedom) accept me into the Corps of Cadets. Even as a daughter of a former Secret Service agent, I cannot imagine needing to have someone responsible for my safety on a twenty-four-hour-a-day basis.

Michael Mentavlos, Jeanie's big brother, struggled against the administration and his fellow cadets over the way they were treating his sister. He did not return to The Citadel for his senior year.

The Citadel spokesman made his best showing of the Whole Man on a *60 Minutes* program that aired on CBS on March 23, 1997. Ed Bradley asked him about the allegations that, among other things, the shirts worn by Mentavlos and Messer had been set on fire. The procedure was a common practice at The Citadel. Lighter fluid is sprinkled on the knob's shirt, a match is struck, and a flame flashes and almost immediately goes out. The practice was against Citadel regulations. However, Leedom replied that the women also broke Citadel regulations: they were caught eating popcorn in Mentavlos's brother's room after hours. What Bradley did not realize was that Leedom, perhaps unwittingly, was simply acknowledging that at The Citadel an infraction for a flash flame on a shirt is a knob ritual well established enough to be equivalent to an infraction for eating popcorn in the barracks. But Bradley, hopelessly from "Off," would have none of it.

"You are going to equate eating popcorn to setting a girl's sweat shirt on fire?" Bradley asked.

In one of the most widely heard retorts in the media after Faulkner's case, Bradley continued, "Are you serious?"

The Citadel PR director and Citadel loyalists were, of course, very serious. Skepticism about the level of hypocrisy at The Citadel is never taken lightly. And Citadel hypocrisy brooks no attempt at humor. Leedom was described in the papers by Jimmy Jones, the BOV chairman, as The Citadel's "sacrificial lamb." Furthermore, Michael Mentavlos' credibility as a witness against the hazing of his sister was itself, according to The Citadel, undermined by his own alleged infractions of Citadel rules.

In spite of the actions of the interim president and the administration, the upshot of the Mentavlos-Messer incident was that The Citadel, again, was not to blame. There were enough petty allegations against the women to allow the faithful to maintain that the women brought it on themselves. In 1998 Messer settled her sexual harassment lawsuit against The Citadel for $33,750. Mentavlos settled her suit for $100,000 without an admission of liability on the part of The Citadel or the TAC officer who was a named defendant. She also settled with two of the five cadets she named as co-conspirators.[2] By January 1998, the Justice Department itself had completed a year-long study of the Messer-Mentavlos incident and, like the State of South Carolina earlier, decided that there was too little evidence to prosecute the male cadets. In any event, although The Citadel admitted that "mistakes were made" in its treatment of Mentavlos and Messer, no one at The Citadel has ever acknowledged that mistakes were also made toward the first woman in the Corps.

"Sure I Would"

> "Why don't you stand up in the classroom or Judge Houck's Court and tell how much you are paid by a certain organization to disrupt The Citadel?"
>
> [Anonymous letter to SRF, Upstate,
> S.C. GMF 293 & 296, February 19, 1994]

The case of *Faulkner/Mellette* lasted nine years, from March 2, 1993, when Shannon filed her complaint until March 28, 2002, when the clerk of court filed an agreed order of dismissal signed by the state and DOJ at the end of court-ordered status reports on The Citadel's assimilation of women that began on October 24, 1997. Litigation on the merits in *Faulkner/Mellette* had effectively ended with the Fourth Circuit affirming in part and vacating in part the district court's order of August 14, 1996, and affirming the district court orders of July 22, 1994, and July 24, 1995—both of which found The Citadel liable for violation of the Fourteenth Amendment—and the district court order of October 3, 1995, which allowed Mellette to intervene.

The fee fight lasted for more than two and half years, from November 1, 1996, when plaintiffs' attorneys filed their petition for fees until their settlement with The Citadel and state on July 7, 1999. That was about the same amount of time the entire litigation on the merits in Johnson lasted, from June 11, 1992, when Pat and Liz filed their complaint until December 5, 1994, when the Fourth Circuit affirmed the district court order of mootness.

The Citadel case was wrapped up enough by November 1, 1996, so that the plaintiffs' attorneys could then file their petition for attorney fees. If plaintiffs prevail in a civil rights lawsuit, they can usually petition the court for fees to pay their attorneys. The plaintiff herself is theoretically awarded the fees which she then pays to her attorneys, so there was some concern whether Shannon would in fact want to get back into the case to slug it out again with The Citadel. After all she had been through, was she willing to step back into the case? I took it upon myself to call Shannon to ask if she would again meet with us in Charleston to discuss her testimony for attorney fees. Her refusal would have allowed The Citadel to argue that the lion's share of fees could not be claimed, but Faulkner gladly agreed to testify. It was like old times at the Renaissance Hotel where we met with a much-relieved Shearman team, and Shannon was happily in charge again.

The Citadel, in the fight over fees, argued that the order of July 22, 1994, pertained only to Faulkner and not to all women and, therefore, was void since Faulkner dropped out on August 18, 1995, and since Nancy Mellette never had standing to take her place. The Citadel, with the aid of *The Post and Courier*, tried to rewrite the history of the case to ignore the July 22, 1994, order. *The P & C* had performed faithfully throughout the litigation, "pandering to almost all of Charleston's worst instincts" as it fanned the fires of "hatred ... one of the state's leading exports," as Pat Conroy observed in his editorial in *The P & C* on August 27, 1995.

"The Citadel Legal Defense Fund Honor Roll Proof" sent to alumni by General Watts listed the names of contributors to the fund as of February 5, 1994: 1465 alumni in classes from 1925 to 1994, 53 friends, 63 corporations (including American Express Foundation), and four parents for a total of 1585 contributors. A deep-throat source told me that the 1993–94 Annual Report of Giving cited alumni, friends, corporations, and foundations that gave a total of $4.4 million, and the Development office allegedly received more than $3.1

million, of which $173,409 was given to the Association of Citadel Men. The funding sources and the amount of money paid for The Citadel's legal defense were later discovered by DOJ in its Finding of Facts dated May 10, 1997, Government Exhibit #41 (Legal Defense Funds Available as of 21 March 1997):

FUNDS PROVIDED:
    Unrestricted Funds:

Williams Fund:	$1,365,137
Citadel Development Foundation:	$500,000
Ted Turner Fund:	$900,085
Other Unrestricted Funds:	$63,088
Restricted Funds:	
Legal Defense Fund:	<u>$846,603</u>
Total funds available:	$3,674,913
EXPENDITURES:	
Attorney fees:	
Faulkner v. The Citadel	$2,349,138
Johnson v. The Citadel	<u>$700,900</u>
Total attorney fees	$3,050,038
Termination of Veterans' Program	$141,699
Cost of Legal Defense Campaign	39,054
Reimbursement to Association of Citadel Men	76,314
Advance payment to Converse College	94,428
Other expenses	<u>171,605</u>
Total Expenses	$3,573,138
FUNDING CURRENTLY AVAILABLE:	$101,775

But the numbers produced by The Citadel in discovery never added up to an easily accessible composite picture of what The Citadel actually spent to remain all-male, and some confusion remains. Collectively, the recipients of The Citadel degree of Honorary Doctor of Jurisprudence made $982,000, close enough to a million dollars. All of the principal defense attorneys were paid over $1.4 million. In the *Faulkner* case alone, the McGuire Woods Battle & Booth law firm got $1,616,861 in fees and expenses, King & Spalding got $349,883, and Shaw Pittman Potts & Trowbridge got $267,958. As the low-dollar Insurance Reserve Fund law firm for The Citadel, Barnwell Whaley Patterson & Helms reported a figure of $131,234 for attorney fees and expenses that included its defense of Terry Leedom and payment of expert witness fees to the Mahans, the husband and wife team of former members of the faculty.

Yet the exact expenditures in the case, to some extent, remain as vague as they did when the president's assistant replied to Senator Holly Cork's inquiry at the outset of the case. The salaries of the five or six attorneys in the office of the South Carolina Attorney General, their three law clerks, and legal assistant, all of whom spent 8000 hours on the case from May 1993, to March 1996, were never made public. Nonetheless, this much was certain—whatever The Citadel and state had to pay the plaintiffs' attorneys and staff would be on top of what it paid its own attorneys and staff. The total for the case, for The Citadel and state, ultimately was over $14 million.

"But we felt we had a justified reason to defend our policy, so if I had to do it over again, sure I would," the chairman of the Board of Visitors Jimmy Jones told *The P & C* on November 2, 1996, the day after plaintiffs filed their petition for fees.

The November 1, 1996, petition for fees and costs filed by the plaintiffs' lawyers asked for $5.8 million. The actual amount awarded to the plaintiffs' attorneys by the district court order on March 30, 1999, was $4,564,204.17. On June 25, 1999, the press announced that a settlement of $3.24 million had been reached, but only after Governor Jim Hodges threatened to appeal any district court award of fees. Thus, the plaintiffs' numbers went down from $6.7 million in their petition on November 1, 1996, to $4.6 million in the district court's order on March 30, 1999, to a $3.2 million settlement three months later.

I hired Gaston Fairey from Columbia to represent me in trying to collect attorney fees under 42 U.S.C. Section 1988. Gaston ended up representing all the plaintiffs' attorneys in collective negotiations to reach a total figure both sides were willing to settle for. Val also hired Malissa Burnette to represent her since Val by that time had already left Shearman & Sterling and had begun teaching at NYU Law School.

Only the attorneys for DOJ, namely Nat Douglas, Sandy Beber, Mike Maurer, and Tom Chandler did not claim attorney fees, pursuant to law controlling the United States in litigation.

Depositions taken under oath followed the calculations of fees claimed. Questions asked of me were soft. To the deposing attorney in the AG's office, I was not worth any contentiousness. The only thing that seemed to have amused him was my lack of income as a result of taking on The Citadel.

Not surprisingly, one of the most difficult problems for me as local counsel was getting attorneys in town to write affidavits and testify in support of my application for fees. Throughout the case, no local counsel offered to help me with litigating the case. Now at the fees stage, nearly everyone dove for cover. I called fellow attorneys in Charleston whom I thought might agree to submit an affidavit to the court supporting my petition for $175 an hour. Senior attorneys in established firms up and down Broad Street and in the most internationally recognized firm in Charleston would not help. Some had legitimate conflicts of interest. One doubted I was worth $175 an hour. Most knew, as Edmund Robinson did in 1988, that collaboration with the enemy could end with a shaved head. Charleston became Hadleyville, the fictitious town in the movie *High Noon*.

"I've been through all this before," I told Gaston Fairey. "I know who's out there and there's no one. I had to go out of state to get help winning the case, and I know I have to go out of town to get witnesses to help claim my fees." I was such a pariah in town that I had to ask Gaston to make some of the phone calls for me.

After one of the most prominent lawyers in Charleston told Gaston that he could not help me claim attorney fees, Gaston did, however, get an equally prominent lawyer in Columbia—Betsy Gray—to serve as a witness and write an affidavit. Henry Weisburg had also gone out of town to Columbia to get attorney George Cauthen to help with the Shearman fees. Then one of the most pleasant events in the case happened. Several local attorneys answered my call for help. They were Bill Regan, Coming Ball Gibbs, Frank McCann, and Drew Epting.

Gaston used depositions and the live testimony of Gibbs and Epting at the hearing on August 6, 1997. One bobble did occur, however. From a telephone booth just outside the courtroom, I took a call from Regan who told me that he would be happy to testify on the stand but that his own hourly rate was less than what I myself was claiming. Since the judge and everyone else would know that I was not one-tenth the lawyer Regan was, I asked him to stay far away from the courthouse.

Certainly these witnesses at the hearing for attorney fees were crucial in getting a favorable ruling by the court, but there may have been another player on the field. A prominent member of the community and owner of a pharmacy had sent her two sons to The Citadel, both superb cadets. Her sister had taken an accounting class in 1949 at The Citadel under Professor Tibbits while she was studying toward a pharmacy degree at MUSC—another part of The Citadel's hidden history of admitting women long before Faulkner. The cadets' mother was always interested in the case and fully supported Shannon. She approached Melinda while shopping at Harris Teeter on East Bay Street and asked how the hearing on fees was going. Melinda found herself answering the question at the very time that Judge Houck was coincidentally only 20 feet away at the end of another aisle.

"Well, I'll go tell him myself," she told Melinda. "Your husband deserves to get paid as much as possible."

Melinda quickly slipped away and saw and heard nothing as my real fee petition may have been pled somewhere amid the rice and beans.

On June 16, 1997, The Citadel filed its proposed findings of fact in which it challenged payment for virtually everything I did in the case and stated that "it might be overly generous to award Mr. Black even as much as $75 an hour ... in view of his limited role in this case."

At the hearing a couple of months later, on August 6, 1997, one of the lighter questions Hood asked Val concerned the costs claimed by Shearman & Sterling for their lodgings during the 1994 trial. That unwittingly opened the door for Val to recount some of the disruptive pettiness with which the New Yorkers had to deal while in the Holy City. One such pettiness occurred when the identity of the Shearman attorneys was discovered during trial. They had rented a condominium on Vendue Range. Residents and the owner construed the attorneys' activity as impermissibly "commercial" and promptly kicked them out.

Gaston Fairey's job at the hearing for attorney fees was to lay it on in praise of his unpopular client. He argued eloquently in court that I ought to receive $200 per hour in attorney fees. Fairey made reference to the "extreme unpopularity" of the case and some of the more wearing events related in my affidavit.

"He took this case knowing or anticipating what would occur," my paid advocate told the court. "He is the person who has knowledge about The Citadel. He is the person that has the knowledge about military affairs. He is the person that has the knowledge about education issues, and he is the person that was willing to accept the case, and then to garner the necessary resources to get it to the state it is today."

Val testified in my support to say that I was key to the case, and Isabelle later observed that I knew what people at The Citadel were going to say before they said it. Fairey accurately portrayed me as the one whose job it was to slop the pigs:

> He is a deep thinker that looks at a problem and comes up with solutions that you and I may miss. He is the one that will get into the trenches, will keep working at something, keep looking at something, will go and call and call people until he finds the witnesses that are relevant to the issues. And that was how he was used in this case.

He was "the architect," Fairey said, quoting Pat Johnson, in a case that

> has been fought like no case I have ever seen. This case has ruined Bob Black. He gave up his law practice to try this case. He made practically nothing in 1993, 1994, and 1995 and in October of 1995 he had to give up his office and move home. He left debts that he still owes his landlord and he accumulated a hundred thousand dollar debt

that he still owes his mother over this case, and that needs to be compensated for. That is a commitment to a case that is something that doesn't occur, I have never had to do that. I have suffered in cases, but I never had to give up my practice or my office.

Under the specter of the appellate court in Richmond, The Citadel and state did an excellent job of getting rid of many compensable hours. As background to settlement negotiations, we were again reminded that Governor Hodges promised to appeal any award to Faulkner's lawyers. The total hours I cautiously withdrew on my own were 300, but the defendants successfully argued during negotiations to delete 1100 of my hours. Those, plus the 550 unique hours from Johnson which I never claimed, added up to about 1950 hours I spent on the case which were voluntarily withdrawn, objected to, or never claimed.

When the judge ruled that certain hours spent in discovery in the veterans' case were not compensable, even though the defendants themselves had, throughout settlement negotiations, already agreed to pay some of them, I was devastated. Initially oblivious to the fact that I could even get paid at all for doing this kind of stuff, I ended up getting paid for the tip of an iceberg. A lot of hours were also spent in matters for which I never billed, the little things that only someone minding the shop, a custodian, must necessarily tend to. They had to be done and took a lot of time to do, but they did not amount to legal work, and I could not charge an attorney's fee to do them or claim costs for a support staff.

I ended up trying to collect fees for over 3000 hours claimed for my work on the *Faulkner/Mellette* case. The court awarded fees for 1868 hours on *Faulkner/Mellette* and an additional 80 hours, out of the 250 claimed, for my time fighting to get them. The court awarded an enhanced fee of $230 per hour, more than I asked for.

In any event, the $449,497 which The Citadel and state were ordered to pay me in attorney fees was reduced in settlement by nearly $50,000, an amount which was immediately cut in half by the 47% tax bracket I was in. The rest of the award soon disappeared after debts and loans were paid off. It was a double whammy. The case ended up as a clean sweep. I made no money. In fact, I lost ground with the loss of a clientele base and from reprisals. Either because of being so completely involved with the *Faulkner* case for so long or because of being a lousy lawyer, I never really had a practice after The Citadel case. Fortunately, I was married to a woman who, while supporting the family, also had a different last name and a different personality that allowed her to continue social and professional contacts with clients and various saints scattered about town. Devils too. When one found out Melinda was married to me, he asked her, "How can you be married to that son of a bitch?"

I eventually had to sell the land in Alabama that my father gave me.

Loyal Sons

"What it is like to be in a battle, is to have men shot down by your side by bullets, machine guns, sharp shooters, air plane bombs, etc. I've heard the bullets sing about my head and the smoke to blind me from the bombs from air planes and the shrapnel whistle in the air and would wonder—is that mine?"

Quillen Orr Johnson, the author's great uncle,
Memoirs of WWI, Battle of the Marne

If most of the local and state bar gave the silent treatment to the *Faulkner* litigation, select members throughout the state rushed to testify against her attorneys in their request for fees. Some of the most prominent members of the bar demonstrated that the power and clout of The Citadel is not limited to members of the General Assembly. A lesson on how South Carolina operates continued into the fee fight. The Citadel hired several lawyers of renown to argue that the plaintiffs' petition for fees was way out of line and that they should be getting much less than what they were asking for, if anything at all. Dewey Oxner from Greenville was a bond lawyer and partner of Sam Applegate in the Haynesworth firm. He had Charlie Condon as a client and regularly represented the state. At the July 1997, hearings Oxner testified that other lawyers in South Carolina or bordering states would have taken the case, so there was no need for me to look to expensive New York lawyers for help.

Harold Jacobs was a senior partner at Nexen Pruet Jacobs & Pollard and also represented the state from time to time. He gamely testified that he would not have taken the *Faulkner* case, although it was not complex and needed only a few lawyers.

It was Donald V. Richardson, however, who was the principal witness hired to attack me. Yet another one of the state's lawyers who did not review all of the plaintiffs' pleadings related to their petition, Richardson testified that he read through the first 80 pages or about a third of my deposition and concluded that I had no active role in the case—just the opposite position from the one taken when The Citadel thought I was so crucial to its case that it named me the first witness at the trial in 1994. In Richardson's opinion, I deserved only

$100 per hour for my very limited work on a simple case that already had a "road map" from the *VMI* case.

In all the affidavits and testimonies, no witnesses for The Citadel and state named any local counsel who definitely would have taken the case, except Ellison Smith. If I had known that, I would have walked the half block from my office to his to seek his help. Or he could have come to me.

After two hearings on attorney fees on July 7–11, 1997, and August 10, 1998, lengthy discovery and countless documents filed, the district court issued its Findings of Fact, Conclusions of Law, and Order nearly two years later on March 30, 1999:

> Robert Black is the spark that started the flame of this litigation. Due to his valor and steadfast determination, Johnson began—and Faulkner was able to continue and win—a battle for equal protection. Black possessed a knowledge of the procedures, policies, philosophies, and background of The Citadel, a depth of knowledge essential to the factual development of the case. He acted as local counsel for the plaintiffs and as a watchdog in South Carolina who updated the other attorneys on daily developments in the case....
>
> Black truly felt the sharpened point of social ostracism by participating in this case. He and his family were the brunt of insults and the object of threats of bodily injury for over three years. They have been cursed at, hissed at, ridiculed, and denounced by the citizens of this state as well as graduates and students of The Citadel. As stated by Black in his affidavit, "[the] pervasive anger and hostility within the community toward us was emotionally draining." Nobody in this litigation except Faulkner has felt the immense undesirability of this case more than Black.

Sometime after I read the order, I remembered an angry man who gave me the middle finger at a restaurant downtown. I went over to him and asked who he was. Like all the others, he refused to tell me his name, only that he was a Citadel graduate. The man's girlfriend led him away before the conversation could continue. Same with The Citadel graduate at the River Dogs' baseball office on Hasell Street who violently cursed me about the case. And the time Melinda and I were nearly hit by a jerk who cursed at us and yelled something about The Citadel as he swerved his car too near the sidewalk in South Windemere. And the good ole boys at the Mexican restaurant on Coleman Boulevard in Mount Pleasant as we tried to have a meal with Shannon one Friday night, and the two business men who smirked and laughed from a car at the corner of East Bay and Broad after the court put a stay on Faulkner. Melinda remembered a man who spat at me. The mild little gestures like suddenly pulling back their hand before a handshake, or the time a well-meaning daughter of a prominent Citadel man arranged a meeting with her father to help me find work after the case was over: the "people lover," as he was called by *The P & C*, couldn't even stand to look at me as I sat in his living room on Rebellion Road. I couldn't even help myself, much less Shannon, and even others who on a much smaller scale had to deal with the same Citadel pettiness day after day— like a friend who stopped me to complain about the "Fuck You" screamed at her by a cadet who saw her "I Support Shannon" bumper sticker on her car parked on Meeting Street. I don't remember all of them. Melinda hasn't told me everything. Fresh incidents still occur periodically, as when an old acquaintance nearly kicked me out of his house in 2008. Gregg Meyers warned me. None, of course, amounted to what Shannon had to deal with.

Nothing ever got out of hand in my own life. Nothing like the great racial struggles in the 1950s and 1960s in Alabama that others went through, the memories of which I constantly used to hone my resolve. Nothing even approximating what Matthew Perry and Phillip Wittenberg went through while representing Sarah Mae Fleming Brown's right to ride in the front of the bus in Columbia, South Carolina, seventeen months before Rosa Parks made the same case in Alabama. Nothing like two lesser-known battles by teenage black girls in Montgomery where in 1955, sandwiched between the protests of Fleming Brown and Parks, 15-year-old Claudette Colvin and teenager Mary Louise Smith stood alone, although not in court, to fight for their right to ride in the front of the bus. All of The Citadel actions were annoyances that swelled into Faulkner's demise and an economic and professional mess for me, but never more. Never the real thing —just having to deal with the petty little acts of bullies and cowards. Were it not for my adolescence in Alabama, I probably would not ever have taken Shannon's case. I was probably about as safe in Charleston as I was in the Sunday School room in Tuskegee in 1958, and for that I am eternally grateful.

An Incomplete Conclusion

After attending Old Dominion and Furman, Shannon Faulkner was graduated from Anderson College with a degree in secondary education in English in August 1999. She quickly earned a reputation as one of the best English teachers at the school where she is teaching now.

The Citadel museum, located just inside Lesesne Gate on the third floor adjacent to the main library, contains an 8 x 10 inch reprint of the senior picture of Charles DeLesline Foster, the first black man to integrate The Citadel in

1966. On December 1, 1996, *The P & C* quoted Larry Ferguson, a 1973 black alumnus of The Citadel and former member of the BOV, who attended the 1992 ceremony posthumously honoring the first black cadet. Because everyone expected a much greater recognition of Foster to be revealed, there was a "major hush" in The Citadel Museum, Ferguson said, when the small framed reprint was unveiled. "People were shocked" at the paltry effort, Ferguson said.[3]

No other commemoration of his service as a civil rights pioneer at The Citadel exists. No scholarship in his name, no nothing. Foster died under mysterious circumstances in a house fire near Dallas on March 29, 1986. Arson was suspected. The case remains unsolved. According to Faulkner's brief public discussion of the matter, those facts concerned her when she decided to leave The Citadel. During the course of litigation, an unknown Citadel supporter reputedly made threatening references to Foster's fate, and it was not worth the risk for Shannon to put her parents and herself in serious danger by remaining at The Citadel.

Faulkner was very aware of the day-to-day suffering by the first black student admitted to the Corps at The Citadel. However, by the time seven black women were graduated from the Corps in the Class of 2002—one of them, Natosha Mitchell of Tennessee—told *The P & C* on May 9, 2002, that the fact that they were women was more of an issue at the school than the fact that they were black. Toshika Hudson of Columbia, Lesjanusar Peterson of Chicago, Geneive Hardney of Staten Island, Renee Hypolite of Philadelphia, Adrienne Watson of Sanford, North Carolina, were some of the others, but it was the mere presence of Jamey McCloud of Wadmalaw Island, South Carolina, that reminded me of the trip to Johns Island High School with Melody Lutz nearly ten years earlier.

In the summer of 2000, The Citadel hired a new Assistant Commandant for Administration and Coeducation, Hedy Pinkerton. She was hired to take the place of a 1980 USAF graduate, who left to study at MUSC for a career in medicine. The USAF graduate whom Pinkerton replaced allegedly left because The Citadel was dragging its feet to recruit women and promote their success. Pinkerton, however, was happy with her job. She told *The P & C* on July 24, 2002, "We don't give cadets any particular history or background on women in the service because we prefer to focus on all the opportunities available to them today."

So I wrote the new assistant commandant the next day and sent a copy to Ben Legare:

> Perhaps in your capacity as an administrator of coeducation and in lieu of giving Citadel cadets a particular history of women in the service, you can begin to make efforts to recognize Shannon in what is represented as historical facts and items of historical interest at The Citadel Museum in Daniels Library. The last time I looked in the museum

there was no mention at all of Shannon. Or no significant mention of her. I will be glad to help you if you wish.

Nothing came of it. Only recently in 2011 has almost casual recognition in The Citadel Museum been given to the first woman admitted to the Corps of Cadets. The small glass showcase contains no photograph of Faulkner, only pictures of later women cadets, including the first black women cadets. The 3 x 6 foot showcase given to the history of women in the Corps is about one quarter the size of an adjacent showcase given to the history of regimental bands.

And to this day the words "Shannon Faulkner" are not spoken on campus. Citadel tradition requires only a reference to "the young lady who made application to the Corps." Former senator Fritz Hollings referred to such a young lady several times in a speech at the Alumni House during a conference on race at The Citadel in 2003. The floor was then opened for questions and comments, and I stood up in the audience and reminded him of her name, with little effect. Alumni still discuss the case as "the single-gender case," not as "Faulkner versus The Citadel" or "Faulkner versus Jones."

By some accounts, Shearman & Sterling agreed to give the ACLU 75% of its fee as a *pro bono* donation, but I do not know what actual arrangements were made, if any. By March 3, 2000, however, Shearman offered another *pro bono* gift, this time to The Citadel. The Citadel accepted the $300,000 gift from Henry Weisburg only on the condition that Faulkner's name not be attached in any way to the gift. It was too small an amount to generate money for a scholarship—certainly not one named for Shannon. The Citadel implied that the money would probably be used for women's locker rooms.

"I do not think Faulkner ever intended to go to The Citadel," James Battle, a 1964 graduate and member of the South Carolina House of Representatives, told Chris Burritt, reporter for *The Atlanta Journal-Constitution*. "For that reason, any gift made by Shearman & Sterling to The Citadel should not have her name on it. She went down there for the publicity."[4]

I drove Henry and the director of media and communications at Shearman & Sterling, to the gates of The Citadel and dropped them off. The Citadel had asked Henry not to bring the former assistant professor in the English Department with him.

A chauffer's job is better than no job at all. Shannon Faulkner won the battle to change the admissions policy, but The Citadel won the war. With the certainty of my not being able to draw a jury in Charleston without risk of reprisal, as the judge observed during a hearing on attorney fees, I became a member of the Colorado bar in 1993 and interviewed for a job with half-a-dozen firms in Denver. But Melinda would not leave Charleston. I eventually left for Montana.

Payback

A few years after the Citadel case was over, I was sued—or more precisely, in the pleadings at least, my client was sued—by The Citadel for allegedly filing a frivolous lawsuit. The suit was a preemptive act to prevent my representing future clients in actions against The Citadel, especially in lawsuits filed with the ACLU. I had met with Emily Martin, Shanti Hubbard, and Namita Luthra in the Women's Rights Project—and Isabelle Pinzler—in New York on June 1, 2005, to discuss another association, this time to represent two women cadets who had been kicked out just weeks before they were to be graduated. Nothing came of it, however, and no complaint was filed.

In a separate case, one which led to The Citadel's complaint against me for filing a frivolous lawsuit, one of The Citadel's top male cadets was suspended for hazing two female knobs. What the male cadet, a squad leader, did was admittedly irrational even if well-intended, but I thought his actions clearly did not constitute hazing under the definitions of hazing in state statutes. The cadet's actions, I argued and The Citadel admitted, were not done with the key element of an "intent to injure or punish" the women knobs, no matter how outrageous the act, as required for a conviction of hazing in the statutes. Also, under a state statute, nothing in The Citadel regulations can be in violation of or inconsistent with state law, including its definitions of hazing. I based the cadet's complaint simply and solidly on three state statutes under the 1976 Code of Laws, as amended, 59-63-275(A)(4), 59-101-200(A)(4), and 59-121-50. The cadet's actions were naïvely intended to bond the two women knobs with the rest of the male cadets in his squad, the only squad which welcomed them as members.

But a defense based on the absence of intent was not a defense to hazing under The Citadel regulations, The Citadel argued. Otherwise, all cadets could avoid a charge of hazing by simply saying that they did not intend to injure or punish a knob. Dawes had the winning argument.

At the hearing on August 18, 2005, at which time the case was found not to be frivolous, the court asked,

> The Court: Is this really against the client or is it really against Mr. Black?
> Mr. Cooke: It's against the client.
> The Court: And Mr. Black made money off of The Citadel in the last litigation, so I didn't know whether this was?

Mr. Cooke: No, but I'll be?

The Court: —turnabout's fair play?

Mr. Cooke: —very candid. What I would like to see is that the next time somebody's sitting in Mr. Black's office and says, "What do I have to lose by suing The Citadel and taking it to the end?" I would like him to say that, There is a chance that you will have to pay attorney's fees.

Earlier, on December 12, 2001, I sat alone in the courtroom at a hearing in *Faulkner/Mellette*. My first appearance with Isabelle Pinzler had been eight years and eight months previously, almost to the day. Before the court now was a joint motion for a consent order to allow The Citadel to file two instead of four assimilation reports per year. They had been washing up at the district court under the careful eyes of Eunice Ravenel, Lisa Walpole, and Pat Chisolm, clerks on Broad Street who helped everybody keep up with the case. Dan Gordon appeared for DOJ and Dawes for The Citadel. Colonel Joe Trez and Brigadier General Emory Mace, former and current commandants, were present. Judge Kiser had dismissed jurisdiction over VMI six days previously, and The Citadel now wanted Justice off their backs, too. Three months later, on March 28, 2002, The Citadel case would be dismissed. DOJ was happy to leave town. Val and Henry had left a couple of years earlier. The motion was granted:

"The court: Mr. Black, do you have anything you want to say?
"Black: No, sir, I do not."

Chapter 9

And Beyond

Whole Man, Whole Woman, Whole University

"Educate and inform the whole mass of the people.... They are the only sure reliance for the preservation of our liberty."

Letter from Thomas Jefferson to James Madison, 1787

The thrust of this book is toward the future, not the past. It discusses the women's lawsuits not only to present them in a proper light, but also to provide a backdrop to understanding The Citadel as it exists today. From this account of The Citadel's fierce resistance toward women, one sees that the same kind of leadership that fought against benefits flowing to the state from the admission of women in the Corps of Cadets also resists similar benefits that would arise from the admission of ordinary citizens into daytime classes.

Any effort to admit ordinary civilians to The Citadel to sit side by side during daytime classes with cadet civilians is, for some, an effort that goes against the prevailing economic winds in South Carolina. That is, some business leaders wish to keep the state fully identified as a source of cheap labor. A population which is not generally well educated best attracts foreign and domestic industry. Alabama and Mississippi, along with South Carolina, are identified as states in which international and American industries can pay adequate salaries for unskilled labor in order to compete with the labor forces of China, Brazil, and India. Ironically, it is this very identity that attracts major industries to South Carolina—most recently The Boeing Company. But Boeing and similar entities located in the state have skilled jobs as well, and the need for engineers and scientists to be educated locally at The Citadel need not be at odds with the prospect of furnishing unskilled South Carolinians a living wage. We need to have engineers and scientists educated in the Lowcountry to complement an existing strong unskilled labor pool.

The arrival of Boeing creates the perfect time for The Citadel to begin to educate ordinary citizens in daytime classes. Prior to its decision to move from

Washington to North Charleston, Boeing no doubt collected data and made analyses of employment strengths and weaknesses in the Lowcountry.

The General Assembly of South Carolina could easily appoint its own committee or ask the Commission on Higher Education to study the validity of initiating courses for ordinary citizens during the daytime at The Citadel that would educate Lowcountry citizens to hold so-called STEM (science, technology, engineering, and mathematics) jobs. Lowcountry workers in the shadow of The Citadel should greet Boeing with more than a broom.

The South Carolina legislature could take the necessary steps to force The Citadel to expand its mission to educate ordinary South Carolinian civilians in STEM jobs that would qualify them to join the nearly 50 cutting-edge research centers at three other public educational institutions—Clemson University, the University of South Carolina, and the Medical University of South Carolina—in South Carolina's SmartState Program. Created by the South Carolina legislature in 2002, the SmartState Program is funded through South Carolina Lottery proceeds. Paying average salaries of $63,000 (twice the South Carolina average), the SmartState Program brought 5000 new high-tech jobs to a state in desperate need of them. In 2010 SmartState research team grants resulted in more than $50 million entering the state. More than 25 companies invest in the SmartState Program, including BMW, Michelin, Timken, Bank of America, Roche Carolina, GlaxoSmithKline Pharmaceuticals, Fluor, Smith & Nephew, the Duke Foundation, and many others. Others, such as Trulite, Protera, and American Titanium Works have relocated their corporate offices to the Greenville area as a result of the SmartState Program. The Citadel is directly causing Lowcountry citizens to miss out on an incredible opportunity to attain economic excellence through the SmartState Program.

South Carolina remains a jewel and a happy place to live for most of its citizens. Yet, South Carolinians are also worn down from hearing that they are last or near last in the nation in categories of health, education, and the general economic welfare of its people. Low rankings ebb and flow with the Atlantic. Improvement is more often marked by relative advances than by absolute scores. The customary excuse is that there is a large illiterate population—black and white—but some people think that the state resists progress because of the good ole boys in power.

At one time or another around the years of the *Faulkner* case, South Carolina was last in the nation in SAT scores, worst in the increase of toxic waste, first in the nation in percentage of mobile homes, first with the largest disparities between mortgage rates paid by minorities and whites, last in percentage of people who vote, last in the nation in relation to women's earnings compared to men's, last in number of women holding elected office in a state legislature, first in the nation in the rate of women killed by men, first in the nation for most violent crimes per 100,000 residents, first in percentage of single mothers working to support children under 18, worst in the nation for students graduating from high school on time, highest in the number of dead-beat dads, highest in alcohol-related fatality rates, and—according to the United Health Foundation—just above Mississippi and Louisiana in a ranking of the least healthy states, and consistently ranking high among the states with the most obese citizens. South Carolina consistently ranked near the very bottom in children's well-being. Two weeks before the *VMI* decision was announced, South Carolina ranked 46th in the number of children in working-poor families. As this book goes to press, South Carolina ranks tenth in the nation for the percentage (18.2) of its population on food stamps.[1] In matters of health and education, rearing a child in South Carolina arguably remains a form of child neglect, if not abuse.

It would appear from bad publicity that South Carolina, standing alone, is a border-line third-world country. For the state's consistent poor placement among the bottom ten states, the Kids Count national assessment is simply that South Carolina cannot compete in the world market.

There are reasons for our poor showing, reasons that education can help address. The tired old saw is true: education is the key to prosperity. The exclusivity of The Citadel's concept of higher education and its supporting structural network of alumni and political clout create what James Madison in The Federalist No. 10 called "the violence of faction" that impedes educational progress.

After the *Faulkner/Mellette* case was over, beginning in 2000, I routinely wrote letters to the editors of *The State* in Columbia and *The Post and Courier* in Charleston supporting the admission of ordinary citizens in daytime classes at The Citadel. Those who would extend a Citadel education to as many people as possible, I argued, are the very ones who have the highest regard for South Carolina and The Citadel. They ask that The Citadel share its rich educational resources with ordinary civilians as it was compelled by law to do with women cadets.

The clear precedent for The Citadel to take a more responsible direction in education is Clemson University. One of my letters, dated May 2, 2004, also urged The Citadel to follow the lead of Texas A & M, Virginia Tech, and North Georgia "to help South Carolina get out of the cellar in education."

The Citadel remains a college with a mission to offer a liberal arts education in a military environment, regardless of its emphasis on "leadership" for purposes of litigation. Yet it does not open its doors widely enough for the state to benefit from the education of all civilians, those civilians who are in the Corps of Cadets and those who are not.

The *Faulkner* litigation showed the weaknesses of The Citadel as well as its strengths. One such weakness is that The Citadel does not serve the state and nation to the greatest extent possible. It still effectively remains a semi-private preserve controlled by the Board of Visitors and alumni, not the General Assembly and not the taxpayers. It operates as a private club. Nearly 20 years after women filed suit for admission to The Citadel day program, The Citadel still fails to share the wealth with all citizens. For more than 150 years, it kept its resources for male cadets only. After *Faulkner*, it still protects its resources for the exclusive use of cadets only, most of whom are from out of state, and, as of 2009, for a very few male and female veterans.

The next step is for The Citadel to open its day program to ordinary citizens.

The critical shortage of college courses in math, science, and engineering in the Lowcountry is apparent. Bills have been introduced in the General Assembly to make more money available for the State's LIFE and Palmetto Fellows scholarships for students majoring in math, science, and engineering. But the bills do not address the need for The Citadel to open its doors to help solve a crisis in education in the state. For fear of reprisals, legislators dare not propose changing The Citadel into a university that has a non-cadet as well as a cadet student body during daytime hours. Any attempt to dilute The Citadel's identity as a cadet-only institution would "have to come across my dead body," a former president of The Citadel, General John Grinalds, was quoted as saying.[2] Internal study groups that met twelve years ago from MUSC, the College of Charleston, and The Citadel have not advanced plans for consolidated advanced Ph.D. degree programs "to lure high-tech industry and boost the local economy."[3] Doctoral programs were proposed in business, education, engineering, and information sciences, as well as marine biology, psychology, and public policy.

The Citadel is no longer in violation of the United States Constitution as it was when Faulkner brought her lawsuits. It is not breaking the law by not sharing the wealth. It is, however, strangling higher education and prosperity in the Lowcountry, state, and nation.

Outside of Citadel classrooms, advanced courses and a large number of undergraduate courses in math, physics, chemistry, civil engineering, and electrical engineering are unavailable or difficult to access in the Lowcountry. In 1998 it was left to Clemson operating out of Trident Technical College in North Charleston to offer master's programs in civil engineering, electrical engineering, and construction science and management.[4] Now TTC offers two-year course-work in engineering and the sciences through various programs.[5]

The Citadel's contribution to the education of ordinary citizens who are not veterans is meager: its "2 + 2" program in which students studying for a bachelor's degree take the first two years at Trident Tech, then switch to more advanced course taught only in the evening courses at The Citadel.

By denying them access to education during the daytime, The Citadel continues to treat non-cadet civilians the way it treated would-be cadet women up until 1996.

The presence of ordinary civilians in day classes will not inhibit the "integrity" of the Corps of Cadets at The Citadel. John Reid was a knob in the fall of 1955 until he tore the ligaments in his knee at the beginning of the semester and was forced to drop out of the Corps of Cadets. He transferred to the College of Charleston where he took English, math, and history for the rest of the semester. But, according to his sister, he continued to take engineering drafting at The Citadel where he began the course because no courses in engineering were offered at the College of Charleston. He sat side by side with the cadets while he was enrolled as an ordinary civilian at the College of Charleston. There are no doubt other stories of such exceptions allowed, but little is heard of them by The Citadel simply because little damage was ever done. The Reids were family friends of Mark Clark.

After *Faulkner*, the basis of power in the Constitution—the people—must change The Citadel to make these courses more accessible to all citizens. Only in response to pressure from citizens will legislators be forced to change the university's admission policy and admit non-cadets from 8:00 a.m. to 5:00 p.m. to sit with cadets in the same courses.

There is no state law that requires The Citadel to be an institution attended only by cadets and a few veterans during daytime classes. A decision to begin preparations for the admission of ordinary citizens to study engineering, math, and the sciences during daytime classes could be made at the next Board of Visitors meeting. In fact, such a decision should have been announced on June 28, 1996. Clemson made its decision to admit women and non-cadets at approximately the same time.

More undergraduates in American colleges and universities—about one in five—major in business than in any other field.[6] At The Citadel, however, that number is much greater. About one in three cadets major in business administration at The Citadel. The Citadel is top-heavy with cadets who are not taking subjects that are as directly needed for future economic prosperity. By a wide margin, fewer graduates of the Corps of Cadets major in math, physics, chemistry, and engineering than in business. Active Duty Students and veterans, those who are not members of the Corps, make up a disproportionate number of the engineering, math, and science majors at The Citadel.

In May 1999, at Nancy Mace's graduation, out of the 399 names of senior cadets listed in the program, three cadets took a B.A. in chemistry and three in math; two took a B.S. in math and four in physics. All but two were from out of state. A comparison of the Class of 1999 with the Class of 2003 shows stagnant figures in the sciences if not in engineering:

Graduating Class of 1999
Total:	399	
Chemistry:	3	(0.1%)
Biology:	21	(5%)
Math:	2	(0.5%)
Physics:	4	(1%)
Engineering:	43	(11%)
Computer Science:	9	(2%)
Business Administration:	141	(35%)

Graduating Class of 2003
Total:	374	
Chemistry:	3	(0.8%)
Biology:	13	(3%)
Math:	3	(0.8%)
Physics:	4	(1%)
Engineering:	21	(6%)
Computer Science:	5	(1%)
Business Administration:	144	(38%)

One hundred forty-one cadets in 1999 took a B.S. degree in business administration. Forty-three majored in either electrical or civil engineering. The rest of the field included 13 in criminal justice, 16 in English, 33 in history, 9 in modern languages, 50 in political science, seven in psychology, 18 in education, and 22 in physical education.

Things were no better at The Citadel graduation in May 2003, which I attended with Shannon Faulkner who made her only return visit to The Citadel to see a family friend graduate. One cadet took a B.A. in chemistry and two in math; two took a B.S. in chemistry, one in math, and four in physics. Of that lot, two were from out of state, two from Taiwan, and a total of five were from South Carolina.

Another way to look at the majors of the graduating senior cadets in 2003, both B.A. and B.S., includes a mere count of 3 in chemistry, 3 in math, 13 in biology, 5 in computer science, 4 in physics, and 21 in engineering for a total of 49 or 13% out of a total of 374 cadets listed in the program. That's 49 in chemistry, math, biology, computer science, physics, and engineering; 181 in criminal justice, English, history, modern languages, political science, psychology, education, and health, exercise, and sport science; and 144 in business administration. Fourteen of the 20 cadets majoring in health, exercise and sport science were from the Palmetto State.

Percentages available on The Citadel website relative to the hard sciences, engineering, and business administration/marketing, among the 483 total degrees conferred in both the Corps of Cadets and the Evening College in May, 2009, are consistent with those from 1999 and 2003. Even counting the Evening College, the hard sciences go wanting, engineering barely makes a showing, and the business of The Citadel remains business. The Citadel website carefully avoids a break-down of the number of biology, physics, and chemistry majors, amounting to less than 5% of the class:

Graduating Class of 2009
Total:	483
Math:	7 (1%)
Physical Sciences:	7 (1%)
Biological/Life Sciences	17 (4%)
Engineering	70 (14%)
Computer and Information Services	5 (1%)
Business Administration/Marketing	154 (32%)

Sensitive to the fact that most cadets are not South Carolinians, The Citadel did not identify graduating seniors in 2011 by their home state or nation. This was a departure from the practice in 1999 and 2003. Nonetheless, the numbers show no improvement in the production of scientists and engineers from those in 1999, 2003, and 2009:

Graduating Class of 2011
Total:	483
Chemistry:	1 (0.2% of the class; a female cadet)
Biology:	21 (4%; 4 female cadets)
Math:	2 (0.4%)
Physics:	3 (0.6%)
Engineering:	59 (12%)
Computer Science:	8 (2%)
Business Administration:	152 (32%)

The reopened Veterans Day Program graduated 17 students, about one third of whom were engineers.

In its use of two of the state's most precious resources—youth and educational opportunities—a large number of majors in the tough subjects like math, science, and engineering are held by foreign or out-of-state students.

In short, any graduation ceremony at The Citadel demonstrates a failure to fully exploit state resources. The Citadel's emphasis on business and its lack of making full use of existing half-empty classes in engineering and the sciences fails the state and its people. One might say that a Citadel education in "leadership" only serves ironically to shore up South Carolina to continue its role as a servant state. The Citadel network cannot support competition in a world market when there are so few Citadel cadets who major in math, science, and engineering.

The Lowcountry Graduate Center at The Citadel is not the only answer. Education in these subjects must, instead, start at the undergraduate level. Such a graduate center is fine for what it does to bring The Citadel together with MUSC, the College of Charleston, and Clemson for programs in social work and educational administration. But it is not an answer to the "screaming need" to offer undergraduate courses in engineering, math, and the wet and dry sciences to everyone.

At a Citadel University in which cross-registration of ordinary citizens from other local colleges and universities flourishes in both directions, students from The Citadel, MUSC, the College of Charleston, and Trident Tech would become eligible for admission to courses taught at any one of those institutions. Shortly after the end of the *Faulkner* litigation, such was the proposed design of a consortium of higher educational institutions in the Lowcountry. But The Citadel refused to join for fear of weakening the "integrity" of the Corps of Cadets.

Occasionally, civic or political leaders in the state make an association between economics and education and urge that legislators do something to raise South Carolina from the 42nd percentile in the national per capita income. In 2005 South Carolinians made only 82 cents on the dollar compared with workers in other states, a hard fact that translated into a reduced tax base and a lower quality of life.[7]

Even though *Faulkner* has shown the immense advantages to be gained by a more open Citadel, The Citadel continues to create a bottleneck in education by restricting its resources to an elite few in a major industrial area which is critical to future growth of the economy of the state and nation. The Port of Charleston is one of the largest on the East Coast, and the 2010 Boeing Effect taking hold in North Charleston looms large in the state's future. To exploit obvious opportunities, ordinary men and women should be allowed to occupy the empty state college desks in courses which are not fully enrolled by Citadel cadets.

Boeing's decision in 2010 to move to Charleston to build part of its 787 Dreamliner only adds to what should be an exciting future for South Carolina. An economics professor at the University of South Carolina predicts, "If Boeing takes off, South Carolina will soar with it."[8] Even before Boeing's arrival in town there was a demand for trained engineers and scientists of all stripes. The Space and Naval Warfare Systems Center (SPAWARSYSCEN Atlantic), a Department of Defense entity under command of the Department of the Navy in Charleston, contracts with hundreds of private contractors. One of them, the Science Applications International Corporation (SAIC), and its subsidiaries have 43,000 employees worldwide. As well as federal and private entities, the South Carolina Research Authority (SCRA) has a conspicuous presence near Boeing at the Charleston International Airport. Force Protection Industries, Inc., makes the MRAP mine protection vehicles in nearby Ladson. Men and women educated in South Carolina colleges and universities should be able to compete for jobs in these industries. As they are presently educated, South Carolinians are apt to get only the low-paying service jobs. Brains are imported. Improving the welfare of citizens of South Carolina requires an expanded sense of service and national defense that The Citadel can make through teaching non-cadets as well as cadets in its daytime classes. Five to six billion dollars flow through SPAWAR each year. Lockheed, General Dynamics, and Northrop Grumman, among other major corporations, have a presence in Charleston.

One official connected to defense contracts told me that a local undergraduate and graduate program in engineering and the sciences at The Citadel would be "very attractive" in meeting the "dramatic growth" that is expected in the near future. Another could only say, "It's a no brainer."

The agreement which The Citadel signed with SPAWAR or SSC on December 11, 2009, misses the boat. It is limited to educating cadets only. According to an announcement by the Charleston Regional Development Alliance,

> The partnership enhances the educational experiences of the cadets at The Citadel by providing access to the staff, expertise, facilities, and equipment related to naval warfare systems technology available at SSC. It will also promote cadets' interest in science, mathematics, and engineering, particularly relating to space and naval warfare systems technology. Cadets can see first-hand a working Department of Defense laboratory.... The agreement allows SSC Atlantic to transfer surplus computer or scientific equipment to the college, loan laboratory equipment to the college, provide academic and career advice to students, and provide laboratory personnel who may teach science courses or assist in developing courses or related educational material, if needed.

The problem of restricted student access to education in engineering, math, and the sciences at The Citadel is that not enough cadets exploit the opportunities provided. Ordinary citizens have to go to a local two-year technical state college which has to fill the gap. The Citadel should shoulder the state educational burden to teach the sciences to ordinary civilian undergraduates, a heavy burden bravely now being carried in its two-year "2 + 2" program by Trident Tech, and by the College of Charleston and, to some extent, the Medical University of South Carolina. Undergraduate enrollment at Trident Technical College in North Charleston in 2010–2011 was second only to undergraduate enrollment at the University of South Carolina in Columbia. More than 15,000 students registered for classes, and those classes did not include access to the kind of vast resources and capabilities reserved for a handful of cadets at The Citadel.[9]

A comparison of Trident Tech's course offerings to those at The Citadel are like the offerings made by SCIL at Converse. The Citadel is simply treating ordinary citizens the way it tried to treat women by relegating them to a separate and unequal program at Converse. More to the point, Trident Tech is not the right place for the kind of scientific and engineering instruction that can be conducted at The Citadel. Clemson and USC are not going to come to the rescue and set up shop in the Lowcountry to do what The Citadel can do better by opening its doors to ordinary citizens during daytime hours. State taxpayers demand a local response to our educational needs.

There are plenty of empty seats at The Citadel for ordinary citizens to sit side by side with cadets and the few active duty and veteran students during daytime hours of instruction when the entire curriculum is offered. For example, from a cursory look one can see that the five classrooms in Grimsley Hall, where physics and electrical engineering are taught, seat a total of 162 students. LeTellier Hall has two labs seating 28 for civil engineering. Byrd Hall has two chemistry labs for 12 students each or a total of 24 seats. Duckett Hall has a 24-person classroom for biology. Only the Registrar's office at The Citadel, of course, knows the exact number of empty seats for students in the sciences, math, and engineering, but it would appear from the apparent numbers of graduating seniors and their majors that cadets simply do not want to fill them up. Courses in business, after all, are much easier than those in the sciences, math, and engineering.

If more professors in math, engineering, and the sciences are needed to teach people who would occupy all the empty seats in Grimsley, LeTellier, and Duckett halls, The Citadel must use its influence and resources to get the necessary funds to pay them. Such funds are far more necessary than those which were sought and easily won to set up a parallel corps of cadets at Converse.

There are six senior military colleges recognized by the Pentagon on a tier below the federal military academies. Four of the six—Texas A & M, North Georgia, Norwich, and Virginia Tech—have already admitted non-cadets into what were historically all-male, military institutions. Only VMI and The Citadel have not welcomed the future.

Virginia Tech, a land-grant university founded in 1872, ceased being just a military college in 1963 when it began to admit non-cadets. It retained its distinctive Corps of Cadets, however, but students could after that time join the Corps as non-cadets. Such civilians are simply cadets in the "Corps Only," participants in what later was called the "Civilian Track," and have no military obligation after graduation. They do, however, wear the uniform, just as cadets with a military option do, and live scattered at random among the ROTC cadets in barracks of a well-defined Corps of Cadets. As full members of the Corps, these non-cadets study leadership skills within a rigorous military environment, but they do not take ROTC. At Virginia Tech, you can be in the Corps without being in ROTC but not in ROTC without being in the Corps. That was the issue the old-guard alumni fought over, not whether women could be members of the Corps. Women had been on campus in daytime classes since 1922. In a Corps of Cadets numbering 710, about 16% are women, compared to about 8% at The Citadel. At Virginia Tech about 20% of the Corps are civilian and 80% ROTC, so about 80% of graduates from the Corps take a commission upon graduation and go into the military, just the flip side of only 20% at The Citadel who serve. At Virginia Tech, ROTC training is for the most part not wasted on civilians who have no intention of entering the military. At The Citadel, four years of ROTC are required, even for those 80% who begin civilian occupations.

In their history, four of the six senior military colleges let non-cadets attend class in the daytime along with male and female cadets and became the stronger for it. But other previously all-male military colleges, outside the six recognized by the Pentagon, have the same history. The great example in South Carolina is, of course, Clemson. To mark the 50th anniversary of the admission of women into Clemson, the president of Clemson celebrated a love of state and nation in a collegiate mission that is greater than love of alma mater:

> The admission of women into the Clemson family is one of this University's great success stories ... moving it from an all-male, all-white military school to a civilian, coeducational, desegregated research university that we can proudly say is among the nation's most outstanding public universities.

What occurred upstate in January 1955, must now happen at The Citadel. The people of the Lowcountry and throughout the state have no choice but to demand that The Citadel follow Clemson's lead and educate ordinary citizens, male and female, in its daytime program. As America is fully integrated into a global market, so must The Citadel be fully integrated—not just with women cadets who followed Shannon Faulkner into daytime classes, but also with civilians in all programs, day or night. And in such an environment, The Citadel could easily retain an autonomous Corps of Cadets.

A new kind of Citadel Corps of Cadets will exist as the centerpiece and pride of The Citadel, but it will exist along-side a smaller daytime, non-cadet student body. The world will not end when students in the existing Evening College, and others, emerge from the shadows and elect to attend day classes as well as evening classes. They will not be zombies stumbling in the daylight across Summerall Field. Everyone thought the world would end when women came to the South Carolina Corps of Cadets. Instead, as the Boo observed, it has gotten better—just as ordinary citizens in the daytime will make The Citadel better.

What will be lost?

A lot, but more will be gained. The *Faulkner* case showed that what's great at The Citadel is in fact not tied to an all-male culture. Admission of ordinary civilians during the day will show that the richness of The Citadel is not tied to a barracks culture. Those who fought so hard against admitting women into the Corps were wrong. The Citadel is greater than they thought. The greatness of The Citadel lies in strengths that go far beyond sex and a uniform. The Citadel will continue to share the wealth. The Citadel will get even better as it has with the admission of women. More South Carolinians will appreciate Citadel ideals and values which will be shown forth in the light of day. A lot is at stake in American education. It's the most serious game in the world in which The Citadel must now play a wider part.

Admission of ordinary citizens into daytime courses will be a patriotic act beyond anything The Citadel has ever done. As at Texas A & M, North Georgia, Virginia Tech, and Norwich, the long grey line will continue to exist as the central part of The Citadel. Only cadets will continue to live in the barracks, but in daytime classrooms they will benefit from contact with non-cadets who are ordinary citizens, not just veterans, and vice-versa. The Corps of Cadets will continue to march and maintain its own collegiate identity, but it will do so within a larger vision of an institution which is fully responsive to the state, the nation, and the world. The administration and Board of Visitors were wrong. The greatness of The Citadel lies in the power of knowledge, not in social and political connections, and it belongs to all the people of South Carolina.

Notes

Introduction

1. 858 F.Supp. 552 (D.S.C. 1994) [*Faulkner I*], *aff'd. as modified and remanded*, 51 F.3rd 440 (4th Cir. 1995) [*Faulkner II*], *cert. dismissed*, 516 U.S. 910, 116 S.Ct. 331 (1995), and *cert. denied*, 516 U.S. 938, 116 S.Ct. 352 (1995).

2. *Briggs v. Elliott*, 98 F.Supp. 529 (E.D.S.C. 1951), 342 U.S. 350 (1952); *Brown v. Board of Education*, 347 U.S. 483 (1954). *See*, Burke, Lewis W. and Belinda F. Gergel, eds. *Matthew J. Perry: The Man, His Times, and His Legacy.* Columbia, SC: University of South Carolina Press, 2004.

3. *United States v. Virginia*, 766 F.Supp. 1407 (E.D.Va. 1991); 976 F.2d 890 (4th Cir. 1992), *cert. denied*; 44 F.3d 1229 (4th Cir. 1995); 518 U.S. 515 (1996). *See*, Strum, Phillipa. *Women in the Barracks: The VMI Case and Equal Rights.* Lawrence: University Press of Kansas, 2002.

4. *Faulkner v. Jones*, No. 2:93-0488-2 (D.S.C. Aug. 17, 1993).

5. *Faulkner v. Jones*, 10 F.3d 226 (4th Cir. 1993), *stay vacated by*, 14 F.3d 3(4th Cir. 1994), *mandamus denied*, 114 S.Ct. 872 (1994).

6. The Citadel Catalogue, 2009–2010 and 2010–2011; http://www.citadel.edu/main/admissions/veteran-day-students.html (last visited October 25, 2011); BOV minutes for June 14, 2008:

"Motion: 'That the Board of Visitors approves the following changes to the Veterans Program at The Citadel:

Cadets who have begun their pursuit of the cadet degree and have elected to pursue or have been called to active military service will be provided the following options if after their tour on active duty they have been discharged honorably with full rights and privileges of a veteran.

Option 1. If they are eligible, they may return to the Corps of Cadets to continue to pursue the cadet degree.

Option 2. They may enroll as civilian students in classes with the Corps of Cadets to pursue a non-cadet degree with non-cadet diploma and ring (the same diploma and ring available for current Active Duty Students and for Veteran Students while that program was active).

If they meet the following eligibility criteria, they may move to the Veteran Cadet Program to complete their Citadel degree in civilian status:

- must have been sworn into the Corps of Cadets at The Citadel;
- must have been honorably discharged from active duty with the full rights and privileges of a veteran;
- must meet academic and disciplinary criteria for readmission to The Citadel.

Students electing this option:

- may enroll in civilian status in classes with the Corps of Cadets;

- may enroll in evening classes in the Citadel Graduate College;
- are eligible to earn the non-cadet degree/diploma and receive the non-cadet ring currently awarded to Active Duty students and undergraduate students in the Citadel Graduate College (and formerly awarded to veteran students) if they have not reached 1A academic classification prior to moving to the Veteran Cadet Program;
- are eligible to earn the cadet degree/diploma and receive the cadet ring if they have spent at least four semesters in the Corps of Cadets prior to moving to the Veteran Cadet Program or if they are ineligible to return to the Corps of Cadets because of injuries received 'in the line of duty' at the time of their injury in accordance with their appropriate service policies and regulations.

     NOTE: Former cadets who earn the cadet degree through the Veteran Cadet Program must complete all ROTC and RPED requirements through appropriate course submissions;

- may not return to the Corps of Cadets after moving to the Veteran Cadet Program;
- may participate in Cadet Commencement in appropriate academic regalia when academically eligible relative to the non-cadet degree or in cadet uniform when academically eligible relative to the cadet degree and if eligible relative to conditions of marriage and dependent children.'"

"Following discussion, the motion passed unanimously."

7. As stated in the Citadel Catalogs, 2009–2010 and 2010–2011, the BOV in its June 14, 2008, meeting "approved the pursuit of the Cadet Degree, Diploma, and Ring through the Veteran Cadet Program under the following conditions: 1. The former cadet has received while on active duty and in combat an injury that precludes readmission to the Corps of Cadets. 2. The former cadet has served at least four semesters in the Corps of Cadets prior to moving to Veteran Cadet status." However, a publication in August, 2011, appears to have dropped "Option 1" of the June 14, 2008, announcement of what is now The Citadel Cadet Veteran Program; they cannot return to the barracks but can still get the Corps of Cadet ring and diploma.

8. Pick-up truck with Florida tag BEM5D.

9. Buckley, William H. *The Citadel and the South Carolina Corps of Cadets.* The Campus History Series. Charleston: Arcadia Press, 2004, p. 116.

10. http://www.citadel.edu/instresearch/ (last visited October 25, 2011).

11. *Id.*

12. *The State*, October 5, 1992.

13. *Mentavlos v. Anderson*, 249 F.3d 301, 316 (4th Cir. 2001).

14. *See*, Blight, David. *Beyond the Battlefield: Race, Memory and the American Civil War.* Amherst and Boston: University of Massachusetts Press, 2002, pp. 3, 4.

Chapter 1

1. *Voices of American Law*; www.law.duke.edu/voices/usva (last visited October 25, 2011).

2. *The New York Times*, January 9, 2010.

3. http://www.citadel.edu/instresearch/ (last visited October 25, 2011). Other data on the same web page indicate 36 "veteran students" enrolled in the spring of 2011, including one woman.

4. *The Post and Courier*, February 24, 2011.

5. http://www.citadel.edu (last visited October 25, 2011); http://www.che.sc.gov (last visited October 25, 2011); http://www.nces.ed.gov (last visited October 25, 2011).

6. Glenn, David. "The B School Blahs." *The New York Times Education Life*, April 17, 2011, p. 17.

7. http://www.citadel.edu/intresearch/ (last visited October 25, 2011). Compare Class of 1999 and Class of 2009 commencement data in final chapter, "And Beyond," below.

8. Conversation with members of Clemson faculty, Spring, 2011.

9. http://www.usma.edu (last visited October 25, 2011).

10. http://www.citadel.edu (last visited October 25, 2011).

11. *Id.*

12. *Id.*

13. Swager, Christine R. *Heroes of Kettle Creek 1779–1782*. West Conshohocken, Pennsylvania: Infinity Publishing Co., 2008.

Chapter 2

1. *Johnson v. Jones*, 42 F.3d 1385 (4th Cir. 1994), a *per curiam* unpublished, non-binding opinion; citation is stuck in the middle of the Reporter within a table of decisions; the text of the opinion, No. 93-2386, is available in Westlaw or Lexis). There are no published opinions in *Johnson v. Jones*, which was double-captioned by the Fourth Circuit with *Faulkner v. Jones* when it was decided on December 2, 1994.

2. The controlling law in the Fourth Circuit's affirmation of the district court's findings about mootness was *County of Los Angeles v. Davis*, 440 U.S. 625, 633 (1979). The Fourth Circuit found that The Citadel met both prongs of the *Davis* standard:

In cases where defendants voluntarily discontinue challenged activities in order to render the challenge moot, they must satisfactorily demonstrate (1) that there is "no reasonable expectation" that the alleged violation will reoccur; and (2) that interim relief or events have "completely and irrevocably eradicated the effects of the alleged violation."

3. http://class1970.citadelalumni.org/ (last visited October 22, 2011); http://class1970.citadelalumni.org/F-Company-Knob.pdf (last visited October 25, 2011); http://class1970.citadelalumni.org/index.html (last visited October 25, 2011).

Chapter 3

1. *The Brigadier*, May 13, 1994.

2. *The State*, December 9, 1986.

3. *The Post and Courier*, June 12, 2011.

4. Kneen, Terry. *The Long Ago Memories of an Old F Troop Knob*. http://class1970.citadelalumni.org/F-Company-Knob.pdf (last visited October 25, 2011), p. 47.

5. *Id.* at 20, 22.

Chapter 4

1. *The Post and Courier,* December 7, 1994.
2. *Id.,* March 16, 2002.
3. *Id.,* January 1, 1993; January 7, 1993.
4. *Id.,* October 25, 1997.
5. *Id.*
6. *Id.,* October 26, 1996.
7. *Id.,* May 8, 1994.
8. *Id.,* October 25, 1997.
9. *The Brigadier,* March 5, 1993.
10. *The Atlanta Journal-Constitution,* February 17, 1994.

Chapter 5

1. *United States v. Virginia,* 766 F.Supp. 1407 (W.D. Va. 1991), *vacated,* 976 F.2d 890 (4th Cir. 1992), *cert. denied,* 113 S.Ct. 2431 (1993).
2. *United States v. Virginia,* 976 F.2d 890 (4th Cir. 1992) *[VMI I],* cert. denied, 113 S.Ct. 2431 (1993).
3. *United States v. Virginia,* 852 F.Supp. 471 (W.D. Va. 1994), aff 'd., 44 F.3d 1229 (4th Cir. 1995) *[VMI II],* cert. granted, 116 S.Ct. 281 (1995).
4. On December 4, 1995, J. William Haynie, Class of 1983, sent "Save the Male" bumper stickers and buttons to The Citadel Archives and Museum on behalf of his wife Connie who, he said in an accompanying letter, coined the phrase and got a registered trademark on it. The group "Women In Support of The Citadel" marketed them for $2.00 each. Mr. Haynie added that his wife's business, Reveille Company, "continued to market the items and shared the profits with The Citadel's Legal Defense Fund. The 'Save the Males' product line was expanded to include tee shirts and sweat shirts," and through mail-order "were distributed to all fifty states and several foreign countries.... It is our hope that ... the items will serve as a reminder of the college's bold, positive defense of its unique system of educating young men to be citizen-soldiers [*sic*] for the good of South Carolina and the United States of America." The Citadel Archives and Museum, box marked "Coeducation, The Citadel," July 13, 2011.
5. *The State,* June 12, 1992.
6. *The Post and Courier,* November 8, 1996.
7. *Id.,* July 16, 2010.

Chapter 6

1. *The News and Courier,* March 25, 1966, as reported by Jerry Adams, Staff Reporter.
2. *The Beaufort Gazette,* March 19, 1995.
3. *The Post and Courier,* May 2, 1995; *The State,* May 4, 1995.
4. *The Post and Courier,* November 24, 1996.

Chapter 7

1. Wyckoff, Max. *A History of the Third South Carolina Infantry: 1861–65*. Fredericksburg, Virginia: Sergeant Kirkland's Museum and Historical Society, Inc., 1965.

2. *Faulkner v. Jones*, 66 F.3d 661 (4th Cir. 1995).

Chapter 8

1. *The Post and Courier*, November 8, 1996.

2. *The State*, November 5, 9, and 16, 1999.

3. *The Post and Courier*, December 1, 1996.

4. *The Atlanta Journal-Constitution*, March 3, 2000.

Chapter 9

1. USDA statistics as of April 29, 2011; Huffpost AOL News, May 14, 2011.

2. *The Post and Courier*, June 30, 1999.

3. *Id.*, October 14, 1999.

4. *Id.*, October 13, 1998.

5. http://www.tridenttech.edu (last visited October 25, 2011).

6. Glenn, David. "The B School Blahs." *The New York Times Education Life*, April 17, 2011, p. 17.

7. *The Post and Courier*, January 9, 2005.

8. Woodward, Douglas P. *The New York Times*, July 1, 2011.

9. *The Post and Courier*, February 24, 2011.

Index

Note: *p* denotes photo.

2 + 2 program, 53, 318–19, 324
52 Percent, 236
60 Minutes, 151–52, 300–301

Aaron, Cooper v., 7
Ackerman, Bill, 24
Ackerman, Connie, 28
ACLU Women's Rights Project, 69
African Americans at The Citadel. *See also* Integration; Racism
    Berra Lee Byrd, 145–47
    Charles Foster, 7, 310–11
    Larry Ferguson, 310–11
    Norman Paul Doucet, 175
    Von Mickel, 144–45, 146*p*
Air Force Academy
    hair cut in, 188
    number of women in, 20
Alverson, Telieff, 55
American Association of University Professors (AAUP), 76
American Civil Liberties Union (ACLU), 49, 278, 312
    debate on *Faulkner*, 138
    women veterans' case and, 56–57
Anderson, Mentavlos v., 6
Anderson, Wallace, 33
Applegate, Sam, 226, 230, 254
Art of Good Taste, The, 292

assimilation plans. *See also Faulkner v. Jones*, assimilation (remedial) plans
    for 1996-97 class, 289, 291–94
    Citadel resistance to making, 289–91
    motion to file fewer, 314
Association of Citadel Men, 303
Astin, Alexander (Sandy), 87, 88, 108, 176
Atchinson, T. & S.F. Ry. Co., McCabe v., 181
athletes at The Citadel, 251, 252
attorney fees, fight for, 302, 304–9

Bailey, George, 42
Bailey, Jimmy, 42, 119
Baker, Kristin, 30
Band Company, 257–58
Banzhaf, John, 22, 28
Barber, Robert, 42
Barkley (Colonel), 97, 165
Barnett, Ross, 14
Barnwell Whaley Patterson & Helms, 71–72, 303
Bates, Daisy, 38
Bates, Steve, 41, 56, 57, 82, 201
Battle, James, 312
Bealle, Fanny, 46

Bealle, William, 46

Beaver, Vanessa, 176

Beber, Sandy, 27, 162, 189, 239, 250, 252

   on Citadel's first assimilation plan, 162

   on Concurrent Resolution, 120

   as cross-over counsel, 164–65

Bell, Griffin, 63, 66, 67–68, 123

Bell, Grove City College v., 231–32

Bender, Paul, 206

Berger, Allen, 164

Bertin, Joan, 57

Bethea, Paula Harper, 175

Betta (Colonel), 199

Bingham (Colonel), 259

Bishop, Jane, 87

Black, Hugo, 69

Black, John, 113, 128*p*, 130*p*, 131*p*, 132*p*

Black, Mary Holland, 21

Black, Ray, 21

Black, William, 128*p*, 129*p*, 130*p*, 131*p*, 132*p*

Blacksheer, Jim, 28, 55

Blight, David, 12

Block, Herbert, 281–82

Blumstein, Ted, 78

Board of Education, Brown v., 4

Board of Visitors. *See* Citadel Board of Visitors

Boddie, John Bennett, 55

Boeing Company, 315–16, 322–23

Boeing Effect, 10–11, 322

Boland, Bill, 66, 176

"Boo, The." *See* Courvoisie, T. N. ("The Boo")

Boren, Craig v., 30, 180

Bowen, Bill, 89

Boykin, Catherine George, 29, 37–38

Bradwell v. State, 183, 224

Bray, Linda L., 33

Bressler, Marvin, 108

Brigadier, The

   on Faulkner, 106, 147–49, 160, 191

   on integration of The Citadel, 153

   on teacher sympathetic to Faulkner, 208–9

   on women and homosexuals, 106

Briggs, Eliza, 63

Briggs v. Elliott, 4, 63, 64

Brinson, Claudia, 124, 159

British Broadcasting Corporation (BBC), 144

Broaddus, Bill, 66, 107, 175, 198

Brookes, Israel, 134, 196, 259

Brown, Darlene, 109

Brown, Henry, 42

Brown, Katherine Lee, 165–66, 176

Brown, Millicent E., 29

Brown, Minnijean, 141

Brown, Oliver, 109

Brown, Sarah Mae Fleming, 310

Brown, Susan, 181

Brown v. Board of Education, 4, 109, 202, 217, 286

Brown, Walter D. III, 218

Bryant, Bear, 142

bumper stickers, 185–87

Bunting, Josiah "Si," 88, 105, 107, 108, 168, 291

Buoniconti, Marc, 114

Burdock, David, 147

Burke High School, 29

Burnette, Malissa, 283, 304

Burritt, Chris, 312

Bush, George H. W., 216

Butler, Marilyn, 107

Byford, Bruce and Betsy, 262

Byrd, Berra Lee, 145–47
Byrnes, James F., 210

cadets. *See* Citadel cadets
Califano v. Goldfarb, 180
Cameron, Averil (college warden), 107, 108
Campbell, Carroll, 63, 94
Campbell, Patricia B., 176
Canada, Missouri ex rel. Gaines v., 181
Canty, Ralph W., 235, 236–37
Carpenter, C. C. J., 37
Carstarphen (Shearman & Sterling attorney), 175–76
Carter, Fred, 290
Carter, Jimmy, 63, 216
cases against The Citadel. *See also* Attorney fees, fight for; *Faulkner*; *Faulkner/Mellette*; *Johnson, Lacy, and Chapman v. Jones*
    Citadel's lack of acknowledgment of, 7–8
    on closing of Veterans Day Program, 78
    documents filed and requested in, 72, 140, 254
    search for lawyers to represent potential plaintiffs in, 27–28
Causey, William, 219
Cauthen, George, 305
Chandler, Tom, 270
Chapman, Angela, 50, 59–61, 77. *See also Johnson, Lacy, and Chapman v. Jones*
Charleston, 11
Chisolm, Pat, 314
Churchill, Winston, 269
Citadel Board of Visitors
    admission of women to Corps (1996), 285–86
    approval of funds for SCIL program at Converse, 227
    closing of Veterans Day Program, 72–73, 76
    DOJ depositions, 162–64
    on federal orders to integrate The Citadel, 218
    reopening of Veterans Day Program, 5–6, 206
Citadel cadets. *See also* Corps of Cadets
    average grades of, 95
    celebration of Faulkner's last day by, 279, 279p
    first-year (knobs)
        1995 hazing out of, 282
        items needed by, 263
    indoctrination of, 115–16
    praise for, 288–89
    pregnant, 180, 294
Citadel Cadet Veteran Program, 5, 6–7
Citadel Development Foundation, The (CDF), 220, 222, 226, 227–28
Citadel Evening College (EC), 50, 51
Citadel Faculty Council resolution on closing of Veterans Day Program, 76–77
Citadel Family Association (CFA), 262–63
Citadel Graduate College (CGC). *See* Citadel Evening College (EC)
Citadel Non-Cadet Veteran Day Program, 5–6
Citadel students, 8–10
    1992 enrollment of, 50–51
    1994 freshmen, 269
    1997 enrollment of female, 290
    active duty, 9–10, 20

Citadel students, *continued*
  lack of documentation on female, 20–21
  majors of, 19, 20, 319–21
  military status of, 8–10
  number of female, 19, 20
  out-state *vs.* in-state, 20
  veterans as, 9–10
Citadel, The. *See also* African Americans in The Citadel; Cases against The Citadel; Citadel Cadets; Citadel students
  admission of four women to, 294–99
  alleged sexual abuse at, 13
  applications and inquiries to, 194–95, 225–26 (*See also* Plaintiffs, potential)
  church sermon about, 287–88, 289
  Civil War involvement of, 245–47
  commission rate at, 44–45
  community support for, 287–89
  expenditures for defense of, 221–22, 302–4
  faculty of, 10, 33–34, 58–59
  lack of educational opportunities for ordinary students at, 10–11
  limited military nature of, 8–10, 33, 44–45
  physical training test at, 248–49
  proposal for educating ordinary citizens at, 315–26
  publicity for, 142–44, 214
  and recruitment plan for women, 218–19
  semi-private nature of, 318
  sexual harassment/discrimination policy of, 200–202, 241, 293–94
  suggestion for recognition of Faulkner at, 311–12
  unequal treatment of non-cadet veterans at, 6
Citadel Trust, Inc., The, 221, 222
Citadel Veterans Day Program, 50, 321
  closing of, 18, 72–78
  reopening of, 18, 78–79, 206
  threat of closure of, in *Johnson*, 67–68
Civil Rights Act Title IV, 30
Civil Rights Restoration Act of 1987, 232
Civil War and The Citadel, 245–47
Clark, Mark, 143, 153, 319
class certification, 58
Clemson University, 88, 89–90, 91
  admission of women into, 181–82, 325
  Harvey Gantt at, 4, 7, 197
  welcome of women to, 197, 197*p*
Clery Act, 278
Clineburg, Bill, 66, 97, 165
Clute, Sylvia, 35, 53
Clyburn, James E., 109
Cobb, Ty, 21
Coe, Suzanne, 110, 113, 114, 135*p*, 136, 157
  Faulkner's last day at The Citadel, 271, 272, 274, 276
  memo opposing Citadel's motion to dismiss lawsuit, 278
Colatriano, Vincent J., 126
College of Charleston, The, 89, 324
Collison, Madeline, 56, 72
Columbia University, 18, 206, 207–8
Colvin, Claudette, 310

Commission on Higher Education. *See* South Carolina Commission on Higher Education

Commission on Women. *See* South Carolina Commission on Women (SSCW)

Compton, Spencer, 31, 127, 130*p*, 131*p*, 160

Concurrent Resolution on single-sex education, 118–21, 177, 178, 182

Condon, Charles, 63, 228, 308
  1995 assimilation plan, 240–41
  memo in support of state funding of VWIL, 228–29

Condon, Irv, 184

Conrad, Clifton Forbes, 175, 176

Conroy, Pat, 82, 85, 223, 281, 295

Converse College. *See also* South Carolina Institute for Leadership (SCIL)
  author's talk to faculty of, 230–34
  fear of forced admission of men at, 66
  Judge Houck's visit to, 242–43

Cooke, Dawes, 54, 72, 113–14, 123, 138, 164, 165, 168, 181, 184, 186, 191, 200, 259, 271
  on anti-Faulkner bumper stickers, 190
  on Citadel's assimilation plan at 1995 hearing, 238–39
  on *Johnson*, 66, 68
  in *Johnson* appeal, 205
  on non-military nature of The Citadel, 10
  on parking permit for Shannon Faulkner, 134
  on Watts' testimony on adversative education, 293

Cooper, Charles J., 126, 255, 256

Cooper v. Aaron, 7

Cork, Holly, 119, 161, 220, 235, 290
  Citadel's defense expenses, 220, 221, 222–23
  Concurrent Resolution, 118, 120
  letter to Bud Watts, 220

Cormeny, George III, 147

Courvoisie, T. N. ("The Boo"), vi, 38–39

Craig v. Boren, 30, 180

Crocker, Virginia, 39

Croft, Edward Jr., 227

Culler, Kristen, 30

Cupp, Ruth Williams, 175

Cureton, Roger, 256

Cutright, Mark, 96

Dandridge, Lori, 164

Darling, Thomas G., 86, 96

Darr, Ken, 231

Davidson College, 88

Davis, Los Angeles v., 203, 205

Davis, Paul, 49

Davis, Susan, 30

Davis, Washington v., 74

de Bury, Richard, 140

defense contractors, 323

demand issue. *See under* Legal issues

Department of Justice (DOJ), 162
  inaction on Patricia Johnson's case, 53–54
  Letter of Inquiry to The Citadel, 27
  role in *VMI* case, 23–24

Derfner, Armand, 24, 27, 28, 56, 113, 189

Dick, Harvey, 267

Dillard, Mary Rammage, 46

Donehue, Doug, 141
Don Quixote, vii
Doucet, Norman Paul, 175
Douglas, John, 181
Douglas, Nat, 26, 27, 31–32, 37, 53, 113, 136
Douglass, Frederick, 235
Dowd, Roddey Sr., 227
Dunne, John, 35

Echo Company, 213–14
ECP. *See* U.S. Navy Enlisted Commissioning Program (ECP)
Education Amendments of 1972, 66
Education Amendments Title IX, 66, 231–32
Edwards, James B., 91, 92, 142, 175
Edwards, Robert C., 91–92, 93, 119, 197
Elliott, Briggs v., 4, 63, 64
engineering program at The Citadel, 51–52
engineers, "home-bound," 19–20
Episcopal Young Churchmen, 21
Epting, Drew, 305
equal protection clause, 30, 74
Ervin (Fourth Circuit judge), 126, 171
Eslinger v. Thomas, 225
Evening College. *See* Citadel Evening College (EC)
Eyrbyggja Saga, 13
Ezell, Patricia, 44, 53, 98

Fabri, Margaret, 166
Fairey, Gaston, 304, 306
Faludi, Susan, 105–6, 264
Family Education Rights and Privacy Act (FERPA), 295
Farris, Jack B., 137–38

Faubus, Orval, 14
Faulkner, Ed, 112*p*, 136, 169, 251, 257, 259, 264–65, 268, 270
and Shannon's last day at The Citadel, 271, 272, 276–77
Faulkner/Mellette, 283–4, 289, 301–2
dismissal, 314
motion to intervene in *Faulkner*, 283, 289
Faulkner, Sandy, 112*p*, 136, 169, 251, 264–65
Faulkner, Shannon, 187–90, 256*p*, 261*p*
ABC TV documentary, 142, 200
appearance on Oprah Winfrey's show, 284
attempt to get into ROTC, 199–200
attorney fee fight, 302
Band Company, 257–58
birthdate, 111
Black/Lucka family, 128*p*, 129*p*, 130*p*, 131*p*
Citadel application form, 114–15
Citadel's failure to forward mail, 160
desire to be accepted in Corps
60 Minutes proposal to secretly tape harassment, 151–52
complaint through proper channels, 153
court's comment on, 157–58
decline of BBC interview, 144
enrollment at University of South Carolina, 125
entry into case, 110–11
first day as cadet, 262*p*
first day of classes, 126, 141
harassment, 112, 137

The Brigadier, 106, 147–49, 160, 191
bumper stickers and t-shirts, 185–87
deposition, 154–55, 202
"Die Shannon" sign, 183–85
Faulkner's complaint through proper channels, 153
forced feeding, 268–69, 270
hate mail, 159–60, 187, 238, 257, 258–59, 263, 301
hearings, 152–58
name-calling by children, 160–61
radio stations, 141–42
verbal hazing, 158–59
hazing out of The Citadel (*See also* Last day at The Citadel (below))
celebrations of, 279, 279p, 280–81
myths about, 281
hospitalization, 269–70
isolation as cadet, 263–65, 265p
knob hair cut, 112p, 158p
lack of acknowledgment of contribution for women's civil rights, 7–8, 296–97, 311–12
last day at The Citadel, 271–79
living arrangements while in day program, 126–27
physical condition (*See Faulkner v. Jones*, challenge over Faulkner's physical condition)
refusal to secretly tape harassment, 151–52
registration day (day program), 134–37, 135p, 136p, 140–41, 144–45, 146p

security precautions, 133–34, 259–62, 262p
silent treatment by church, 161–62
support
bumper stickers, 187
churches, 161
Citadel faculty member, 208–9
offer to shave head, 188–89
rally, 236–37
steel workers, 166
teaching career, 310
testimony on issue of demand, 176–77
training for physical test, 257
Virginia Gourdin's comments, 211
Faulkner v. Jones, 215. *See also* Attorney fees, fight for; *Faulkner/Mellette*
aftermath, 5–6
assimilation (remedial) plans (*See also* Assimilation plans)
1994 plan, 179–80
1995 plan and hearings, 238–42
Citadel's lateness in filing plans, 253
first assimilation plan, 162
Lewis Spearman's deposition, 138–39
SCIL plan and depositions, 240, 253–54
challenge over Faulkner's physical condition, 192–93, 247–52, 255, 260
Concurrent Resolution, 118–21
conference on hostile environment, 190–92
court order for security for Faulkner, 195–97
cross-over counsel, 164–65

Faulkner v. Jones, continued
  defense motion for clarification of
    security for Faulkner, 260–62
  defense motion to dismiss lawsuit
    following Faulkner's hazing out,
    278
  defense's post-trial motions,
    177–79
  "demand" issue, 176
  depositions, 253
  district court order to admit
    Faulkner into Corps (*Faulkner I*),
    180–83
    Fourth Circuit's first stay of, 183
    Fourth Circuit's second stay of,
      198
    hearing on implementation of,
      180
  district court order to admit
    Faulkner into Corps (July 24,
    1995), 254–55
  district court order to admit
    Faulkner into Day Program,
    121–23
    appeal of Fourth Circuit's stay
      of Judge Houck's order, 125
    defense's petition to Supreme
      Court, 126
    defense's request for rehearing
      en banc, 126
    Fourth Circuit's stay of Judge
      Houck's order, 123
  Fourth Circuit affirmation of
    Faulkner I and *II* (1998), 286
  Fourth Circuit affirmation of
    Faulkner I (*Faulkner II*), 215,
    216–18
  hearing and deposition on harass-
    ment, 152–58

  hearing on allowable student ac-
    tivities, 150–51
  hearing on conditions of Faulkner's
    admission to Corps, 190
  initial complaint, 113
  "manufactured" evidence of de-
    mand, 166–68
  overview, 4–5
  parallel program issue brought up
    in *Johnson*, 204–5
  petition for *certiorari*, 285
  publicity, 214–15
  remedy phase, 172–77
  significance, 4
  strategy, 111
  Supreme Court decision not to
    grant stay (1995), 255–56
  U.S. motion to intervene as plain-
    tiff, 113
  VMI, 198
Federal Bureau of Investigation (FBI),
  106
*Feeney, Personnel Administrator of
  Massachusetts v.*, 74, 180, 203
Feiger, Collison, and Kramer, 72
Felder, James L., 236
Ferer, Barbara, 29, 30
Ferguson, Larry, 311
Figg, Eugene Jr., 227
Fighting Tiger Battalion, 90
Fine, Michelle, 176
Fix, Sybil, 296
Fleming, John, 64
Fonda, Ann, 184
Ford, Gerald, 216
Ford, Robert, 161
Forrest, Nathan Bedford, 54, 142
Foster, Charles D., 7, 310–11
Foster, John Franklin Marion, 246,
  247

Fourth Class System, 266, 268, 293
Fowler, Sandra, 115
Fox-Genovese, Elizabeth, 88, 98, 175, 207, 280
Frazier, Herbert, 146
Frederick, Caroline, 40
Fulmer, Ron, 41, 42, 86–87

Gallager, Robert C., 175
Gantt, Harvey, 4, 7, 197
Garrity, W. Arthur, 177
Gaskin, Ron, 134
General Dynamics, 323
George, Catherine. *See* Boykin, Catherine George
Germain, Mark, 189
Gibbs, Coming Ball, 305
Gibler, John, 268
Ginsburg, Ruth Bader, 55, 170, 171, 218, 285
Glover, Maggie, 235
Glover, William, 24, 25
Goldfarb, Califano v., 180
Gonzales, Stephen, 42
Goodpaster (General), 72, 293
Gordon, Dan, 314
Gordon, Jane, 71, 98, 99
Gourdin, Virginia, 40, 209–11, 211*p*
Gray, Betsy, 305
Green, December, 106
Greenberg (chief of police), 183–85
Greenberg, Jack, 109
Greenblatt, Jonathan, 70
Grimsley, Alex, 109–10, 188, 268
Grinalds, John, 318
Gross, R. H., 193
Grove City College v. Bell, 231–32
Gunnells, Charlene, 144

Halford, Celia, 98

Hall, K. K., 73, 126, 171, 204, 216, 255
    concurrence in appeal of Fourth Circuit's stay in *Faulkner*, 125
    concurrence in *Faulkner II*, 217–18
    dissent in Fourth Circuit's stay of *Faulkner I* order, 183
    dissent in Fourth Circuit's stay of Judge Houck's injunction in *Faulkner*, 123
Hall, Ruby Bridges, 196
Hallman, Harry, 42, 234
Hamilton, Clyde, 73, 171, 183, 204, 216, 217
    concurring opinion in *Johnson v. Jones*, 75–76
    defense's request for *en banc* hearing in *Faulkner*, 126
    dissent in appeal of Fourth Circuit's stay in *Faulkner*, 125
    dissent in orders to admit Faulkner to Corps, 255
    impact of closing of Veterans Day Program on plaintiffs in *Johnson*, 79–80
    stay of Judge Houck's preliminary injunction in *Faulkner*, 123
Hamilton, Mary, 69
Hampton, Wade, 246
Hansen, Chris, 202
Hardney, Geneive, 311
Haring, Marilyn J., 176
Harris, Frederick III, 227
Hart, Nancy Ann, 46
Haskins, Terry, 41
hate mail
    to author, 133, 245
    to Faulkner, 159–60, 187, 238, 257, 258–59, 263, 301

hazing, 116–18, 265–68. *See also*
  Faulkner, Shannon, harassment
Hazlett, Karen, 164
Henderson, Marilyn, 30
Herrnstein, Becky Hoover, 283
Higdon, Cantey, 227
Hipp, Francis, 227
History of Education in Antiquity, 105
*History of the South Carolina Military
  Academy*, 246
Hodges, James, 119, 304, 307
Hogan, Joe, 53. *See also Mississippi
  University for Women v. Hogan*
Hollings, Fritz, 14, 37, 63, 86, 312
Holmes, Allan, 189
Holt, Don, 42
homosexuality among Citadel cadets,
  105–6
Hood, Bobby, 113–14, 176, 181, 249
  on Concurrent Resolution, 120–21
  on lack of demand for all-female
    military institution, 173
Hood Law Firm, 72
Horn, Peggy, 21, 38
Horner, Randy, 78
Houck, C. Weston, vi, 63–65, 64p,
  109, 259, 260, 291
  court's controlling orders, 286
  dismisses case, 289
  preliminary injunction in *Faulkner*,
    121–22
  on resistance by Corps, 267
  rules on *Faulkner I*, 180–82
  U.S. Marshals on Citadel campus,
    195–96
  on *VMI I*, 170
Houck, William S. Jr., 119
Howe, Arthur G., vi, 64, 177
Hudson, Toshika, 311
Hughes, Jackie, 188

Hypolite, Renee, 311

integration. *See also* African Americans in The Citadel; Racism
  in The Citadel, 218
  in South Carolina, 14

Jacobs, Harold, 308
Jefferson, Thomas, 315
Jenkins, Clauston, 88
Jennings, Peter, 200
Johnson, David Cromwell, 28
Johnson, Frank M. Jr., 108–9, 177
Johnson, George D., 226, 227, 228,
  231
Johnson, Harriet McBryde, 35
Johnson, Julius F., 42, 45, 164
Johnson, Lacy, and Chapman v. Jones
  ACLU involvement, 56–57
  aftermath, 5–6
  appeal to DOJ for help, 53–54
  attorneys, 62–63, 70–72
  author's argument on public pol-
    icy, 68
  author's search for witnesses for
    public policy hearing, 86–91,
    93–94
  closing of Veterans Day Program,
    73–77, 79–80
  comity, 108–10
  complaint, 49–50, 56, 57–58
  defense arguments, 66–68
  defense lawyers honored by Citadel
    with doctoral degrees, 123–24
  defense motion to moot case and
    plaintiff's appeal, 73–77
  defense witnesses, 98–101, 105,
    107, 108
  defense witnesses for public pol-
    icy hearing, 88

first hearing (motion for preliminary injunction), 61–69
plaintiff's appeal to Fourth Circuit, 202–6
plaintiffs' depositions on public policy, 92–93
press conference after filing of complaint, 58–59, 59p
searches for lawyers, 55–56, 69–70
value of single-sex education, 65–66
Vergnolle's testimony on Citadel experience, 82–85
VMI lawyers' interest in case, 63
Johnson, Patricia, 49, 50, 51–52, 52p, 59p, 134. *See also Johnson, Lacy, and Chapman v. Jones*
closing of Veterans Day Program and, 77
first veteran woman plaintiff, 49
Johnson, Quillen Orr, 308
Jones, Faulkner v. See Faulkner v. Jones
Jones, Jimmy, 22, 58, 69, 137, 138, 226, 228, 241, 286, 301
Jones, United States v. See United States v. Jones
Jones v. Faulkner, 126
Jordan, Mary, 159
Jordan, Pamela, 166, 176

Kamensy, Robert J., 32
Karnow, Stanley, 78
Kaup (Admiral), 86
Kaynard, Gerald, 28
Keel, Don, 230–31
Keith, Judith, 54, 83
Kennedy, Bill, 177
Kern, Candy, 41, 119
Keyserling, Harriet, 39, 40
Kilpatrick, James J., 49

Kim, Ty, 151
Kimmel, Michael Scott, 175
Kinard, Bobby, 86
King, Ed, 28
King, Martin Luther Jr., 21
King & Spaulding, 63, 71, 221, 303
Kinloch, Jerome, 78, 118
Kirsh, Herbert, 119
Kiser, Jackson, 49, 54, 169, 170, 174, 255
Kneen, Terry, 85
knobs. *See* Cadets, first-year (knobs)
Kotakis, Paul, 43, 95

Lacey, Elizabeth, 49, 52p, 53, 59p, 77. *See also Johnson, Lacy, and Chapman v. Jones*
Lafayette, 77, 116
Lake, Michael, 106
Land (Senator), 235
Lane Report, 188
Latimer, Edwin, 227
Lawrence (Admiral), 188
lawsuits. *See* Cases against The Citadel
Lazaro, Karen, 106
Leedom, Terry, 193, 242, 247–48, 300–301, 303
legal issues
basic issues, 30–31
comity, 108–10
demand by women to enroll in The Citadel, 47, 93, 166–68, 173, 176, 218–19
Faulkner's physical condition, 247–52
informed consent, 284
justification in *Faulkner*, 171
liability in *VMI* and *Faulkner*, 172
military nature of The Citadel, 44–45

legal issues, *continued*
 remedy in *Faulkner*, 171–72
legal strategies
 Zentgraf strategy, 31–35
Legare, Ben, 41, 280
legislation. *See* South Carolina Leg-
 islature
Lever, Jo Ann, 234
Lions Head, 107
Little Rock Nine, 141
Lloyd, Virginia Crocker, 178
Lockheed, 323
Lords of Discipline, The, 85
Los Angeles v. Davis, 203, 205
Losey, Clyde, 205
Lovetinska, Petra, 190, 286–87, 290,
 295
Lowcountry Coalition of Women, 29
Lowcountry Graduate Center (The
 Citadel), 322
Lucka, Melinda, 17–18, 22, 31, 105,
 127, 131*p*, 160, 177, 261*p*, 277,
 305, 309–10
Lucy, Autherine, 21, 133
Luttig (Fourth Circuit judge), 126
Lutz, Melody, 46–47, 97–98, 166,
 311
Lyons (Colonel), 221

MacArthur Award, 94, 164
Mace, Anne J., 296, 297
Mace, Emory, 314
Mace, Nancy, 8, 192, 264, 286, 287,
 290, 296–99
Mack, David J. Jr., 24–25
MacMillan, Richard, 227
Maddox, Lester, 14
Madison, James, vii, 3
Mahan, Alice, 88, 98, 303
Mahan, Tom, 88

Mandelbaum, Sara, 83, 135*p*, 136,
 175, 202, 204–5
Manegold, Catherine, 106–7
Manly, Sarah G., 39–40, 46, 119
 bill to admit women in The
 Citadel, 39–42, 178–79
Mannes, Elena, 200
Marchant, T. Easton, 87, 168, 175
Marine Enlisted Commissioning Ed-
 ucation Program (MECEP), 9–10,
 60
Marion, Francis, 109
Marks, Barry, 188
Marrou, Henri, 105
Marshall, Thurgood, 21, 64, 109
Marshals. *See* U.S. Marshals
Martin, Daniel Sr., 42
Mary Baldwin College (MBC) paral-
 lel program. *See* Virginia Women's
 Institute of Leadership (VWIL)
Massachusetts Maritime Academy, 30
Mathis, Bland, 87
Mauer, Michael, 138, 175, 214, 291
McCabe v. Atchinson, T. & S.F. Ry. Co.,
 181
McCann, Frank, 177, 305
McClain, Ray, 81, 168
McCloud, Jamey, 311
McConnell, Glenn, 119, 234, 290
McCuller, Carson, 105
McDaniel, Thomas R., 175, 206, 207,
 231
McDowell, Judy, 181
McGill, Yancey, 234, 290
McGuire Woods Battle & Booth, 62,
 63, 71, 165, 221, 303
McKnight, Cuyler, 97
McNair, Robert, 210
McNair, Williams v., 24
Meade, George Gordon, 54, 246

MECEP. *See* Marine Enlisted Commissioning Education Program (MECEP)

media. *See also Brigadier, The*; Publicity

60 Minutes show on hazing of Mentavlos and Messer, 300–301

ABC TV documentary on Faulkner, 142, 200

articles critical of hostile behavior at The Citadel, 105, 106

coverage of author, 80

Faulkner's appearance on Oprah Winfrey's show, 284

Faulkner's rejection of *60 Minutes* interview, 151–52

Faulkner's rejection of BBC interview, 144

radio stations' harrassment of Faulker and author, 141–42

reaction to hazing out of Faulkner, 280–82

Medical University of South Carolina (MUSC), 324

assistance with public relations for The Citadel, 142–43

proposal to train nurse cadets at The Citadel, 42–46

Meenaghan, George, 34, 89

Meggett, Linda, 80

Mellette. See Faulkner/Mellette

Mellette, Nancy, 7, 283, 286, 287, 302

Mentavlos, Jeanie, 190, 287, 290, 291, 295, 299–301

Mentavlos, Michael, 300, 301

Mentavlos v. Anderson, 6

Meredith, James, 133

Messer, Kim, 190, 287, 290, 291, 295, 299–301

Metts, Spike, 62, 78

Meyers, Gregg, 32, 310

Michael (Fourth Circuit judge), 171

Mickel, Von, 144–45, 146*p*, 148–49

Mikolajcik (Colonel), 86

Military College of South Carolina. *See* Citadel, The

military colleges, 89–90, 324–25

Mill, Rick, 114, 123–24

Miller, Emilie, 39

Mississippi University for Women v. Hogan, 7, 30–31, 44, 93, 180, 181, 224, 286

Missouri ex rel. Gaines v. Canada, 181

Mitchell, Natosha, 311

Mitchell, Peter T., 175, 207–8

Mitman, Ed, 196, 259

Mood, Francis "Frank," 119, 120, 121, 175

Mood, George Jr., 265–68

Mood Report, 120, 188, 265–68

Moon, Dan, 141

Morris Brown AME Church, 161

Morrison & Forrester, 35

Motley, Constance Baker, 21

Motley, Tony, 295

Motz, Diana Gribbon, 170, 171, 217

Moultrie (General), 285–86

Muhlenbeck, Jack, 94

Murnaghan (Fourth Circuit judge), 171

Murphy, Tom, 63

Murray, George Mosley, 37–38

MUSC. *See* Medical University of South Carolina (MUSC)

Musgrove, Mary Bobo, 46

NAACP. *See* National Association for the Advancement of Colored People (NAACP)

Nance, James D., 247

National Association for the Advancement of Colored People (NAACP), 25, 236
Naval Academy
hair cut in, 188
number of women in, 20
student majors in, 20
Nelkin, Carol, 32
Nesmith brothers, 109
Nesmith, Kevin, 109–10, 117
Nettles, Dana, 257
News and Courier, The
on racial integration of The Citadel, 153
Nielsen, Barbara, 72–73
Niemeyer, Paul V., 73, 123, 125, 126, 171, 183, 204–5, 216, 217, 255
Niketas, Alexia, 236
Norman, Curtis, 7, 256
North Georgia College (NGC) Corps of Cadets, 96–97
Northrop Grumman, 323
Norton, David, 177
Norwich College, 95
nurse cadets, proposal to train at The Citadel, 42–46

O'Connor, Sandra Day, 30, 224
O'Dell, Billy, 234, 290
Olivas, Michael, 55
Omicron Delta Kappa, 165
Orangeburg Massacre, 14
Owens, Bill, 33
Oxner, Dewey, 308

Palmer v. Thompson, 74–75, 114–15, 203
Palmetto Brigade, 9
Palms, John M., 89, 137

parallel programs, 5, 169, 170–71, 204–5. *See also Faulkner v. Jones*, remedy phase; South Carolina Institute for Leadership (SCIL); Virginia Women's Institute of Leadership (VWIL)
Parker, Kathleen, vii
Parks, Rosa, 109
Paschall, Douglas, 107
Pascoe, Pat, 33
Passailaigue, Ernie, 234, 290
Patterson, Kay, 161, 176, 235
Patterson, Robert, 54–55, 62, 66, 72, 123, 249
Pembroke College Oxford, 68
Penn State, 13
Perry, Matthew J., 4, 310
Personnel Administrator of Massachusetts v. Feeney, 74, 180, 203
Peterson, Lesjanusar, 311
Phi Beta Kappa, 165
Phillips, J. Dickson, 170, 171, 216, 217
Phillips, Olin R., 40
Philobilon, 140
Pinkerton, Hedy, 311
Pinzler, Isabelle, 62, 110, 113, 306
on additional counsel for women veterans' case, 69–70
at first hearing of women veterans' case, 65
Johnson and, 49, 56, 57
plaintiffs, potential
fear of reprisals against, 81–82
Karen and Tonya as, 25–27, 28–29
Poole, Clifton (vice president of The Citadel), 134, 136, 136p, 241, 262
on assimilation plan for 1996-97, 289

and Faulkner's last day at The Citadel, 272, 274–77, 278
Porter-Gaud School, 160–61
Powell, Alma, 21
Powell, Colin, 29–30, 97
Prioleau, Buddy, 218
Provence, Tiffany, 35, 36–37
publicity. *See also* Media
  for The Citadel, 142–44, 214
  for *Faulkner* case, 214–15
public opinion on women in The Citadel, 174

racism. *See also* African Americans in The Citadel; Integration
  and "Die Nigr" sign, 213–14
  sex discrimination equated with, 68, 75
Rae, Bob, 282
Rainsford, Bettis, 227
Rama, John, 42
Ravenel, Arthur Jr., 86, 220
Ravenel, Eunice, 314
Rawson, Jessica, 107, 108
Reagan, Ronald, 49, 216
Reeder, Adam, 149
Reed v. Reed, 180
Reflections in a Golden Eye, 105
Regan, Bill, 305
Regan, Scott, 142–43, 200
Rehnquist, William, 123, 125, 126, 256, 285
Reid, John, 319
Reilly, Rick, 106
Reno, Janet, 144
Reserve Officers' Training Corps (ROTC)
  and Citadel programs for ROTC students, 9
  in colleges and universities, 90

Faulkner's attempt to enter, 199–200
and proposal to train nurse cadets at The Citadel, 42–46
and quality of students in relation to participation in all-male Corps of Cadets, 94–96
at Virginia Tech, 325
ReVille, Louis "Skip," 13
Rice, Condoleezza, 21
Rice, Tandy, 297
Richardson, Donald V., 308–9
Richardson, Richard C., 88, 175
Richter (Senator), 290
Rickson, Terry, 49, 141, 189
Rieger, Richard, 226
Riesman, David, 88
Riley, Dick, 218
Riley, Joe, 86
Ripley, John, 88
Rittenberg, Charles, 127
Rivers, Nelson, 236
Robertson, Tony, 81
Robinson, Bill, 213
Robinson, Edmund, 24, 305
Roffey, Nina, 183
Rogers, Tim, 119
Rosenlieb, Ed, 106, 185
Rose (Senator), 290
Ross, Mary Jane, 297
ROTC. *See* Reserve Officers' Training Corps (ROTC)
Rugby School (England), 107
Rush, Wayne, 113
Russell, Donald, 24, 171
Russell, Robert, 227

Salley, Eulalie Chaffee, 210
Sandler, Bernice, 202
Sansom, William, 227

Sawyer, Diana, 200

Scalia, Antonin, 126, 216, 255, 256, 285

"Scarlet Pimpernel." *See Brigadier, The*

Schoettler, Gail, 33

scholarships, all-male, 286

Schroeder, Patricia, 33

Schwarzkopf, Norman, 86

Schweiger, Susan, 71

Science Applications International Corporation, 323

SCIL. *See* South Carolina Institute for Leadership (SCIL)

SCUM. *See* South Carolina Unorganized Militia (SCUM)

SCWLA. *See* South Carolina Women Lawyers Association (SCWLA)

Seignious (General), 72

Self, James, 227

settlement award, 304

Sewanee, The University of the South, 88

sexism, 292

sexual harassment
Citadel handbook, 200–201, 241
lawsuits against The Citadel, 301
policy at The Citadel, 200–202, 241, 293–94

Shaw Pittman Potts & Trowbridge, 303

Shearman & Sterling, 70–71, 202, 306, 312

Sheheen, Fred, 234

Sheheen, Robert, 42, 119, 121, 177

Shepherd (Major), 94

Sherman, William T., 70, 246

Shields, Greg, 205

Shores, Arthur, 21

Short (Senator), 290

Shott, Hugh II, 96–97

Siegfried, Tom, 86

Silver, Jessica, 54, 83

Simmons (Lieutenant), 199, 226

Sinisi, Kyle, 246–47

SmartState Program, 316

Smith, Bruce, 165–66

Smith, Ellison, 309

Smith, Mary Louise, 310

Smith, Mic, 279

Snead, Allison, 164

South Carolina
"horse race" in, 253
ownership of The Citadel by, 326
socioeconomic rankings of, 316–17, 322
as source of cheap labor, 315
women's socioeconomic status in, 40

South Carolina Commission on Higher Education, 20, 50, 234

South Carolina Commission on Women (SSCW), 29, 30, 93–94

South Carolina Institute for Leadership (SCIL), 5, 175, 206–8. *See also* Parallel programs
and assimilation plans in *Faulkner*, 240, 253
author's talk to Converse faculty on, 230, 231–34
Converse faculty vote on, 231, 234
district court 1996 opinion on, 289
funding for, 226–30
opposition to legislature's appropriations for, 225
Senate's vote against funding for, 234–35

South Carolina Legislature
agreement with Converse on funding for SCIL, 228

bill to admit women into The Citadel, 39–42

bill to increase bond spending on Citadel barracks, 290

committee to study single-gender education for women, 178

Concurrent Resolution on single-sex education policy, 118–21, 177, 178, 182

role in opening up The Citadel to ordinary citizens, 316

Senate vote against funding for Converse SCIL program, 234–35

South Carolina Research Authority, 323

South Carolina Sportsmen's Coalition, 283

South Carolina Unorganized Militia (SCUM), 10, 33–34, 58–59

South Carolina Women Lawyers Association (SCWLA), 223–25

Space and Naval Warfare Systems Center, 323

Spearman, Lewis (Citadel president's assistant), 22, 61, 136, 137–40

Spees, Wade, 279

Starks, Fernando Xavier, 175

Starr, Ken, 35

State Insurance Reserve Fund, 221

STEM (science, technology, engineering, math) courses, 318

Sterling, Ross N., 32

Stockdale (Admiral), 87, 265, 266, 268

strategy. See Legal strategies

Stroble, Fred, 109, 177, 198

St. Stephen's Episcopal Church, 161

Suitt, Howard, 227

Summerford (Citadel nurse), 98

Suter, William, 256

Suu Kyi, Aung San, vii

Swift, Tom, 71, 107, 176

Talbot (Colonel), 87

Talbot, Donna, 164

Terry, Mary Sue, 62, 108

Texas A & M University, 164

average grades of cadets of, 95

lawsuit against, 32

Thomas, Clarence, 174, 284–85

Thomas, Eslinger v., 225

Thomas, John Peyre, 246

Thomas, Sandra, 228, 229, 230, 231, 242–43

Thompson, Joseph G., 24, 25

Thompson, Murray, 271

Thompson, Palmer v., 74–75, 114–15

Thomson, Danger, 286

Thorp, Willard, 33

Thurmond, Strom, 32

Title IV of Civil Rights Act, 30

Title IX of Education Amendments, 66, 231–32

Toal, Jean, 210

Toffler (Colonel), 165

Top Trainer Award, 94, 95

Trez, Joe, 314

Trident Technical College, 19, 53, 60, 318, 324

Turner, Ted, 228

Tyson, Cynthia, 88

United States Military Academy (USMA). See West Point

United States v. Jones, 289

United States v. Virginia, 169–71. See also Virginia Military Institute (VMI)

United States v. Virginia, continued
  The Citadel's legal posture following Supreme Court case, 6–7
  hearing on VMI's declaratory action against DOJ in *VMI I*, 54–55
  Supreme Court granting of *certiorari*, 284–85
  VMI I, 49
  VMI I as precedent for *Faulkner* case, 121–22
  VMI II, 215
University of South Carolina, 89
U.S. Army ROTC. *See* Reserve Officers' Training Corps (ROTC)
U.S. Department of Justice. *See* Department of Justice (DOJ)
U.S. Marines. *See* Marine Enlisted Commissioning Education Program (MECEP)
U.S. Marshals, 195–97, 259–62, 262*p*
U.S. Navy Enlisted Commissioning Program (ECP), 9–10, 60, 205

VA. *See* Veterans Administration (VA)
Vail, Charles, 92, 93, 168, 175
Vanier, Jean, 77
Van Tassel, Emily, 42
Vargyas, Ellen, 53
Vasilew, Eugene, 58
VEAP. *See* Veterans' Educational Assistance Program (VEAP)
Vergnolle, Ron, 82–85, 175
Veteran Cadet Program. *See* Citadel Cadet Veteran Program
Veterans Administration (VA), 60–61
Veterans Day Program. *See* Citadel Veterans Day Program
Veterans' Educational Assistance Program (VEAP), 60

Virginia Military Institute (VMI), 5. *See also United States v. Virginia*
  1997 female enrollment in, 290
  average grades of cadets of, 95
Virginia Tech, 86
  average grades of cadets of, 95
  education of civilians at, 325
Virginia, United States v. See United States v. Virginia
Virginia Women's Institute of Leadership (VWIL) at Mary Baldwin College (MBC), 5, 172. *See also* Parallel programs
  filing of plan for, 253
  funding of, 228–29
  Judge Houck's visit to, 242
  VMI II ruling on constitutionality of, 169, 170, 171
VMI Alumni Association, 62
VMI Foundation, Inc., 62
Vojdik, Valorie K., 70, 113, 125, 134, 135*p*, 153, 175, 176, 189, 252, 256, 256*p*, 304, 306
  plaintiffs' lead attorney, 4
  1995 hearing on assimilation plan, 239
  Concurrent Resolution, 120
  Mellette as intervening party, 289
  memo opposing Citadel's motion for stay, 250
  testimony on Tony Motley, 295–96

Wagner, Eileen, 53
Wagner, Robert E., 175
Wallace, George, 14, 68, 108
Wallace, Mike, 151
Walpole, Lisa, 314
Walters, Barbara, 200
Ward, Hiram H., 216
Waring, Waties, 63, 64, 121, 198

Warlick, Anderson, 227
Warren, Estelle, 38
Warren, Mary, 71, 176
Washington and Lee University, 88
Washington, Dorothy, 123
Washington, George, 77
Washington v. Davis, 74
Waters, Sam, 81
Waters, Wesley, 78
Watson, Adrienne, 311
Watson, Elwood, 236
Watts, Claudius E. Bud, 22, 86, 137, 138, 147, 148, 175, 227, 228, 246, 289
    adversative education, 293
    Citadel behavior on Faulkner's registration day, 280
    meeting Holly Cork, 220
    report on publicity for The Citadel, 143–44
    ROTC's proposal to train nurse cadets at The Citadel, 42–43
    Shannon Faulkner's registration day, 136–37
Weisburg, Henry, 71p, 176, 256, 270, 271, 305, 312
    plaintiffs' ultimate shot-caller, 70–71
West, John, 91, 92, 175
West Point, 20
West, Wally, 115, 173, 175
Weston, Tucker, 227
Whipper, Lucille, 39, 40, 42, 115, 161
Whitehurst, Darrell E., 218–19
White, J. B., 246
White, Rebecca, 127, 187
Whitmire Report, 188
Whittemore, Ann Marie, 66, 72, 123, 176, 230, 231

Widener (Fourth Circuit judge), 126, 171
Wilder, Douglas, 62–63
Wilkins, David, 119
Wilkinson (Fourth Circuit judge), 171
Williams, Angela, 98
Williams, Bruce, 297
Williams (Fourth Circuit judge), 126
Williams, John, 42
Williams v. McNair, 24
Willkins (Fourth Circuit judge), 126
Wilson, Michael, 227
Wilson, Sam, 88
Winfrey, Oprah, vii, 281, 284
Winthrop University, 88, 89, 92–93, 181–82
Withers, Claudia, 53
Wittenberg, Phillip, 310
Wofford, Sandra, 42
women
    1997 admissions to VMI and The Citadel, 290
    Citadel recruitment plan, 218–19
    Citadel's attitude toward women in classroom, 34
    civil rights in South Carolina politics, 209–11
    sexist stereotypes disguised as manners, 292
    socioeconomic status in South Carolina, 40
    soldiers, 46
    suffrage in South Carolina, 210
    supporters of women's admission into The Citadel, 80, 81, 101
Women Against Rape, 236
Women's Rights Project. *See* American Civil Liberties Union (ACLU)
women veterans' case. *See Johnson, Lacy, and Chapman v. Jones*

Woodington, Ken, 295
Woods, James, 44
Wotkyns, Jeanette Kellogg, 35, 55–56, 284

XMD status, 238, 267, 268

Young, Annette, 42
Young, Roger, 42, 119

Zentgraf, Melanie, 32
Zentgraf strategy, 31–33
Zerillo, Bill, 134, 259
Zimmerman (U.S. Marshal), 196
Zinzer, Roy R., 43, 164